Adel Guindy

A SWORD OVER THE NILE

A BRIEF HISTORY OF THE COPTS UNDER ISLAMIC RULE

AUSTIN MACAULEY PUBLISHERS™

LONDON • CAMBRIDGE • NEW YORK • SHARJAH

Ordering Information:
Quantity sales: special discounts are available on quantity purchases by corporations, associations, and others. For details, contact the publisher at the address below.

Publisher's Cataloging-in-Publication data
Guindy, Adel
A Sword Over the Nile

ISBN 9781643787602 (Paperback)
ISBN 9781643787619 (Hardback)
ISBN 9781645365099 (ePub e-book)

Library of Congress Control Number: 2020902962

www.austinmacauley.com/us

First Published (2020)
Austin Macauley Publishers LLC
40 Wall Street, 28th Floor
New York, NY 10005
USA

mail-usa@austinmacauley.com
+1 (646) 5125767

To the ordinary and unsung Copts,
in their towns and villages,
for their quiet perseverance
and heroic steadfastness
over the centuries.
A testimony to resilience.

To Congressman (ret.) Frank Wolf
and Lord David Alton (U.K.),
for their remarkable efforts
to promote global religious freedom.

Table of Content

Foreword

February 2015 was the first time many in the West heard of the Copts, Egypt's indigenous, Christian inhabitants. Then, the Islamic State published what subsequently went viral—a gory video of their jihadi members savagely carving off the heads of 20 Copts and one Ghanaian by the shores of Libya because they refused to renounce Christ for Islam.

Little known, however, is that, well before the Islamic State targeted and unwittingly "popularized" the Copts, countless other Muslims in modern Egypt—individuals, mobs, sheikhs, organizations (the Muslim Brotherhood, the Salafi Front), and even governmental authorities—had persecuted or at the very least discriminated against the nation's Christian minority.

Such oppression is often seen and presented in the West as an aberration. After all, have Muslims and Christians not lived in peace for centuries in Egypt? Does the fact that Copts comprise at least 10 percent of Egypt's population not bespeak of tolerance—a Muslim willingness to live and let live for 14 centuries? Indeed, was it not the Copts themselves who initially called on the Arabs to enter and 'liberate' Egypt from the Byzantine yoke in the seventh century?

All these observations that invariably arise in response to the "Coptic question" suggest that current discord is rooted to temporal matters—poverty, ignorance, tribalism—anything and everything other than religion.

The problem, however, is that these observations are built atop a faulty first premise—and, as always, false first premises always lead to false conclusions. Put differently, they are built atop a pseudohistory that has long dominated the West's understanding of Islam's history vis-à-vis non-Muslims in general, the Copts, for our purposes, in particular. A corrective is needed.

Enter the current book in your hands. I first read an earlier version of *A Sword Over the Nile* in Arabic and found its contents so useful as to urge its author, Adel Guindy, to translate it into English. Not only did he comply—

to the benefit and subsequent edification of English-language readers—but he greatly enlarged the original work, tying it to the current era and supplying several useful appendices.

A Sword traces the history of the Coptic people under Islam, from the seventh century on to the present era. Most of it is a chronological translation of lengthy selections of the compendious *History of the Patriarchs of the Egyptian Church* and other Coptic primary sources, some translated here for the first time. Although the *History of the Patriarchs* was first rendered into English in the early twentieth century, most editions are out of print; existing copies tend to be exorbitantly priced. But Mr. Guindy has not only provided an accessible and fresh translation; he has spared the reader the agony of culling through the *History of the Patriarchs'* many volumes—as might be imagined, hundreds of its pages make for dry and irrelevant reading—to find the most applicable selections for inclusion.

As such, *A Sword's* merits are many. Unlike the well-known and dominant Muslim historiographical tradition, which is largely hagiographical—that is, meant to put a "saintly" veneer on Muslim conduct vis-à-vis non-Muslim subjects—the Coptic sources used for this book tend to more accuracy. For example, whereas the oldest Muslim history of the Arab invasion and subsequent conquest of Egypt was written *two centuries* after the facts (by Ibn 'Abd al-Hakam, d. 870), the Coptic sources relied on in this book are contemporaneous with the events they record. That alone suggests that their narrative is more authoritative. Moreover, by relying heavily on Coptic sources, this book offers the added benefit of presenting the story of Egyptian Christianity under Islam through the eyes of the vanquished, not the victors, the latter hitherto being the traditional guardians of the "narrative."

Less academically, the great achievement of *A Sword* is that it gives the lie to the aforementioned and popular Western view that whatever the Copts are currently suffering has nothing to do with Islam. The next few hundred pages of source document translations make clear that everything modern Egypt's Copts are currently suffering—including the burning and bombing of their churches, sporadic bouts of violent persecution, the abduction and forced conversion of Coptic girls, and a myriad of other forms of entrenched social discrimination—was suffered by their Coptic ancestors over the course of fourteen centuries. The continuity is staggering; think what the Islamic State has been doing to Christians and others but on a prolonged and sometimes exponential scale (for instance, under the Mamluks). Moreover, the persecutors were not fringe "radicals" but often the very rulers of Egypt, whether Arabs, Fatimids, Kurds, Mamluks, Turks, or Egyptians.

Lest the Coptic chronicles appear too sensational or exaggerated, it is worth observing that Muslim sources sometimes confirm them. For instance, in Taqi al-Din al-Maqrizi's (d. 1442) authoritative history of Egypt, anecdote after anecdote is recorded of Muslims burning churches, slaughtering Christians, and enslaving Coptic women and children—often with the compliance if not outright cooperation of the authorities. The only escape then—as sometimes today—was for Christians to convert to Islam.

Indeed, after recording one particularly egregious bout of persecution in the eleventh century, when, along with the countless massacres, some *30,000* churches, according to Maqrizi, were destroyed or turned into mosques—a staggering number that further indicates how Christian pre-Islamic Egypt and the Middle East was, a point to be addressed anon—the Muslim historian makes an interesting observation: "Under these circumstances a great many Christians became Muslims."

This leads to the all-important question, one that *A Sword's* chronological approach clarifies: how and why did Egypt go from being overwhelmingly Christian in the seventh century, to being overwhelmingly Muslim in the twenty-first century? To understand the significance of this question—and because few in the West comprehend pre-Islamic Egypt's profoundly Christian nature—a brief primer is in order:

Before Islam invaded it, Egypt was home to some of Christendom's earliest theological giants and church fathers, including Clement of Alexandria (b. 150), Origen the Great (b. 184), Anthony the Great, father of monasticism (b. 251), and Athanasius of Alexandria (b. 297), the chief defender of the Nicene Creed, which is still professed by all major Christian denominations. The Catechetical School of Alexandria was the most important ecclesiastical and learning center of ancient Christendom.

Writing around the year 400, and further indicative of how thoroughly Christian pre-Islamic Egypt was, John Cassian, a European, observed that "the traveler from Alexandria in the north to Luxor in the south would have in his ears along the whole journey, the sounds of prayers and hymns of the monks, scattered in the desert, from the monasteries and from the caves, from monks, hermits, and anchorites." Some Europeans, such as the British historian and archaeologist Stanley Lane-Poole (d. 1931), even claim that

Coptic missionaries were first to bring the Gospel to distant regions of Europe, including Switzerland, Britain, and especially Ireland. Most recently, both the oldest parchment to contain words from the Gospel (dating to the first century) and the oldest image of Christ were discovered in separate regions of Egypt.

In short, something very dramatic, very cataclysmic—namely, violent persecution, as made clear by the Coptic sources translated here—is responsible for transforming Christian Egypt into Muslim Egypt. Yet physical violence was not alone in making such a fiercely Christian nation become Islamic. The *dhimma* system, Islam's discriminatory rules for governing Christian and Jewish subjects (based largely on Koran 9:29 and the so-called *Conditions of Omar*), while providing some religious freedom, also stipulated a number of fiscal burdens (*jizya*), social inequality, and a host of other disabilities that, decade after decade, century after century, saw more and more Copts convert to Islam to alleviate their burdens and achieve some semblance of equality.

Thus, in his *The Arab Conquest of Egypt* (1902), historian Alfred Butler mentions the "vicious system of bribing the Christians into conversion," before elaborating:

> [A]lthough religious freedom was in theory secured for the Copts under the capitulation, it soon proved in fact to be shadowy and illusory. For a religious freedom which became identified with social bondage and with financial bondage could have neither substance nor vitality. As Islam spread, the social pressure upon the Copts became enormous, while the financial pressure at least seemed harder to resist, as the number of Christians or Jews who were liable for the poll-tax [*jizya*] diminished year by year, and their isolation became more conspicuous… [T]he burdens of the Christians grew heavier in proportion as their numbers lessened [that is, the more Christians converted to Islam, the more the burdens on the remaining few grew]. The wonder, therefore, is not that so many Copts yielded to the current which bore them with sweeping force over to Islam, but that so great a multitude of Christians stood firmly against the stream, nor have all the storms of thirteen centuries moved their faith from the rock of its foundation.

Such is the forgotten history of the Copts' diminution: that ten percent of Egypt is *still* Christian is not a reflection of Muslim tolerance but intolerance. While the lives of many Christians were snuffed out over centuries of violence, the spiritual and cultural identities of exponentially more were wiped out. (Such is the sad and ironic cycle that plagues modern Egypt: those Muslims who persecute Christians are themselves often distant descendants of Copts who first embraced Islam to evade their own persecution). In short, if it were not for the Copts' stubborn resilience and endurance, Christianity would have been wiped out altogether from Egypt—just as it was in the rest of North Africa, which, before the seventh century Islamic conquests, was also thoroughly Christian.

In connection, it is interesting to note that, according to the Convention on the Prevention and Punishment of the Crime of Genocide (adopted by Resolution 260 (III) A of the U.N. General Assembly on December 9, 1948), both violent *and* nonviolent pressures are deemed factors of genocide. "Killing" and causing "serious bodily or mental harm" to members of any group of people—in this case, "infidel" Copts—are the first two legal definitions of genocide. The third definition of Resolution 260 encapsulates the "slow-motion genocide" that typifies Coptic history under Islam: "Deliberately inflicting on the group *conditions of life calculated* to bring about its physical destruction in whole or in part" (emphasis added).

That is precisely what the aptly called *Conditions of Omar* did (see *Crucified Again* pp. 24–30 for my translation and analysis of this historically pivotal document). It imposes negative "conditions of life calculated" to prompt the Copts to abandon their Christian identities/heritage in order to reap the benefits of joining Islam—which includes the cessation of persecution and discrimination.

Mr. Guindy's achievement, it should be noted, is not simply to document the historic persecution of Copts. At the end of every chapter he analyzes the translated material's significance; additionally, a comprehensive essay providing a synthesized overview—with suggestions on moving forward and solving the Coptic question—appears at the end of the book. In his analyses, and to his credit, Mr. Guindy not infrequently calls out some of history's individual Copts, often clerical leaders, for their complicity or at least acquiescence to their flock's treatment—a phenomenon he traces to the modern era.

It is for all these reasons and more that *A Sword over the Nile* is a most welcome book and contribution to the existing literature. Here in one volume we have the largely unknown historical experiences of Egypt's Coptic Christians under Islam—and from the most primary if previously inaccessible or untranslated sources. Not only is it a window to the past; it may be an ominous look to the future.

Raymond Ibrahim is author of *Sword and Scimitar: Fourteen Centuries of War between Islam and the West* (2018); *Crucified Again: Exposing Islam's New War on Christians* (2013); and *The Al Qaeda Reader* (2007). He holds fellowships at the Middle East Forum, the Gatestone Institute, and the David Horowitz Freedom Center.

Introduction

The Copt has acquired a certain notoriety over the years—occasionally earning a spot in international news, depending on the sympathy-value of the occasion's bombing of a church or lynching in communities. Islamic State's 2015's glossy, dynamic beach-front production featuring the beheading of twenty Egyptian and one Ghanaian Christians horrified the world in its polished perversity. Still, it compounded what is essentially diminutive: Copts are mere terror-targets.

Very little is known of the Copts—even less of their history.

Inside Egypt, oftentimes discussions about the Copts' real history, and the history of Egypt through them, elicit peculiar reactions. While only a few respond rationally, most people react with unfathomable and unjustifiable animosity and antagonism. Or, perhaps after all it may be understandable, because one would be treading too closely to some taboos.

The *official* (hagiographic) and dominant narrative of Egypt's history in the past fourteen centuries roughly goes like this:

Christians in Egypt's sixth and seventh centuries were persecuted by their fellow Christians and occupiers, the Byzantines. In 640 A.D., the light of Islam shone on Egypt (as it did on the rest of the region) and the Arab-Muslims liberated the Copts from their oppressors, allowing them to worship as they wish. Shortly after, most Copts converted freely to (the superior) Islam and Egypt became a Muslim country. Ever since, the minority of Copts (who continued to freely practice their faith) along with their fellow Muslims, lived happily together. Of course, there were some bad episodes, but Muslims and Copts suffered alike under oppressive rulers.

Clearly—or at least that is what we hope to prove in this book—this is not *History*. Nor is it in any way part of the 'collective memory.'

But is this a *myth*?

Historical, social and political studies offer a mass of writings on historical myths and the important role they play in the creation of a nation-state, as they would help hide, or efface, the violence which is, in general, associated with such a creation. In fact, when it comes to forming one people, it would sometimes be preferable to opt for the myth, rather than the real history.[1] However, even a myth is supposed to be no less factual than history, even though it acts as 'a story that simplifies, dramatizes, and selectively narrates the story of a nation's past, and embroidered to explain the present.'[2]

So, the above-mentioned narrative would not even qualify for a myth. It would, in fact, be closer to what we call these days 'alternate facts'—or to give it a colloquial (if anachronistic) flavor, 'fake news.'

On the other hand, while being aware of the adage that history is written by the victors, historical memory cannot be taken away from the losers, for the 'losers cannot afford to forget; they need to brood over the past, on what went wrong and why, in the vain hope of standing once more at the decisive crossroads.' Also, the losers may 'want to turn the page of history, but (they) don't want to leave it blank.'[3] So, history is important after all, and it must be written by the losers, as well as by the winners, before the page can be turned. There is a need to protest against historical injustices and/or the way in which these have been glossed over.

Many of the reactions to any discussion about the history of the Copts also reflect a great deal of 'lack of knowledge' with regards to elementary information about the history of Egypt and Egyptians. This ignorance is due to the *counterfeit* method of presenting history employed by the 'Establishment' containing a great deal of misinformation, which is part and parcel of a system of deceit. This system forbids challenging any of its particulars for fear that the entire structure would come crumbling down.

We, however, see a necessity for discussing some topics that have been avoided for far too long. But before we can do that, we need to make some preliminary remarks:

1. No one is capable of recreating history; the past is the past. Current reality is the result of that past, and we cannot hold present-day people responsible for the sins of their ancestors. To use a geological analogy, history may be viewed as comprised of consecutive strata deposited one on top of the other, without a single layer cancelling or abrogating another.

2. History should not be sacred, but rather, a subject to continual research. First, this is done to scrutinize past events based on new data and

sources of information that become available. Second, it is done to reanalyze historical givens from various perspectives. The purpose of such endeavors is not purely academic, rather, it is to discover how the past impacts the present and the future. After all, he who controls the past controls the future.[4] It would also be appropriate to admit to, and even apologize, for past mistakes and crimes committed by the previous generations, not only to cleanse the collective conscience, but more importantly, to show determination not to repeat them.

3. The issue of religious discrimination in Egypt is not unrelated to history; rather the opposite is true. Discrimination did not descend upon us from another planet; it is not the doing of genies and devils, or just the practice of an 'evil few,' nor is it just a result of some (often-ridiculous) laws that need amending. Instead, *doctrinal*, *historical*, and *cultural* roots nourish religious discrimination for the governing and governed, educated and uneducated alike. This triad also justifies and normalizes religious discrimination, almost making it inevitable. This highlights the importance of dealing with this issue squarely from all angles, in an effort to heal its sores and eradicate its root cause.

It should also be noted that improving the future of Egypt cannot not happen until backward values put off.

The next and more important question is how did the Copts fare since the Arabs came to Egypt?

To give a fair answer to this question, it is necessary to delve deeper into certain details and events, to which this book will be dedicated.

For starters, there will be some who may agree, for the sake of argument, that the entrance of the Arabs was an 'invasion' rather than a (happy) *fat'h,*[i] but they will quickly remind that the nature of wars are determined by the eras in which they are fought. Also, given that Egypt was occupied before the Arabs, they will question the singling out of the Arabs, when, in their view, the Arabs were better—or at least, not worse—than other invaders.

But there are a few points that we must address in order to answer the above question:

---

[i] The term *fat'h,* used in Arab-Islamic annals, is usually translated as 'conquest,' but it literally signifies 'opening,' with an implicit sense of being peaceful, and bringing in civilization and good news (Islam) to the 'opened' territories.

1. Did the actual status of the Copts, since the Arab conquest, match the portrait drawn by the 'official' (hagiographical) history books that make a variety of claims ranging from 'the Copts having invited' (or 'called upon'!) the Arabs to deliver them from the Byzantine rule, to the Copts being blessed the entire time with a life filled with tolerance, brotherliness, and good care?

2. To what extent did the Copts *enjoy* rights (religious or otherwise)? Did these rights even meet the terms of the treaty signed by the Arabs at the time of invasion that stated, "[..] Amr Ibn Al-Aas granted safety to the people of Egypt, as it relates to their lives, religion, churches, farm lands, and Nile; nothing more and nothing less (to be imposed) [..] and the people of Egypt were to pay the *Jizya* at the Nile flood time [..]"?

3. How did the Muslim rulers deal with the Copts in the context of *Dhimmitude, Jizya, Kharaj*, and other forms of exaction?

4. How did the policies and practices of those Arab rulers impact the life of the Copts, as well as the nature and rates of Copts converting to Islam?

5. What was the impact of the invasion on the language, religion, identity, and civilization of the Egyptians?

In sum, there should be a minimum level of agreement over what took place when the Arabs invaded Egypt and what happened since then. It is important to cleanse the national memory, and for all to be reconciled with their history, both the good and the bad.

***

In an effort to deal with this subject dispassionately, we will make use of long excerpts and quotes from the *History of the Patriarchs*.[i] This huge document was initiated by Sawiris (Severus) Ibn al-Muqafa'. Born around 915, he was a senior government scribe before quitting to take a monastic vow. He researched manuscripts and became most knowledgeable in Coptic history and theology. During the reign of the Fatimid Caliph Al-Muizz li-

---

[i] There is another *History of the Patriarchs*, falsely attributed to Yousab, bishop of Fuwah in the Delta. But actually, it is a work composed in the 18th century, by an anonymous author, and preserved in a single manuscript in the Syriac Monastery in Wadi al-Natroun. It is based on the above-mentioned *History of the Patriarchs,* and completed by using additional sources. (S. Moawad, 2006).

Din Allah, he was a well-known figure. He became bishop of Ashmounein,[i] and died around 1000. Sawiris referred to masses of manuscripts and diaries (chronicles) of the Church and monasteries covering the time from the first days of Christianity in Egypt, some ten centuries earlier, to his time. He compiled the material, and then wrote his book in Arabic, which he seems to have reasonably mastered, even though he must have had great difficulties translating from his own sophisticated (rich in phonetics and grammar) Coptic language to the invaders' relatively primitive language[ii]. This may explain why, in many cases, his Arabic expressions appear to be clumsy, or too reliant on vernacular expressions.

The work of Sawiris was later taken by Mawhūb Ibn Manṣūr Ibn Mufarriğ al-Iskandarānī, who seems to be its first compiler, and insured its continuation till 1088. Afterward, chroniclers continued the task, all the way to the early 20th century. As a result, then, we appear to possess eyewitness accounts of well-placed (but not necessarily neutral) observers of the events.

The *History of the Patriarchs* is, of course, known to academics and specialists, and they often quote it as part of their narrative. However, we chose to offer long excerpts from this huge work and 'let it speak' for itself, in order to provide broader insight into the mindset of its chroniclers across the centuries.

Only one complete copy of the *History of the Patriarchs* is known to be in existence; it is in the French National Library at Paris[iii]. A photographic

---

[i] Or Eshmounein, about 300 km south of Cairo, whose old name was Hermopolis Magna. It was, until 1826, the capital of the now-called Asyut province.

[ii] Arabic was a dialect, or rather a number of dialects, part of a family of Semitic languages which includes Aramaic and Hebrew. The oldest known written edifice was an inscription found in Namara, Syria, written in the Nabatean script, dating back to 328. It was found in the tomb of Umru' al-Qays, of the Lakhmid dynasty (in south west of current-day Iraq and Kuwait), and the text tells about his military exploits. The first inscription in the Arabic alphabet, which derived from the Nabatean one, was written in 512, and found in Syria. The Arabic grammar, diacritics, and vowel marks were only formulated at the end of the 8th century by the Persian linguist, Sibawayh.

[iii] Bibliothèque Nationale de France : *Compilation des sources coptes et rédaction en arabe traditionellement attribuée à Sawīrus Ibn al-Muqafa', reprise par Mawhūb Ibn Manṣūr Ibn Mufarriğ al-Iskandarānī. Il semble que ce dernier soit en fait le compilateur primitif et continuateur partiel.*

copy of this original is kept in the Egyptian National Library and Archives. Partial copies exist in the Coptic Patriarchate Library and the British Museum.

It is important to emphasize that these texts, which can be considered an official history of the Coptic Church, should be defined not as one book representing a structural unity, but rather as tradition of historical writing. In various epochs, Coptic authors have recorded the history of their church and their country, each one of them continuing the work of his predecessor.

As for the contents, most records are much more than a biography of a Patriarch. The authors endeavored to record all kinds of events, including those belonging to political or social history. But there is no uniformity on this point. Some of the authors concentrated on the Patriarch's personality, whereas others limited themselves to using the Patriarch's reign as a general framework in which other events are dealt with. At any rate, the *History of the Patriarchs* constitutes our main literary source for Coptic history, and if used with some caution, an important complimentary source for Egyptian history in general.[5]

Such texts naturally portray the mindset of the chroniclers, the environment, and the era. However, they sometimes look astonishingly modern—including an incredible dose of political correctness, albeit 12th-century style. On the other hand, the chroniclers had the advantage of being first-hand witnesses and even involved in the current events of their times.

We should also note that even though the chroniclers of *History of the Patriarchs* focused to a great extent on events related to the Patriarchs, history researcher Abdul Aziz Gamal Al-Din, who researched, verified, annotated, and provided explanatory supplements to the original text[6], recognized the great importance of these manuscripts, and thus titled his book, *The History of Egypt Through the History of the Patriarchs Manuscript*.[i]

Initially, we feared that such chronicles might have been written in an apologetic manner that forgoes objectivity, meaning they might, for instance, offer too idealistic images of the figures covered, or justify the defeat of the

---

(http://data.bnf.fr/12472388/histoire_des_Patriarches_de_l_eglise__d_alexandrie/).
[i] *The History of Egypt Through the History of the Patriarchs Manuscript*, by Abdul Aziz Gamal Al-Din, research, verification, and annotation. Publisher: Madbouly—Cairo, 2006, six volumes (6100 pages).

defeated, while exaggerating the blame placed on the invaders, stressing their flaws, and disregarding their good deeds. Nevertheless, in general, we find that exaggerations are avoided, and that there is no hesitation in praising those worthy of praise or in being self-critical. Furthermore, Gamal Al-Din frequently makes reference in the footnotes to writings of other, particularly Muslim, historians, who seem to confirm the events recorded in *History of the Patriarchs*, and, at times, go beyond them.

Translation to English of the first half of the *History of the Patriarchs* was made in 1904–1915, by Basil T. A. Evetts, under the title, *History of the Patriarchs of the Coptic Church of Alexandria*, then, in 1943 onwards, by Abdel-Messih.[i] This translation, known to academics but not to the general public, is unique and valuable. However, in writing this book, we opted for a fresh interpretation of the selected Arabic quotes abiding by a simple rule: faithful translation, but seeking clarity of the intended sense as best as one can from the text and context. Hopefully, both the academic and the general, non-specialized reader, will be reasonably content with the outcome.

Numerous other sources have naturally been consulted in order to present as complete a picture as possible, for the period that spans some fourteen centuries. These include several texts that are translated into English for the first time.

***

Far from being a book about the Copts *for* the Copts, it is essentially meant for a global readership with broad interests, especially in the West. The hope is to shed light on what befell the Copts, an indigenous population descendant of the oldest civilization in the world (the 'Cradle of Civilization'), and to help understand how they ended up where they did today. Moreover, the Copts' experiences under Islam are more generically useful in that they are paradigmatic of the experiences of other non-Muslims—many of whom have essentially become extinct—under Islam. The history lessons to learn from are many. An implicit—but perfectly applicable to several parts of the world—lesson would be: 'Our past is your future.'

---

[i]http://www.tertullian.org/fathers/severus_hermopolis_hist_alex_patr_00_intro.htm

Note to the reader:

—The chapters of this book are divided into historical eras as we saw their significance. However, we also retained concurrently an arrangement according to the Patriarchs, as they shape the history of the Coptic Church and the Copts.

—The 'factual' chapters, which are meant to highlight historical events, are followed with two final chapters that offer the author's overall analysis and conclusions.

—At the end of the book, we have added seven appendices. Five of them provide some focused discussions that might have become distractive if left in the main body. The sixth enlists the Coptic Patriarchs. The last is a glossary.

—In the following chapters, quotes from *History of the Patriarchs* will always have deep indents.

—In addition to the customary use of [..] to denote abridged parts of extended quotes, we will, at times, add a word or more for clarification, and these are indicated by the standard use of brackets [like so]. This may be done in certain instances to use a more modern expression in place of an archaic one that is difficult to understand, to summarize a long irrelevant section, or for the purpose of clarification of the background or context to the reader.

—There were instances when a quoted text needed additional, more lengthy, clarification or supplementation, and those are indicated by using an asterisk (*), signifying that a paragraph or more have been added below, rather than as a footnote, due to the importance of such additions, which usually come from other sources.

—In some instances, we will use transliterated original words (e.g. Sultan, *Wali*, *Archon*, etc.). Apart from rendering authenticity to the text, this choice was made because quite often, no single equivalent word would provide an exact translation. A glossary at the end provides definitions for the words used.

—Names of persons and places are transliterated from original languages. Their spelling is kept consistent across the book, but occasionally the rule may be missed.

—Unless otherwise indicated, the dates are A.D. (C.E.). Dates given in the original texts according to Coptic (*Anno Martyrii* which starts with the first year of Emperor Diocletian accession in 284 A.D.) or *hijri* (lunar, starts in 622 A.D.) calendars are converted to A.D. and shown only as such. In fact, almost all dates in the *History of the Patriarchs* are according to the Coptic calendar, but we opted for showing only the dates according to the standard C.E. calendar.

—Notes giving references are at the end of the book, while explanatory notes are kept at page bottom for ease.

Who Are the Copts?

The word 'Copt' comes from the known derivative '*Aegyptus.*'

In the old kingdom, Egyptians called their country '*Kemet,*' meaning 'the dark land,' most likely because of the color of the soil, due to the silt brought by the annual flood of the Nile.

They also began to call it '*Hwt-ka-Ptah,*' meaning '*house (temple) — spirit — (of/for) Ptah,*' which was the religious name for Memphis, the ancient capital of Egypt. For them, *Ptah* was the god of creation, manufacturing, and art, and he was the main deity in Memphis. With the arrival of the Greeks[i], the name morphed into '*Aígyptos*' (Αιγυπτος), and then '*Aegyptus,*' which became the known name everywhere in the ancient times. This name appears in Greek mythology and is mentioned in Homer's epic, *The Odyssey.*

For the Semitic peoples in the region, the country is called *Miṣr,* after *Miṣrāyim* the son of *Ham* of the Genesis. But the inhabitants of Egypt were referred to in a dual way. Thus, the Arabs called them '*Gbṭ*' or '*Qbṭ,*' and that was undoubtedly prior to the invasion. Notice also that in Upper Egypt, the Copts are being called, and they even call themselves, '*Agbat,*' where the 'g' goes back to the original pronunciation and not a morphing of the 'q' in the more formal '*Aqbaṭ.*' This is unlike the case with people of Cairo and the Delta, who pronounce it as '*A'abat,*' (replacing 'q' by 'a').

Therefore, the terms '*Aqbat,*' '*Agbat,*' '*Qebt,*' and '*Copt*' (*Copte, Kopten, Coptos,* in different languages) are linked to '*Egypt,*' (which is the country's name used in other languages, even in Japanese and Chinese) in that all these terms have the same root '*Aegyptus,*' which is derived from a genuine Egyptian root.

---

[i] Alexander the Great came to Egypt in 332 B.C. He adopted the Egyptian deity and declared himself to be the son of Zeus-Amon. He founded Alexandria and left for Assyria in 331 B.C.

Three centuries after Alexander's descent, Egypt came under Roman rule (in 30 B.C.),[i] and was submitted directly to Rome. However, the Hellenistic influence remained unchanged and Egypt was never Latinized. In fact, Alexandria remained, for centuries, the leading cultural center of the Old World, around the Mediterranean, and took over from Athens as the capital of Hellenistic thinking. It was once the center of the Hellenistic Empire, and the hub of scholarship and commerce in the ancient world. Greek scholars, Roman emperors, Jewish leaders, fathers of the Christian Church, mathematicians, philosophers, scientists, poets, and other intellectuals flocked to Alexandria. One of the main attractions was the Alexandrian Library and Museum. In *Alexandria: City of the Western Mind*, Theodore Vrettos wrote that Alexandria was special and different from other large, ancient cities of the Mediterranean. Carthage, Rome, and Sparta were all considered important military centers; Alexandria was a city of the mind. A curious capital that became not only the largest Greek city of the time, but more than anything else, a very important center for culture and learning.

Alexandria was also a center for biblical studies. The chief librarian commissioned the *Septuagint*, which was the oldest Greek version of the Old Testament. The Jewish community in Alexandria was large and had its own separate quarter in the city, overseen by an *ethnarch*.[ii] The *Septuagint* made Judaism accessible to people of other faiths, who were curious about the basis for the Jewish religion. Greeks, Romans, and Jews constituted the majority of people living in Alexandria in its heyday, but there were also many thousands of Egyptians, Persians, Syrians, and many Asiatic. Alexandria was a melting pot of people from all over the ancient world. The outcome of having so many cultural and religious ideologies coming together in the city was that Christianity was able to rise out of the Hellenistic movements of magic and superstition, philosophy, mystery religions, and Judaism. It was the Hellenized Jewish philosophy typified by St. Paul and Philo of Alexandria—the fusion of Jewish and Greek thought—that formed the basis of modern Christianity, through Clement and St. Augustine.[7]

---

[i] Octavian (the future emperor Augustus) defeated his rival, Mark Antony, deposed Queen Cleopatra VII, and annexed the (Ptolemaic) Kingdom of Egypt to the Roman Empire.

[ii] A leader of the ethnic group of Jews in the city.

Then comes another conventional question: who said the term *Copts* was, or is still, limited to Egyptian indigenous *Christians*?

After the Arabs invaded Egypt, they called all the natives Copts, bearing in mind that, as mentioned above, in Egypt resided a Greek community, a sizable Jewish community, not to mention others who had assimilated and became part of the native 'Copts.'

In *The History of the Patriarchs*, Christian Egyptians are referred to in several ways. Sometimes as the 'Orthodox' Christians (to differentiate from the 'Chalcedonians,' who followed the Byzantine doctrine), and other times as the 'Natives' (or 'Indigenous'), who were the original inhabitants of the land. Later, the new Arabic expression 'Nazarenes' was used, thus appropriating such a derogatory term that was applied by the Arabs, irrespective of denomination, most probably thinking that it was simply an Arabic translation of 'Christian.' Occasionally, misleading terms such as 'Jacobites' (after Jacob Baradaeus, Patriarch of Antioch, sixth century) or even 'Monophysite' (rather than 'Miaphysite,' as it should be) are used. Here, it is the Chalcedonians' terms (which are normally reserved for heretics) that are curiously used for self-describing.

Those who converted to Islam are called *Muslemani* or simply Muslims, whereas the term 'Arab' is reserved for the invaders.

The expression *Copt* appears for the first time around 750, i.e. more than a century after the invasion, to specifically refer to the native Christians of the land. Even if it may be *technically* correct to currently use the designation '*Copt*' to refer to every Egyptian irrespective of religion, nonetheless, the expression has come to describe specifically and exclusively Christian Egyptian natives (i.e. not every Christian living in the country, even if they had the Egyptian nationality, such as Armenians, Syriacs, Maronites, Greeks, etc.). This term is, hence, almost as a good as a *definition*, given its continued usage over the centuries.

Copts are then the direct descendants of the Ancient Egyptians. Gamal Hamdan [i] said that the Ancient Egyptians were an indigenous (autochthonous) people that had not migrated from anywhere else, and even if miscegenation (racial mixing) had taken place, it did in the context of racial continuity across the ages and even prior to the dating of Pharaonic dynasties

---

[i] A renowned Egyptian geographer and anthropologist who authored '*The Character of Egypt.*'

(32 centuries B.C.). Contemporary Egyptians are (regardless of their religion) descendants of the Ancient Egyptians intermixed with traces of Arabic, Semitic, Caucasian, European, and other genes (not that genetic composition is of any importance in itself). In fact, according to a recent National Geographic genographic study, modern day Egyptians carry particular blends of regional affiliations: 68% North Africa, 17% Southwest Asia and Persian Gulf, 4% Jewish Diaspora, 3% from each of Southern Europe, Asia Minor, and Eastern Africa.[8]

***

Modern Copts are not only 'genetically' descendants of Ancient Egyptians, but retain some tangible cultural heritage such as language, music, and more.

Coptic language is the latest stage of the Ancient Egyptian language, which was initially written in hieroglyphic, then 'Demotic' characters. The hieroglyphic (which dates back to around 3300 B.C.) combined logographic, syllabic, and alphabet elements, with a total of some 1,000 distinct characters. The Demotic (popular) was a simplified form of the hieroglyphic. The passage of the writing of the Egyptian language to Coptic started in the first century A.D. The Coptic alphabet is identical to the Greek alphabet, with the addition of six or seven characters to represent specific sounds[i]. Coptic and Demotic are grammatically closely related to Late Egyptian language (New Kingdom, around 1350 B.C.). Coptic flourished as a literary language from the second to 13th centuries. It was supplanted by Egyptian Arabic as a spoken language toward the 16th century. But by the middle of the 17th century, Coptic was still at least 'as much a part of the education of a well-bred Copt as Latin or Greek is of an English gentleman.' Coptic was still taught regularly in the Coptic schools.[9]

In fact, learning Coptic was instrumental in Champollion's success in deciphering hieroglyphs, and he was convinced that spoken Coptic evolved from ancient Egyptian. A Coptic priest and scholar, Youhanna Chiftichi, taught Champollion the secrets of Coptic language.[ii]

---

[i] These are *Sh, F, Kh, H, J (dzh), Tsh, Ti.*

[ii] He was born in Cairo in the last quarter of the 18th century and died in France, sometime after 1825. In a letter by Champollion written in Paris to his brother, he

In its *Bohairic* dialect, Coptic continues to be the liturgical language of the Coptic Orthodox Church. But not only, as it still survives through the current colloquial Egyptian. Many people claim that this colloquial language is simply a slang and distortion of the classical Arabic. But nothing is farther than reality in this interpretation, which derives from considering classical Arabic a 'sacred language,' because it is the language of the Quran. The fact is that colloquial Egyptian has its own grammatical rules that differ distinctly from those of Arabic.[i] Furthermore, hundreds of words (estimated to be over 800 roots) are simply 'Egyptian' (Coptic), while many others found their way into Arabic and related roots were created.[10]

In the Coptic Church, all traditional rites and services are sung. Even the afterlife is believed to be an eternal musical celebration in the presence of God. Copts believe that their liturgical hymnody, as it is sung during worship services, helps to create momentarily a sense of heaven on earth, as music is the medium that bridges the everyday mundane life with a higher, spiritual realm.[11]

The percussion instruments used in the Coptic Church are unusual among Christian liturgies. Since similar instruments appear in ancient

---

says, "I am going to visit a Coptic priest at Saint-Roch, rue Saint-Honoré, who celebrates Mass...and who will instruct me in Coptic names, and the pronunciation of Coptic letters... I am devoting myself entirely to the Coptic language, for I want to know the Egyptian language as well as my own native French. My great work on the Egyptian papyri will be based on this [ancient] tongue."
(http://ccdl.libraries.claremont.edu/cdm/ref/collection/cce/id/454)

[i] Most linguists agree that there are at least three Arabic 'languages': a) Classical Arabic (C.A.), on which they still differ; not even the Quran would be written in C.A., given the fact that about one third of its vocabulary is mere transliteration of Aramaic; b) Modern Standard Arabic, which is learned through formal education and used for official sermons and news broadcasts, but nobody speaks it in their daily life; c) Colloquial Egyptian. Taha Hussein (the renowned 'Dean of Arabic Literature') goes as far as saying that, "For Egyptians, Arabic is virtually a foreign language; nobody speaks it at home, school, in the streets, or in clubs. (..) People everywhere speak a language that is not Arabic, despite the partial resemblance to it." (*The Future of Culture in Egypt,* Cairo, 1936). Unlike Italian and French, which could be qualified as descendants of Latin, Colloquial Egyptian did not emerge from a degradation of C.A. (see Ibn Warraq, *In Search of Avocado*, reproduced in *Christmas in the Koran*, Prometheus Books, 2014).

Egyptian frescoes and reliefs, the tradition must have deep roots that survived over the centuries. Most of the Coptic melodies are unique and had been adopted from Ancient Egyptian rites. If one listens, for example, to the hymns chanted during the annual Good Friday services, one cannot but imagine burial practices of great Pharos.[i]

Coptic art has distinctive features related to Ancient Egyptian art, albeit with Hellenistic influence. Though the Coptic Church has suffered more from persecution, and the terrible tortures too often consequent to it than any other Church in the world, they have not destroyed the tender hopefulness of her religious life. Go where you will in the poverty-stricken Egyptian churches, you will not find one representation of hell or torture, no grinning skull or ghastly skeleton. Her martyrs smile calmly down from the walls, as if the memory of their sufferings were long forgotten.

The Coptic art strongly influenced the Islamic art and architecture with many features that are now integral in the Islamic art. In fact, the architects, engineers, and artisans were all natives of the country, and for some centuries, Christians as well. Copts were the ones who mostly built the beautiful mosques which are quoted as examples of Islamic architecture.[12]

More details on the contributions of the Copts to Western Civilization, especially in the area of philosophy, can be found in Appendix one.

***

Then comes the question about the Copts in religious terms. Are they an ancient 'sect'? Are they different from other Christians in the world, and how?

To start with, it is important to clarify that referring to 'Copts' usually implies the followers of the 'Coptic Orthodox Church.' Then, we need to look at a bit of history to understand the background.

St. Mark, the writer of the Gospel that carries his name, introduced Christianity in Egypt. He was one of the Seventy Apostles of Jesus Christ, and the Cenacle, where the Last Supper took place, was owned by his mother.

---

[i] The ancient Coptic liturgy was orally transmitted until ethnomusicologist, Ragheb Moftah, notated 13 volumes of songs in the 1920s and recorded the entire Hymnal. His collection is now at the Library of Congress.

He was a relative of St. Peter[i], and followed him closely during the early years of preaching as a companion, secretary, and interpreter (to Greek). According to tradition, St. Mark wrote the Gospel attributed to him based on St Peter's sermons. St Mark's mission in Egypt started in Alexandria and Babylon (Old Cairo), probably less than fifteen years after the Resurrection[ii]. He was martyred in 68, in Alexandria.

The new faith gained ground rather quickly, as it appeared to culminate the values of the Ancient Egyptian religion. Less than two centuries later, Christians became a numerical majority, despite the persecution of the Romans. The Alexandria papal seat was soon to become a pillar of Christianity. In fact, only the bishops of Rome and Alexandria could be given the title of 'Pope.' Already by 260, the Pope of Alexandria used to issue before every Easter a Paschal letter, which was a sort of General Epistle, and thus notified to the church, in general, the day on which Easter would fall that year.[13] The 'Catechetical School of Alexandria' was a major center of studying theology in the Late Antiquity. Some of the Coptic theologians were instrumental in formulating the Universal Church's 'creed': in particular, St. Athanasius (at the First Council of Nicaea[iii], in 325) and St. Cyril (d. 444), who presided over the Third Ecumenical Council at Ephesus (431), and is counted among the 'Fathers and the Doctors of the (Universal) Church.'

---

[i] Peter's wife and Arestopolos, Mark's father, are cousins.

[ii] The exact year in which he made his first visit to Egypt cannot be stated with any certainty (43–45 A.D.?). He seems to have been accompanied as far as Babylon by St. Peter, whose first General Epistle was sent from 'Babylon.' Absolute proof, indeed, cannot be given that the Babylon of the Epistle is the Babylon of Egypt, and many attempts have been made by Western writers to prove that the city referred to is the ancient (and extinct) Babylon of Assyria, or else a metaphor signifying Rome. But it is fair to say that the balance of evidence is in favor of the more natural supposition that St. Peter wrote from an important and well-known town, largely inhabited by Jews, in the country where his master had taken refuge (..). Refer to Butcher, Vol. 1, Ch. 3. Also, several recent articles, such as,

https://www.billkochman.com/Articles/AMysterySolvedPeterBabylon.html

It may be interesting to note here that Pope Clement of Rome mentioned in a letter (October, 1602), to the Coptic Pope, Ghobrial VIII, that "*the Alexandrian Church of St. Mark was of Petrine origin.*"

[iii] Nicaea, now known as Iznik, in Turkey.

The Coptic Church split as a result of the first ecclesial schism that followed the Chalcedon Council of 451, over the theological formulation of nature of Christ. It is beyond this book's scope to analyze the issue in any detail, but it is important, jumping over the centuries, to describe the current situation.

The Coptic Orthodox Church, along with the rest of the 'Oriental Orthodox family' of churches (Armenian, Eritrean, Ethiopian, Malankara[i], and Syriac), differences with Roman Catholic and Byzantine Orthodox Churches date to the great Christological controversies of the fifth and sixth centuries[ii]. Efforts were made over time to bridge these differences, but the greatest of developments were initiated by a series of unofficial theological consultations established in 1964, by Franz Cardinal König, Archbishop of Vienna. There is agreement that the Christology expressed by these churches should not be considered a separating factor as, in fact, the different theological formulas seek to express the same reality.

As a result of these consultations, the Coptic Orthodox Pope Shenouda III visited the Vatican for the first time ever by a Coptic Pope, and met, for the first time in over fifteen centuries, with the Roman Catholic Pope Paul VI and, on May 10, 1973, they signed a common declaration that states their common confession. [14] On February 12, 1988, the Commission of Theological Dialogue between the Catholic Church and Oriental Orthodox (non-Chalcedonian) Churches issued a common document with more explicit terms of what both Churches confess and anathemize.[15]

Consultations continue between the Coptic Church and each of the Greek Orthodox (Byzantine) Church and the Vatican, but progress has not ended all the outstanding issues necessary to restore common communion. Clearly, centuries of disputes have left a gap that is still too large to bridge.

***

At this point, it is important to note that the 'Coptic Orthodox' represent about 85% of the 'Copts' in Egypt, but there are other denominations too, the largest of which are:

---

[i] Of India.

[ii] These confessional divisions were also indirectly linked to regional, ethnic, and linguistic affiliations.

- Protestants, or 'Coptic Evangelicals.' Their roots go back to the work of American Reformist Presbyterians who came in 1854. Today, they number over one million.
- Coptic Catholics. They have almost identical rites to the Coptic Orthodox, but obey the Roman Catholic Pope, who appoints their Patriarch (who is sometimes an ordained cardinal). Their roots go back to early 19th century, and currently number about 200,000. The Vatican appointed the first Coptic Catholic Patriarch in 1895.
- Greek Orthodox, or Melkites [i], who continued to follow the Byzantine faith, unlike the 'Coptic Orthodox,' after the Council of Chalcedon.

***

In terms of geographical extent, it is important to highlight the presence of the Coptic Church in Africa. Though the Roman or Byzantine rulers of Egypt had never really established themselves for any length of time beyond the limit of Philae (Aswan), the bloodless conquest of paganism by Christianity in all these southern countries had been going on steadily for centuries. Christianity was steadily progressing through the Nubian kingdoms, till, in the fifth and sixth centuries, it had become the dominant religion from Alexandria to the furthest confines of Ethiopia or Abyssinia.[16] There were a number of politically independent Christian kingdoms between Aswan and Abyssinia, which, on the whole, was never so well-settled, well-governed, and well-cultivated as at this time.[17]

The Christian religion, at the time of the Arab invasion, was professed not only in the valley of the Nile, but far down to the southern frontier of Abyssinia, on the eastern side of the African continent. All these countries acknowledged the head of the Coptic Church of Egypt as their Pope. There were a number of politically independent Christian kingdoms between Aswan and Abyssinia.

To the west, the church of Alexandria extended its spiritual reach over the 'five western cities' (Pentapolis) of north Africa, located on the coasts of current-day Libya and Tunisia.

---

[i] From *Malek* (king), in reference to being loyal to the Byzantine kings.

***

The number of Copts in Egypt is, for some reason, a well-kept secret by the country's authorities.[i] However, there is consensus that they represent 10–15% of Egypt's total population. This makes them the largest non-Muslim population in the Middle East. Their number is conservatively estimated to be (currently) over twelve million[ii].

The Copts live everywhere in Egypt, but their percentage is higher in Upper (south) Egypt, especially in the governorates of Minya and Assiut, where they amount to 25–30% of the population. Although rare, some villages are still almost entirely inhabited by Copts. Copts are also significantly present in Cairo and Alexandria.

Copts started to emigrate from Egypt in the late 1950s, but their major exodus came following the 2011 uprising which resulted in empowering the Islamists. Today, their diaspora grew to represent 15–20% of their total population. These are mostly in the U.S.A., Canada, and Australia, with growing numbers in Europe.

---

[i] It is sometimes reported that the Copts 'constituted about 160,000 out of a population of around three million' at the time of the French Expedition (see for example *The Copts* by Abdel Latif El-Menawy, Gilgamesh Publishing, U.K., 2017, P. 34), maliciously implying that if they represented barely 5% of the population at the dawn of the 19th century, they can only be less than that at present. However, this figure was based on the number of the *Jizya*-paying adult male Copts (i.e. excluding women, children and ailing elders). Hence, the real total number of Copts would be three-to-four times as much. Indeed, according to *La Description de l'Égypte* prepared by the French Expedition, the Copts represented 15–20% of the total population (refer to chapter titled *Bonaparte's Knocks at the Door*).

[ii] To put things in prospective, Copts' number would be more than the current population of Finland (5.5 million), Lebanon (6.1 million), Israel (8.5 million), Sweden (10 million), U.A.E. (10 million), the state of Michigan (10 million), or North Carolina (10.4 million).

A Peaceful or Forceful Conquest?

The term 'conquest' is the usual translation of '*al-Faṭ.*' However, this Arabic expression, which literally means 'opening,' has a different connotation: one with an implicit sense of being *usually* peaceful and, more importantly, bringing in civilization and good news (Islam) to the *opened* territories. The question put in the title above has been raised numerous times over the centuries—but not for mere historical accuracy. As we shall see in this chapter and the ones to follow, the main issue was about the *rights* of the people in the *opened* lands.

***

First, we need to look at the political, administrative, and religious situation in Egypt.

Since coming under Roman rule (in 30 B.C.), Egypt was submitted directly to Rome or, at times, to the Eastern Administration. However, in 554, about a century prior to the Arab invasion, the Byzantine Emperor, Justinian (527–65), changed Egypt's administrative structure by dividing it into four provinces under the control of the general ruler of the East (Constantinople). These four provinces (or duchies) were: *Aigyptiaca*, which included the West of the Delta and Alexandria; *Augustamnica*, which included the East of the Delta reaching Arish (northern Sinai); *Arcadia*, which included central Egypt reaching Al Bahnasa; and *Thebaid*, which included Upper Egypt, from Hermpolis (El-Ashmunein) to the far South. It is needless to mention that this division was one of the reasons behind the defeat to both the Persian and later the Arab invasions, since it divided the accountability, etc.

At the top of these provinces, the ruler was often referred to as *Pagarch* (prefect), who was the civil governor, to whom the whole administration was confided. Only the army and the clergy were exempt from his control.

Under the emperor Theodosius the Great (380–95), Christianity became the official religion of the empire. A state religion usually finds itself liable to state control, and the emperors were anxious to ensure uniformity of belief, as well as uniformity of laws. Doctrinal arguments for long distracted the church. The creed to which Egypt's Athanasius gave his name (in 325) has become the symbol of Christian orthodoxy for the entire church, but a century later, a schism took place at the Council of Chalcedon (451) and the Church in Egypt became known as 'Miaphysite' (often referred to, erroneously, as 'Monophysite.') This doctrine became adopted as a badge of nationalism. The emperors continued their effort to realign the Coptic Church, but without much success. Under Justinian, a rival Patriarch was brought to Alexandria (around 543), but the effort to install him was followed by a riot. Henceforward, there were to be two Patriarchs in Egypt, one ('Melkite') supported by the imperial authority and a part of the Copts (mostly Alexandrians), and the other usually to be found in one of the monasteries and enjoying the support of the mass of the people.

Like other provinces of the Byzantine Empire, Egypt had been occupied by the Persians between 619 and 629 or 630, when it had just been recovered by Heraclius. When Amr and his troops came in 639, the country was still disorganized, and rival factions were taking advantage of the dynastic troubles engendered by the internal divisions of the Byzantine state.

***

The invading army is said to have included units from various Arab tribes, especially from Yemen, who would represent its majority. It included also many apostates (*murtad*), who left Islam after the death of the prophet, whom the first Caliph, Abu-Bakr, fought to force them back into Islam (*Riddah* wars). They were strongly encouraged by Caliph Omar Ibn Al-Khatab to join the conquests, as a way to tempt them to gain bounty, to keep them away from seditious activities. But these Arabs numbered only a few thousands. On the way to Egypt from Palestine (through northern Sinai, along the Mediterranean cost) numerous Arab Bedouins (from the inhabitants of Sinai and the Eastern desert), bandits, and vagabonds joined the foray, as well as some Nabateans[i] (who mainly helped as guides and

---

[i] Inhabitants of northern Arabia and southern Levant, in current day Jordan.

translators), [18] Amr enticed these various groups by promising them war booty, spoils, and captives in return for their help in the battles leading to the invasion. It is estimated that the army numbered between twelve and fifteen-thousand men.

The *History of the Patriarchs* deals with the savage Persian invasion that was brought to an end by Heraclius, who later installed 'Cyrus'[i] as Patriarch of the Byzantine (Melkite), Church of Egypt, and (a de facto) governor over the Alexandrian province, *Aigyptiaca*. His goal was to try to revert the Copts back to the Byzantine doctrine, being convinced that doctrinal differences threatened the unity and security of the empire. This was when Abba Benyamin I (the 38th Patriarch) fled to Upper Egypt.

The *History* then mentions the news that the Egyptians heard of the appearance of Islam and the commencing of invasions in the Levant:

[..] An Arab man from around the *Qibla*[ii] in Mecca, by the name of Mohammed, was stirred up and turned back the idolaters to the worship of Allah alone and to confessing that Mohammed is his messenger. His people (*umma*) were circumcised by the flesh, not by the Law (*Nomos*), and they prayed toward a place they called the *Kaaba*. He ruled over Damascus, the Levant, and across the Jordan. The Lord delivered the Roman army into his hands because of their corrupt [faith] and the anathemas of the Early Fathers that affected them as a result of the Council of Chalcedon [..].

Amr and his army entered Egypt after some battles on the way. Then, after winning over a garrison in Heliopolis and then another one at Tendunias[iii], he set siege of the Byzantine stronghold of the Babylon[iv] Fortress (in what is currently called 'Old Misr,' or 'Old Cairo,' located south of Cairo) in September, 640. This must have brought home to the population

---

[i] Refer to Appendix two.

[ii] *Qiblah*, is the direction that Muslims face when they do their prayers.

[iii] On the eastern bank of the Nile, in current-day Rod Al-Farag.

[iv] Babylon, considered the key of the south of Egypt, was founded in the early days of the Persian conquests (525 B.C.), and was enlarged and strongly fortified by the Romans. Trajan (around 100 A.D.) extended the Ptolemaic canal (linking the Nile to Red Sea) to there, and built the great fortress, on which ruins now exists Qasr Al-Sham' (Candle Castle) that encloses six of the oldest churches in Cairo.

that this was no mere ephemeral raid; the threat was real. There were some skirmishes, but perhaps most damaging to the morale of the besieged was the news of the death of the emperor, Heraclius, and also the ensuing struggle for the succession, which made it unlikely that help would come from Constantinople any time soon. So, when Amr promised that the lives of the troops garrisoning the fortress would be spared, they decided to surrender and evacuated their positions on the second day after the feast of the Resurrection, in April, 641, after a siege of some seven months.

The *History* then says,

[..] So when the heads of the of the city [Misr] saw these things, they went to Amr, requesting safety for their city lest it be plundered. And these are the words of the command that their leader, Mohammed[i], issued to them: "The area of Misr and its city shall remain with its people [as long as] you are paid the *Kharaj*. If they pledge compliance to your rule, make a pledge with them, and do not treat them unjustly; as for those who refuse [to pledge compliance] and oppose you, plunder and take them as [war] prisoners." That is why they kept their hands off the city and its people, but they destroyed the Romans and their Patriarch, called Maryanos, and those who survived escaped to Alexandria, shut its gates, and took refuge there.

[..] Three years after Amr took control over [the city of] Misr, the Muslims overpowered Alexandria and destroyed its walls and burned many churches, including the Church of Saint Mark, by the sea, where his body was laid to rest [..] They also burned all the convents around the church. A wonder took place during the burning of the aforementioned church (the head of St. Mark was retrieved unscathed) [..].

Alexandria finally surrendered in September, 642.

***

---

[i] Not clear who is 'Mohammed,' as it cannot be the prophet of Islam, who had died seven years earlier. Unless this would be in reference to some general perception of the prophet's 'guidelines' to his companions when embarking on war expeditions (*ghazawat*).

It is instructive here to refer to what Yohanna Al-Nakyousi (John, Bishop of Nikiu[i]) recorded as a contemporaneous witness of these events, in his annals written in Coptic (693-700). These were later translated into Arabic (in the Middle Ages), and some of these were then translated into Ethiopic in 1594[ii]. As the only extant copies, the Ethiopic manuscripts were translated into English, in 1916.[19] It is to this translation that we now turn for some brief quotes regarding the course of the battles and the affairs of Egypt:

Then, a panic fell on all the cities of Egypt, and all their inhabitants took to flight, and made their way to Alexandria, abandoning all their possessions and wealth and cattle. (Chapter 113, section six).

[..] *The Moslem took as a booty all the possessions of the Christians who had fled, and they designated the servants of Christ enemies of God.* (Chapter 114, section one).

And Amr, the chief of the Moslem, spent twelve months in warring against the Christians of Northern Egypt, but failed, nevertheless, in reducing their cities. (Chapter 115, section one)

Al-Nakyousi describes how Amr destroyed all the inhabitants of the city of Al Bahnasa, near Faiyum, when it fell into his hands:

...and they put to the sword all that surrendered, and they spared none, whether old men, babe, or woman. Faiyum and Bawit suffered the same fate. And thereupon the Moslem made their entry into Nikius, and took possession, and finding no soldiers (to offer resistance), they proceeded to put to the sword all whom they found in the streets and in the churches, men, women, and infants, and they showed mercy to none. [..] And after they had captured (this) city, they marched against other localities and sacked them and put all they found to the sword.

---

[i] Nikius, of which John was bishop, is situated in the Delta, between two branches of the Nile, in the district of Menouf. Its Egyptian name was Pshati.

[ii] According to the very precise note of the translator, an Egyptian monk living in Abyssinia, 'in the year of the world, 7594; in the year of Alexander, 1947; in the year of our Lord, 1594; in the year of the Martyrs, 1318; in the year of the Hegira, 980, or 1010 by their lunar computation.'

Then, he sorrowfully adds:

Let us now cease (from talking), for it is impossible to recount the iniquities perpetrated by the Moslem after their capture of the island of Nikius, on Sunday, the 18ᵗʰ day of the month, Genbôt...

Then, he describes what took place after the capturing of Kîlûnâs, which was done by the help of a certain (Jewish) individual:

...they had cast down the walls of the city, they forthwith made themselves masters of it, and put to the sword thousands of its inhabitants and of the soldiers, and they gained an enormous booty, and took the women and children captive and divided them amongst themselves, and they made that city a desolation (lit. destitute). (Chapter 118, sections 9, 10, and 11).

Lastly, the besieged Babylon Fortress was surrendered on the day after Easter,

And Egypt also had become enslaved to Satan. A great strife had broken out between the inhabitants of Lower Egypt, and these were divided into two parties. Of these, one sided with Theodore (the Roman commander), but the other wished to join the Moslem. And straightaway, the one party rose against the other, and they plundered their possessions and burnt their city... (Chapter 119, section one)

And subsequently, the Patriarch, Cyrus, set out and went to Babylon to the Moslem, seeking by the offer of tribute to procure peace from them and put a stop to war in the land of Egypt. And Amr welcomed his arrival, and said unto him: "Thou hast done well to come to us." And Cyrus answered and said unto him: "God has delivered this land into your hands: let there be no enmity from henceforth between you and Rome: heretofore, there has been no persistent strife with you. And they fixed the amount of tribute to be paid." (Chapter 120, sections 17 and 18)

And the Romans were to cease warring against the Moslem, and the Moslem were to desist from seizing Christian Churches, and the latter were not to intermeddle with any concerns of the Christians. And the Jews were to be permitted to remain in the city of Alexandria. And while things were in this condition, the Moslem came to receive the tribute, though the inhabitants of Alexandria had not yet been informed (of the treaty). And the Alexandrians, on seeing them, made ready for battle. But the troops and the generals held fast to the resolution they had adopted, and said: "We cannot engage in battle with the Moslem: rather, let the counsel of the Patriarch Cyrus be observed." Then the population rose up against the Patriarch and sought to stone him. But he said unto them: "I have made this treaty in order to save you and your children." And plunged in much weeping and grief, he besought them... (Chapter 120, sections 20–26)

And the Egyptians, who, through fear of the Moslem, had fled and taken refuge in the city of Alexandria, made the following request to the Patriarch: "Get the Moslem to promise that we may return to our cities and become their subjects." And he negotiated for them according to their request. And the Moslem took possession of all the land of Egypt, southern and northern, and trebled their taxes... (Chapter 120, section 28)

And Abba Benjamin, the Patriarch of the Egyptians, returned to the city of Alexandria in the 13th year, after his flight from the Romans, and he went to the churches and inspected all of them. And everyone said: "This expulsion (of the Romans) and victory of the Moslem is due to the wickedness of the emperor, Heraclius, and his persecution of the Orthodox through the Patriarch, Cyrus. This was the cause of the ruin of the Romans and the subjugation of Egypt by the Moslem." (Chapter 121, section one)

> In the same vein, the *History of the Patriarchs* says,
> Amr found out about the hiding of Abba Benyamin, so he wrote [upon the request of the Coptic *Archons*[i], or leaders] a pact guarantying his safety and peace, and he returned to Alexandria after thirteen years. When Amr saw him, he treated him with dignity and respect.

Yohanna Al-Nakyousi again says,

"And Amr became stronger every day in every field of his activity. And he exacted the taxes which had been determined upon, but he took none of the property of the churches, and he committed no act of spoliation or plunder, and he preserved them throughout all his days. [..]"

And he increased the taxes to the extent of 22 batr of gold, till all the people hid themselves owing to the greatness of the tribulation, and could not find the wherewithal to pay... (Chapter 121, sections three and four).

---

[i] Greek, for ruler or holder of senior public office. Used here to designate community leader, who is usually more affluent and holder of a post in the administration.

And none could recount the mourning and lamentation which took place in that city: they even gave their children in exchange for the great sums which they had to pay monthly. And they had none to help them, and God destroyed their hopes, and delivered the Christians into the hands of their enemies. (Chapter 121, section seven).

Yet, this crushing situation was not deemed as final, for Al-Nakyousi closes his narrative with some hope in future:

But the strong beneficence of God will put to shame those who grieve us, and He will make His love for man to triumph over our sins, and bring to naught the evil purposes of those who afflict us. (Chapter 121, section eight).

***

Modern scholars often argue, on the basis of later witnesses, that the Egyptians who were anti-Chalcedonian (that is, they rejected the creed agreed upon at the council of Chalcedon in 451) welcomed the Arabs and only the Chalcedonian Egyptians opposed them. However, John of Nikiu never once intimates that he or his fellow non-Chalcedonians were in any way well disposed toward the conquerors. He also makes clear that the Arabs themselves were indiscriminate in their slaughter and that the disunity among the Egyptians lay not in sectarian differences, but in how to face this challenge: whether it was better to submit and make peace, or to stand and fight. "A great strife had broken out between the inhabitants of Lower Egypt, and these were divided into two parties." Of these, one sided with Theodore, the commander-in-chief of the army in Egypt, who was determined to resist, whereas the other side felt that their interests were best served by negotiation and accommodation with the invaders. And this indecision seemed to grip the very highest echelons of government. The elder son of Heraclius promised to send Theodore a large force in the autumn of 641, with which to repel the enemy. However, upon his premature death, his younger brother chose not to respect this promise, and furthermore, he reappointed Cyrus, who had been Chalcedonian Patriarch of Alexandria during the 630s, but who had been sacked for his conciliatory stance toward the Arabs.[20]

***

From the testimonies of Sawiris and Al-Nakyousi, it appears that the Copts, generally speaking, were somewhat happy to be rid of the Byzantines, but at the same time, they (with some individual exceptions) did not help the Arabs; rather, they were wary of them. Egypt was always vulnerable to raids from the Arab Bedouins, and others living in bordering countries who targeted it for looting and pillaging. Since, in the past, those invaders went away upon accomplishing their 'mission,' perhaps the Copts expected the new invaders to eventually do the same...

As the dust settled after the invasion, a clearer portrait of the invaders began to emerge. Although Amr sought a policy of accommodation toward the national church and its leading clergy and refrained from seizing their property, conceivably to avoid fueling any uprisings, he nonetheless treated the populace in a completely different manner, especially as related to exaction of taxes.

Al-Nakyousi summarizes these conditions by frankly stating,

For Amr had no mercy on the Egyptians, and did not observe the covenant they had made with him, for he was of a barbaric race... (Chapter 120, section 36)

According to the Muslim chronicler Ibn Abdul Hakam,[21] Amr told the Copts: "If someone conceals his treasure (his wealth) from me and I come to know about it, I will kill him." Amr heard about a man named Botros, from Upper Egypt, who had 'a treasure,' and when Amr questioned him, Botros denied it. When Amr verified the truth of what he had heard, he killed Botros. So, the Copts began bringing out all their wealth for fear of being killed.

According to the same source, when one of the Copts asked Amr, "Inform us of the value of the *Jizya* for each of us so that we may pay it accordingly," Amr replied, "Even if you paid me from the floor to the roof, I will not tell you exactly what you owe. All of you are our treasury, when we are asked to deliver more (money as requested by the Caliph), we impose more on you, and if less is demanded from us, we lighten your burden."[i]

Furthermore, after things settled down militarily for the invaders upon seizing full control of the country, a question was raised, "Was the conquest

---

[i] Ibn Abdel Hakam, P. 153. Strictly speaking, Amr refers to what his superior (the Caliph) would order him to collect, and whether this goes up or down.

of Egypt peaceful or by force?" The likely answer was, "By force," the presence of Copts in the Byzantine armies being evidence of the natives' resistance to the invaders. In addition, the army divisions in Babylon and Alexandria requested the fighting to cease only when circumstances got out of control; this further demonstrated that the locals resisted the conquest. In fact, while sitting one day in the mosque, Amr said, "I sit in this position and none of Egypt's Copts can make demands of me with regards to treaty or pact [..]; if I desire, I kill, if I desire, I keep the fifth, and if I desire, I sell."[i] And when a man who converted to Islam during the time of Omar Ibn Al-Khatab requested to be freed from his obligation to pay the *Jizya*, Omar said, "No, the conquest of your land was by force."

***

Ironically, the oldest known seal of the Islamic era belongs to Amr. This seal represents a *charging bull*. It appears on an Egyptian papyrus[ii] dated according to the Coptic calendar to what corresponds to January 8th, 643. It was Amr who, conforming to his personal totem, had taken the initiative of the conquest, putting the Caliph Omar before the fait accompli.[22]

It is interesting to add that Amr left Egypt afterward and was replaced by Abd Allah Ibn Saad. Because of his past experience, he was ordered by Caliph Uthman to return back to lead the fight against the Byzantines who tried to regain Alexandria. Having succeeded in his mission, the Caliph asked him to stay as the army chief, while Ibn Saad remains as a *Wali* on the *Kharaj* (taxation). It is then when Amr made his famous statement, "I would then be like someone who holds a cow from its horns, while another one milks it," and refused to accept the position.[23]

But were the atrocities committed in Egypt unique? Not so, if we just take the example of what took place in Palestine a few years earlier. Sophronius, the Patriarch of Jerusalem, in the letter he wrote in 634, he rails against 'the Saracens who, on account of our sins, have now risen up against

---

[i] Al-Balathury, *Futuh al-Buldan* (Conquests of Countries), P. 217. Splitting the booties taken from the *Kuffar* in Islamic *ghazawat* is regulated according to Quran and Sunna rules.

[ii] The document is addressed to the pagarch (*pagarchos*), the Byzantine chief of a district.

us unexpectedly and ravage all with cruel and feral design, with impious and godless audacity.' Later in the year, the security situation was so bad that he could not travel to Bethlehem and was obliged to give his Nativity sermon in Jerusalem. He laments, "So now the army of the godless Saracens has captured the divine Bethlehem and bars our passage there, threatening slaughter and destruction."

The Patriarch's last and most detailed description of the Arab attacks appears in his sermon on the Holy Baptism, which he delivered on the feast of the Epiphany, December 6th, of either 635 or 636. He urges his congregation to eschew sin, for this is the reason 'why the vengeful and God-hating Saracens, the abomination of desolation clearly foretold to us by the prophets, overrun the places which are not allowed to them, plunder cities, devastate fields, burn down villages, set on fire the holy churches, overturn the sacred monasteries, and oppose the Byzantine armies arrayed against them.'[24]

***

As time passed, it became clear that, in addition to the 'customary' looting and pillaging, the invasion of Egypt took the form of an actual colonization.

Regarding the deteriorating conditions in Egypt after the conquest, it is enough to quote the sad and sobering statement of Alfred Butler:

"...One might also sketch the decline of those great and splendid cities which the Romans had left in Egypt: for Alexandria, though first among the cities of the East, if not of the world, was only one among many which reached from Syene (Aswan) to the Mediterranean. One would find that temples and palaces were suffered to fall into ruins; that precious marbles were quarried for building or burned for lime; that bronze statues were melted down and turned into coin or domestic vessels..."[25]

In fact, Amr was almost aghast at the wealth and splendor of Alexandria, and wrote to Omar in extravagant terms of his conquest, "I have taken a city of which I can but say that it contains 4,000 palaces, 4,000 baths, 400 theatres, 12,000 sellers of green vegetables..."[26]

But though he writes much of the baths and the shops, he says nothing of the books or the works of art which still adorned that city, and the well-known story of the destruction of the Library of Alexandria. Gibbon[i] throws doubt upon its destruction, but his only good argument against it is the silence of the contemporary writers, and this is by no means conclusive. It was not until they had lived among the Egyptians for a century or two that the Arabs realized what they had done. At the time, it must have seemed to them a most trifling incident. One of the most learned of the Alexandrian scholars of that day sought an interview with the barbarian conqueror, and entreated that the books of the Alexandrian library should not be dispersed or destroyed, but might be delivered to his guardianship. Amr, we learn, was inclined to grant his request, but inquired with curiosity what he could possibly want with the musty old parchments. The scholar replied indignantly, but incautiously, that some of them were worth all the riches of Alexandria put together. Amr replied that, if so, he was not empowered to give them to the first man who asked for them, and referred the question to Omar.

The Caliph's decision was simple, "If these books contain nothing more than that which is written in the book of Allah (Quran), they are useless; if they contain anything contrary to the sacred book, they are pernicious. In either case, burn them." It is written that the books sufficed for six months' fuel for the public baths of Alexandria.[27]

***

Another question seldom asked is why, in the first place, the Arabs embarked on their conquest? What really motivated them to do?

An answer comes from none but Amr Ibn Al-Aas, to whom is attributed the following account (in a moment of truth?), as related by the Sunni Arab scholar and historian, Ibn Asakir (1106–1175) in his book, *The History of Damascus*, where he devotes a chapter to Amr. This rare account goes as follows:

An army of Muslims of which I was the general (amir) went on conquest. We arrived at Alexandria. One of their leaders[ii] said, "Bring someone to me, so I can speak to him and he speaks to me." I said, "*N*o one but me will see him." I went there, accompanied by an interpreter. He himself had an

---

[i] Edward Gibbon (1737–1794), author on the history of the Roman Empire.

[ii] No specific date of the incident, but it could be around 641–2. Nor the name of the leader is given, but it could by Cyrus.

interpreter. He arranged two high seats (minbar). Then, he asked, "Who are you?"

I said: "We are Arabs, people of thorns and acacia. And we are the people of the house of Allah. We were the poorest of the earth, the most miserable when it came to the way of life. We ate the bloodless dead flesh. We were attacking each other. We led the most miserable life among men. But there came among us a man. He was not, then, the most noble of us, nor the richest. He said: 'I am sent from Allah to you.' He commanded us what we did not know; he forbade things we did, and our fathers did. We treated him with scorn and called him a liar. We refused his words. But other people came to him and said to him, 'We believe that you speak truth and we believe in you. We will follow you and fight those who fight you.' He went (to live) with them. We stood up against him and we fought him. He fought us and he overcame us and defeated us. And he undertook the Arabs who were nearby him; he fought them, and he defeated them. Now, if the Arabs I left behind knew what kind of life you have, none of them would ever stop coming to share it with you."

Amr continues,

Then the other (Byzantine) person laughed. Then, he said, "Your prophet truly spoke. Our prophets came to tell us what your prophet has come to tell you. We followed them. But some kings appeared among us; they began to make use of all of this according to their own passions, diverting the commandments of the prophets. As for you, you have supposedly taken into account what your prophet ordered. But when none of us fought you, here you are coming to fight and overcome us, while none of us was trying to steal from you, you are here to take away what is ours. If you forsake the order of your prophet and act as our kings did according to their own passions, then the matter is now between us. You are not more numerous than us, and you have no more strength than us."

And Amr concludes: "I have never spoken to a man more odious than this man."

In this story, Amr, the 'hero,' is trying to explain—not to justify—the conquest. The crux of his argument is about the situation of the Arabs. Before the coming of their prophet, they were miserable and without law. The prophet finally commanded them laws which he imposed by the arms. The Arabs bowed. Having then become a strong people, they come to claim their place and their share of the wealth enjoyed by others, and they do this by conquest.

The response of Byzantine governor is strictly on the same grounds. It is not a religious apologetic debate — 'your prophet against ours': all the prophets have, according to him, the same function, which is to give laws so that people stop attacking each other. He points out to Amr that in the end, by his unjustified conquest — "No one of us fought you or stole from you" — he (Amr) is reproducing the pattern of earlier kings: these had diverted the laws given by the prophets by putting them at the service of their own interests. If it is so for some as for the others, then the speeches about the prophets do not matter at all; we can only laugh, and let the strongest win! Stung by the argument, Amr concludes: "What a heinous man!" This moral fable is indeed remarkable.[28]

Se non è vero… (even if it was not true, it is a good story!)

***

In conclusion, this is what we can say about the conquest of Egypt:

1. The Arabs embarked on their conquest for no other reason than to share in—or rather, take for their own—the 'good life' of other people. They came uninvited and aggressed those who never did them any harm.

2. Taking advantage largely of a situation that the Byzantines mastered badly, the conquest of Egypt was the result of successive military actions led by Amr, then in parallel or jointly by other generals, such as Al-Zubayr Ibn Al-Awwam, sent for assistance by the Caliph.

3. The country was conquered by the sword; the conquest was an alternation of combat followed by massacres, taking captives and booty, and then surrender, more easily obtained and followed by peace treaties in which the conquerors imposed their conditions on the conquered populations. It ended in 642 with the first surrender of Alexandria, when a comprehensive peace treaty was concluded. In 645, taking advantage of the murder of Omar, the Byzantines took back Alexandria and some localities of the Delta. But Amr ended up chasing them again in 646.[29]

4. Egyptians did not help the Arabs and, for the most part, resisted the invaders. When the Romans (the Patriarch Cyrus and the generals of the army) sensed impending defeat, they chose peace and negotiated with Amr, and handed the country over to him. The people of Alexandria were angry

because of that surrender treaty, but it was too late to do anything about it. Regardless, for the invaders, the conquest of Egypt was 'by force.'

5. During his rule, Amr dealt with the Patriarch and the national Church in a generally reasonable manner, precisely to win them over…

6. Amr did not honor any pacts or treaties pertaining to the treatment of the populace or the *Jizya* dues, and he rushed to increase taxes and used violence and abuse in exacting these funds.

7. Civilizational deterioration and the destruction of the country began with Alexandria, the 'first among the cities of the East, if not of the world…'

Rapacious Umayyads

The Umayyads established their state in Damascus in 661, after the killing of Caliph Ali in the major inter-fights that tore the Muslims apart for five years (and ultimately led to the split of Sunnis and Shia). Amr Ibn Al-Aas was sent again to Egypt as a *Wali*, as a reward for his support of the winners in that conflict, where he remained until his death in 664.

In reference to the days of Abba Yoannes III (677–686), who was the 48th Patriarch, the *History* says,

In the days after the death of Yazîd Ib Muawiya[i], a king (Caliph) named Marwan[ii], rose from the lands of the Muslims, like a hungry lion coming out of the forest, devouring and trampling everyone in his sight, and he installed his son, Abdul-Aziz, as a *Wali* over Misr [..]. In his first year, he went to Alexandria, but his arrival was not publicized, so unaware of his arrival, the Patriarch failed to welcome him. Some snitched on him to the *Wali*, who angrily called the Patriarch to his palace. The Patriarch's explanation of the situation failed to convince the *Wali*, who handed him over to be held by his officials until he pays one-hundred-thousand dinars [pieces of gold].

He was then delivered on the first day of Easter week, to a cruel and heartless man named Saad, who kept torturing the Patriarch, demanding

---

[i] In the days of Yazîd Ibn Muawiya, who was the second Umayyad Caliph (installed 680), Al-Husayn, the son of Ali Ibn Abi Talib, was slaughtered and his head was sent to the Caliph. The Umayyads trampled his body with their horses until they crushed his back and chest in a strangely vicious manner. In his days, 'The (Copts) experienced great severity and their anguish and calamities were multiplied, and the corrupt people pursued them, killing and looting them.' Refer to *Al-Kafi fi tarikh Misr al-qadim wa-al-hadith* by Mikhail Sharubim Bek, First edition (1898), Second edition in the series of *Safahat min Tarîkh Misr* (Pages from the History of Egypt), 2004, Publisher: Madbouly, Cairo.

[ii] Ruled November 683–685.

that he pay the money. The Patriarch responded, "You ask me to pay one-hundred-thousand dinars, and I do not even have 100 dirhams [..], do what you want to do, my body is in your hands, but my soul and my body together are in the hands of my Lord, Jesus Christ." Hearing these words, the infidel[i] was enraged and gnashed his teeth, and ordered that the Patriarch's feet be placed in a copper bowl filled with burning coals [..]. He then brought the Patriarch back and threatened that if the money was not paid, then he would dress him in Jewish garb, smear his face with ashes, and parade him around the city. The Patriarch told him: "Even if the Lord, my God, does not deliver me from your hands, you will not be able to do anything to me except what He wills." So, Saad told him: "I will take off fifty-thousand dinars from what you owe, and I will let you go beg for the rest." The Patriarch replied: "I can only afford the clothes on my back." As the bargaining continued, the amount of money demanded reached ten-thousand dinars, and when the [Coptic] scribes designated in Alexandria heard of it, they told the Patriarch to accept, and we will have the bishops, scribes, and Divâns pay the sum in installments. [..] So they informed the *Wali*, who threatened them and released the Patriarch on Maundy Thursday[ii], to go collect money from the Christians [..]. After he collected the demanded sum of money, the *Wali* helped him in rebuilding the Church of St. Mark [which was burned down by Amr].

***

In the days of Abba Ishak[iii] (686–689), the 49th Patriarch, who was previously a monk in the Monastery of St. Makarius, it so happened that he

---

[i] Sawiris used the term 'infidel' many times for people irrespective of their religion, referring to a 'harsh, haughty, and unjust' person (this is how the term is often used colloquially by Egyptians even today).

[ii] He went straight to the cathedral to take part in the ceremony of washing the beggars' feet and celebrated the Holy Communion before returning to his residence.

[iii] The *Wali* had sent orders that election should take place in Babylon, which now formed the southern suburb of Al-Fustat, instead of Alexandria. After this date, the election of the Patriarch generally took place at Babylon, but the consecration was always performed in the Church of the Angels at Alexandria, until the end of the 11th century.

wrote to the kings of Abyssinia and Nubia[i], asking them to reconcile. Christianity (according to the Coptic doctrine) was the prevalent faith in these two countries, and thus the Coptic Church wielded spiritual authority over them, even ordaining their bishops. The fallout was partially due to the Nubian kingdom conducting raids against Abyssinia to kidnap people, who would then be used as slaves to meet the quota required by the *Wali* of Egypt, according to the treaty they signed in the days of Caliph Uthman. The *History* says,

> [..] But this [the Patriarch's intervention] extremely angered the *Wali*, Abdel Aziz[ii], who ordered that the Patriarch be brought and killed [..], but when the Patriarch's messengers were brought to him, he did not find such letters [because they had discarded them]. Therefore, he let the Patriarch go back to Alexandria, but he would not allow him to come in his presence again. In addition, he ordered that crosses, including gold and silver ones, in all the cities of Egypt be destroyed, and this unsettled the Christians in Egypt. He also wrote on several scraps 'Mohammed is the great prophet of Allah, and Isa also is a prophet, and Allah neither begets nor is born,' and he nailed these to the doors of the churches.

***

In the days of Abba Simon (689–701), who was a Syrian by birth, and greatly respected by the Nitrian monks' community[iii],

---

[i] Nubia extended beyond Egypt's southern borders to cover most of the current-day Sudan. As attempts by Arabs to occupy Nubia failed, a treaty was concluded (about 660), in which Arabs agreed not to invade Nubia. In return, the Nubians were to allow a mosque to be built in Dongola for those Arabs who might desire to settle there, and to see that no harm was done to it, and no Moslem annoyed. The worst feature of the treaty was the clause, which laid the foundation of the Arab slave trade—so different an affair from the domestic servitude which has existed from time immemorial in Oriental countries. Three hundred and sixty slaves from the interior, of both sexes, among whom should be found no old man or old woman or child below the age of puberty, were to be brought every year. (Butcher, V-1, p 380).

[ii] Son of Merwan, the Caliph.

[iii] Natroun Valley, or Shehit, south west of Alexandria. After taking the office, he appointed a superintendent of the Egyptian monasteries; this was John of Nikius, the known historian.

The *Wali* ordered the banning of holy masses [church services],[i] and he called the Christians misguided for claiming that Allah has a wife and a child. Afterward, a priest arrived from India, asking the Patriarch to ordain a bishop for India, and since the people of India were not obedient to the Muslims, the Patriarch replied: "I cannot do that without the approval of the *Wali* of Egypt." The priest left to meet with the *Wali*, but, while on the way, a group of 'Gaianites'[ii] met with him, and they ordained for him a bishop and two priests. After travelling 20 days on their journey back, they were arrested by the Muslim road guards, who sent them to Caliph Abdul Malek, who amputated their hands and feet[iii]. He then sent them to Misr and wrote to (his brother), *Wali* Abdul Al-Aziz, rebuking him, saying, "It appears that you are unaware of what is going on in your domain: the Christian Patriarch who resides in Alexandria sent Egyptian clergy to India, and you must administer two-hundred lashes and take from him one-hundred-thousand dinars and bring the money to us quickly." So, the *Wali* brought the Patriarch [..], and after a while, he discovered the truth and crucified the one responsible for ordaining the bishop [and released the Patriarch]. Abba Simon was diligent all the days of his life to avoid conflicts between the Christians and the Muslims.[iv]

***

---

[i] We do not know for how long this prohibition was in effect.

[ii] A sect not associated with the Coptic Orthodox Church, followers of the heresy of Eutychius.

[iii] The Caliph probably regarded their journey as evidence of conspiracy between the Christians of Egypt and India against the Muslim dominion.

[iv] During the reign of this Patriarch a question arose about divorce. Some had become infected by the practice prevailing amongst the Muslims, and declared, like them, that it was lawful to divorce a wife at pleasure. A Council was held in 695 at Babylon, attended by sixty-four bishops—of whom the greater part belonged to the (National) Coptic Church, but among whom were Gaianites and Barsanuphians, as well as Chalcedonians or Melkite bishops, who discussed their common affairs without any outbreak of ill-feeling between the different parties. (Butcher, V-1, P. 391)

In the days of Alexanderos II (705–730), the 43rd Patriarch, the *History* says:

> *Wali* Abdul Aziz had an older son called Al-Asbagh, who was believed to be the next in line to become *Wali*, after the death of his father, so he made him in charge of collecting the Kharaj over the whole area. Being the son of the *Wali*, the priests obeyed him in fear, but he despised Christians and was a ruthless killer, an evil man, like a wild lion. Some people slandered a group of monks to him [Al-Asbagh], so he sent and registered all the monks in all the areas and stipulated a one [gold] dinar Jizya per person, which was the first Jizya imposed on them. He also ordered them not to allow the ordination of more monks that have not been included in the registry. Then, he imposed the payment of two-thousand dinars per year on the bishops of the areas, and he acted horrendously and forced people to pray as he did [..]. Many beyond count had to convert to Islam, including Botros [the governor of Upper Egypt], his brother, the son of Mariout's town chief, and many clergy and seculars. On Saturday of the Holy Week, he [Al-Asbagh] entered a monastery in Helwan, and when he saw a picture of the Virgin Mary and Christ, he spat on it and said, "If I have time, I will wipe out the Christians from this area." He [allegedly] died the following day, and his father died 40 days later.

> Then, Caliph Abdul Malek sent his son, Abdullah (* see below), to rule over Egypt. He too acted wickedly and created devices with which he tortured people. He was like a wild beast, even finding joy when people were killed in front of him and their blood spattered over his plate of food. At that time, the Patriarch travelled [from Alexandria] to Misr [the old city, next to which Al-Fustat was built] to greet the *Wali,* as it was customary to do. Upon seeing the Patriarch, Abdullah said, "What is this?" They told him, "This is the Abba and Patriarch of all the Christians." So, he took the Patriarch and delivered him to one of his janitors and instructed him: "Humiliate him whichever way you desire, until he pays three-thousand dinars." For three days, the Christians were requesting that he be freed, and great fear came upon the bishops and priests. Deacon Gerga went to the *Wali* and asked him, "O my Lord, do you seek the Patriarch's life or money?" So, he said, "I want the money." So Gerga replied, "Entrust him to me for two months, and I will go

around with him asking for money." Abdullah gave him the Patriarch, and they toured the cities and towns, collecting money from believers in Christ, until they came up with the amount. Additionally, the *Wali* would assemble bishops, clergy, and monks to mock them arrogantly with hard words, and he would say to them, "To me, you are like the Roum [Byzantines]; whoever kills any of you will be forgiven by Allah, because you are the enemies of Allah."[i]

(*) In the days of Abdul Malek Ibn Marwan, according to another source,[30]

(...) The Copts experienced great hardships. Patriarch Alexanderos was detained twice for he had to pay a combined sum of six-thousand dinars, and this was the first time Jizya was collected from the monks, in opposition to the treaty. *Wali* Abdullah Ibn Abdul Malek became more severe in his treatment of the Copts in Egypt and harassed them. In so doing, he inspired Qurra Ibn Shreek (who succeeded him as *Wali*) to act the same way, so both killed, burned, destroyed, and shed much blood, and inflicted great atrocities on the Christians that were never experienced before that time. Therefore, these days were filled with calamities, disasters, and tribulations.

Abdul Malek was known for being [..] a lover of haughtiness and quick to shed blood [..] And that is why his *Walis*—Al-Hagag in Iraq, Mohammed Ibn Youssef (the brother of Al-Hagag) in Yemen, Mohammed Ibn Marwan in Gezira, and all the rest of them—were haughty, tyrannical oppressors.

> We return to the *History,* which continues,
> When he [Abdullah] collected the Kharaj from the people, he raised the amount by two-thirds of a dinar on top of every dinar. This caused many churches to go bankrupt. He loved money very much. So, the people were in great trouble and some were killed because of that. He also seared the hands and foreheads of strangers he found and exiled them. There was great anxiety and turmoil in the land, and he ordered that the dead not be buried until their Jizya was paid.

---

[i] During Abdullah's reign, the Christians found themselves worse off than ever. He invented new tortures for them, and it is said that one of his amusements was to invite a Christian to dinner and then cause his head to be struck off as he sat down. (Butcher, V-1, p. 395).

After two years, [Caliph] Abdul Malek died, and his son, Al-Walîd (705–715), became Caliph and made Qurra Ibn Shreek *Wali* over Egypt [in 708] (*see below). Qurra afflicted the people with great troubles.

When the Patriarch came to greet Qurra and congratulate him for becoming *Wali* [as was the custom], Qurra arrested him and said to him, "Pay me the same amount you paid Abdullah Ibn Abdul Malek." The Patriarch replied and said that was because of calumny by evil men, and that he does not have the money. So, the *Wali* replied, "This talk will not do. Even if you have to sell your flesh, you must pay three-thousand dinars; otherwise, you will not be delivered from my hands." Then, he released him to go from town to town in Upper Egypt to collect the money, and the Patriarch experienced great difficulty and loneliness. After accusing the Patriarch of hiding some money, Qurra brought him and wanted to kill him. He placed him in iron chains and threw him in prison, and after seven days, he compelled him again to come up with the three-thousand dinars. With great difficulty and under severe troubles, the Patriarch gathered one-thousand dinars after two years. Qurra was also known to take the money of any dead clergy. Because of his grave injustice and the calamity that he inflicted on the populace, the people smuggled their women and children from place to place. Fatal epidemics spread, and Qurra and his household ended up dying during one of them [..].

And the *Walis* [of provinces] removed the colored and marble pillars from the churches and carried them away.

(*) '[Qurra] was an unjust, tyrannical despot...and the land was filled with injustice... In the days of [Abdul Malek], they were running out of space in the treasuries because of the abundance of accumulated money. So he ordered that mosques be built, and he built the Mosque of Al-Fustat in Misr city, which was originally a Roman fortress...'[31] This indicates that the grave injustice in the exacting of money was not due to a lack in finances, but was 'violence for the sake of violence.'

After the death of Qurra Ibn Shreek, the *History* continues,

Osama became the *Wali* of Egypt's Kharaj, and he was determined to do evil. He ordered that no one should shelter a stranger in the churches, inns, or wharves, and the people were afraid of him and drove out the strangers who were in their houses. He counted the monks and branded each one with a metal ring on his left hand so that he and his church may be easily identified. If any monk was seen without this identifying mark, his leg would be amputated, and those who were mutilated were countless. He also shaved the beards of many monks, killed some, mercilessly plucked the eyes of others, and some he killed by scourging to death. Osama told his provincial *Walis*, "I have delivered to you the souls of the people to take from them as much as you can, whether they be bishops, monks, churches, and everything you can find." (*see below) Thus, there was, in the year 96 of the Hijra (715), anxiety among the monks and anguish among the faithful.[i] The distress was so great that people were forced to sell their children, and instead of showing mercy, the *Wali* oppressed the people even further. Anyone wandering, or getting in or out of a carriage, who did not have his record (**see below), would be apprehended and his carriage looted and burned. Even if a record was damaged because it was eaten by a rat, water damaged, or burned, and only a small part remained, a new one would not be issued unless five dinars were paid. [For example], a widow had a child who went down to the Nile for a drink of water and was grabbed by a crocodile with the record tied to him. His mother was crying bitterly for him, but when she went and informed the *Wali*, he did not have mercy on her. She had to sell everything she owned and go from one town to another, begging for money until she was able to pay the ten dinars.

(*) Caliph Sulayman Ibn Abdul Malek wrote to Osama, the *Wali* overseeing the *Kharaj* of Egypt: "Milk the udder until it dries out, and milk more until the blood runs dry."[32]

(**) It was no longer permitted for anyone to travel or resettle in another area without a specific approval (a 'passport') to ensure the paying of the *Jizya*. That was the response of the Arab authority against the Copts' passive resistance movement that took the form of forsaking their farmlands and migrating en masse to other places in order to escape the tyranny of *Jizya* and taxation. This was especially the case after resorting to monasteries no longer exempted them from their financial obligations. Lands were confiscated for Arab tribes, and Coptic farmers were forced to tend the land

---

[i] This is the first occurrence of a *Hijri* date in the *History of the Patriarchs,* earlier reckonings being according the Coptic calendar. This suggests that it was significant.

without compensation. As for the land tended by the Arabs, it was considered 'tithing land,' meaning that no *Kharaj* was owed on it, only the *Zakat*.[33]

Then, he inspected the monasteries and discovered a group of monks without [identifying] marks, so he beheaded some, and some were scourged to death. He then nailed the doors of the monastery shut and asked for one-thousand dinars. He gathered the head monks and tortured them, asked each one of them for a dinar, and threatened to destroy and tear down the monasteries and to send them [as sailors] to the fleet ships (*see below). The older monks became so worried, and all they could do was pray and make supplications. Shortly afterward, Caliph Sulayman Ibn Abdul Malek died, and Omar Ibn Abdul Aziz took his place.

(*) Arabian Fleet ships traveled with Egyptian [Coptic] soldiers who were forced to work onboard these ships until their death, away from their families and homes. In fact, thousands of ship builders, along with their families, were (eventually) exiled in order to build a fleet of ships in Africana prior to the invasion of Andalusia. These exiles called their new town after the name of their hometown, Tanîs, which became Tunis.[34]

[Omar Ibn Abdul Aziz] began his rule (*see below) by lifting the *Kharaj* over churches and bishops, and abolishing exactions, and, as a result, Christians started to find peace and quiet. Then, he began to act wickedly and wrote to the *Wali* of Egypt ordering that, "Everyone who desires to remain (employed) by me and to remain in his country has to be on the religion of Mohammed." (**see below) So, the Christians turned over their jobs to the Muslims and became an example to many. Then, the *Walis*, tax officials, and Muslims began to lord it over the Christians everywhere, old and young, rich and poor. He [Omar] also ordered that the *Jizya* be collected from all the people [even those previously exempted from paying it] who did not convert to Islam. God did not delay and destroyed him quickly[i].

(*) During the Caliphate of Amir al-Muminin (Commander of the Faithful) Omar Ibn Abdul Aziz, who was alleged to have been 'pure, pious,

---

[i] He stayed as Caliph for less than three years and died at the age of 40 by an unknown disease.

devout, worshipful, a man of faith, righteous, and honest…' the 'Pact of Omar' was issued. This Pact of Omar (sometimes referred to as the Conditions of Omar) is the well-known historical document that codified the abasement and humiliation of the *Dhimmis*[i]; some historians claim it was wrongfully attributed to Omar Ibn Al-Khatab, the second caliph. Other researchers argue that it was produced by ninth-century scholars who credited it to either 'Omar' to make it authoritative.

The *Conditions* did not take the shape of administrative orders. Rather, they were in the form of a letter supposedly written *to* Caliph Omar by the Christians of a Syrian city, seeking his approval to the letter's contents. The following is the text of the letter[35]:

When you came to us, we requested of you safety for ourselves, our offspring, our wealth, and sons of our community. We have pledged that no new house of worship or a monk's cell will be built in our city or its environs, and that none of the collapsing churches or monasteries will be renovated; and that we will not hide any of these buildings located in the Muslim districts; and that we will not prevent any Muslims from residing in our churches for three nights full-board; and not to allow into our homes and churches a spy; and not to teach our children the Quran; and not to display shirk (polytheism) nor invite anyone to it; and not to prevent our relatives from converting to Islam if they want to; and to respect Muslims and to leave our seats for them if they want to sit down; and not to emulate them in their dress, in their caps and turbans, and in their parting of their hair; and not to talk like them, nor use the same surnames they use; nor ride on saddles or carry swords or any other arms; and not to engrave Arabic on our stamps; and not to sell alcohol; and to shave the front parts of our heads; and to abide with our religion wherever we go; and to wear girdles around our waists and not have crosses on our churches; nor should we pursue the ways of Muslims nor emulate their behavior; nor should we ring our bells in our churches except lightly; and not to raise our voices when reciting in our churches or in presence of Muslims; nor we go out in Palm (Sundays); and not raise our voices nor light fires at funerals — especially in the streets and markets of Muslims — nor should we bury our dead close to Muslims; nor

---

[i] *Dhimmis* are non-Muslims treated as second-class citizens under Muslim rule. Refer to the Glossary.

should we take slaves selected by Muslims; nor should we meet them in their homes. [..]

This will be our obligation and [that of] sons of our community; and in return, you will ensure our safety. If we did otherwise, we will have no Dhimma (pact), and you might do to us what you do to people of obstinacy and dissention.[i]

(**) Caliph Omar Ibn Abdul-Aziz hated employing *Dhimmis*, and told his governors, "The *moshrekîn*[ii] are filth, and Allah made them the soldiers of the devil and made them the greatest losers as to their deeds; they are those whose efforts are in vain in this worldly life, while they think that they are doing good. I swear, they are those upon whom the curses of Allah and the damnations of the cursers descend. In the past, when Muslims went into a city populated with *moshrekîn*, they made use of them only because they were knowledgeable in matters relating to tax exaction, writing (record keepers), and administration. They only remained for as long as Allah willed it. If [now] I knew of a scribe, or a tax collector, or any other worker who was not a Muslim, I will get rid of him and replace him with a Muslim man, for to destroy their work is to destroy their religion. It is more befitting to degrade them to the level of abasement and servility that Allah has degraded them to. Do this and report back to me how you have done it."[36]

Omar Ibn Abdul-Aziz ordered the collection of *Mokous* (imposts on goods and on commerce), whose rate for *Dhimmis* was the double of that for Muslims (5% instead of 2.5%).[37]

The *History* then carries on,

Yazîd became Caliph after Omar (*see below), and perhaps it is best that we do not explain what happened during his days nor even mention

---

[i] Al-Qalqashandi added to the *Conditions* a reminder of the other 'standard' conditions imposed upon the *Dhimmis* thereafter: "To pay *jizya*, to host (traveling) Muslims for three days, to submit to the Muslim administration of justice, to ride donkeys by putting both legs on one side of the donkey, to allow Muslims to head meetings and lead the way, to wear different dresses from Muslims, not to allow their buildings to be higher than those of Muslims, and not to build a new church in countries newly invaded by Muslims."

[ii] Those who practice *Shirk* (idolaters or polytheists).

him because of all the trouble and harm he inflicted, since he went down the path of Satan and deviated from God's path. Immediately upon taking power, he reinstated the Kharaj that Omar Ibn Abdul Aziz had lifted from churches for only one year. He burdened the people with a heavy yoke, and everyone was in agony. He also ordered that crosses everywhere be broken, and he scratched out all the images inside churches. He died two years and four months after taking power.

(*) Caliph Yazîd sent a letter to *Wali* Oqba Ibn Muslim, ordering him to smash Pharaonic 'idols and statues,' and he did his best to oblige,[38] which undoubtedly was catastrophic to the Pharaonic artifacts...

[Yazîd's brother], Hisham, became Caliph after him. He feared God according to the way of Islam, and he loved all people [..]. He ordered, for the sake of fairness, that a deed be given to whoever paid the Kharaj (*see below). And he made Ubayd Allah, a *Wali*, in charge of Egypt's Kharaj. When he arrived, he ordered that a census be taken of all people and cattle, to size the land, and to place a lead collar around the throats of males aged 20 years old and up [..]. He doubled the Kharaj, committed grave injustices, and kept on searing marks on the hands of Christians. The *Wali* of Alexandria arrested Patriarch Alexandros to sear him [too], but he refused and appealed to see Egypt's *Wali* [in order to protest the searing matter], and he was sent to Misr under guard to Ubayd Allah. When Ubayd Allah found out that this was with regards to searing, he insisted that the Patriarch be seared. So, the Patriarch asked to be granted three days, and during these three days, he prayed, asking God to remove him from this world quickly, and he became sick quickly and died. Ubayd Allah then arrested the Patriarch's scribe, because he transported him [from prison] to die on his chair, and asked for one-thousand dinars, but he could not pay. So, the *Wali* delivered him to some Berbers who were like wild lions. They dragged him to the gates of Saint George's Church, stripped him, dressed him in sackcloth, hung him from his arms, scourged him with whips, and tortured him for a week, until the people were able to collect 300 dinars. Then, Ubayd Allah released him when he was as good as dead.

(*) During the Caliphate of Hisham Ibn Abdul Malek;

'...Abdullah Ibn Al-Higab, who was the *Wali* in charge of collecting the *Kharaj*, increased the harassment severely against the Copts in relation to the exaction of the *Kharaj*. He added one carat for every dinar, and when the people asked for leniency, he refused. So, the Copts in the eastern side[i] revolted against him, and he fought back. He killed, took captives, looted, destroyed, and shed enough blood to fill a sea. Before him [..], Osama Ibn Yazîd Al-Tanoukhi [..] treated them harshly and entrapped them. He took their money and seared the hands of the monks with a metal ring that had the name of the monk, his monastery, and date etched on it. And if he found monks without those identifying sear marks, he amputated their hands and publicly defamed them. He also wrote to all the provincial governors that if any Christian was found without his (identification) papers, he had to pay ten dinars. In addition, he raided the monasteries and arrested many monks who had no identifying sear marks; some he beheaded, and the rest, he scourged to death with whips. At his behest, churches were looted and burned, making for dreadful sufferings. News of these events reached Hisham Ibn Abdul Malek, so he wrote [..] that Christians are to pay taxes in accordance with the pact in their hands. However, Hanẓala Ibn Safwan (yet another *Wali*) would not follow Hisham's orders. Rather, he acted more severely with the Christians [..] and increased the *Kharaj*, took a census of the people and cattle, and seared every man with an image of a lion. He also pursued them, and if he found anyone without a burn mark on his hand, he amputated that person's hand. Suffering mounted and continued this way for many days, and the people were on the verge of uprising across the entire country; therefore, the provincial governors stopped their actions out of fear, and a relative calm returned.'[39]

As a result of these heavy financial burdens, the Copts started for the first time to forgo passive means of resistance and to oppose the ruler. They rioted in (725), in the north and south of Egypt, so *Wali*, Al-Khor Ibn Youssef, sent an army to fight against them, and many of the Copts were killed.[40]

When Al Walîd Ibn Refaa was installed *Wali* over Egypt by (Caliph) Hisham Ibn Abdul Malek, he went out to take a census accompanied by scribes and assistants. He stayed in Upper Egypt for six months, and in the north for three months. Over ten-thousand villages were registered, and in the smallest villages, they registered no less than 500 men who were

---

[i] Not clear what does this refer to; perhaps the east of the Delta.

obligated to pay the *Jizya*; this indicates that there was a minimum of five-million adult men.[41]

One of the most remarkable documents available from a medieval Egyptian Patriarch is a paschal letter of Abba Alexandros II, announcing the date of Easter for the year 724. Writing with theological sophistication (in elegant Greek), he insists on the reality of the incarnation and crucifixion, in a way that would surely resonate in a special way with Islamic criticism of those fundamental Christian doctrines. The letter also addresses present difficulties, as the Patriarch refers to 'misfortunes the Church was experiencing, one on top of another,' and prays that God may 'gentle the hearts of those who oppress us, and abate the disturbing storms that lower over us.'[42]

The Patriarch adds that he thought it was that the world might be 'coming to the End Time which will destroy all things.'[i] In that he was not alone, as a number of Coptic writers were interpreting the current events as the opening act of the drama of the End. If earlier Copts had been tempted to see Islamic rule as a passing phenomenon, like that of the Persians (at the beginning of the seventh century), that was no longer possible now. For some writers, the most plausible explanation of God's agonizingly mysterious ways in history was that God was about to bring history itself to its end.[43]

***

In reference to the days of Abba Tawadros[ii] (731–743) the *History* says, Ubayd Allah tortured and afflicted the people with great troubles and losses. When he went too far, a group of Muslim expeditors rebelled against him and complained about him to [Caliph] Hisham, which resulted in his removal from office.

After Ubayd Allah, his son, Al-Qassem, became *Wali*, and he was even more evil than his father. He was removed from office, and at the same time, Tawadros died. On Al-Qassem's way back to Damascus, bishops and a group of Christians caught up with him, requesting permission to ordain a new Patriarch. He asked them for money, but they did not pay,

---

[i] See Appendix five.

[ii] In Greek, *Theodhoros* or *Theodosius* means talent, or gift, of God.

and when Ḥafs Ibn Al-Waleed Al-Hadrami became *Wali*, Khail was ordained.

During the Caliphate of Alwalîd Ibn Yazîd Ibn Abdul Malek, who became known for his 'apostasy, heresy, imbibing of alcohol, and hedonism,'

[..] The Copts of Upper Egypt rose up against the injustice of the *Kharaj* collectors and revolted (broke with their obedience). War broke out between them and the soldiers residing in Misr. They fought for many days and many lives were lost. Then, Yuḥannes, the Copt, a man of strength and an esteemed leader of the people of the city of Samnûd, went out to fight the *Kharaj* collectors. The fighting was fierce, and the unrest lasted many days. The Muslims intensified their mistreatment of Christians, and the tug-of-war was prolonged and spread north and south. The fighting came to an end with the death of Yuḥannes and many others, and this was a time of great turmoil for all the Christians [..].[44]

However, the uprisings of the Copts continued, and the people of Upper Egypt fought the *Walis' Kharaj* collectors (in 738). The *Wali* of Egypt, Hanẓala Ibn Safwan, dispatched an army that killed many and defeated them.[45] The Copts then rose up in Samnûd (742), so *Wali* Abū Awan sent out an army to fight them. The Copts were defeated and their leader, (Abū Mina), was killed.[46]

***

In the days of Patriarch Khail I (744–768), the 46th Patriarch,

Wali Ḥafs (744–745) ordered that everyone in Misr and dependent districts pray the prayers of the Sunna, and that whoever recants their faith and converts to Islam is to be absolved from paying the *Jizya* thenceforth [..]. Because of this advantage, many Egyptian Christians strayed and renounced their faith, and some even joined the [Muslim] army. The Patriarch observed with tears of sadness [..], and *Archons* [community leaders] came and said to him, "Pray and persevere, the number of those who converted to Islam in Misr and its dependent districts on the hands of this *Wali* is twenty-four thousand persons."

Ḥafs died by fire in al-Fustat and Ḥawtharah was installed as *Wali* by Marwan Ibn Muhammad, who had usurped the Caliphate from Ibrahim

Ibn Al-Walîd. He loved the Orthodox Christians, hence peace and quiet
came upon Egypt for five years, after which he was removed and
replaced with Abdul Malek Ibn Marwan [..]. He despised the Christians
and was very arrogant. He laid heavy burdens on the people of Egypt.
Then, a disagreement arose with the Roum[i] regarding [the ownership of
some of] their churches, and the *Wali* was bribed by the Roum. He was
removed and replaced with one of the sons of the Muslim judges named
Aba Al-Ḥassan. He was elderly, meek, impartial, and rejected bribes.
He spoke wisely and judged evenhandedly; [he acted equitably toward
the Copts].

Abdul Malek brought Abba Khail to Misr regarding the *Kharaj* of his
churches,[ii] and he asked him for a sum of money that he could not afford.
As a result, Abdul Malek incarcerated him, placing his legs in wooden
stocks and a metal ring around his neck. Moussa, Bishop of Ausîm, and
Tadros, Bishop of Misr, were also with the Patriarch, and were placed
in a windowless prison cell with no view of the sun. The Patriarch was
under stress because he was in iron chains for one month. In the same
prison, there were also 300 men and women; and the women were in
even more dire conditions. The sick, Christians, Muslims, and even
Berber, came to the Patriarch so that he may bless them [..]. Then the
Wali brought him and asked for the money and harassed him, so the
Patriarch asked for permission to go to Upper Egypt saying, "However
much the Christians pay and support me with, I will bring to you." So,
he let him go. The people of Misr were exhausted from all the injustices,
losses, and *Kharaj*.

When Marcurius, King of Nubia,[iii] learned of what the Patriarch of
Egypt went through, he sent a messenger to Abdul Malek in order to set
him free, but Abdul Malek imprisoned his messenger. So Marcurius
marched with a great army of one-hundred-thousand cavalry, and when
they neared Misr, they descended upon Ḥabash Lake, plundering and

---

[i] Roum, or Melkites, the followers of the Greek Orthodox (Chalcedonian) rites.

[ii] *Kharaj* is a tax on farmland and the buildings on which they stand, where
applicable. It seems that churches and monasteries were sometimes exempted, but
often not.

[iii] There were several kingdoms in 'Nubia,' which extended over modern day Nubia
and Sudan, all the way to Khartoum.

killing Muslims, as they had done to the Muslims of Upper Egypt [on their way up to Misr]. When Abdul Malek learned of the arrival of Marcurius, he released his messenger, because he could not fight him. Abba Khail [who had been released by the *Wali* to collect money] wrote [to Marcurius], requesting that he return to his country without warring. He then returned after he had plundered much from the Muslims. [But, prior to these events], Muslims [from Egypt] used to abduct Nubians and sell them [in the slave market].

The land of Egypt knew no comfort or repose during the reign of Abdul Malek. He did what is impermissible toward the monasteries because of his loathing of Christians. Interestingly, he had a four-year-old daughter who was demon-possessed. He asked Abba Khail to pray for her, which he did, casting out the evil spirit. After this, Abdul Malek began to like Christians.

In these days, the soldiers of [Caliph] Marwan used to continuously fight and kill one another. Abdullah Abu Muslim Al-Khurasani [leader of the Abbasids] rose up against him. So, Marwan smuggled a lot of money, jewelry, and ammunition out of Damascus, and burned the rest [to prevent these things from falling into the hands of the Abbasids]. And en route [fleeing] to Egypt, he visited an elderly monk, seeking to know what would befall him. So, the monk said to him, "If I tell you the truth, you will kill me, nonetheless, I will tell you what God has revealed to me. With the measure you used, it will be measured to you, and as you have made mothers childless, so will your mother become childless and your kingdom usurped by him who pursues you now." Upon hearing these words, he dragged the elderly monk and burned him alive.

Marwan arrived in Egypt in 751. Prior to his arrival, Abdul Malek faced a revolt by some of the Peshmurians (*see below), led by Mina Ibn Bakirah, allied with others from Shobra Sanbūṭ, who controlled the area and refused to pay the *Kharaj*. When Abdul Malek sent his soldiers to subdue them, he was defeated. After Marwan arrived [to Egypt], he dispatched a great number of Muslim Egyptian soldiers, as well as others who had accompanied him on his journey. However, they still failed to reach the Peshmurians, because they had taken up fortified positions in *Alwaḥlat* [northern Nile Delta muddy swamps and lakes].

(*) After trying passive resistance and escaping in large numbers, the Copts began staging numerous revolts in the north and south. The most forceful were the ones carried out on several occasions by the people of Peshmur, which is the sandy coastal area in the northern Delta. The first revolt was in 87 Hijri (706) in the Delta, the second occurred in Upper Egypt, and it was forcefully put down. A third revolt was during the reign of Hisham Ibn Abdul Malek in 120 Hijri (738), and the fourth was in 122 Hijri (740), and it was led by Yuḥannes (John), the Copt in Samnûd. The uprisings persisted [i] in Rshîd, during the reign of Marwan, the last of the Umayyad Caliphs. The Copts revolted again in the days of the Abbasids in Sakha in 767 and 773.[47]

These events reveal that the relationship between most of the rulers and the cities they occupied was exploitative ('milking until the udder bleeds'), violently oppressing whoever stood in the way.[48]

[Then] Marwan arrived in Egypt along with eight-thousand [of his men], and ordered his subjects, "Anyone from the people of Misr who does not convert to my religion, pray the way I pray, and follow my views, I shall kill and crucify; but whoever converts to my religion, I will favor, dignify, enrich, and fix his name in my Divân." Immediately, one-thousand people prayed as he prayed [converted to Islam], so he paid each one of them ten dinars [..].

Marwan's armies went into Alexandria, led by Ḥawtharah, killing many, looting their rich *Archons*, taking captive their women and children, and all their belongings. He then asked Abba Khail, "How could you allow your Christian children [the Peshmurians] to fight us?" and he imprisoned him. He also imprisoned the Melkite Patriarch, but his people collected one-thousand dinars in five days, so he was released.

Ḥawtharah asked Abba Khail for money, but he replied, "My church has nothing, so do to me as you will." So, he pushed him to his knees and beat him with a stick 200 times on his head. Then they dragged him like a silent lamb, and he [Ḥawtharah] ordered that they behead him. As the executioner raised his sword, he changed his mind, saying, "Let us carry him to Rshîd and let him write to them [the Peshmurians, to stop disobeying]."

---

[i] As we will observe in the coming chapter.

The Peshmurians then went out and killed Marwan's soldiers. News of this and of the approach of the Abbasids, his enemies, reached Marwan. He wrote to his defeated soldiers, "Come to me quickly because I have need of you; pillage and kill the people of every town you come across on the way." These infidels then went to Upper Egypt and killed a group of *Archons* and looted their possessions, took captive their women and children, burned convents, and took nuns captive [..].

The Patriarch arrived under guard [to Al-Fustat?], and Marwan ordered that he be brought to his tent. The infidel, Ḥawtharah, was telling Amr, "This Patriarch told the Christians to remain strong because God will deliver Marwan's kingdom to his enemies." Upon hearing this, Marwan asked the Patriarch [through his translator], "Are you the Patriarch of Alexandria?" and he replied, "Yes, my Lord," Marwan responded, "[Rather], you are the leader of the enemies of our doctrine [religion]." The Patriarch replied, "I am not the leader of evil men, and my people do not make mischief, but troubles wore them out, forcing them to sell their children." Then Marwan ordered his assistants to pluck the Patriarch's beard, which was long and came down to his chest.

Meanwhile, the Khurāsānians[i] were at the eastern shore of the Nile, without a way to cross over [because Marwan had previously burned all the ships]. Later, Marwan was informed that they had found a way to cross over [..], so he ordered that the Patriarch and those with him be held until the following day. At sunrise, the Patriarch was brought before him and was left standing for about ten hours, surrounded by drawn swords and weapons of war. With the Patriarch was also ten [bishops and scribes] being tortured by soldiers who deliberated over them [..].

---

[i] I.e. 'from Khurasan,' referring to the Abbasids. Khurasan is a historical region in northeast of Persia. In early Islam, it was regarded to include the territory of the old Sasanian Empire, east of Persia proper. Note that the Abbasids revolution against the Umayyads began in 747 by Abu Muslim near Merv, in Khurasan. In 749, they took Kufa, and Abul-Abbas (al-Saffah), who claimed to be a cousin of the prophet, was made Caliph. Note that according to some modern Islamic studies, Marwan, the Umayyad Caliph, is thought to have originated in Merv (his name being '*Mervan*;' since the letter '*waw*' in Arab-Persian alphabet is pronounced 'v' in Persian). In other words, the Umayyads also might have come from northeast Persia, thus putting in question a lot of givens in official Islamic history…

Abdullah Ibn Marwan asked his father to set them free, suggesting, "The enemies are approaching, and if things get worse, we will flee to the Sudan, [black followers], of this old man [the Patriarch], so if you kill him, they will rise up against us." Instead, he put them in iron chains and imprisoned them in the Giza prison.

Marwan then ordered his followers to kill, take captive, and loot the people. He dispatched a group to Upper Egypt and killed [many] Christians. They also raped many women and young virgins. After this incident, a group of people showed the Khurāsānians a way to cross the Nile River. Immediately, they pursued Marwan's followers and fought them. So, Marwan gathered his women and money and escaped secretly. Marwan then released the Patriarch and those with him [..] with the iron [chains] still on their feet. And as God is witness, a group of Muslims dismounted their horses, unchained them, and took them to the Church of Saint Peter [in Giza].

The Khurāsānians pursued Marwan and his companions, and crucified him upside down [?] after killing him.

After being pursued by Saleḥ Ibn Ali, Abu Awn [an Abbasid] found Marwan hiding in a church in Abu Ṣir, in Upper Egypt, and that his friends have been dispersed, with only very few remaining. So they killed him and sent his severed head to Ṣaleḥ, who ordered that his tongue be severed, and when they did and cast it aside, a cat came and took it... Ṣaleḥ returned to the Levant and delivered Marwan's head to the Slaughtering Caliph, so he bowed down and worshiped Allah.[49]

***

With this bloody background, we reach the end of the rule of the Umayyads and come to the arrival of the Abbasids to Egypt, with obvious support from Egyptians, and perhaps from the heavens as well,

The Nile rose everyday about an arm's length[i], and the people were saying that the hand of God was with the Khurāsānians.

***

---

[i] A length measurement, about 58 cm.

A century after the 'opening' of Egypt, and as the Umayyads are about to be replaced by new conquerors, the Copts were facing uncertain future. They aspired to liberate themselves from their domination, but they sought—above all—an explanation of the nightmare they have been subjected to. Attempts to understand came in the form of prophecies attributed to famous Church Fathers.

Apocalyptic writings[i], that became popular, attributed the events to God's wrath because of excessive sins by the people and — especially — their clergy, and linked the lot to the imminent return of the Messiah. A particularly important text was the 'Prophecy attributed to St Athanasius about the Arab Conquest' (or the 'Pseudo-Athanasius'). Dated to early-to-mid eighth century, it is thought to be written by an anonymous monk. He recounts (putting words into Athanasius's mouth) how a certain Ishmaelite people, who are cruel, ferocious, and merciless, would descend like locusts and dominate the land and plunder it. He recalls the 'Fourth Beast' mentioned in the Bible's Book of Daniel, considering it to be a reference to the Arabs. He even links the text on the Umayyad's new currency coins[ii] to the 'Mark of the Beast [..], whose number is 666.'[50]

For Christians, it was of crucial importance to account for the successes of the Muslims, who had done so much damage [..], and to divine what would be their outcome. In answer to the first question, they pointed to the laxity of their members, and in response to the second, they reinterpreted and recast earlier apocalyptic scenarios. Christians viewed Arab rule as the time of testing before the 'final peace,' when 'the churches will be renewed, the cities rebuilt, and the priests set free from tax.' The ousting of the Muslims and regeneration of the religion was to be achieved by a savior figure. [..] Apocalypses thus offered an interpretation for historical change, thereby rendering it more meaningful, and hope for redemption in the near future, thereby encouraging steadfastness.[51]

---

[i] Refer to Appendix five.
[ii] Dinars coined by Caliph Marwan II portrayed the Islamic *Shihada*.

The Abbasids Squelch the Resistance

The Abbasids came to rule Egypt with the help of the Copts, who saw in them 'saviors' from the Umayyads, and promised to relieve them from paying the *Jizya* and other heavy penalties. They treated Abba Khail with dignity and honor, and they also exempted the Peshmurians from paying *Kharaj*.

But did things continue this way?

The *History* says,

Marwan [the last Umayyad caliph] had burned the books and the account logs kept by the Divâns. Shortly after [the Abbasid's victory], Abu Awn [Ibn Abdul Malek Ibn Yazîd] became the new *Wali* of Egypt, and two officials were sent from the Caliph's Divâns: Atta Ben Sharhabeel and Safi. These two ungodly men, who were without mercy, reinstituted the accounts of Egypt to the state that had been under Marwan. They were authorized to do as they pleased, and not only did they detest us Christians, but they had great love for money. The annual [tax] returns from Egypt at the time amounted to two-hundred-thousand dinars[i], after deducting the soldiers' pay, the expenses of the Sultanate, and the kingdom operating expenses, with the unused funds going to the treasury.

After being in power for three years, the Khurāsānians [Abbasids] began breaking their promise to the Christians and, in fact, doubled the *Kharaj*. Caliph Abdullah [Abul-Abbas, also known as '*Al-Saffah*' or 'the Slaughterer'] wrote to his subjects across the entire kingdom that 'anyone who adopts his religion and prays the way he prays is to be exempt from the *Jizya*.' The excessiveness of the *Kharaj* and the inordinate financial burdens made many, rich and poor, abjure the faith

---

[i] That is about 800 kg of gold.

of Christ.[i] Abba Khail [the Patriarch] went to Abu Awn, the *Wali*, and addressed him, regarding the ordeals committed against Egypt instead of the good that had been promised. Abu Awn responded by saying that the Caliph ordered these things because some wicked advisors told him that if the people of Egypt found rest for just one year, they would plot and war against him, just as the Peshmurians had done against Marwan. So, Abba Khail asked him to act leniently regarding the *Kharaj* imposed on the churches. Abu Awn transmitted the request to his scribes, but they rejected it and instead, acted to harden his heart.

In the days of (the Caliph) Abul-Abbas, according to other sources, the graves of the Umayyads in Damascus were vandalized, and when the corpse of Hisham was found not decomposed, it was crucified and burned with fire.

'During this Caliph's days, the Copts from the city of Rashîd (Rosetta, located on the Mediterranean) rebelled because of the injustice and despotism of the provincial governors. So, Abdul Malek Ibn Musa Ibn Nusair, who was then the *Wali* of Egypt, fought them, but they fought back fiercely, until he finally defeated them. Abdul Malek also arrested and imprisoned the Patriarch, Khail, and imposed on him to pay an exuberant sum of money. The Patriarch, along with the bishops, traveled across the provinces of Egypt, looking for financial contributions from the people, but instead, he found them in destitution and under the yoke of unbearable slavery. He returned to Al-Fustat, where Abdul Malek resided, and paid him whatever he was able to collect and thus gained his freedom, but only to be arrested again three days later. Abdul Malek subjected the Patriarch to great hardship and assaulted the Christians with the sword. Misr (Old Cairo) was set ablaze with all its crops, many nuns were abducted, and their convents were looted and destroyed. Abdul Malek attempted to seduce one of the nuns, but eventually she tricked him into beheading her. He then understood that she chose death over acting impurely (fornication). The Slaughterer (the Caliph) removed Abu Awn and replaced him with Saleh Ben Ali as *Wali*, but then, he reinstated Abu Awn...'[52]

---

[i] Meanwhile, to make up for the reduction in exaction resulting from conversions, it was emphasized that revenue be maintained by raising the *Jizya* and *Kharaj* on those who did not convert (to Islam).

***

In the years 767–799, the *History* records nothing out of the *ordinary* harassment and slander.

But, as other sources indicate, in the days of Abba Mina, 767–775, the *Walis* and provincial governors treated the Copts with greater harshness and further degradation. So, in 770, some of the Copts from the region of Sakha (in the Delta) rose up and expelled the provincial governors and the tax collectors. In response, Yazîd Ibn Hatem Ibn Qubaisah (the Prince, or army commander, of Egypt) dispatched a great army, which the Copts defeated. As a result, the Christians in the southern and northern provinces were subjected to even greater persecution and greater harassment to the point where they were forced to eat animal carcasses and the dead to survive. The churches in Misr were destroyed.

In the days of Abba Yohanna (775–799), the Copts of Balhêt rebelled, so Musa Ben Ali, the *Amir* (army commander) of Egypt, dispatched an army to quell their rebellion. The fighting protracted until eventually the rebellion abated. The provincial governor tried to treat the Copts with more kindness to placate them. Thus, things went back to how they were, with the Copts being peaceful and obedient...[53]

Afterward, the *Wali* gave permission to Abba Morcos II (799–819) to rebuild the churches that were torn down in Al-Fustat, Misr (Old Cairo).

The *History* then says:

> After that, a tribe named the Andalusians[i], with a great cohort from other Roman cities, invaded Alexandria. On their journey, they continued looting until they reached Misr, and brought Christian captives to Alexandria to sell them as slaves. This selling of souls, as if they were cattle, and the conversions of many to Islam, saddened Abba Morcos.

---

[i] Pirate Saracen (Arab-Muslim) bands, which dominated the Mediterranean starting late 8th century. They were Andalusian Muslims who had set up their own Umayyad caliph, and owed no allegiance to the Abbasids. For a few years, around 820, Alexandria even became their base for raids. Refer to : Pierre Guichard, '*Les débuts de la piraterie anadalouse en Méditerranée occidentale (798–813)*' (http://www.persee.fr/doc/remmm_0035-1474_1983_num_35_1_1981 , esp. Pp 66–69)

Some had mercy on these salves and bought from among them, specifically monks, priests, deacons, virgins, and mothers, and after each purchase, immediately issued a deed of emancipation.

The *History* then describes the fighting of the Andalusian pirates and others, and the chaos that ensued, saying,

They killed everyone in sight from the citizens of the country: Muslims, Christians, and Jews. [..] As they reached the church of the Savior [the *Soter*], they found some of their companions who were killed by Muslims and their bodies thrown at its doors, and they became extremely enraged. One Sheikh appeared to them, looking at the road, and he was Satan appearing in a man's likeness, and said to the Andalusians, "I saw [this] to whom the church belongs, and he killed your companions." So, they threw fire on the church, which was burnt, as well as many nearby buildings. [..] They killed uncounted numbers of people and looted and burned many places, [..] and Abba Morcos was crying while reciting the Psalm[i] [..]. He then left [Alexandria], and moved from place to place in tribulations for five years.[ii]

At that time, great trouble came upon the (monasteries in the) wilderness of Wadi El-Natroun [Scetis] as the Arabs looted, took the monks captive, tore down churches and hermitages, causing the dispersion of the elderly saints in every area of the earth.

---

[i] Ps 79, 1–3: "O God, the nations have invaded your inheritance; they have defiled your holy temple, they have reduced Jerusalem to rubble.[2] They have left the dead bodies of your servants as food for the birds of the sky, the flesh of your own people for the animals of the wild. [3] They have poured out blood like water all around Jerusalem, and there is no one to bury the dead."

[ii] One pious *Archon*, Maqar, secured the approval of the *Wali* of the East of the Delta, for the Patriarch to stay in Nabaruh, a town in the Delta, near current-day Al-Mansourah, because of the destruction of his seat in Alexandria. Along with the near-by Dimayrah, they served as temporary residence till 1047, when the Seat was relocated to Al-Muallaqa Church, in Old Cairo. It was moved to the Church of the Virgin Mary in the alleyway of Zwailah, in Cairo, around 1300, the Church of the Virgin Mary in the alleyway of the Roum in 1660, then to Saint Mark's Church in Al-Darb Al-Wase' (Clot Bek) in 1800, and then to the area of Abba Ruwais, Cairo, in 1968.

This exile represented a turning point in the story of the Patriarchs of Alexandria. Their connection with their city, while not completely severed, would never be quite the same. Also, the *History of the Patriarchs* presents Abba Morcos in the portrait of a figure like Jeremiah, an exile who gives voice to his people's laments over the destruction wrought in the 'holy temple' (Alexandria) or the 'Holy of Holies' (Scetis).[54]

During these chaotic days, Abba Morcos cared for all Christians, without distinction of Monophysite or Melkite, and had the courage to seek out the leader of the Andalusians and offer to ransom all the prisoners he had made in Egypt and intended to export as slaves. It is recorded that in this way, he redeemed no less than six-thousand captives, Egyptians and Byzantine Christians; men, women, and children. To each of these, he presented a deed of freedom, and provided them with necessaries for their return to the homes from which they had been torn. Some who had lost all, he provided for in Alexandria.[55]

During the infighting between Al-Amin and Abdullah, the sons of Haroun Al-Rashîd, the Christians in Alexandria were looted and much of their property was burned down. Wadi El-Natroun monasteries were also burned down until there were only a few monks left—it was a great adversity.[56]

***

In the days of Abba Yacoub (819–830), who was the 50th Patriarch, the *Wali,* Abdul Aziz Al-Garwi, sent a certain individual to the Patriarch and ordered that he be ordained a bishop, but the Patriarch refused to bypass the laws of the church. The *Wali*, therefore, wrote the Patriarch, threatening that he would destroy all the churches and kill all the bishops everywhere if he did not meet with him.[i] Then, a stone fell on the *Wali* and killed him. His son, Ali, governed after him and prosperity returned to Alexandria after a bad wave of severe rise in prices. Also, the monks of Abi Makar returned to their monastery.

---

[i] Not only were the Copts not allowed to choose and ordain their Patriarch without the rulers' approval, but the rulers tried to impose whomever they wanted, which is a blatant violation of the church's rules and traditions.

In 826, a new *Wali*, Abdullah Ibn Ṭaher, was sent to Egypt from the Caliph of the Muslims. He was a kind, merciful, and pious man, who loved justice and hated injustice. Then, he started to get tougher with the Patriarch in his demand for the *Kharaj*, but the Patriarch did not have enough to pay because of how poor the church became as a result of numerous wars [attacks]. Instead, the Patriarch [had to] give the church communion utensils as a *Kharaj* to [this] violating nation.

*** *

As for Abba Yousab I (830–849), the 52nd Patriarch, the *Wali* of Alexandria (Abdullah Ben Yazîd) prevented his ordination until he paid one-thousand dinars. The *History* says:

Ahmed Ibn Alasbat and Ibrahim Ibn Tamim were the *Kharaj* collectors. And despite the scourges people suffered, these men demanded the *Kharaj* without mercy, and the people became extremely poor. Egypt experienced a sharp rise in prices, to the point where a quarter *Ardabb*[i] of wheat was sold for a dinar, which caused the death of innumerable people, including women, children, old, and young. The tax collectors abused the people everywhere. In particular, they severely tortured many Peshmurian[ii] Christians, to the point where they were forced to sell their own children in order to pay the tax. They were also tortured by being tied to mills, taking the place of beasts, and beaten in order to grind, and so it went on until they would die.

But they started to revolt. This was the time of Caliph Abdullah Al-Mamoun[iii], the son of Haroun Al-Rashîd. When he heard about the situation in Egypt, he sent an army under the command of Al-Afsheen, killing the rebelling Peshmurians, starting from the east of Egypt and ending with the great city of Alexandria. There, he wanted to kill all its inhabitants because they had enabled the enemy to enter their city [but he was prevented by God]. Al-Afsheen even killed the innocent for the guilt of the lawbreakers. He also killed some of the *Archons* of the

---

[i] A quarter *Ardabb* is almost ten gallons.
[ii] Living in the area of Peshmur, mostly made of water marshes, in the north of Delta.
[iii] He is said to have been an Arab of the old type; illiterate, unable even to read or write, passionate, sensual, but a great warrior.

Christians in every place. The Patriarch was saddened to see all this trouble caused by plagues, severe inflation, and the sword.

The Peshmurians successfully plotted to manufacture weapons and fought the Sultan [*Wali*], refusing to pay taxes. The Patriarch was saddened, as he perceived their inadequate power to resist the Sultan. He wrote, warning them so they would repent and stop resisting the Sultan. He did not cease writing to them day after day, quoting to them chapters from the Books (from the Epistle of Saint Paul), but they insulted the bishops who delivered his letters.

Al-Afsheen wrote to the Caliph [..], so he came to Egypt, accompanied by the Patriarch of Antioch [Dionysius][i]. Abba Yousab, along with all the bishops, went to greet him at Al-Fustat. Al-Mamoun was satisfied when he found out about his [the Patriarch's] writings to the Peshmurians, deterring them from defying the Caliph's orders. He said, "Behold, I order you and your companion [the Patriarch of Antioch] to go to these people [the Peshmurians] and deter them, so that they would return to being obedient to me." So, the two Patriarchs did accordingly and went to the Peshmurians, offering advice and rebuke, but the Peshmurians did not yield. So, the two Patriarchs returned and told Al-Mamoun, who in turn ordered Al-Afsheen to take his soldiers and go fight them. But Al-Afsheen could not overpower them because of their fortified positions; rather, the Peshmurians were killing several of Al-Afsheen's soldiers daily.

Al-Mamoun then marched with his army and ordered the gathering of everyone who knew the ways of the Peshmurians from the surrounding cities and villages. When his army succeeded to reach the Peshmurians, they annihilated them, killing them with the edge of the sword, pillaging, destroying, and burning their homes with fire, and destroying their churches. When Al-Mamoun saw that so many were killed, he ordered his soldiers to stop the killing. The remnant alive, both men and women, were taken into captivity to Baghdad (*see below).

When the Patriarch of Antioch found out that the rebellion was because of the tax collectors, he approached Al-Mamoun and spoke to him about the reasons behind the rebellion. When Al-Mamoun heard these words, he told the Patriarch, "Excuse yourself and leave Egypt at once, because

---

[i] Based in Syria, doctrinally united with the Copts.

if my brother [Ibrahim Al-Motasem] hears this, he will kill you,"
because the tax collectors were actually sent by him. So, the Patriarch
left Egypt immediately. Ibrahim indeed became very angry when he
heard what the Patriarch said. After Al-Mamoun died and Ibrahim [Al-
Motasem], his brother, took his place as Caliph, the Patriarch of Antioch
escaped, until Ibrahim promised him that he would not kill him.

Most likely the Patriarch knew the reason for the rebellion beforehand,
but he did not expect the disciplinary campaign to morph into a gruesome
bloodbath. The question that remains is why did Sawiris not mention the
Coptic Patriarch's (Abba Yousab's) pathetic reaction to these events?

Patriarch Dionysius of Antioch reports the story as follows,[57] "Al-
Mamun said, 'Take all the bishops of Egypt with you and go meet with the
rebels. Negotiate with them on condition that they surrender, and come with
me and my army where I shall resettle them. If they refuse, I will kill them
with the sword.' When I talked to the Caliph at length about the Peshmurians
subjecting themselves to his authority, on condition that they are left to live
in their own country, he refused and said, 'No, either they leave the country
or expose themselves to death.' When we met their leaders, [..] they said that
the *wali* responsible for collecting the *Kharaj* forced them to pay *Jizya* that
they could not afford. He imprisoned them, tied them to the mills, beat them
severely, and forced them to grind the grain like animals. When their wives
came carrying their lunch, his servants raped them. Many of them were
killed. [..] When we reported to the Caliph, he said, 'I am not responsible for
the policy of my *walis* because I did not dictate to them the measures they
took.'"

(*) Some sources mention that the remainder of the Peshmurians (who
were taken captive) were made to settle in the swamps of Ahvaz (Shatt Al-
Arab), in southern Iraq, to work the marshlands. The climate was
inhospitable, and the land was infested with malaria (..), and perhaps the rest
joined the Zanj or 'Negro' revolt.[58] Other sources mention that after the
battles, there were about 3000 prisoners who were taken to Baghdad. Some
died on the way; those left were taken as slaves and distributed among the
Arabs. About 500 of these were sold as slaves in Damascus.[59] The area where
the Peshmurians had lived in the northern Delta became de-Christianized, as
whoever escaped the fate of the rebels either immigrated to other regions or
converted to Islam.

After that defeat, the Copts were demeaned in their own land, and the Muslims defeated them and intensified the persecutions and harassments, furthering their abasement and humiliation. So, they made tax-record keeping a profession in order to support themselves in this new (and unfortunate) situation, after once being the masters of the country, the owners of its fields, farms, and orchards.[60]

It is worthy of note that after the massacre carried out by Al-Mamoun (with the unintentional help of some Copts), a Coptic leader approached Al-Mamoun and requested to be made the *Wali* of the city of Bourah (near Damietta). In response, Al-Mamoun suggested that he convert to Islam in order to be assigned to this office, so the Copt responded, "Amir of the Faithful commands ten-thousand *Mouwali* Muslims,[i] should he not have under his charge one Christian loyal?" and he was assigned the office he requested.[61]

Certain accounts indicate that Al-Mamoun asked one of his friends, called Amr Ibn Abdullah Al-Shaybani, about the origin of the Copts. He replied that they are descendants of the ancient Egyptian Pharaohs. Then (as a result of the complaints of some of the converts to Islam), he reminded him that Caliph, Omar Ibn Al-Khatab, ordered not to employ them in government and scribal work. So, when Al-Mamoun returned to Baghdad, he ordered the expulsion of all the employed *Dhimmis* and imprisoned many of them.[62]

The Patriarch then turned his attention to the troubles in Ethiopia and Nubia [..]. Wars had broken out between them and the Muslim *Walis* until Ibrahim [Al-Motaṣem] became *Wali*. He [Ibrahim] wrote to Zachariah, the King of Nubia, [demanding from him] the *Kharaj* of the previous fourteen years [in the form of slaves], lest he go to war with him. The *Wali's* scribe in Upper Egypt was a deacon by the name of Gerga, and he wrote to the Patriarch [advising him], so the Patriarch wrote to the King of Nubia, [..] saying, "My sin prevented me[ii] from writing to you because of the wars and transgressions of the Peshmurians against the orders of the king [Caliph], until he killed them

---

[i] *Mouwali*, literally signifies loyal, supporter, client; refers to local converts to Islam who had to appear as loyal follower to one of the Muslim Arabs (individuals or tribes) and paid dearly for that. Even so, they were considered second-class Muslims.
[ii] A way of humbly apologizing for not writing earlier.

and destroyed their homes and churches [..], so my beloved, you must pay your dues to these kings [..]." When the scribes arrived, Zachariah said, "What should I do [..] and who could collect [taxes] due for fourteen years in souls, [slaves] in order to send to him [Al-Motaṣem]?" So, he sent his son to Egypt and then to Baghdad. As a result of this visit and the pledging of their obedience to Al-Motaṣem, he relented from demanding the 14-year tax.

  Despite the Patriarch's efforts to appease Al-Motaṣem and to influence and convince the King of Nubia to be obedient to him,

[..] the King [Caliph, Al-Motaṣem] ordered all the marble pillars in all the churches in Misr be taken, and [the person in charge of this matter] was a Nestorian named Eliazer [Lazarus] [..]. When he reached [the monastery] of the Martyr Saint Menas in Mariout, he took all the pillars and rare marble [despite the Patriarch's pleas] and sent everything to Alexandria, in order to be sent to the Caliph's city [Baghdad, which greatly saddened the Patriarch].

Days later, a severe plague came upon the cattle, [..] to the point where people were unable to walk the streets without holding their noses because of the great number of carcasses. Farming came to a halt, and the land of Egypt experienced great sorrow. The people became infected with the same plague and ultimately perished [..]. The period of the plagues then came to an end.

There was a certain judge in Misr named Mohammed Ibn Abdullah who was feared by all. No one could contradict him because he was perceived by the Muslims to be a jurist and an Imam, who is well-versed in their doctrine. [But] he committed sordid deeds in secret, and he loved drinking wine and listening to singing. He also owned beautiful female slaves and loved hedonism and fornication. He had no fear of God and felt no shame for his actions before the people [..]. He was relentless in his ignorance and insults of [all] Christian doctrines. He approached the Patriarch several times, shaming him [..].

Then, Malek Ibn Naṣer Al-Ḥidr became *Wali* over Alexandria in 848, and he was worse and more unjust than his predecessor [..]. Several days later, he rode in and arrived at the [residence] of the Patriarch, accompanied by his concubines. He toured the entire residence and finally came to the bedroom in which this Patriarch, and previous

Patriarchs, slept. He threw the Patriarch out of his own bedroom, brought in his concubines and commenced to eat, drink, and sleep with them, in the very room where there was incense and perfume from the prayers of the Patriarchs. The Patriarch was sorrowful and wept bitterly [..]. After committing these filthy acts, he left and returned to his home.

That very day, Sawiris says, the *Wali* fell sick, almost to the point of death, and his doctors failed to stop his bleeding or to cure him.

Then, some people slandered the Patriarch, saying, "He corresponds with the Byzantine kings, [who] send him large sums of money, so [Al-Hadir] brought the Patriarch and imprisoned him in a tight space. He also determined that as punishment, [the Patriarch] had to pay one-thousand dinars (then he reduced the amount) to 400 dinars, which his disciples collected and paid, freeing the Patriarch [..]."

The *Wali* died seven days after receiving the payment.

***

In the days of Abba Qozmas II (851–859), the 54th Patriarch, the *Wali* of Alexandria multiplied his acts of tyranny, which forced the Patriarch to move his residence and seat to the city of Dimayrah[i], east of Misr [in the Delta].

The King of the Muslims, Jafar Al-Mutawakkil [the Abbasid Caliph, who came to power in 847] brought immeasurable trouble on the churches everywhere. He ordered that all churches be torn down and prevented Orthodox Christians [Copts and followers of the Antioch Seat], Melkites, Nestorians, and Jews from wearing white garments; rather, they were to wear dyed clothes in order to stand out among the Muslims. He also ordered that frightening images[ii] on wooden boards be nailed to the doors of Christian homes, and he compelled the majority to convert to Islam.

He also decreed that no Christian whatsoever be allowed to serve the Sultanate [administration, Divâns], but only Muslims and Muslim converts (*see below). As a result, the love and patience in the hearts of many diminished to the point of renouncing Christ; some because of

---

[i] North of current-day Al-Mansourah.
[ii] Possibly demonic or pagan images.

worldly rank and love of this world, and others because of the poverty that came upon them. When the Sultan[i] saw such ugly procedures applied in other lands, he began to do likewise in Egypt [..]. So, he sent an individual named [Anbasah] Ibn Ishaq and made him the *Wali* in charge of Egypt, including its *Kharaj,* and ordered him to do to the churches of Egypt and the Christians as it was done in the city of Baghdad and the east.

When he arrived, he started with the Christians and afflicted them with great trouble, and humiliated them with numerous sorrows [..]. Then, he began [to prevent] the display of all crosses, and he broke all the crosses in churches in bulk [..]. He persecuted us and our denomination [community], to the point where Christians could not pray in churches unless in a hushed voice that is inaudible from the outside. He also prohibited the prayer over deceased Christians and put an end to the ringing of church bells. Then, he began to prevent Christians from attending mass and from congregating in groups for mass [..]. And this tyrant continued to add to the heavy yoke on Christians because of his hatred of them [..]. He then expelled the Christians from the Divâns and replaced them with Muslims. Moreover, he forced the Christians and Jews to dye their clothes. As was done in the eastern countries, he attached to their doors frightening images displaying a devil with many heads and faces, with fangs riding on the image of a pig. Furthermore, he then prohibited Christians from riding horses. He did all this [in order to] force the Christians to renounce their faith. Many of them could not withstand the pressure [and converted to Islam].

(*) Caliph Al-Mutawakkil ordered that Copts wear a light-brown head covering, tighten their sashes, and ride on wooden saddles (identified by forming two balls on the back of the saddle). Further, they were to have two patches, the size of each is that of four fingers across, and each made of a different color, on the men's garments that contrast with the color of the garment. And women were also to wear light-brown, long (wrapping) skirts

---

[i] In charge of the executive governance under the Caliph. Initially, the sultan was some kind of prime minister, but over the time, the Sultan in the Abbasid state and later in the Ottoman state, became the de facto ruler, while the caliph became a mere religious figurehead.

when in public, and were prohibited from wearing waist belts. He also tore down new churches (built after the Arab's conquest) and decreed that a tax be collected from the houses (equaling a tenth of their value) and that frightening wooden images of devils be nailed to doors of houses. He banned Copts from working for the Sultanate and prohibited them from teaching Muslims, although in that day, Copts were the ones with knowledge of the various sciences. In addition, he prohibited the display of crosses on Palm Sunday, and the lighting of torches for travel. He ordered that the graves of their dead be leveled to the ground so as to not reveal a trace of their existence. Then, he ordered that (Copts) be confined to riding mules and donkeys, and not horses. He further engineered different types of hardships and troubles.[63]

In those days, the *Wali* [Anbasah] proceeded to build ships in all the coastal areas of the country, because the Roum [Byzantines] had reached Damietta and left after a three-day plundering excursion. For this reason, many ships were built [..], and they sailed in these ships to the lands of the Roum and waged war against them. A lot of money was spent on the fleet every year. As for the Copts, they were forced to work on these ships without receiving a single dirham to compensate their travel expenses and necessities. They were only given a daily ration of food. The *Wali* did these things because of how much he hated the Christians. He would also enumerate and register the people across the country and designate the number of men from each hamlet to work on his fleet. He did not provide them with weapons [they had to purchase weapons], and he would inspect them; if he found any of them without a weapon, or missing a part of a weapon, he would treat that person harshly, fining and forcing him to purchase weapons for fighting. He would even take weak [individuals] without strength and without maritime or fighting knowledge. [Some of the Copts] used to pay what they owned [to individuals who would accept to go instead of them]. After those drafted Copts complained, the *Wali* ordered that each Christian be given two dinars, but those who found a Muslim substitute [had to supplement this sum] had to pay fifteen dinars. Because of the intensity of the persecution, they desired death [..].[i]

Then, Anbasah was summoned to Baghdad.

He had married in Egypt, had many concubines, built houses, fathered children, owned countless blessings, but he was immediately struck with hemiplegia and died several days later.

***

Based on the aforementioned and on the previous chapter, we especially note:

- There is no difference between the Umayyads and the Abbasids in regard to viciousness, greed, and barbarism.
- The Arab rulers, of all sorts, over a period of two centuries, did not care about the Church's peaceful attitude; on the contrary, they were violent, slandering and extorting as they pleased. In fact, out of the fifteen Patriarchs ordained from the time of the Arab invasion to the above-mentioned Abba Qozmas, six were arrested, imprisoned, tortured, and humiliated.

---

[i] This section reveals the movement to mercilessly enlist, or rather exploit, the Copts into the military fleet, and how they were treated with savageness exceeding that used with slaves. Researcher Gamal Al-Din also mentions that the Fatimid Caliph Al-Muezz later used Copts after occupying Egypt.

The Turkish Walis: More Sorrows

Anbasah was the last *Arab* to rule Egypt since the Arab invasion, a period that lasted a little over two centuries. This was followed by the period of the Turkish *Walis*, starting with Yazîd Ibn Abdullah Al-Turki (856).

The change came about when the Abbasid Caliphs in Baghdad began to recruit the Turkish tribes of central Asia as slave soldiers, to protect themselves from Arab and Persian opponents. Caliph Al-Motaṣem was the first to recruit Turks in his army because of their strength, violence, and war expertise. The reason for this was that the Arabs apparently began to lose fervor once they experienced the comforts of easy living.

The Turks' influence grew rapidly, and one of their own became the leading minister, referred to as the 'Sultan,' a title more influential than 'Vizier' as it derives from the root verb denoting authority and dominance. The Sultan eventually became the de facto ruler who sent *Walis* (usually Turks) to the provinces, while the caliph gradually moved from being an actual ruler to becoming a mere religious figurehead to bestow legitimacy on the Turks.

It is worth noting that historians divide the time between the Arab invasion (639) and the Ottoman invasion (1517) into three main periods: the *Walis'* era (Arabs and then the Turks), the Fatimid era, and the Ayyubid-Mamluk era.

***

Were things different for the Copts under the Turkish *Walis*?

Regarding the days of Abba Shenouda I (859–880), the 55th Patriarch, the *History* says,

> In those days, Jafar Al-Mutawakkil was Caliph, and his son, Mohammed [Al-Muntasir], rose up against him and usurped his rule. After taking power, he exiled all the *Walis* commissioned by his father [..], and he

sent Ahmed Ibn Mohammed Al-Mudaber to Egypt. This was a harsh and difficult man [..] and did things that were not done by anyone before him. He had resided in Palestine for a long time, and he afflicted the people with many trials and great trouble [..]. When he arrived at Egypt [..], he sent emissaries to monasteries in all places registering the number of monks and imposing on them the *Jizya* and *Kharaj* for the grass, palm trees, and other trees. When news of this reached Abba Shenouda, he wept bitterly and said, "O Holy Mountain, Wadi Hebeb [Shehit, Al-Natroun], port of lost souls[i], how did the devil lay on you all this trouble that befalls those who live in you?" This unjust man [the *Wali*] summoned the Abba [the Patriarch] to take him [as hostage] in order to guarantee the payment of all that pertains to this Wadi and all the monasteries in Egypt [..], but he escaped [..].

Because of his evil, he [the *Wali*] sent out to all the churches to bring whatever they possessed [..], and he ordered that churches in Misr [Old Cairo] be shut down, with the exception of one church. His emissaries gathered the wardens of churches everywhere, locked them up, put them in iron chains, and carried them away to Misr [..]. During this time, he gathered money from the churches, bishops, and monasteries [..].

The Patriarch remained a fugitive for six months; however, when he saw that the [*Wali's*] anger was not abating, but rather intensifying, he made preparations to turn himself in for the sake of the churches and the bishops [..]. He travelled in secret to a house [of a Copt] in Al-Fustat and wrote to the *Wali*, requesting a pledge of safety to turn himself in [..]. So, he responded cunningly and said, "If you come to me before any of my people who are looking everywhere for you arrest you, then you will be set free and forgiven of the trouble that I had planned for you and the churches. But if someone arrests you and brings you to me, then I will do to you what I had intended and worse."

---

[i] This desert wadi (valley), situated southwest of Alexandria, has been, and still is to this day, the area where Egypt's key monasteries exist. Till the Arab Conquest, it is said to have had hundreds of monasteries.

So, the Patriarch went to him, and he (the *Wali*) compelled him to pay the *Kharaj* of the two years prior to his arrival to Egypt. The sum owed was seven-thousand dinars[i].

This was the beginning of the affliction caused by the exorbitant *Kharaj* imposed on the churches, bishops, and monasteries in all the cities of Egypt [..]. Even a poor individual who was incapable [of securing] his daily wage was forced to pay [two dinars], to the point where the people of Egypt growled from this great torment. Many Christians abjured their faith [renounced their religion and converted to Islam] because of their abject poverty [..]. So, the bishops held a meeting in Fustat, Misr, and committed themselves to pay in installments [what the *Wali* had compelled the Patriarch to pay] to the extent of their ability [..]. The cities of Egypt experienced great distress and the bishops and monks became poor because of these penalties.

[Caliph] Al-Muntasir Ibn Al-Mutawakkil, who had killed his father, died in these days, and God repaid him for what he had done to his father [..]. Al-Mustaîn ruled after him, and he was a righteous man who did good in his days [..].

Then his brother, Al-Motaz, rose up against him and usurped his power and ruled in his place. The two brothers fought each other for three years. After the victory of Al-Motaz,

sermons were given in his honor[ii], and [everyone] rejoiced because of fear over the fate of the country, since the Arab [Bedouins] spelled corruption in the land of Egypt. They [the Bedouin], who reside in mountains and wildernesses, ruined Upper Egypt with pillaging and killing. The Monastery of Abba Shenouda, the Monastery of Al-Qalmoun in Faiyum, and the Monastery of Abba Pakhoum in Taha, were only some of the places that were looted [..]. They also burned forts, robbed businesses, killed [many] monks, and violated a group of virgin nuns, some of whom they killed by the sword. They did other perverse

---

[i] That is 28 kilograms of gold, currently worth $1.2 million.

[ii] In Friday religious sermons, an Imam prays for the prevailing Caliph or ruler.

things, which, to explain the simplest of these actions, would require much time, and the reader should comprehend.[i]

The evil *Wali*, Ibn Al-Mudaber, did not pay any mind to these wars, nor to the fear that befell the country; rather, he resolved to do evil to the people and keep collecting money.

During the days of Lent, the Patriarch went to the wilderness of Shehit (the monasteries of Wadi Al-Natroun).

Then, the wicked Arab [Bedouins] arrived. They came down from the land of Upper Egypt to the countryside [of the Delta], after their livestock spring season, [and they took over] the Patriarch's church-monastery, the dwellings and forts, looting everything inside and removing the people under the threat of the sword on Easter Thursday [..].

During this period, a Muslim man, from the tribe of Al-Madlagah, a resident of Alexandria, rose up and was joined by his fellow fighters [..]. They burned many towns and killed many [..]. When they became more powerful, they also took control of the surrounding farms of the Monastery of Abba Mina in Mariout and the Monastery of Abba Maqar, and they plundered these places while eating and dividing all their produce among themselves. When they had committed great transgressions [..], they surrounded the city of Alexandria and demanded that it submit to their looting, just as they had looted other cities, enslaved women and children, killed their men, and took their money [..]. The siege protracted [and the people nearly starved if it were not for] the people of Rshîd[ii], sending boats with grain for aid [..].

[..] Then a man rose up from the King's race[iii] and mobilized a large group of fighters [Qarmatians][iv]. He marched to the place, which is now called Mecca, in the land of Hejaz, called Al-Kaaba and [seized it]. He

---

[i] It is difficult to speculate what the chronicler is referring to here, as he has already listed a number of abominable acts.

[ii] A port city, some 40 km to the east of Alexandria.

[iii] Racially Arab, like the ruling Abbasid Caliph, as opposed to those warriors of Turkish origins, whose influence in the state was growing.

[iv] Their name derives from 'frowners,' denoting their angrily zealot stance.

also seized the house to which Muslims go for *Hajj*[i]. It is said that only nobles [decedents of the prophet] may enter it, because it is held in high esteem by Muslims. When this rebelling man took control of it, he burned it [..], and the Muslims were greatly saddened because of the destruction of the house.

[The Caliph] sent a *Wali* named Ahmed Ibn Mozaḥem [Ibn Khaqan] to Egypt, who was righteous and pure according to his faith. He was knowledgeable of the statutes of his religion and just in his ways[ii]. He was also accompanied by an army of Turks, who were brave fighters, an insurmountable force, because unlike the weapons used by the people of Egypt, they were archers [..]. They fought those who created the sedition [Al-Madlagah] and killed them by the sword [..]. As a result, safety returned to the land of Egypt and its people rejoiced.

As for Ibn Al-Mudaber, the tyrant whom we mentioned, he did not relent from his wicked deeds. He decreed that everyone in the land of Egypt be charged double the *Kharaj* that year, and he doubled the *Jizya* of each Christian. So, the people relapsed into poverty [..], and even the rich were unable to afford bread [..]. He [Al-Mudaber] set his anger upon the Patriarch and asked him for the *Kharaj* for the [monasteries' farms], as well as what belongs [to the Church] in Alexandria, Saint Menas Church, and the monasteries. The *Jizya* amount that he set for the monks, which he required the Patriarch to pay, was seven-thousand dinars, which was paid after much anguish and distress [..]. Ibn Al-Mudaber continued his wicked actions against monks in the wildernesses, including his exorbitant requests that could not be met. Some could not bear it any longer and gave in to their lust, got married, and left [..] the wilderness of Abba Maqar. Our Abba looked on these things with burn in his heart, constantly making prayers and requests to the Lord [..].

The King [Caliph] sent to the land of Egypt a *Wali*, to oversee the *Kharaj*.[iii] When he arrived, he performed good deeds and through his

---

[i] The Muslim pilgrimage to Mecca that takes place in the last month of the Hijri year, and that all Muslims are expected, if they afford it, to make at least once during their lifetime.

[ii] He stayed in power for two months only (died in 254 Hijri/867 A.D.).

[iii] Does he mean Ibn Khaqan, mentioned earlier? Notice the chaos in the previous and coming sections resulting from attempting to trace the *Walis* with their various

actions, revealed his fear of God [..]. A certain saintly monk travelled to the city of the King [the Caliph, in Baghdad] and sought the assistance of some Christians [employed in his Divân]. He asked the Caliph regarding the *Jizya* and *Kharaj* of monks, so he was issued a letter [..]. When he returned to Egypt, the *Wali* was happy with this letter because of his leniency toward the monks and fulfilled the King's orders. He quoted from the Quran (*see below) that whoever resides in the mountains is exempt from paying *Kharaj* or *Jizya*. [..].

(*) This (around 860) is the Quran's first mention in the *History of the Patriarchs*. It appears that it was not known or widespread prior to this point (?)

The *Walis* [of the provinces] were Turks; they were frightening in appearance and despised the Christians. They used to neigh at the women like horses, kidnap and defile children without fear, steal and slaughter the cattle for food [..], constantly ate, drank, and engaged in debauchery. They did other disgusting acts that ought not to be explained for the sake of prudence. The bishops were so scared that they dressed in secular clothing [to disguise themselves].

[A former monk from among the Peshmurians] snitched on the Patriarch's whereabouts, so the cavalry went to his place of hiding[i], arrested him, and carried him to Misr [Al-Fustat]. When he arrived, the *Wali* ordered that he be thrown in prison with thieves, murderers, and other evildoers. [He was sick, in pain, and suffered from gout.] He suffered greatly, and all the Muslims and Christians heard his news. The *Wali* forbade anyone from visiting him, except one of his disciples who brought him food; however, the Patriarch was not allowed to speak to that disciple or give any instructions concerning his wishes [..]. He [the *Wali*] arrested bishops from all over the land of Egypt. He defamed them, stripped them of their religious garb, and dressed them in other clothes, leaving only the monk's headwear. He would also make them ride on beasts without saddles and humiliate them before the people of the city [..]. Abba Shenouda was held in these dire conditions for 40

---

responsibilities; some were *Walis* for the *Kharaj* (responsible for the exaction), while others were *Walis* of 'Prayer' (responsible for the general administration and security), etc.

[i] Not clear why, nor since when, was he hiding.

days[i], and was then released by the *Wali*, who asked for an exorbitant sum of money that the Patriarch could not pay [..]. He also set free the bishops who were on their way to Egypt.

The *History* chronicler dedicates many pages to tell the story of another monk (who was turned down for an ecclesiastical position that he coveted) who went before the *Wali* and accused the Patriarch, saying, "He charms a group of Muslims in order to baptize them." The *Wali* ordered that this charge be investigated, and he sent his scribe and soldiers to the Monastery of Abba Yuḥannes in Wadi Hebeb.[ii] They arrested one of the monks on the charge of being a former Muslim, but he asserted that he is a son of a Christian and has been a Christian all his life. The scribe brought false witnesses and promised to pay money to the monk if he converted to Islam, but he refused. The scribe then sent a group of Turkish soldiers (unfamiliar with the Egyptian tongue) to bring the Patriarch to Misr. They carried him from his sickbed with their own hands and placed him in a carriage. They looted all they could find in his hermitage (residence), including church books, for he cared much for books and employed several transcribers. They arrived to Al-Fustat at night, and imprisoned him in a tight cell with thieves and murderers. Several days later, the scribe asked him for money in return for his freedom, but he had no money to pay. So, they brought Sam'an, the Bishop of Banna, who was accused of hiding the Patriarch's money. At the scribe's behest, Sam'an was thrown on his stomach, beaten until he bled, and then imprisoned. After 30 days, the *Walis* verified that the monk had been a lifelong Christian and released them.

A group of well-known Muslim traders from Alexandria (who visited the monasteries to purchase mats and other items) found out about what happened. So, they spoke to the *Wali*, which led to the arrest and yearlong imprisonment of the monk who made the initial accusation against the Patriarch.

---

[i] Ironically, his homonym, Pope Shenouda III was held by President Sadat (in Sept. 1981) under confinement — de facto arrest — in a monastery, until he was released 40 months later by Mubarak in January, 1985.

[ii] Currently there is no such monastery in the area; it must have perished over the years.

***

Regarding the days of Abba Khail III (880–894), the *History* says that after the Bishop of Sakha was removed from his office by the synod of bishops (for some wrongdoings).

He went to the Amir, Ahmad Ibn Ṭūlūn, [..] and complained to him about the Patriarch, whom he claimed was exceedingly rich. This made Ibn Ṭūlūn happy (*see below), because he desired to replenish what was spent to mobilize the Levant soldiers. So, he brought the Patriarch and said, "You know the sums of money we need to send to the Caliph in Baghdad, since he is the owner of this land, especially with all the wars he has to deal with. And you, leaders of the Christians, live in peace, and have no need of gold and silver, [but only] bread to eat and clothes to wear. I have been informed that you are in possession of large sums of money and countless gold and silver utensils, and silk garments. I like you and revere your old age [..]." So, the Patriarch replied, "[..] I am a humble man; I do not have gold, silver, or any of the things that you were told were in my possession. Your highness knows that we are a people who are commanded [by our religion] not to lay up for ourselves treasures on earth [..]. I am in your hands, do as you please, for you have authority over my body, but my soul is in the hands of its Maker." When Ibn Ṭūlūn heard these words, he became angry and said, "Truly, because I honored you, you withheld your money from me. Everyone who is not of our religion, if honored, does not understand honor." Then he ordered that he be imprisoned [..], and the jail was extremely crowded. After spending a year in prison, the Patriarch paid some money to the jailer in order to make him [a toilet] [..].

(*) Ibn Ṭūlūn (a son of a Mamluk from Turkistan) ran the affairs of Egypt on behalf of Bakbak, to whom the country was bestowed by the Caliph in a feudalistic arrangement. Ibn Ṭūlūn did the same on behalf of Bakbak's successor, Yargookh, thus becoming somewhat of a de facto independent Sultan over Egypt. He was tyrannical in imposing taxes and purchased many slaves; Turks, blacks, Abyssinians, and white inhabitants of the Mediterranean Islands. He cared for architecture, and when he began to build a town (Al-Qaṭāei), he ordered that Christian and Jewish graves be ploughed through. He then began building where these graves once stood.[64] He built a

mosque that was unparalleled in any of the Islamic counties. During the
course of building this mosque, he needed 300 pillars, and he was told that
he would not be able to find that many anywhere, unless he took them from
churches. Meanwhile, a Coptic architect[i] heard of this and wrote to Ibn
Ṭūlūn, suggesting that he can build the mosque using only two pillars for the
front section. Ibn Ṭūlūn, therefore, released him from prison, clothed him,
and provided the finances needed for construction. So, the Coptic architect
built and decorated the mosque.[65] The Ibn Ṭūlūn Mosque stands as a jewel
till this day.

Worthy to note here is that the mosque of the first few centuries of the
Muslim era was a plain unroofed court, which, though rich materials were
sometimes used in the construction, had no pretensions to architectural
beauty. They soon, however, began to build cloisters round them, with pillars
taken by force from the Christian churches, which no Arab was capable of
carving for himself. It is the same with almost all of the columns of Al-Azhar
mosque, and indeed with every mosque of any age throughout the country.
If, in visiting, Egyptian villages known to have possessed fine churches in
the early centuries, one finds no church still occupying the ancient site, one
has only to look into the village mosque, and will find the pillars of its nave
looking sadly out of place, and very often upside down. Also, the fountain
for ablutions, which all the primitive churches in Egypt had, has now become
pre-eminently the characteristic of a mosque. [66]

***

Ibn Ṭūlūn's Vizier, Ahmed Ibn Al-Mazrai, had a scribe named Yoannes
[John], who approached him regarding the Patriarch [..]. The Vizier then
communicated the status of the [imprisoned] Patriarch to Ibn Ṭūlūn, who
replied back to him, "I will kill him, because he was aloof with me."
[However, the Vizier persuaded Ibn Ṭūlūn, so he released the Patriarch,
pending the determination of the amount he must pay.] After many
inquiries and numerous correspondences, he settled on the sum of

---

[i] Named Katib Farghani, who was jailed in an underground prison because the
Sultan's horse had stumbled over his workman's rubble. He was martyred in a later
persecution; beheaded on his refusal to renounce his faith and convert to Islam.

twenty-thousand dinars to be paid in two installments: the first would be ten-thousand dinars which must be paid within one month, and the remainder was to be paid within four months. [Ibn Ṭūlūn ordered that a deed be issued, making Yoannes, the scribe, and his son, Maqar, responsible for the sum of money that was determined.] [..] The *Archons* became worried when the end of the first month neared, and the Patriarch still had nothing. So, they counted the number of vacant dioceses [a total of ten] and [selected] ten bishops for them. After imposing a monetary sum on each one, the ten were ordained by the Patriarch. Yoannes and his son brought two-thousand dinars and borrowed [the remaining amount] from Muslim scribes. They then delivered the ten-thousand dinars to the *Wali* by the end of the month [..].

The Patriarch met with the synod and discussed the matters of the borrowed and remaining money that must be paid to the *Wali*. They eventually decided to return to their seats and collect one carat of gold from each [priest]. In so doing, they went against the law of the Apostles and Church teachers who said, "No gold or silver is to be taken in exchange for [ecclesiastical] positions [to prevent the laying on of hands]."[i] They eventually gathered the agreed upon amount from the ten [new] bishops. The Patriarch also went to Wadi [Shehit] [..] and collected one dinar from each monk. Then, he went to Alexandria and asked the priests to gather and sell objects from their churches in order to obtain money. However, the priests did not obey him, and finally, it was decided that dependency buildings of the churches be sold on the condition that the Patriarch pay them one-thousand dinars every year and for this to be binding on all future Patriarchs who sit on Saint Mark's Seat [..]. Thus, through these different avenues, he was able to collect [to pay back] what he had borrowed, but he was still short ten-thousand dinars and knew of no way to come up with such a sum[ii] [..]. He became depressed because of what took place.

---

[i] Or, more precisely, simony, which is the buying or selling of ecclesiastical privileges.

[ii] When the Patriarch failed to pay half of the sum of money requested of him, Ibn Ṭūlun arrested and imprisoned him. *Al-Kafi*, Part two, P. 290.

In those days (around 877), having finished the building of his city and mosque, Ibn Ṭūlūn next proclaimed jihad against the Greeks (the subjects of the Byzantine Empire). He marched through Syria, receiving the submission of the governor of that country on his way, and began a conquest in Asia Minor, taking Antioch, Mopsuestia, Adana, and Tarsus. During the course of the war, each side took captives. When two Roum kings wrote to Ibn Ṭūlūn asking to exchange captives, he refused.

> The two kings wrote to him, saying, "Peace be unto you, in accordance with the measure you deserve. We received your response to what we wrote with regards to the captives and found in it contradictory words [..]. You even insulted our doctrine [our religion], and this is improper [..]. You ought not to insult our doctrine when no flaw is identified with it. We have also viewed past correspondences with your predecessors, since the appearance of your religion, and did not find any of the vulgarities with which you insulted our doctrine. Hence, we knew that your predecessors were more honorable than you [..]."[i]
>
> Ibn Ṭūlūn travelled to Damascus and died there (883), and his son, Khamaraweih, took his place [..]. The Patriarch returned to his hermitage [after being released and exempted from paying the remainder of the money], praising God. But he was also sorrowful for disregarding the laws of the church, for his future successors who will have to deal with simony, and for what happened between him and the people of Alexandria.

***

Abba Ghobrial, the 57th Patriarch, (910–921) came, after the St. Mark seat had been vacant for sixteen years. In his days, the problem of simony got worse because of the ruler's continued financial pressures. He spent most of his days as Patriarch in Wadi Hebib (Al-Natroun). During his tenure, Ibn Ṭaghg Al-Akhshîd multiplied his demands, and the people suffered greatly under him, and hardships spread. [67] Things did not get better in the consecutive years, and the circumstances of the church kept deteriorating.

---

[i] Notice Ibn Ṭūlun's arrogance in this instance; because of his lack of concern to retrieve his captives (Mamluk slaves who made up his army), he preferred, instead, to insult Christianity in correspondences that were completely unrelated to religion.

At that time, the great Church of the Resurrection in Alexandria was burned down (912?) and not one stone was left upon another. It was highly esteemed by Christians.[i]

***

Abba Mina took the reins (956–974), and he was the 61st Patriarch.

Ibn Ṭaghg Al-Akhshîd was the *Wali* over Egypt, who was formerly one of the Ṭūlūnian commanders. He tried to establish a state that was somewhat independent of the caliphate, as the Ṭūlūnians had done. However, he faced competition from Saif Al-Dawlah in the Levant, and the Fatimids in Morocco, attempting to enter Egypt. In his days, Egypt became one of the biggest markets of black and white slavery in all the Islamic lands. During his rule, a new job appeared: *muḥtaseb*[ii]. As usual, the harassment of Copts continued.

Al-Akhshîd travelled to Palestine and died there. His sons, Abu Al-Qassem and Abu Al-Ḥassan, took over after him, along with their father's teacher, Kafour. Kafour had been taken captive [as a child] from Nubia, and his master sent him to be taught calligraphy and literature. When he grew older and was perceived to be smart, his master gave him responsibilities over his kingdom.

Both sons died after seven years, and Kafour took the reins, but then, he died [after only 100 days]. The senior officials of the country mummified his body. [In an effort to keep his death a secret], they seated him on a highchair in his palace and dressed him in a garment with extremely long sleeves that reached to the doors of the throne room. They also designated servants who prevented visitors from coming in by claiming that their master ordered that people kiss his sleeves and greet him from the outside of his throne room, because he felt weak [..]. They had [someone] behind his chair move his head and sleeves when

---

[i] Originally, this was a temple of Saturn, built by Cleopatra VII, the Queen of Egypt. As Christianity became prevalent, it was not destroyed, but converted into a church. *Al-Kafi*, Part two, P. 307.

[ii] *Muhtaseb*: A person assigned to ensure that the rules of Islamic *Sharia* are enforced, and polices public conduct. This includes tasks like inspecting commercial market dealings.

someone came to greet him. No one in his palace [except for his two private teachers, his concubines, and Abu Qazman Ibn Mina [his Coptic scribe] knew about this arrangement. This continued for three years, while his Vizier exacted the *Kharaj* and administered the country's affairs. However, news of this arrangement was leaked by some who wrote to the King of Maghreb, Moed Abu Tamim Al-Moez li Din Allah [..], so he sent his commander, Gawhar, with a great army [..], and he took over the land of Egypt (in 969).

***

With this macabrely absurd ending, the curtain goes down on the rule of the Turkish *Walis* who succeeded the Abbasid Caliphate—only for a new sorrow-filled chapter to begin.

This period was notorious for its sustained barbaric tactics and the spreading of corruption by the Arab Bedouins. In addition, it appears that the more than 300-year vicious war of attrition against the Copts began to produce results in the form of snitching, backstabbing, and internal conflicts...

The Fatimids and the Adventures of Al-Ḥakem bi-Amr Allah

After Gawhar Al-Siqilli became the ruler of Egypt (in 969)[i], Caliph Al-Muizz li-Din Allah arrived from Maghreb (in 973), and Egypt became the headquarters of the Fatimid Caliphate.

The history of the Fatimids with the Copts is filled with terrible contradictions. In the beginning, they were inclined to be friendly toward the Copts (who still constituted the majority of Egyptians at that time). This was because the real enemies of the Fatimids were the Sunnis who supported the Abbasid Caliphate, prior to the conversion of the Egyptian Muslims to the Shiite doctrine after the Fatimid's arrival. Moreover, that friendliness was out of concern for keeping the administration of the country's affairs afoot (for example, Gawhar retained Quzman Ibn Mina as an administrator, because he had a reputation of being trustworthy and honest). But things did not continue on the same trajectory.

---

[i] In 893, a strong body of Arabs, followers of Ismaili Shia and known as the Fatimid party because their head claimed descent from Fatima, the daughter of Mohammed, had made themselves masters of Pentapolis and the surrounding districts (current day Tunisia and western Libya), and sixteen years later, their leader assumed the title of Caliph in opposition to the Sunni Omayyad Caliph in Spain, and the Abbasid Caliph at Baghdad. The Fatimid Caliph fixed his capital at Cyrene. Having consolidated his power, the Fatimid Caliph determined to conquer Egypt, always the richest prize of the Oriental world. In the year 913, he marched into that country at the head of 40,000 men, seized Alexandria, and laid siege to Al-Fustat. He was, however, driven back from the interior with great loss, and, though he held possession of Alexandria for some time, he was ultimately forced to retire to his own country. The Christians suffered, as usual, and the great church of the Cesareum in Alexandria was burnt down. Invasion attempts were repeated in 919–921 and 935–936.

It is worth noting that Sawiris was a scribe in the Divân at that time, known for his extensive knowledge and voluminous work (authoring more than 20 books). He learned the Arabic language and created for himself an Arabic-to-Coptic dictionary to aid in the writing of *History of the Patriarchs* in Arabic. Finally, he left behind the cares of this world and entered the monastery, before becoming a bishop over the Ashmunîn. He died at the turn of the tenth century (around 1000).

Shortly after the entrance of the Fatimids into Egypt, Gawhar, the commander of the invading forces, decreed the building of a new city north of Al-Fustat. For its location, he chose the old city, *Ka-Hi-Ra*,[68] which morphed into the name, *Qahirah*, (then 'Al-Qahirah' or Cairo), meaning 'the Victorious' in Arabic.

> The country did not fare well as the *History* observes:
> In the first year of the rule of these Maghrebis [the Fatimids], there was a drought over the land of Egypt [..]. Costliness persisted for seven consecutive years [..], to the point where the city of Misr became deserted because many people died [..], and the price of a tenth of a sack of wheat reached one dinar. Many dioceses lay desolate, because the number of people plummeted, and were, therefore, conjoined to the adjacent dioceses [..]. The Patriarch did not enter Alexandria for one year [..].

***

The *History* says that Abba Abraham (Ephraim) the Syriac, also known as Ibn Zar'ah (974–978), the 62nd Patriarch, who was from Levantine origins, ended simony.

> When some of the *Archons* pleasured themselves with concubines and had children with them, he excommunicated them, and they repented [..]. It is said that a certain *Archon*, known as Abi Alsrour Al-Kabir, had a high standing in the country, and that he had many concubines. When he was ordered by the Patriarch to cast out his concubines, he refused, so he was excommunicated [..], [and later, God punished him].[i]

---

[i] Notice how some of the rich Copts began to be influenced by the customs of the occupiers.

The Vizier of Caliph Al-Muizz was a Jewish man named Abu Yaqub Ibn Killis. He arrived with Al-Muizz from Maghreb and converted to Islam under the influence of Al-Muizz. Ibn Killis had a Jewish friend named Mousa (..), who asked Al-Muizz to debate the Christians.

So, they sent to him the Bishop of the Ashmunîn, Sawiris, known as Ibn Al-Muqafa', who was a scribe prior to becoming a bishop. God gave him grace and power in the Arab tongue [..], and on many occasions, he debated judges from the Muslim *Sheikhs*, at the king's behest, and defeated them [..].

On the day set for the debate with the Jewish interlocutor, (Ibn Killis) challenged the Christians with the Gospel verse that says, "If you have faith the size of mustard seed, you will say to this mountain, 'Move from here to there,' and it will move."

So, Al-Muizz said, "Here you are, myriads of thousands of Christians in this country [..], now I want a practical demonstration of this verse [..], or I will annihilate you by the sword."

Then, the *History* recounts the miracle that virtually every Copt still remembers of moving the Mukattam Mountain, after which Al-Muizz said, "O Patriarch, I have recognized the soundness of your faith." Then he said, "Ask for anything," and the Patriarch replied, "I ask God to establish your kingdom and give you victory over your enemies." However, Al-Muizz insisted that he ask for something, so the Patriarch asked for the rebuilding of several churches: the Church of Abu Marqoura, Al-Muallaqa (Suspended) Church, and others. Al-Muizz ordered that a letter be issued, granting these requests and that money from the treasury be dispensed for the building projects. The Patriarch accepted the letter, but (declined) the money.

When the letter was read at the Abu Marqoura Church location, the Muslim merchants and riffraff exclaimed, "Even if we are all killed by the sword, still, we will not allow anyone to place one stone on top of the other in this church." So, the Patriarch returned to Al-Muizz, who was angered by what happened [..], and he ordered the commencement of the foundational digging [..]. After that, no one dared utter a word, with the exception of one *Sheikh*, who was the Imam of the mosque that the merchants attended. He was the one who rallied [and incited] the mobs. He threw himself in the pit dug for laying the church's foundation and proclaimed, "I would rather die than let anyone build this church."

When Al-Muizz found out, he ordered that the Imam be buried under the stones and the church be built over him. After he saw stones being thrown at him, he tried to get out, but he was prevented [by the soldiers of Al-Muizz]. When the Patriarch saw this, he went and had a discussion with Al-Muizz and asked that the *Sheikh* be pulled out of the pit [..]. Afterward, no one dared utter a syllable until the church was built, along with the Al-Muallaqa Church located in *Qasr al-Sham'* [i] and the churches in Alexandria that were dilapidated.

Stepping outside Church affairs, the *Chronicles* recounts this anecdote:

[..] Often, whenever Al-Muizz desired to enact something as he used to do [in Maghreb], he was prevented by Gawhar, who would pleasantly and diplomatically tell him, "The people of Egypt are cunning and shrewd, and nothing is hidden from them, as if they know the unseen." [Al-Muizz wanted to test them], so he ordered that large sheets of empty paper, resembling a letter, be folded and sealed [..]. Then he ordered that a trumpet be sounded in front of him and that a crier call the people to gather and hear the contents of the letter. Meanwhile, Al-Muizz dispatched his spies to find out how the Egyptians would respond. It was reported to him that some people were telling others, "Do not bother yourselves, there is nothing to be read, it is an empty letter." Al-Muizz marveled when he found out.

***

In the days of Abba Filotheos (979–1003), the 63rd Patriarch, Sawiris says that he reverted to taking money from those whom he ordained as bishops (simony), and some accused him of ordaining the unworthy.

The *History* recounts the story of Alwaḍeḥ Ibn Alraga. He was a young Muslim man who studied Islam and was in the habit of attending the Judicial Council (Court). One day, he saw soldiers gathering wood to burn a Muslim man sentenced to death for converting to Christianity.

Many people gathered to watch him. [Ibn Alraga] was very zealous for his religion [..], so he approached this individual and said, "What

---

[i] The Castle of Candle,' the Wax Palace, or 'Castle of Beacon.

compels you to destroy your soul for a religion where you become a *Kafir* [unbeliever] to Allah and commit *Shirk* [idolatry] by worshiping another [Christ/the Trinity] besides him? By this, you will hasten the fire of this world and the fire of the hereafter, in hell, because you make Allah out to be a third of three [gods] [etc.]. Now listen to me, forgo this *Kufr* [unbelief], come back to your religion, and I will make you a brother to me, and you will be honored by everyone." He replied, "Do not accuse me of *Kufr* [..], for we worship one God [..], and the mystery of our faith is wonderful, but it is hidden from all of you, because your minds cannot withstand it, and your heart is dark [..], but in a little while, I see the light coming close to you and filling your heart with light [..]." Upon hearing these words, [Ibn Alraga] became enraged [..], and he took off his shoes and hit him over the face [..]. Then they beheaded him and burned his body.

The *History* recounts in detail how this incident was a turning point for Ibn Alraga, leading to his baptism, after great vacillation, and his eventual fleeing and suffering. He also gives details of how the two of them (Sawiris and Ibn Alraga) became friends, and how he wrote two polemical books: *Al-Waḍeh* (The Clear) and *The Wonders of the Interpreters* responding to the critics' books (written by Muslim apologists).

The King of Abyssinia (Ethiopia) asked the Patriarch to ordain a Metropolitan[i],

---

[i] The Patriarch of Alexandria was the spiritual leader of these countries. Furthermore, the almost daily decline in the Patriarch's authority in Egypt did not diminish the respect that he enjoyed in Ethiopia. We know how the Negus (Ethiopian emperor) overlooked the Patriarch's declining prestige and respectfully asked the Egyptian authorities to send him a bishop. Ibn Fadl Allah al-Umari describes how the rulers of Ethiopia received the person who was delegated by the Coptic Patriarch: "The statesmen, the priests, and the notables received him at the boundary of the country, carrying incense burners. When the delegate arrived in Amhara, the Negus received him personally and abstained from using royal decrees from that moment, until the Sunday after the arrival of the delegate. Then, the Negus, the clergy, and the statesmen held a meeting in the church courtyard to listen to the (Patriarch's) message. The Negus listened to the message while standing." Tagher. P. 252.

because he feared that the Christian faith will be extinct and void [in Abyssinia], explaining, "Six prior Patriarchs did not pay attention to our country, and now, we are without a shepherd. The bishops and priests died, and the churches are in ruins [..]." [The Patriarch] honored his request and ordained a priest from the Monastery of Abba Maqar and sent him to be their archbishop [..].

For all intents and purposes, it appears that Copts lived in peace during the days of King Al-Muizz, until his death (975). His son, Al-Aziz Billah[i], succeeded him.

But in these days, the Muslims of Jerusalem (which was under Abbasid control) rose up against the Church of the Resurrection (Al-Qeyamah), looting and burning it until nothing of worth remained. Egypt's Muslims also began to treat the Copts with greater harshness, pillaging and destroying many of their homes, and harassing them. The days of hardship protracted, affecting almost all parts of the country, but then they came to an end.[69] After the death of Al-Aziz Billah, Al-Hakim bi-Amr Allah took his place.

***

Sawiris died prior to 1000, and other chroniclers throughout history picked up where he left off to continue writing *History of the Patriarchs*, sometimes employing different styles.

***

Regarding the time of Abba Zakaria (1003–1032), the 64th Patriarch, the chronicler (Mikhail, who became the Bishop of Tannîs) paints a bleak picture of

> the deeds of some of the bishops at that time [..]. They became like the *Walis*, lording it over the priests, making excuses to collect money, and selling [priestly offices] for gain [..]. However, God did not delay, and unleashed His wrath on the churches because of them [..]. In their days, church teaching ceased, and no one deterred another [..]. Those with understanding and wisdom accounted for nothing if they were poor, while those who were ignorant and lacked understanding were honored

---

[i] One of his wives was a Christian Egyptian of the Greek (Melkite) Church.

[..], if they were affluent. [While it appears that the Patriarch himself was virtuous, he was nonetheless weak.] His disciples controlled him, and it was they who took the money.

[..]

As for the Caliph [Al-Ḥakem bi-Amr Allah], he was a young boy when he took the reins of the kingdom [in 996]. He started to rule officially [at the age of 16] and loved bloodshed more than a ferocious lion. The number of those whom he killed was estimated at more than eighteen-thousand souls [..].

Al-Ḥakem had many adventures with the Copts…

[..] The Caliph took ten [Coptic] *Archons* and scribes, among whom was Abu Alnagaḥ Al-Kabir, and he said to him, "I want you to leave your religion (for) my religion. I will make you my Vizier, in charge of my kingdom's affairs." Al-Kabir said in response, "Give me until tomorrow." So, he went away [gathered his family and friends, bade them farewell, and encouraged and strengthened them. Then, he returned on the following day to inform the Caliph that he will not renounce his faith]. Al-Ḥakem endeavored, through persuasion and intimidation, to sway his decision, but could not. So, finally, he ordered that they strip off his clothes and drag him to the *Hanbazin* [a vicious torturing device][i]. They lashed him 500 times until his flesh was torn [..]. Then he was lashed 300 times more, and he said, "I thirst," [..] so Al-Ḥakem said, "Give him a drink only if he converts to our religion." Al-Kabir refused and died. Although Al-Kabir was already dead, Al-Ḥakem ordered that he be lashed until one-thousand lashes had been administered.

Another man from the ten *Archons*, named Al-Rayes Fahd Ibn Ibrahim, who [Al-Ḥakem] had promoted over all his scribes and Divân officials, was brought to him. Al-Ḥakem told him, "You know that I chose you over all the others, so listen to me and join my religion, and I will exult you further, and you will be like a brother to me." But he did not yield, so he [Al-Ḥakem] ordered that he be beheaded and then his body burnt [..].

As for the rest of the ten [*Archons*], when he asked them to renounce their faith, they refused. So, he ordered that they be tortured, and they

---

[i] Hemetarim, a vicious torturing device.

were lashed. When the beatings increased, four of them converted to Islam, but the rest were tortured to death. One of the four died that same day, and the other three reverted back to Christianity after the times of frenzy were over.

Although many of those who ruled Egypt since the occupation employed such barbarous methods, Al-Hakem bi-Amr Allah stands out for his psychotic personality. He

[..] did things no one had ever heard of [..]. His opinions and beliefs were in constant flux, and his appearance resembled a lion. He could make a person shake [out of fear] just by looking at him, and his voice was loud and terrifying. He used to look at the stars, seek esoteric wisdoms, and served [worshipped] Saturn, as he claimed. He often walked around the eastern mountain [Al-Mukattam] by night, along with three horse riders. He also walked the streets by night, eavesdropping on the people's homes to find out what they were saying about him. He had many spies and informants who relayed the news to him [..]. He forbade women from leaving their homes [..], forbade the eating of Mulukhiyah[i] [..], forbade anyone from drinking wine, and wine containers were smashed everywhere. One day, a dog jumped in front of the donkey he was riding, which startled the donkey, so he ordered that all the dogs in Egypt be killed [..].

He forbade the ringing of [church] bells in Egypt, and a short while later, he ordered that crosses on top of church domes be destroyed and that [tattooed] crosses on the people's hands be erased. Then, he ordered Christians to tighten the sashes around their waists, wear black turbans on their heads [..], carry crosses handspan long, and then he increased the length to an arm and a half [..]. He also forbade *Dhimmis* from entering bathrooms along with Muslims [..]. He affixed crosses on the doors of bathrooms used by Christians and wooden tree stumps on the doors of bathrooms used by Jews. He then ordered that crosses [carried by Christians] be made of wood, weighing five pounds each, stamped with a lead stamp, and hung around their necks with fiber ropes [..]. Anyone found without a stamp on his cross was [taken] to jail. Thus,

---

[i] Popular Egyptian meal, made of leaves of Corchorus olitorius, sometimes known as 'Jew's mallow.'

many Christians and Jews were jailed, from the greatest to the least of them, and they could not bear up under this shame and misery [..].

Once, a monk wanted to be made bishop, but his request was denied. So, he went to Al-Ḥakem and complained about the Patriarch.

So, he [Al-Ḥakem] ordered that all churches be shut down and summoned the Patriarch. Even though the Patriarch was advanced in years, Al-Ḥakem imprisoned him.

On the second day of the Patriarch's imprisonment, Al-Ḥakem wrote to the *Wali* of Jerusalem, saying, "By the Caliphate's authority, you are ordered to demolish the *Rubbish*. Level it to the ground."

Rubbish refers here to the Church of the Resurrection in Jerusalem (more known in the West as the Saint Sepulcher). This derogatory designation is based on a linguistic play, given that the two words rhyme in Arabic and are identical except for one letter: Al-Qemamah (rubbish) vs. Al-Qeyamah (the Resurrection). Also, historically, the church was built on top of a trash heap, under which Helena (Constantine's mother) found the Cross of Jesus. At any rate, the destruction of this world-renowned church sent shockwaves across the Christian world in the West. It was certainly one of the leading factors fueling the Crusades that broke out a few decades later.

Days later, Al-Ḥakem sent edicts to all the provinces of his entire kingdom, ordering them to tear down churches, bringing all their gold and silver utensils to his palace, and to collect money from bishops everywhere. It was also decreed that nothing was to be sold or purchased from Christians anywhere. Therefore, some Christians renounced their faith [converted to Islam], and most of the Egyptian Christians removed their identifying clothes, crosses, sashes, and dressed like the Muslims [..].

Abba Zakaria [the Patriarch] remained in prison for three months. During this time, they terrorized him daily, threatening to burn him alive or throw him to the lions if he did not convert to Islam. They told him, "If you convert, you will be greatly honored and made the chief judge," but he paid them no mind [..]. [Eventually, Al-Ḥakem released him] and the Christians rejoiced and suggested that he go to the wilderness [monasteries of Shehit]. He agreed and spent nine years there [..], and most of the bishops resided with him [..]. At that time, Christians went to the wilderness twice a year, to celebrate the Feast of Epiphany, and to celebrate the Resurrection [to receive communion]. These nine years were filled with great hardships for Christians, because they were evicted, insulted, and spat upon, by Muslims [..]. If a Christian passed by Muslims, they would hurl insults at him and say, "Break this cross, and convert to this great religion."

There are many other similar instances. It is worth noting that the Coptic language received a strong blow at the hands of Al-Ḥakem bi-Amr Allah, since he issued strict orders completely prohibiting its use in homes, roadways, or schools. Those who failed to comply had their tongues cut off. He even ordered that if mothers spoke to their children in Coptic, they too were to have their tongues cut off. He personally walked the streets and eavesdropped on Coptic homes to find out if anyone was using the Coptic language.[70]

The faithful Christians could not bear staying away from the sacraments and used to bribe the [provincial] *Walis* in order to be allowed to secretly go at night to the torn-down churches [..].

[Years later], Al-Ḥakem reversed his edict, [preventing all trade] with Christians, and issued an edict, allowing Christians to travel to the Roum [Byzantine] territories, Abyssinia, Nubia, or any other place [..], and it appears that many left to escape the persecution.

A group of Christians, who had converted to Islam, appeared before Al-Ḥakem, asking for his approval to revert back to Christianity.

He said to each one of them, "Where are your sashes, crosses, and clothes?" So, they brought these items out from under their clothing, and he issued each one of them a letter [..]. Thus, many who had converted to Islam converted back to their religion.[i]

---

[i] It is the irony of ironies that Al-Ḥakem bi-Amr Allah, during one of his irrational moments, allowed Muslim converts to go back to their pre-conversion religions, while, ten centuries later, droves of people, who wish to revert back (or convert) to Christianity, are waiting for a similar 'irrational' moment from present day rulers of Egypt. Hopefully, one day they will realize that we now live in the 21st century.

One of the Muslim converts, who reverted to his religion, was a monk by the name of Benyamin. He asked Al-Ḥakem to allow him [to rebuild] the Monastery of Saint Mercurius [in Old Cairo]. After rebuilding it, Benyamin stayed there with his fraternity of monks. Al-Ḥakem used to visit often and eat their beggarly food [..].

On one occasion, Benyamin reminded him of the situation of Abba Zakaria. [On the next visit], Benyamin revealed the Patriarch to him [he brought him out of the wilderness of Shehit, where he was hiding]. So [the Patriarch] greeted him with a king's greeting, blessed and prayed for him, so Al-Ḥakem asked, "Who is this?" [and he was informed of his identity], so he gestured with his hand and greeted him. Now the Patriarch was accompanied by a group of bishops [who were elderly and venerable], so Al-Ḥakem said to them, "Is he the leader of all of you?" They replied, "Yes, our Lord, may the Lord establish his rule." Al-Ḥakem marveled and asked, "Where does [his rule] end?" They responded, "In the lands of Egypt, Abyssinia, Nubia, the five western cities, and elsewhere." He was more bewildered and asked, "How do all of these obey him, when he is without an army or money to spend?" They answered, "By one Cross," and he asked, "What is this cross?" They responded, "By the example of the Cross on which Christ was crucified" [..]. He said, "Truly, there is no stable religion in the world like the religion of the Christians. Here, we are shedding blood, expending funds, driving out armies, and yet we are not obeyed, and this old, haggardly and unsightly man is obeyed by the people of these countries, with nothing more than a word." Then he said to the Patriarch and the bishops, "Remain here until I tend to your needs" [..].

He then returned with a great edict [nine years after his previous edict], allowing the reopening and visiting of churches, and the return of all the wood, pillars, floors, and orchards to these churches [..]. He also exempted them from the special dress code and compulsory cross-carrying.

One night, during the year these events took place [1021], Al-Ḥakem went around the Mukattam Mountain [as was his custom], dismounted his horse, and ordered his rider, "Leave and go back to the palace," so he left as he was ordered. In the morning, everyone in the palace was looking for him, but they could not find him and did not know what happened to him [..]. His sister, [Sitt al-Mulk], took the reins of power until his infant son grew up and became king. They named him Al-Zāhir li-Izaz Din-Allah.

Historians have come up with many theories regarding what happened to Al-Ḥakem bi Amr Allah; however, the general consensus is that his sister, Sitt al-Mulk, arranged his assassination because of his erratic behavior.

***

Mikhail, the chronicler and bishop of Tanîs, says that during the days of Abba Shenouda II (1032–1046), the 65th Patriarch, the people of Alexandria made an agreement with the Patriarch to put an end to simony, but he

> broke the agreement, loved money, and gathered a considerable sum [..].
> The people of Assiut prevented their bishop from ministering to them for three years, [because he had paid money in exchange for his ordination].

The chronicler offers a partial excuse by clarifying,

> "The Coptic Patriarchs and the fathers acted according to the commandment [of Christ, about freely receiving, and therefore, freely giving], until the time when pressures placed on them were multiplied by the Muslim *Walis*, from the days of Ahmed Ibn Ṭūlūn, to the days of Al-Ḥakem, along with other factors which would take too long to explain. Therefore, it was out of necessity that they took money in order to pay what was demanded from them and deal with the burdens that were laid on their shoulders."

> In these days, King [Caliph] Al-Zāhir, and his Vizier, Al-Gergai, filled the prisons with people, men, and women, to the point where women were giving birth in prison.

Indeed, in these days, the people suffered great hardships, and the provincial governors (*Walis*) committed innumerable acts of oppression and injustice.[71]

***

According to the next chronicler (Deacon Mawhoub Ibn Mansour Ibn Muffrig Al-Iskandarani), Abba Khristodolos (1046–1077), who was the 66th Patriarch, enacted many laws and rules to regulate church life. He also mentions that at the start of his tenure, around 700 monks resided in the wilderness of Shehit (Wadi Al-Natroun). He moved his headquarters from Alexandria to Al-Muallaqa (Suspended) Church in Egypt.[i]

A Christian young man [age 22] in Misr, named Fam Ibn Baqourah, converted to Islam [..], then he converted back [to Christianity]. He intended to take the vows of the Monastery of Abba Maqar [but first, he wanted to confess Christ, Whom he had previously denied]. So, he tightened his sash [to prove his Christianity] and walked in the markets of Misr [Al-Fustat]. His father, Baqourah, a wool merchant, [worked for] Adat Al-Dawlah Rifq, who was the leader of the Turks, caretaker of the palace and also close to the Caliph [Al-Mustanṣir bi-Allah]. When the Muslims saw Fam's sash after his conversion to Islam, they ganged up against him and took him to the police, where he was arrested and harassed. So, his father, [Baqourah], went to his friend, Adat Al-Dawlah, and promised to pay him a large sum of money if he delivered [his son]. But he responded, "I cannot do anything, unless your son agrees to pretend that he is crazy. Then I can send witnesses to his prison cell, who would hear his crazed words, and only then can I release him as a Christian." [..] But when the witnesses went to his cell, Fam spoke to them rationally and confessed that he is a Christian [..]. The *Wali*, along with the witnesses, went to the Vizier [..], who ordered his execution.

The Sultan's janitor and the *Wali* went, spoke to [Fam] in prison, showed him kindness, and informed him that they were ordered to execute him; nonetheless, he remained steadfast [..]. So, they took him out of police custody, and many inhabitants of Misr, soldiers, and others, followed with sticks and torturing devices in their hands [..]. When they arrived at a bridge, the *Wali* dismounted his mule, and on it was a saddle and bridle with heavy ornamentation. He then placed his shiny sword on the saddle and said to him, "Take this mule and everything on it, and I will establish your name in the Sultan's Divân and dispense a yearly [salary] for you, but first recant what you have done." So, Fam replied, "Even if you offered me the rule of Egypt, I still would not be swayed," so he slapped him [..]. [The executioner drew his sword], so Fam got down on his knees, turned his face to the east, made the sign of the cross over his

---

[i] The Pope's Seat was moved from Alexandria to different temporary residences in the Delta before settling on Al-Muallaqa.

own forehead, and offered his neck to the executioner. The executioner jabbed him so that he would turn and face the Qibla, but he would not turn. Fam then asked for water, but was given none, and he was beheaded [..].

The chronicler has someone to blame for the disasters that befall his Coptic people: themselves:

> When all the leaders of the kingdom, Divân administrators, those in charge of all the affairs, and those in the helm of power were Christians, they, and all the Christians in Egypt, became fat, insolent, and haughty. They became arrogant and prideful, and they hated and envied their leaders. They became obsessed with worldly things, such as adornment, and one-upmanship. So, heavenly rebuke from Christ, the Lord, descended upon all the Christians, [as it did] on other nations, to take revenge against them for all their sins in this world and to deliver them in the world to come [..].

Then, he starts to recount what proves his point,

> The first thing to happen to the Patriarch was when [a person] wrote to Vizier Al-Yazouri, [accusing the Patriarch of] preventing the King of Nubia from sending gifts [to the Vizier] [..]. So, the Vizier arrested [the Patriarch] and brought him to Cairo [..]. The Patriarch arrived at the Vizier, accompanied by Abu Al-Beshr, the [Coptic] physician of Al-Aẓmeyah[i], [and proved to him] that nothing of what was reported to him was true. Thus, the Vizier released the Patriarch, who returned to Damru[ii].

> A leading man among the certified witnesses[iii] in Egypt was called Abu Al-Ḥassan Abd Al-Wahab Al-Sirafy. He was removed from an assignment in Misr, then appointed to and removed from judgeship in Alexandria, and was employed in different positions in the countryside. This man hated Christians. When he arrived to Damru, and the Patriarch failed to pay him [what he demanded], he wrote to the Vizier, Al-

---

[i] *Lit.* 'the haughty places,' probably referring to the caliph's palace.

[ii] A temporary residence for the Patriarch at that time, situated in the Delta.

[iii] Witnesses who are required, according to *Sharia* rules, in courts, marriage, execution of penalties, etc. They must be Muslims and of 'good reputation.'

Yazouri, telling him [..], "This Damru is the second Constantinople. It
has seventeen churches, and most of them are newly built [after the Arab
Conquest] [..]. The Patriarch has built a place to inhabit, and etched on
its door words of *Kufr*, insulting Islam and its people." [..] The Vizier
responded by asking him to confirm his findings by certified witnesses.
So, he rode with a group of official witnesses to the residence of the
Patriarch, where etched on his door were the words, 'In the name of the
Father, and of the Son, and of the Holy Spirit.' So, he scratched off these
words, prompting the Patriarch to ask, "If you scratch off these words
from the door, can you scratch them off my heart?" After this incident,
Vizier Al-Yazouri ordered that all the churches in Egypt be shut down.
His assistant in implementing this was a man named Abi Al-Farg Al-
Babili, one of the leaders of the government, and a keeper of the Divâns.
Naṣer Al-Dawlah Ibn Ḥamdan was the *Wali* over the two provinces of
the eastern and western countryside [Delta], and he shut down the
churches. He also demanded from the Patriarch and the bishops a sum
of seventy-thousand dinars.[i] Because of this, and the shutting down of
their churches, the Christians faced great oppression and hardships.

It appears that the *Wali* of Alexandria, Al-Amir Al-Moayed Ḥiṣn Al-
Dawlah Abu Torab Al-Kani, sympathized with the Christians. In fact,
Yohanna Ibn Ṣaed, known as Ibn Al-Qalzami, the writer of this section of
the *History*, was the *Wali's* business partner. He helped negotiate the sum of
money imposed on the Alexandria Christians down to two-thousand dinars.
He writes,

> We thanked and prayed for him. We then raised the issue of the churches
> that had been shut down. As a result, he turned over the key to the
> Church of Mar Gerges [St. George], which, in the past, had been the
> house of Ananias, the Shoemaker, who was the first Patriarch after Saint
> Mark. He said to us, "Pray there in secret and pray for me," so we did
> [..]. We then delivered to him [the demanded sum of money, after
> gathering it]. Several days later, he called us in, along with one of his
> [Coptic] friends who worked for him in handling shipments of products
> from the Levant, and asked us, "How much did [we contribute to] the

---

[i] This is the equivalent of 280 kg of gold, worth over 12 million dollars in today's
reckoning.

demanded sum of money that was paid?" We responded, "200 dinars."
So, he paid us 200 dinars, saying, "I have collected this sum for you
from the Christians of Rshîd and Idku, so take the money to cover what
you paid." We prayed for him and thanked him, and we said, "Our Lord,
this is not lawful for us, because [the requested sum was collected from]
the widows and as well as those who cannot afford it, so how can we
reclaim what we paid?" He responded, "These dinars are yours, do with
them as you please." We thanked him and used the money to buy clothes
and wheat, which we distributed to the needy Christians.

The shutting down of churches in the time of Vizier Al-Yazouri took
place on Friday, the fifth of the month of *Baūnah* of the 776th year of the
Coptic martyrs, [1059]. The Patriarch and bishops were arrested and
asked for money. Three of the bishops [the Bishop of Maṣîl, in Beheira,
the Bishop of Samnûd, and the Bishop of Al-Khandaq, near Cairo] were
also tortured to death. Our Syriac brothers, in Antioch, also faced the
same circumstances [..], and their sobbing and tears intensified.
Afterward came a man by the name of Ibn Al-Qaed Al-Raḥîm, who was
in charge of collecting [the *Kharaj, Jizya,* and the like] in the countryside
[of the Delta]. He was a very evil man who hated Christians. Christians
were greatly abased and faced many hardships at his hands [..].

Then a war broke out between the sons of Ḥamdan and the ruling Turks
on the one side, and Naṣer Al-Dawlah Al-Ḥamdani on the other [..]. So,
the Fatimid Caliph, Al-Mustanṣir Billah, expressed disdain for the sons
of Ḥamdan and their accomplices. One of their groups, the Kurds,
resided in Cairo and Misr [Old Cairo, Al-Fustat], and numbered around
five-thousand, [and he pursued them] [..]. Naṣer Al-Dawlah and his
cohorts were defeated, and arrived in Alexandria and formed an alliance
with Qays and the Lowatians.[i] The soldiers marched from Misr at his
charge [..], but they were overpowered by the sons of Ḥamdan and their
cohorts who ruled the entire eastern and western towns in the

---

[i] Bedouin tribes (of Berber/Amazigh origins?) coming from eastern Libya, who
spread in the western desert of Egypt. They attacked the farmlands and the cities,
particularly in the western Delta. They spread corruption, looting, pillaging, and
killing. Footnotes, Part three, P. 958.

countryside [the Delta]. They also looted and destroyed the inhabitants of these towns, defiling and slaughtering the children in their mothers' arms. Additionally, they plundered and destroyed the churches, and defaced whatever icons that were left. The Lowatians then expelled the Patriarch from his residence and looted it [..]. Circumstances worsened even further, and the Lowatians dominated the country [..].

Prices continued to rise, and the people were increasingly in fear. There was such a shortage of wheat that people began to eat the dead [carcasses]; therefore, they perished by pestilence, inflation, and the sword[i], and only the affluent survived [..].

The Lowatians controlled [the entire Delta] and numbered around forty-thousand horsemen, in addition to their cohorts. Having the towns of Egypt under their control, they farmed freely [..]. They also looted, destroyed, and killed the monks of the monasteries of Wadi Hebib [Al-Natroun], and only some escaped. The people were in immense sorrow because of the adversity they experienced in the days of Ḥamdan and his cohorts [..]. The Lowatians further established their dominance over the countryside, and no one was permitted to farm except them [..]. The land of Egypt became destitute, and the people could no longer find [wheat], and began to eat the carcasses of mules and donkeys [..]. In the midst of these hardships, God destroyed Ibn Ḥamdan and his cohorts. He was killed in the area where the Turks lived in Egypt, by the hands of Baldacore[ii] and his maritime Mamluk associates, in the lunar year 465 (1072 A.D.). A year after he was killed, Amir Al-Gyoush ['Commander of the Armies,' Badr Al-Gamali] arrived, and God eased the burdens of the people [..].

As Amir Al-Gyoush was on his way to conquer Upper Egypt, he was approached by a man named Ali Al-Qifṭy, who alleged that Boqṭor [Victor], the metropolitan of Nubia [ordained by the Patriarch], had torn down a mosque in Nubia [..]. In response, Amir Al-Gyoush wrote a letter to his son [in Cairo], ordering him to arrest the Patriarch, which he did. The Patriarch remained in prison until a messenger, who had been

---

[i] This is what historians have dubbed the 'Almustanṣirya Distress,' which came upon Egypt at that time.

[ii] His own son-in-law or brother-in-law.

dispatched by Amir Al-Gyoush to the King of Nubia, returned and
refuted the account of Al-Qifṭy. Upon his [Amir Al-Gyoush's] return to
Cairo, he summoned the Patriarch to his quarters [..]. He also brought
Al-Qifṭy, who admitted that he had told a lie. Then, he summoned the
judges, witnesses, and scholars, and asked them, "What should be the
fate of this lying Al-Qifṭy, who [caused the rift] between two kings?"
Their verdict was execution. Then, Amir Al-Gyoush asked the Patriarch,
"What do you say?" He responded, "In our religion, we do not kill, or
repay evil for evil, but you are the Sultan, and the verdict is yours." So,
he ordered his [Al-Qifṭy's] execution.

The Patriarch then sent a letter [to the King of Nubia] carried by one of
his bishops, who was accompanying a messenger, called Saif Al-Dawlah,
from Amir Al-Gyoush,

[..] requesting the extradition of an army commander named Kanz Al-
Dawlah, who [led a mutiny] in Upper Egypt. Kanz had looted and
destroyed Upper Egypt prior to the arrival of Amir Al-Gyoush, and
escaped to Nubia. The King of Nubia obliged and delivered [Kanz Al-
Dawlah] to them. After arriving to Egypt, he was killed by Amir Al-
Gyoush, and crucified at Bab El-Hadeed [..]. Amir Al-Gyoush honored
the Patriarch exceedingly and treated him with respect. In his days,
prosperity returned, the roads were restored, and trade carriages
continued coming into Egypt from the east and west.

***

In the days of Abba Kyrillos II (1078–1092), the 67th Patriarch, the
chronicler, Abu Al-Barakat Ibn Zouin, writing in the *History of the
Patriarchs*, recounts that the Patriarch went to visit the Caliph, Al-Mustanṣir,
in his palace.

When he arrived, he was greeted by Mamun Al-Dawlah Anbar Al-
Harani, Al-Ostaz [the Professor], who said to him, "Amir al-Muminin,
[Commander of the Faithful, the Caliph], sends his greetings." He then
bowed toward the ground and took him in to our Lord, where his mother
and sister were present [..]. They said, "Bless us," so he blessed them,
prayed for them, and ordered Botros, the Bishop of Duqmayrah, to read

the prayer [..]. Then, he headed to the house of Amir Al-Gyoush and was most kindly received, so he prayed fervently for him.

Now, the Patriarch had put an end to simony, but some of the northern bishops and Misr's (Al-Fustat) *Archons* asked him to dismiss some of those who surrounded him. They argued,

"they corrupt the affairs of the people, and these types should not accompany you anywhere, because they will bring shame upon you."

They had arguments with him concerning this matter [..]. They then sent their complaints to Amir Al-Gyoush through Benyamin Al-Kholi, who was the Sultan's gardener.

Amir Al-Gyoush summoned the Patriarch, along with all his bishops. So, he went to his large grove outside of Cairo, accompanied by 47 bishops, 22 from the North and 22 from Upper Egypt, and those from Misr, Giza, and Al-Khandaq. This took place on the 23rd of Masrá [year 802 of the martyrs], [1085]. Amir Al-Gyoush spoke to them firmly with words given to him by God. He ordered them to organize and present to him the entirety of their [church and monastery] laws [..]. Then, the most exalted Amir Al-Gyoush summoned the Patriarch and bishops once more [..], and said to them, "You must all agree to one law. Do not dispute, and obey your leader. Be like him, and do not store up for yourselves silver or gold, and be truthful in all circumstances, as you were commanded by Christ. I have no use for these laws that you have presented to me. I asked for them in order for you to go back to using them" [..]. His words to them were inspired by God, since God allowed him to speak because he is a king, as the wise Solomon said [..]. So, they left him, feeling cheerful [..].

Afterward, a monk named Farag wrote [a letter] to Amir Al-Gyoush, [accusing] all the bishops without exception of holding deposits for the *Hypocrites*.[i] So he ordered to summon him and the bishops [..]. He then levied [a penalty of] four-thousand dinars [to be equally divided between

---

[i] This incident, perhaps, indicates that the 'Hypocrites' (dissidents and those who opposed the ruler) would sometimes deposit some of their wealth with the bishops for safekeeping and to temporarily hide it.

the Delta and Upper Egypt] [..]. [They all paid the penalty] with great difficulty [..]. Then, Amir Al-Gyoush published a decree that Farag, the monk, be entitled to five dinars per year from each of the northern bishops [..].

Abba Kyrillos sent the laws that he had drafted to the people of Upper Egypt. When these laws were read in the churches and various provinces in Egypt, the people rejected them. [His assistant] said to him, "You have warned them, so leave them alone."

In 1086, a decree was issued and read in the palace's large hall, stipulating that all Christians and Jews tighten their black sashes, and that sashes worn by Jews must have yellow tips, to be distinguished from the Christians.[i] It also decreed that the *Jizya* be increased on everyone by one and a third and a quarter dinar [i.e. one and seven-twelfths of a dinar].

Amir Al-Gyoush warred [to repel the attacks by the Turkish Oguz], who ruled over Al-Sharqiyah. Some of the Turks went to Al-Mahalla [Al-Kubra][ii], and they pillaged and murdered most of its inhabitants, and ruled from Al-Gharbeyah[iii] all the way to [near Tanta] [..]. Amir Al-Gyoush returned victorious to Cairo, and most of his soldiers were Armenians.

The following year,

[..] The Armenian Patriarch[iv] arrived from Constantinople and stayed in the Melkite [Byzantine] Church of Saint Mary, which is near the Jacobite [Coptic], Abu Qozman Church [..], between Cairo and Misr [..]. The Armenian Patriarch then met with Abba Kyrillos and confessed to him the correct Orthodox faith, which is also the faith of all of us, the Jacobites [non-Chalcedonian] [..]. And all people came to know the truth

---

[i] It is unclear why the Copts went back to being harassed. Notice that Coptic women were forced to wear two sandals with different colors (usually white and black) to be distinguished from a Muslim woman. Notice the resemblance between the yellow tipped sashes that the Jews had to wear and what Nazis did to them centuries later.

[ii] A town in central Delta.

[iii] Al-Sharqiyah and Al-Gharbeyah are the eastern and western provinces of the Delta.

[iv] The reason for the visit was because of the large number of Armenians in the army of Amir Al-Gyoush Badr Al-Gamali (who was of Armenian origins himself).

of the unity of the Copts, Armenians, Syriacs, Abyssinians, and Nubians, over the correct faith that was agreed on by the honorable saintly Fathers, which was contradicted by Nestor, Leo, and the Council of Chalcedon.

The brother of Abyssinia's metropolitan arrived and brought a gift to Amir Al-Gyoush, which he did not enjoy or appreciate. Amir Al-Gyoush then summoned the Patriarch, who arrived with ten bishops. He said to them, "You ordained this man's brother as Metropolitan of Ethiopia, and he owes us money. He had also [vowed] to build mosques in Abyssinia and bring gifts and many other things, but he did not." [..] He then added, "You must send to them two bishops who are to assure the building of mosques and propagation of [Islamic] *Dawah*[i] [..]. Furthermore, the Abyssinians are committing acts of highway robbery against Muslim and other merchants. The Patriarch [must therefore] prevent them from these acts, or else." The Patriarch responded, "My Lord, what do I have to do with highway robbery? I am not a patrolman."

So, Amir Al-Gyoush threw the Patriarch and ten bishops out and ordered that the Metropolitan's brother be imprisoned [..]. He also compelled the bishops to pay two dinars per day [per person, until they obliged] [..]. So, they decided to send the bishops of Giza and Sinjar to carry letters [to Abyssinia] [..]. The children of baptism [the Copts] were terrified because of the might of Amir Al-Gyoush and because of what he did; however, God had mercy when a good gift was sent by Basîl, the King of Nubia [..]. Then, Amir Al-Gyoush brought the Patriarch and bishops and treated them kindly [..]. He said to the brother of Abyssinia's Metropolitan, "Your brother promised to build four mosques for us in Abyssinia and did not." He responded, "My Lord, [the Metropolitan] built, in the areas where he could, seven mosques, and this is well known, [but] the Abyssinians tore them down and wanted to kill him. And when the king heard what happened, he arrested and imprisoned the Metropolitan." [..] [Amir Al-Gyoush] asked the Patriarch and bishops, "What did you do?" They responded, "We wrote [letters] in Coptic and Arabic; order whom you will to read and interpret [translate]

---

[i] *Da'wa* is the proselytizing or preaching of Islam.

them before you." [..] The bishops then left his presence, glad and thankful to God [..].

Amir Al-Gyoush wrote to the King of Abyssinia, saying, "If you do not do such and such, I will destroy the churches in Egypt." He [the king] responded by saying, "If you remove one stone from the churches, I shall carry to you all the stones and rocks of Mecca, and if a single stone is lost, then I shall send you its weight in gold."

Note the extent to which the Coptic Church was being blackmailed, and how the propagation of Islam and building of mosques in Abyssinia and Nubia became church tasks. At any rate, it appears that the stern response of Abyssinia's king managed to stave off trouble for now.

The *History*'s chronicler continues,

[..] Amir Al-Gyoush forbade anyone from living in Al-Hosayneya, which is in Al-Zaher, outside of Cairo, except for the Armenians [..]. A group of Armenians took a written request [to Amir Al-Gyoush], which stated that they are left without a church to pray in, and that, meanwhile, there are several churches in the Al-Khandaq Monastery that are not being used by their fellow Jacobites [Copts]. And since those churches are shut down, then they must not need them [..]. So, Amir Al-Gyoush verified this information, and ordered the [Coptic] bishop to give these churches to the Armenians to pray in, and it was done accordingly [..].

The above implies the dwindling numbers of the Copts due to conversions, etc. Nonetheless, they continued to make up the majority. As was observed by the Andalusian scholar Abu Al-Salṭ, who visited Egypt when the Vizier was Al-Afḍal, the son of Badr Al-Gamaly (Amir Al-Gyoush), during the Caliphate of Al-Âmer bi-Aḥkam Allah (see the coming sections): "The inhabitants of Egypt are a mixed people, of different types and races: Copts, Roum, Arabs, Kurds, Deylams [i], Abyssinians, and others, but the majority are Copts."[72]

---

[i] Possibly from northern Persia.

The Decay and Demise of
the Fatimid State

By the end of the 11th century, the Fatimid State began to weaken and decay. We now turn to what the chroniclers of *History of the Patriarchs*, who appear to have shifted their main emphasis from internal church matters to the general state of affairs in the country.

In the days of Abba Mikhail IV (1092–1102), the 68th Patriarch, Yuḥanna Ibn Ṣaed Al-Qalzami, the chronicler, states that disagreements arose between the Patriarch and a number of bishops and *Archons*.

In the second year of the Patriarch[..]'s ordination, the exalted Amir Al-Gyoush (Badr Al-Gamaly) died[i], and his son, Al-Afḍal, became Vizier. This was during the days of the Caliph, Al-Mustanṣir bi-Allah.

In those days, Roum [Byzantines] and Frankish soldiers from the Roum and Frankish countries arrived in the Levant in great numbers [a reference to the First Crusade]. They ruled Antioch and beyond, as well as the northern Levant, which, at the time, was in the hands of the Khurāsānian[ii] Turkish-Oguz, leaving only Damascus and beyond under the control of the Oguz. They then ruled Jerusalem [in June, 1099], and we, Christian Jacobite Copts, were prevented from performing our pilgrimage there, or even from getting close. This was because of their hatred of us, and their claim that we are heretics. They also ruled all the

---

[i] Starting the days of Al-Gamaly onwards, the Fatimid state entered the phase whereby the Vizier would hold the real power, over and above the caliph, which is similar to what sultans did in the Abbasid state. This post became the envy of all, and only the more powerful could attain it — often through assassination of the incumbent.

[ii] From Khurasan (*lit.* 'The land of the rising Sun') which lies in northeastern Persia, near the borders between current-day Iran and Turkmenistan. This is where the Abbasids started their 'revolution' three and half centuries earlier.

Levant forts, except for Sûr [Tyr] and Ashkelon, which remained under the control of Al-Afḍal's *Walis* [..]. Al-Afḍal went to battle with them, going far, and spending much, but God's will was not favorable. His Name's glory is sufficient for us; may He favor us by His mercy.[i]

***

Abba Makarius II (1102–1128), the 69th Patriarch, was ordained during the rule of Al-Ḥakem bi-Amr Allah, and remained in his office during the days of Vizier, Al-Afḍal, and, after his death, Al-Mamoun.

[..] [The Patriarch and his companions] arrived at the house of Exalted Master Al-Afḍal (*see below), and upon entering his residence, the Patriarch prayed intensely for him. Al-Afḍal found the Patriarch to be meek, virtuous, handsome in appearance, and eloquent. Thus, God made the Patriarch find favor in the eyes of Al-Afḍal, who seated and honored the Patriarch [..]. He ordered that an official notice be issued and sent to the *Walis* of Alexandria and others, whom the Patriarch will encounter on his journey. He exempted him from paying the fee [imposed on newly ordained Patriarchs].

His ordination had taken place in Saint Mark's Church [..] after many problems with the Alexandrians regarding the fee owed to them by whoever sits in the Patriarchate [..] He said to them, "I am a monk; I have nothing, nor do I write [a pledge] to pay anything. I will pay you whatever I can yearly. If you accept this, good and well, otherwise, let me go back to where I came from [the monastery]. This is better and more favorable to me than what you have called me to." [..] These exchanges continued several days, until he wrote [a pledge] to pay 200 dinars each year [..].

---

[i] This marks the beginning of the 'Frankish Wars,' which western historians, at the end of the 17th century, dubbed 'the Crusades' (*Croisades*). Modern Arabs refer to them as the Crusader Wars or, literally, 'Cruciform Wars.' Notice that during their presence in Jerusalem, the Franks prevented the Copts from performing their pilgrimage. On their part, Copts could never forget the Chalcedon Council, nor forgive the deposition of the Coptic Patriarch Dioscorus, who was regarded in the West as a heretic, while the Copts considered him one of their Saints.

(*) Vizier Al-Afḍal ordered, that very year, the destruction of the Church of Saint Mikhail (Michael) in the Rhoda Island (in Cairo), because it was located in the middle of a garden that he had purchased. Additionally, a chronicler of the church, at that time, mentioned that Abu Al-Yamin Ibn Abd Al-Masiḥ, a prominent Divân official, had renovated the Church of Abi Qdamah in Al-Fustat, which was on the verge of collapsing, without the Sultan's approval. So, when Vizier Al-Afḍal heard of it, he was irate. He rode to the church with his army, judge, and witnesses. He also brought Muslim *Sheikhs*, and all witnessed (affirmed) the renovation. So, he tore down the church, leveled it to the ground, and built a mosque in its place.[73]

In [the month of] *Epep,* 834, year of the Coptic martyrs [1117], 'Bardwell' [Prince Baldwin], the chief of the Franks, arrived with a great army to Al-Farma[i], and proceeded to loot and burn it. He had also planned a surprise attack on Egypt, but he fell ill [..] and died in Al-Arish. The exalted Al-Afḍal had gathered together a great army to fight them. So, when Bardwell died, Al-Afḍal's army pursued them to the Levant and then returned. And God protected us from them; we ask Him, glory to His Name, for His continued mercy [..].

At the end of Ramadan lunar (November, 1121), Al-Afḍal was murdered.

When the news reached our Lord, [the Caliph] Al-Amer bi-Aḥkam Allah, he went to the kingdom's house [the residence of Vizier Al-Afḍal] and put his hands on all the money he could find [..]. On the third day, he released Al-Afḍal's casket, and the people walked around it barefoot [mourning]. Our Lord, Al-Amer, may God prolong his rule, walked behind the casket, in washed clothes and a Hamdany turban, until he arrived at his father's burial plot outside of Cairo and Bab El-Nasr. There, he prayed over his body and buried him. Our Lord then returned to the house [of Al-Afdal] in Misr, and stayed there for seventeen days, until he carried off [to his palace] all the money, jewelry,

---

[i] Pelusium, also known as Pirimu, and situated in Sinai, to the east of current-day Port Said.

gold, silver, clothes, furnishings, furniture, and devices.[i] It is reported that the money visible in moneybags amounted to four-thousand-thousand [i.e. four million] dinars [..].

* * *

Abba Ghobrial II (Ibn Tureyk) (1131–1145), the 70th Patriarch, was of an honorable lineage of noble scribes. He was an avid reader of books, diligent in interpreting their meanings, and a capable Arabic and Coptic transcriber. In his days,

[..] a great war broke out between the black[ii] slaves and the soldiers [Turkish and other mercenaries], in a place called Kom Al-Darb, south of Misr, in Atfih[iii]. Many of the blacks were killed [..].

Hassan, the army commander [the son of the Caliph], arrested the Patriarch and imprisoned him in a cell until [Coptic] scribes [collected money] for him. With the help of [Coptic] merchants, they were able to gather and pay one-thousand dinars, and God delivered the Patriarch from his hands [..].

A group of Hassan's soldiers rose up against him and went to the *Wali* of Al-Gharbeyah,[iv] a Christian-Armenian man named Bahram, and given the title Tag Al-Dawlah[v]. He was Armenian, the race of their kings, who had come with Amir Al-Gyoush Badr Al-Gamali, from Acre, during the days of [Caliph] Al-Mustansir. He continued to serve the state and was promoted and made (a provincial) *Wali*, while remaining a Christian [..]. So, the soldiers went to him and asked him to become Vizier and Sultan, and he conquered Cairo [..]. Hassan, the army commander, escaped and went out of sight. Then, [Caliph Al-Hafez]

---

[i] Al-Afdal was murdered by Abd Allah Al-Batyehi, by the order of Caliph Al-Amer bi-Ahkam Allah, and he was rewarded with governorship. Notice how the Caliph murdered his victim, walked in his funeral procession, and then seized his inheritance.

[ii] 'Sudan,' *lit.* Black *people*; later became the name of the country.

[iii] South of Giza.

[iv] A province in west of Delta.

[v] *Lit.* 'Crown of the State.'

returned to his former position[i] and made Bahram Vizier, even though he was a Christian [..].

Tag Al-Dawlah Bahram remained Vizier [for about two years], and the Muslims verbalized their disapproval of him because of his faith. They envied him because the Caliph liked him, and because his word carried more weight than theirs. In his days, the Christians had high esteem, and their words were authoritative. They were treated honorably in the Caliph's large Divâns, and they ran the ministries. Many of them were the administrators and supervisors across all of Egypt [..]. Seeing their significance slip away in favor of the Christians, the Muslims conspired to target the source of this plague, in order to [get rid] of them, by bringing the Viziership of Tag Al-Dawlah Bahram to an end. So, a group of Amirs [princes; army commanders], soldiers, and a conglomerate of people filled with zeal called upon Raḍwan Ibn Al-Wakhshi, the [new] *Wali* of Al-Gharbeyah, and said to him, [..] "Only you can deliver the Muslims from the insults of the Armenians; if they grow any stronger, many Muslims will convert to Christianity."

Because of their pleas, he went with them and assembled Bedouins and the country's warlords, and cried out, "O Mujahedîn against the *Kuffar*," and he attached Qurans to the ends of spears before the soldiers and began to march. He assembled a great and innumerable army of Muslims, and continued to rise [in power] by the word of Islam [..] When news of this reached Bahram, he wanted to spare lives and said to his men, "I do not [want] God to call me to account for the blood of any of you. God has delivered this country into the hands of Muslims, so I should not, nor has God permitted me to, fight this people over their own kingdom and take away their rights. If the Caliph had not sought me out, because of what his son did to him, and if he was not pleased with the actions I took serving him, then I would not have devised anything on my own. Rise, take your children and as much of your money as you can, and let us go to Qous[ii] [where his brother, Basak, was a provincial *Wali*], and then go back to our countries, leaving this kingdom to its people, for we have no reason to fight them." But [when the Armenian

---

[i] The Caliph had imprisoned Al-Baṭyeḥi, after four years as Vizier, and directly assumed all the executive responsibilities, until appointing Bahram.

[ii] A town, 30 km north of Luxor.

soldiers refused], he disagreed with them and immediately went to Qous
[..]. However, he learned that the news of Ibn Al-Wakhshi had already
reached the people of Qous, who killed his brother and buried him in the
manure of his livestock at the state house [..]. So, he, instead, went and
resided in the White Monastery [west of Sohag[i]] [..].

Notice from the above accounts: (1) The difference between Bahram's
behavior and that of Ibn Al-Wakhshi and his peers; (2) Bahram was the first
non-Muslim 'Prime Minister' since the Arab invasion, and doubtlessly, this
counts as a positive point for the Fatimid Caliphate; (3) However, Bahram
was an Armenian; therefore, a Coptic native of the land was never made
Vizier. This was the case when Copts made up the majority of the population,
or became a minority, and this continued until the end of the 19th century.

> The chronicler of the *History of the Patriarchs* continues,
> As for Ibn Al-Wakhshi, he conquered Cairo, and the Caliph installed
> him as Vizier. He then pillaged the churches in Cairo and Al-Khandaq.
> Muslims also burned the Armenians' monastery, known as Al-Zahri,
> and killed their Patriarch and all their monks. Ibn Al-Wakhshi gave
> orders that Christians be prohibited from assuming any offices, such as
> administrators and supervisors, in the large Divâns. He also forced
> Christians to tighten their sashes around their waists and prohibited them
> from riding horses. In addition, he also tripled the *Jizya* of the Jews and
> Christians [..].
> Ibn Al-Wakhshi remained in office until soldiers and army commanders
> rose up against him, and then he escaped [..]. He stayed with [Bedouin
> tribes, east of Cairo], who took him to the Levant [..]. Then, our Lord,
> Caliph Al-Ḥafez, asked Bahram [retreating in the monastery] to return
> to his Viziership, but he refused [..].
> The King of Abyssinia wrote to the Patriarch and the Caliph of Egypt,
> requesting the ordination of some bishops for him [a number greater
> than what was customary]. The Caliph ordered the Patriarch to answer
> the request, but he apologized, saying, "My Lord, if any more bishops
> are sent to the Abyssinians, they will be emboldened to seek a
> metropolitan for themselves, and they will [no longer] obey the Patriarch

---

[i] A town, 200 km north of Luxor, or 470 km south of Cairo.

of Egypt [..][i]. This, in turn, will lead to antagonism and wars against their neighboring Muslim countries, which will disrupt orderliness and increase wars." [..]

***

In the days of Abba Yoannes V (1147–1166), the 72nd Patriarch, who assumed his office during the reign of Al-Hafez (around 1149), the chronicler was Morcos Ibn Zara'ah (he later succeeded Abba Yoannes as Patriarch). He says,

Negm Al-Deen Ibn Maşal was made Vizier in the days of Al-Zafer. But Ibn Salar, the *Wali* of the port of Alexandria, revolted against him, defeated and killed him, along with many [blacks]. He severed Ibn Maşal's head and paraded it on the edge of a spear all over Cairo. Ibn Salar then took his place as Vizier. He ordered Christians in Cairo and Misr [Old Cairo] to tighten their sashes and take off their turbans [headbands] [..]. This was caused by a group of [Muslim] religious scholars who hated Christians.

Ibn Salar remained in his office until [his janitor?] Naşr Ibn Abbas walked in and killed him, taking his severed head and defaming it between the two palaces. Abbas [Naşr's father] was the *Wali* of Al-Sharqiyah [..], then [the Caliph] installed him as the Vizier.

The Christians had rebuilt a ruined church in Al-Matareya, where there was a balsam well, from which they extracted the chrism for anointing [..]. But the Muslims tore that church down and built a mosque in its place.

After several bloodbaths between the rulers, Naşr Ibn Abbas was accused of having improper relations [..] with the young Caliph, Al-Zafer. So, he assassinated Al-Zafer [in 1154]. The child son of Al-Zafer was made Caliph, and surnamed Al-Faez.

Talaye' Ibn Razîk was installed as Vizier, and was surnamed Al-Şaleh ['the Righteous']. He loved to exact money and caused the death of many [..]. He befriended [astrologers] and listened to them. He hated

---

[i] By the church canons common to both Egypt and Abyssinia, a minimum number of twelve bishops was required for the legitimate consecration of a Patriarch.

Christians, along with some Muslim sects, since he was a follower of the *Imamah* [Shiite] sect. He also prohibited Jews and Christians from having tips to their turbans [which was only allowed for the Fatimids] [..]. In his days, cows began to die [of murrain, for the first time in Egypt].

Then, Imam [Caliph] Al-Faez died [in 1160, at the age of 20], and his uncle took his place, and was surnamed Al-Aded ['the Sustainer']. [Then, the Vizier, Razîk, was killed], and his son took his place, and was surnamed Al-Agal Magd Al-Islam ['the Honorable Glory of Islam'] [..]. He then began to act tyrannically [and became rich], and then Shawer, the *Wali* of Qous, [rose up against him with the help of Maghrebi soldiers and Bedouins], so Magd Al-Islam escaped [..]. Glory to God, He brings whom He wills into power, He exults whom He wills and humbles whom He wills [..]. Then, Shawer took office, and he was surnamed Amir Al-Gyoush ['Prince, or Commander, of the Armies'] [..]. On [the last] Friday of the month of Ramadan, a high-ranking official named Dargham and surnamed Saif ['Sword'] Al-Mujahideen, conspired against Shawer [..], and gathered a sizable army and opened [one of the] gates of Cairo.

Shawer escaped from Bab al-Futuh [one of Cairo's gates] and travelled by night, until he arrived at the dwellings of his clan, Bani Sad. Thus, Dargham became ruler [..]; meanwhile, Shawer travelled to Damascus and met with Nour Al-Deen Mahmoud Ibn Zinky. He stayed with him for a while, and they assembled soldiers [under the command of] Asad Al-Deen Shirkuh, [to help him reclaim his office], and returned to Egypt and arrived at Bilbeis[i]. Then, Dargham's brother, Nasser Al-Muslmeen, went out to fight against them with a great army [..], but he was defeated by Shawer and Shirkuh [..], who then marched toward Cairo and besieged it. Dargham was killed while attempting to escape [..], and the gates of Cairo were opened to them. As soon as Shawer settled in, he heard that Shirkuh was planning to betray him. So, he took precautions and locked down all the gates of Cairo. However, Shirkuh fought and surrounded him.

---

[i] About 60 km, northeast of Cairo, in the Delta.

The above accounts may appear to have little value for the readers, but they are left in order to show how bloody and chaotic the situation was.

The chronicler goes even further:

Then, the Oguz [Kurds] spared no one from the people of Misr. They went after the Christians, Sudanese [blacks], Armenians, Turks, and Egyptians. They killed many and sold others. If they were able to sell someone, [they would, otherwise] they killed him. They robbed the people of their money and took their women. When they had a Christian, they would call out, "Who wants to buy a *kafir* [infidel]?" [..]. They sold them cheap: 20 dirhams for a Christian, ten dirhams for a Turk, and five dirhams for a black. A monk from the monastery of Abba Maqar was martyred at their hands when he refused their offer to convert to Islam [..]. They also looted and tore down many churches in the suburbs of Cairo.

As Shirkuh's siege of Shawer in Cairo continued, Shawer sent a large sum of money to the Frankish King, 'Mari.'[i] When Shirkuh [found out] that Mari was approaching, he and the Bedouins [who were his allies] left for Upper Egypt. When King Mari finally arrived with his soldiers in Bilbeis, large sums of money and presents were carried to him from the Caliph and [Shawer], the Vizier. Mari rested in Bilbeis for one month, and then he took his soldiers around Cairo, and they marched, along with Muslim soldiers, against Shirkuh.

He was overtaken [south of El Minya[ii]], and many were killed and taken captive [from both sides], but he [Shirkuh] fled to Alexandria and took up fortified positions there. Yet, King Mari, his soldiers, and the Egyptian soldiers followed him and surrounded him there. When the siege protracted, he [Shirkuh] left Alexandria by night and returned to capture Cairo [..]. After negotiations, they [paid him] money, at which point he returned to his country [..]. Then, King Mari returned [to his kingdom], after realizing that he had made a big mistake by bringing his soldiers into the land of the Muslims [..].

---

[i] Amalric, King of Jerusalem (1163–1174). Notice how the Muslim rulers formed alliances with the 'infidels' to fight each other; the opposite also holds true, as was the case sometimes during the 'Crusades'.

[ii] 270 km south of Cairo.

During these days, a Jewish man by the name of Abu Al-Fakhr Ibn Azhar converted to Christianity in Misr. He was a man of preeminence among his people, an expert, and a scholar. He learned to speak the Coptic language in record time, and he debated with the Jews in Hebrew. He became skilled and more knowledgeable of the Christian doctrine then those who were lifelong Christians. He died [40 years after his conversion] as a believer in Christ, after he had suffered greatly at the hands of Muslims and Jews.

A letter came from the King of Abyssinia to [the Vizier], Al-Adel Ibn Al-Salar, and to the Patriarch, requesting the ordination of a metropolitan [instead of the current metropolitan, who had rebuked the king for unlawfully taking power]. The Patriarch refused, [as this was against the canons of the Church], and because of this, Al-Adel became angry at the Patriarch and imprisoned him [..]. Because of the confined space and stench during his prolonged imprisonment, the Patriarch suffered greatly in that prison, until Al-Adel was killed.

***

Abba Morcos III (Ibn Zara'ah) (1166–1189), the 73rd Patriarch, was
> [..] of honorable lineage, whose name prior to his ordination was Abu Al-Farg Ibn Abu As'ad. His [origin] was Syriac, from the people of the Levant. [Prior to his ordination], he was well-thought of by Muslims and Christians, who attested that he was virtuous and religious [..]. He did many good deeds [..].
> His days saw difficult circumstances, exhausting troubles, bloodshed, and the death throes of the [Fatimid] State [..] until its final demise in the days of Al-Adid, [after] 275 years, of which 201 years were spent in Egypt [..].

In [1160], Mari [Amalric], king of the Franks, attacked Bilbeis and destroyed it.[i] Caliph Al-Adid wrote to Nour Al-Deen Mahmoud Ibn Zinky,

---

[i] The war started as a result of the succession crisis in the Fatimid Caliphate which began to crumble. The specific reason was that Egypt had never paid the yearly

the King of the [Kurdish] Oguz in Damascus, to inform him of what happened to the Muslims in the lands of Egypt. He also requested aid. Ibn Zinky responded by sending..

[..] Assad al-Din Shirkuh, [who had fled Egypt earlier], with many Oguz soldiers, [and they chased out the Franks], and then he went to Al Louq and surrounded Cairo. The Caliph was hospitable to Shirkuh, took off his sword [in honor of] him and those army commanders who arrived with him, [paid them] large sums of money, and provided them with tents and equipment. [..]

On Friday, first day of Rabi Al-Awwal, 564 lunar [December, 1168], the Caliph sent the sword of blood with the Caliphate trustee, Jawhar Al-Ostaz, and ordered him to behead Shawer, his Vizier, so he slaughtered him [..]. Then, Shirkuh entered Cairo and the Caliph ordained him Vizier [..]. And it was an illustrious day like no other in the world. After spending one month in power [as Vizier], he proclaimed in Cairo that Christians were to lift the straps off their turbans and tighten their sashes, and that Jews were to [place] a yellow rag on their turbans[i].

[Sixty days after becoming Vizier], Shirkuh died, and the Caliph ordained in his place Youssef Ibn Negm Al-Deen Ayoub, Shirkuh's nephew, who arrived with him as an assistant, or deputy. He was surnamed 'Al-Malek Al-Naṣer, Ṣalaḥ Al-Donia wa Al-Deen, Sultan Al-Islam wa Al-Moslimeen, Game' Al-Iman wa Qame' 'Abadet Al-Solban, Moḥye Dawlat Amir al-Muminin' ['The Victorious King, Uprightness of the World and Religion, The Sultan of Islam and Muslims, Unifier of the Faith, Oppressor of the Cross Worshippers, The Reviver of the State of Amir al-Muminin] — known as Saladin [..].

On the day he was ordained, a decree was signed by the righteous judge, Abd Al-Raḥîm Al-Bysani, who was a virtuous scholar [..], and loved by everybody [..]. But as human nature is not perfect, since only God is perfect, nothing was found to taint him except that he signaled that

tribute that it had promised Baldwin III in 1160. Amalric was hoping to gain control of Egypt and break Muslim unity, invaded Egypt.
(https://www.britannica.com/biography/Amalric-I).

[i] It appears as if one of the rulers' favorite pastimes was to control how the *Dhimmis* dressed.

Christians should not be used as administrators over the state's finances
or supervisors [..]. Therefore, during the rule of Ṣalaḥ Al-Deen and his
progeny after him, Christians were not employed in administration or
supervision.

We are not sure here if the chronicler enjoyed dark humor, or if this
is an example of the victim adopting the view of its oppressor.

In Jumada Al-Akhar, 566 lunar [January, 1171], Al-Naṣer Ṣalaḥ Al-
Deen was informed that Jawhar, Ostaz[i] of Al-Aḍid, left Cairo [and was
on his way] to the Franks, seeking to bring them to Cairo in order to help
fight [Ṣalaḥ Al-Deen], because when he ascended to power, the Caliph
and two Ostazs became fearful of him [..]. So, Al-Naṣer delegated Al-
Ṭawashi [black eunuch] Qaraqosh along with 100 cavalries to pursue
Jawhar. When he overtook Jawhar and summoned him, [he refused to
go back with him], so Qaraqosh surrounded him and killed him. He took
his [Jawhar's] head and returned to Cairo. When the Sudanese [blacks]
heard of it, they assembled and marched to fight the Sultan [Al-Naṣer].
But God gave him victory, and he defeated them. [However], he did not
kill any of them, but said, "I do not blame them, because they were
fighting for their Caliph and master." [He won them over and offered
them] to reside wherever they pleased, so they left Cairo and went to the
countryside and Upper Egypt. They dispersed all over the land of Egypt.
One night, Shams Al-Dawlah, who is Ṣalaḥ Al-Deen's brother, entered
the palace and sought the Caliph. When they informed the Caliph of his
presence, he sucked his own poisonous ring [..] and died. [..]
[This is the backstory:] One of the palace men recounts that prior [to his
death], he drank wine with Ṣalaḥ Al-Deen and Shams Al-Dawlah, and
listened to singing in their presence, and when the gathering was
concluded, he was alone with his concubine [..]. She asked him to give
her the gold brocade ornamented with jewelry that was fastened to his
trousers [and he did]. She then brought that brocade to show it off to
Ṣalaḥ Al-Deen, who in turn took it and brought it before the judge,
witnesses, and scholars [..]. He then asked them for a legal opinion, "Is

---

[i] Professor, adviser, or confidant.

it permissible for the Caliph to imbibe wine[i] and live in debauchery?" The scholars opined that if this was proven to be true, then the Caliph must be removed from his office. So Ṣalaḥ Al-Deen asked his brother, Shams Al-Dawlah, to go to the palace and mercifully kill the Caliph [and he went, as seen above].

The death of Al-Aḍid li-Deen Allah, who was the 14th Fatimid Caliph, took place in 567 lunar [1172]. Al-Malek Al-Naṣer [Ṣalaḥ Al-Deen] took over the palace and everything in it. He took from the estate and furniture what was useful for him and his women, including clothes, precious stones, jewelry, etc. What he had no desire for, things like books, pots, etc., he ordered to be sold. He made Judge Ibn Banan the trustee overseeing the selling of these items.

As for the people, he [imprisoned] the Caliph's concubines and children in Dar Al-Muẓafar, in the Borgwan alleyway under guard, and sent them daily sustenance [..]. As for the Caliph's family and relatives [..], he gathered over 200 men, placed their feet in iron shackles, and imprisoned them in the hypocrites'[ii] jail located in the palace courtyard. When, out of kindness, the people of Cairo and Egypt brought forth alms [to those imprisoned], then the daily sustenance for those imprisoned [from the palace] was withheld. Many of them died and were buried in their shackles. Glory to Him Who never dies, He brings low whom He desires, and He exults whom He desires. As for the female slaves and servant slaves, he sold them along with the rest of the estate.

And just like that, with utter frivolity, the Fatimid State came to an end, and orders were given that during Friday prayers, preachers were to begin praying [..] for Imam Abu Mohammed bi-Nour Allah, the Abbasid Caliph in Baghdad...

***

---

[i] Remember that Ṣalaḥ Al-Deen partook in drinking wine with him in that very instance.

[ii] '*Munafiqun*,' those Muslims not deemed Islamic enough by their more-zealous coreligionists. The term may also refer to political opponents in a general sense.

In conclusion, the Fatimids had many mixed dealings with the Copts, ranging from vicious persecution to clemency—which was, at times (truth be told), far better than the actions of their predecessors and successors. For example, Palm Sunday and the Coptic (i.e. Egyptian) New Year were recognized as National holidays. Nonetheless, generally speaking, the Copts embarked on the next chapter of their history with a deteriorated and diminished status in their own country.

The Wars of Ṣalaḥ Al-Deen Against the *Kuffar*

After terminating the Fatimid State in 1172, Ṣalaḥ Al-Deen (Saladin) began to strengthen the pillars of his rule in Egypt. He first annihilated the Fatimid supporters. Then, he rearranged the structure of the army, making the bulk of his fighters Kurds and Seljuks, replacing the Sudanese (blacks), Berber, and Armenians. In 1175, the Abbasid Caliph in Baghdad conferred on him the title 'Sultan.'

The day of his ordination was memorable. His garments were made up of a turban covered with brilliant white gold, clothes embroidered with gold, a shawl embroidered with gold, a ten-thousand-dinar gem chain around his neck, and an ornamented sword. His eight-thousand-dinar horse had a saddle made of gold and opulent jewelry, ten-thousand gems on its head, and four gem chains on its legs.[74]

Soon after, border skirmishes started between the Muslims and Nubia's Christian kingdoms, as the Nubians were targeted by plundering raids, doing incalculable damage to the inhabitants. Then, in 1176, Copts in the town of Qeft[i] revolted, but were promptly suppressed by Al-Adel, brother of Salah Al-Deen, who inflicted upon the town the most terrible reprisals; 3,000 of the inhabitants were hanged on the trees which surrounded the town, using their own girdles and turbans for ropes.[75]

When things settled down for Ṣalaḥ Al-Deen, his heart yearned to conquest, waging *Jihad*,[ii] and invading other towns and countries. So, he assembled a very great army and prepared for battle.[76]

The chronicler of *History of the Patriarchs* says,

---

[i] About 40 km north of Luxor.

[ii] A war fought by Muslims to defend or spread their beliefs.

In [1182], Ṣalaḥ Al-Deen assembled soldiers and marched to Damascus, after the death of Nour Al-Deen Ibn Qasîm Al-Dawlah. So, he conquered it and took full control of all its surroundings. He then headed to Aleppo and encircled it, but he could not conquer it, so he conquered Homs, Baalbek, and crossed the Euphrates and conquered many cities in the area of Mosul [..]. He then returned and conquered Aleppo [..]. Later, he conquered Nablus, and after ruining it and taking a large sum of money and many captives, he returned to Egypt [in 1184].

Once Ṣalaḥ Al-Deen became the mightiest ruler in the Islamic world, he decided to wage *Jihad* against the enemies of Islam, and he directed the state's resources to the warfare against the Franks.

He dealt kindly with his Egyptian subjects [..]. He put an end to injustice, shut down entertainment parlors in all of Egypt, prohibited all abominations, and instituted the *Sharia Ḥudud* [i] [..].

This is the first time the *Ḥudud* are mentioned in the *History of the Patriarchs*. It is peculiar that the chronicler does not provide any details about such a major event. For example, what were these exactly? Was it the first time since the Arab Conquest to apply them fully or partially? How and to what extent were they used? Were they applied to the Copts or Jews, and if so, how? What were the reactions to their use? What were their repercussions? These and other questions still need serious historical research.

The clouds thickened, and Ṣalaḥ Al-Deen's Islamic zeal entered a critical phase. The chronicler recounts the battle of 'Kom Ḥaṭîn' between Ṣalaḥ Al-Deen and the Franks (July 1187):

They kept fighting, but God granted Ṣalaḥ Al-Deen victory over them, so he demolished them, and some, he took captive and some, he killed. The people of good will rejoiced because they believed that God knew that this was for their own good. When Ṣalaḥ Al-Deen defeated them, [they brought before him] Prince Arnat [Renaud de Châtillon], head of

---

[i] These are five *Sharia* bodily retributive punishments of thieves, adulterers, etc. They include flagellation, hand (and, sometimes, foot) amputation, crucifying, and stoning (or hanging).

the city of Al Karak[i], and Ṣalaḥ Al-Deen spoke to him harshly [..]. Then, he slaughtered him with his own hands and washed his hands in his blood.[ii] Count Godfrey was present during this incident, [but Ṣalaḥ Al-Deen comforted him and explained that the reason he killed Prince Arnat was because he had raided Muslim caravans travelling near his cities]. Then, he released the Count [..], who left for Cyprus [..].

Ṣalaḥ Al-Deen wrote to his son, Al-Aziz, whom he made vice Sultan over Egypt, to describe the situation:

[..] We write this to convey Allah's great victory, His manifest fat'h, which led to this victory that has [wiped out] any trace of the idolaters, bringing healing to the believers' burning bosoms [..]. It shows that almighty Allah perceived the intent of the Sultan to make His religion victorious, and knowing such intent, He granted victory; He perceived his strong will, and so, enabled and supported him, made him victorious, and supported him with his soldiers against those who deny His oneness and embrace Kufr. With his sword, he killed and buried the sultan [domination] of Shirk [..] and proclaimed the profitable victory that placed Allah's adversary on his heels. Among Allah's blessings, in all this, is that the Franks were battled, and were vanquished, leaving the countries free of them. This has also united the tyrants of Kufr with their mother, [in] the abyss of hell, and has made them taste the blazing fire. On Sunday, I took over Tiberius and killed Prince Arnat [Renauld] by the mighty sultanate hand, [and took others captive] [..]. On Tuesday, the sultanate troops went up against the city of Acre, and on Thursday, a peaceful fat'h was achieved, and Islam settled back into its homeland and returned to its dwelling. On Friday, the beginning of Jumada I [hejir month], the Islamic sermon was preached in its mosque, and the Muezzin[iii] stood in place of the [church] bells, proclaiming the words of Tawhid [iv] [..]. Then came the fat'h of Nazareth, Haifa, Hula,

---

[i] Karak city-castle, situated to the west of the Dead Sea (Jordan).

[ii] Ṣalaḥ Al-Deen also ordered the execution of about 200 captive knights. He preserved the lives of the remaining captives in exchange for a ransom.

[iii] A Muslim crier who calls for the daily prayers.

[iv] The Muslim doctrine of the oneness of God.

Iskandarouna[i], and Nablus. And I point out that the number of those killed and taken captive exceeds twenty-thousand people [..], but no more than ten Muslims were lost.

Ashkelon surrendered [in August, 1187] [..], the best bride in the world, and was delivered from the hands of Kufr [..]. There, the flags of Islam were raised on its towers, and it became inhabited by Mowahedeen[ii] and [ridding it] of its Moshrekîn and Kuffar.[iii] The number of Muezzins became abundant in all its parts, and the signs of the cross are nowhere to be found, and the [Muslim] preacher declared that there is no deity but Allah from its pulpits.

One of the stories of this fat'h, is that when the city encountered the capable Nasiriya[iv] armies of Islam, joined by the supporters of the believers and Tawhid, and the wrath of Allah engulfed its Kuffar, the Moshrekîn resorted to fleeing, so we set up for them the weapons of war and made them taste the curses of stabbing [..]. So, when they feared our torment, they chose peace [..], and I took the city and planted the flags of Islam over it [..].

The Sultan arrived at Jerusalem on Thursday [..], and organized the army, surrounding the city from all sides. The [Muslims] prayed on the mountain around it on Friday, and marched to fight after the prayer [..]. The Sultan asked Balian[v] to peacefully surrender the city, but he refused. Meanwhile, there was a Jerusalemite Christian-Melkite[vi] man named Yusuf Al-Batît, who had previously lived in Damascus, and knew Salah Al-Deen, his brothers, and his uncle, Asad Al-Deen Shirkuh, when they served Nour Al-Deen Mahmoud Ibn Zinky. When Salah Al-Deen ruled Egypt, [Al-Batît] came to them, and he was taken in by Salah Al-Deen's brother, Al-Malek Al-Adel, and treated well [..]. Salah Al-Deen used to

---

[i] Iskenderoun, also known as Alexandretta, in south Turkey, close to the Syrian borders.

[ii] Those who embrace *Tawhid*, i.e. Muslims.

[iii] Interesting to note that these words are all still on the mouths of modern jihadis.

[iv] Armies of Al-Nasser Salah Al-Deen. Also denotes being 'victorious,' coming from the same root as 'Nasser.'

[v] The Frankish Knight who was leading the garrison.

[vi] Followers of the Byzantine (Greek) Orthodox rites.

send him as an envoy to the Frankish kings, and he [Al-Baṭīt] came to know these countries' circumstances and their most prominent knights. [So now], when the Sultan realized that this was a hard battle, and that he could not overcome Jerusalem, he summoned Yusuf Al-Baṭīt. He arranged for him to correspond with the Melkite Christians, promising to do right by them if they refused to help the Franks in battle and surrendered their side of the city to Ṣalaḥ Al-Deen [..]. When Balian heard [of this offer], he feared the annihilation of all the Franks by the edge of the sword, if the Melkites agreed to surrender, knowing that the number of Melkite Christians in the city exceeded that of the Franks (*see below). Thus, he acquiesced to peace [..] and negotiated a [ransom] with the Sultan for every man, woman, and child.

(*) The pivotal role that the Jerusalemite Christians played in the Frankish surrender of Jerusalem to Ṣalaḥ Al-Deen is rarely mentioned in the writings of Muslim historians.

On the other hand, Jerusalem was in no condition to resist. Enormous numbers of the poorer people had flocked into the city, but there were hardly any soldiers, and only fourteen knights, to be found. The priests and deacons fought bravely, regarding the defense of the Holy City as a lawful cause in which to bear arms, but the populace surrounded the Patriarch and the queen (Amalric's wife), clamoring for a capitulation; and after the hopeless struggle had lasted fourteen days, the queen yielded, on condition that the Christian inhabitants of the city should be held to ransom and not sold as slaves. To this, Salah Al-Deen agreed, fixing the ransom for each man at ten dinars, for each woman five, and for each child two dinars. Some fourteen-thousand, however, were unable to pay, and half of these Salah Al-Deen, convinced of their uselessness, set free without ransom; the other half were reduced to slavery.[77]

Ṣalaḥ Al-Deen wrote to Naṣr Al-Deen Ibn Bahram, the *Wali* of the western provinces, telling him what happened, using his assonance-filled style and typical vanity:

We write to the Honorable and Grand Amir Al-Asfahslar [commander of the armies], the defender of religion, the pride of Islam, and the dean of Mujahedîn [..]. Our flags have been mounted on the walls of Jerusalem, and to our decrees, all have succumbed, the days of our Kafir enemy are gone, and to our days people say, come, come! By the support of Allah, our feet are secure. The days of confrontation were thirteen, and the days of battle were seven, no more. The mangonel catapulted until its walls were ruined; utterly destroying its walls, leveling them to the ground. The word of Tawhid has been firmly established, and the greatness of the rituals of this true religion have been put on display; for how can perversion coexist with the truth? [..]

The Kuffar kept experiencing misery and trouble from the day of confrontation till the day of surrender. Then, as their zeal died down [and they realized that] the days of their rule are over, and that [the Jerusalemites] will cast them into the hands of the allies of Allah [the Muslims] where they will be judged by sword and fire, and that Al-Aqsa Mosque has worn the two garments of joy and rejoicing [..]. And when it was Thursday, the sixth day of battle, the believers marched, and the Mowahedeen advanced, with cups of certain death in their hands [..]; it was then that they sought the safety of a truce and sent to inquire [about the determined ransom].

Decisions were made that brought joy to the prophet, the prayers of Allah be upon him, in his tomb. The tongue uttered the right opinion with frankness [about the ransom]: ten dinars for a man, five dinars for a woman, one dinar for a prepubescent boy or girl. And there are about one-hundred-thousand people or more in this city. They also pledged a ransom of thirty-thousand dinars for seven-thousand infirm men, which their elders offered as charity. Praise be to Allah who had muted their cause and uprooted their sedition with the victorious Nasiriya swords [..].

When Sultan Al-Naṣer Ṣalaḥ Al-Deen took Jerusalem,[i] through the agreement of a truce and payment of ransom in Rajab, 583 lunar [September, 1187], he resided in it until he fasted all of Ramadan and prayed during the Eid [..]. In his Eid sermon, the preacher said, "Praise be to Allah, Allah Akbar, for what He has facilitated and made easy, for the *fat'h* and victory that He accomplished, for granting us the purified

---

[i] News of the fall of Jerusalem came as a huge shock to Western Europe. This started a rallying cry for a new campaign, and those involved included prominent feudal lords and knights.

Aqsa Mosque, for the expelling the *Kufr* and *Al-A'lag, sons of yellow* [i]
out of it. He has disbanded, dispersed, and destroyed them, and He has
given to the Islamic sect the Holy Land, the land of [Latter Day]
gathering and resurrection [..]. Praise be to Allah for replacing churches
and hermitages with mosques, for replacing bells with the *Azan* [ii] and
holiness, and for turning the glorification of the cross and crucified to
the praise of Him Who never dies." [..]

Then, Ṣalaḥ Al-Deen besieged and took Al-Karak [iii]. He then proceeded
to Sidon, Beirut, Jubaila, and continued the *fat'h* of cities and fortresses
along the coast. Most of his *fat'h* was accomplished through truces
rather than the sword. He kept his promises, did not go back on his word,
and did not act deceptively. The Frankish knights, their princes, and their
notables left their forts, taking all their money, cattle, women, children,
and everything they owned from money, horses, mules, camels, male
and female slaves, and even their Muslim captives. Some agreed to sell
their Muslim captives [to Ṣalaḥ Al-Deen], and those who chose not to
were told by Ṣalaḥ Al-Deen, "Take your captive, but act kindly toward
him, as I have toward you." Many knights handed over their prisoners
and insisted not to receive any compensation in return [..].

When the *fat'h* of the entire coast was completed, Ṣalaḥ Al-Deen gave
innumerable cattle, captives, and clothes as gifts to his soldiers, friends,
and the Muslim kings and their army commanders who supported him.
I [the chronicler] was told by a young soldier that he took a Frankish
man captive and sold him to a beer brewer for a single cup of beer. Later,
it was revealed that this was a high-ranking knight. So, I take refuge in
God against the cessation of blessings and the dawning of curses [..].

---

[i] Very difficult to guess what is meant here by Saladin's preacher. *A'lag* could mean
Kuffar, well-built people, or zebra. Also, not sure why call the Franks 'sons of
yellow,' unless it's about their fair skin. In any case, this seems to be part of a
rambling string of swears and insults.

[ii] The Muslim call to ritual prayer, typically made by a Muezzin from the minaret of
a mosque.

[iii] Karak, (or Crac) derived from 'Castle of the Kurds (*Akrad*).' There are three
Crusader castles carrying this name. The most important, Crac de Chevaliers, is
located near Homs, in northern Syria. It was built in 1142, on an earlier small
Kurdish castle. The other two are al-Karak (Crac de Moab), and a close-by Crac de
Montréal; both on the southeast of the Dead Sea, in today's Jordan.

Now, we return to explain God's support for Ṣalaḥ Al-Deen, and why He enabled him to have the victories and dominance he had, and what God did with the enemies of his religion and his state. We first quote the Torah that says, "If you see the donkey of someone who hates you, fallen down under its load, do not leave it there; be sure you help them with it." Now, we quote the Gospel, which goes even further, saying, "Love your enemies, bless those who curse you, pray for those who mistreat you, and do good to those who hate you." Ṣalaḥ Al-Deen acted in accordance with these two statutes without prior knowledge or reading, but by the inspiration of God. This explains [the blessing of peacefully] dying on his own bed, and the good that followed him and his progeny.[i] While the war raged [with the Franks], the German King [Frederick Barbarossa] assembled six-hundred-thousand [??] javelin lancers, and after one full year, he reached [near Antioch]. When he wanted to cross the sea to Constantinople, the King of the Roum assembled his army against him (* see below). But [Frederick] vanquished him, besieged Constantinople, and exacted taxes from all its cities and towns [..]. He then marched toward Jerusalem, and on his way, he attacked, by the sword, all the towns of the Roum, Armenians, Muslims, and Franks. No one was able to stop him, but when he neared Antioch, King Al-Moẓfer Taqey Al-Deen blocked the water of Al-Kalb River, which flooded all the roadways. So, [Frederick] sailed across the sea in his ships from Antioch to Acre and stayed there with the Frankish soldiers [..]. Then, he, his son, and many of his friends died because of the change in climate. He is no longer spoken of, his plans were frustrated, and it is as if he never existed; praise be to the living God [..].

(*) The thrill of horror that ran over Europe when it was known that Jerusalem, after 96 years, was once more in the hands of the Muslims, gave birth speedily to a fresh Crusade. The Emperor of the West, Frederic Barbarossa, took the Cross himself, and wrote Ṣalaḥ Al-Deen a defiance in which he assumes himself to be the direct descendant of the ancient Romans and natural lord of their empire both in East and West. Ṣalaḥ Al-Deen replied to this letter in terms no less defiant and arrogant, assuring him that not only were the Muslims prepared to meet the Christians in the East, but that he

---

[i] Notice the *Dhimmi* flattery by the Chronicler.

intended to cross over to Europe, 'and will take from you all your lands, in the strength of the Lord...'[78]

When Ṣalaḥ Al-Deen received substantiated news of the new campaign by Frederick, he returned to strengthening his relationship with the Byzantine Emperor to secure his support. The number of gifts that he sent to the emperor exceeded that of any previous occasion. Ṣalaḥ Al-Deen promised the Byzantines that all the churches in Palestine will conform to the Byzantine doctrine. Likewise, the emperor, for his part, promised that the Constantinople mosque would be in the hands of the Sunni sect. Based on this agreement, the Emperor placed stumbling blocks in the way of the German campaign. Whenever he failed to stop the Germans, he would update Ṣalaḥ Al-Deen on their whereabouts.

There is no end to the descriptions and explanations [..] of what took place between the Muslims and the Frankish over Acre and other places. The chronicles of our forefathers, which remain superior to this one, present the answer by looking at God's unchanging character: to every nation that deviates from [God's Laws] and commits acts of corruption, God sends another more powerful and merciless nation to drive it out by the sword, take it captive, make it suffer starvation, pillage it, and sell its women and children [..]. This is because God desires that the king maintain [in his kingdom] purity, justice, a good reputation, along with prayers and charity, as David did [when he ruled his kingdom].[i]

War did not cease between the Franks and the Muslims in Acre [from 1189–1191]. Then, the Frankish King[ii] arrived by sea with his soldiers and joined the Frankish soldiers [near Acre] and arranged for a joint attack against Acre. Now, Ṣalaḥ Al-Deen had sent new soldiers to Acre, made up of high-ranking and well-known army commanders, Kurdish and Mamluk Ṣalaḥite [followers of Ṣalaḥ Al-Deen], Mamluk Assadites [the soldiers of Assad Al-Deen Shirkuh], and Turkmen.[iii] The Frankish

---

[i] Notice that the chronicler appears to strictly adopt the approach that all historical events are acts of, or allowed by, God, according to His own purposes.

[ii] King Philippe II Auguste.

[iii] It is clear, contrary to prevalent misconceptions, that *Egyptians* had no significant human involvement in Ṣalaḥ Al-Deen's wars against the Franks, reclaiming

King intensified the siege and took Acre at noon on Friday, mid-Shabaan. A man told me [the chronicler] that when Ṣalaḥ Al-Deen first took Acre, he found that its mosque had been turned into a church by the Franks. So, he gathered the Frankish captives and made them wash the walls, scratch all the images off the walls, and paint over everything, leaving no trace of what was there. Likewise, when the Frankish King [previously] took Acre, the Franks took their Muslim captives to the mosque and made them wash it and restored the original images and paint to its former state.

Praise be to God who is sovereign over everything, He exalts whom He pleases, demeans whom He pleases, and repays each one for his deeds [..]. Then, the King of the Francis [French] sailed back to his country and [Richard, Lionheart] the King of England arrived. He was a brave, fearless, and dauntless hero [..]. He left Acre and headed to Haifa, [and the wars continued for a while].

While Ṣalaḥ Al-Deen was strategizing, and God was giving him success, he favored a truce and a settlement to spare the bloodshed from both sides. A 40-month long armistice was agreed upon, stipulating that Muslims keep what they have gained during the *fat'h* of the coastal cities, and that Franks keep the towns they had [..]. As for Jerusalem, it was to remain with the Muslims. Ṣalaḥ Al-Deen allowed the Franks to perform their pilgrimage to Jerusalem, but only if they were unarmed (*see below) [..].

After this truce, the Franks and Muslims were like brothers, and so it went with the kings and Ṣalaḥ Al-Deen. He sent them money and gifts, and they sent him gifts, horses [and shields], German swords, and spears. Praise be to God who brings closer distant hearts and opposing customs. [..] As for the captives on both sides, nothing had been decided with respect to them [..]. [Richard] returned to his country, and Ṣalaḥ Al-Deen went to Damascus and circumcised his fifteen children—not from the same woman, but several [they are the ones he set as rulers over all the parts of his vast kingdom].

Jerusalem, and others. These were carried out by Mamluk (slave) soldiers, as well as Kurdish and some Seljuk Turk mercenaries.

(*) In fact, Ṣalaḥ Al-Deen was compelled to make terms for an honorable capitulation. The city of Acre, the 'true Cross,' two-thousand noble Christian captives, and 500 of inferior rank, were to be given up and a ransom paid of two-hundred-thousand dinars as well...but neither captives nor money [nor the true cross] were sent. The Christian captives, in spite of Ṣalaḥ Al-Deen's bad faith, were freed after all. They were being sent to Egypt under the escort of a Turkish force, when King Richard suddenly came upon the convoy, as he was reconnoitering the country nearby. He had but a few soldiers with him, but the fame of his deeds had already struck such terror into the Turks that at the mere sight of his banner, the escort abandoned their prisoners and fled for their lives. King Richard pursued and slew some of the soldiers, took 20 of the officers alive, and speedily released the Christians.[79]

On the other hand, the Byzantine Emperor asked that control over the holy sites be returned to the Byzantine Christians, as Ṣalaḥ Al-Deen had formerly promised. But Ṣalaḥ Al-Deen refused to relinquish control and make one sect supreme over the others; instead he made himself the arbiter and judge between the different sects. He said that the emperor must pay two-hundred-thousand dinars if he desired to acquire the (actual) Cross of Christ.[80]

All the days of his reign were pleasant, and the ways of the parish were affable. He did not act unjustly like his predecessors. The roads were safe, and circumstances were favorable. Ṣalaḥ Al-Deen died in his castle in Damascus [February, 1193] at the age of 70.

After giving this historical account filled with adulation for Ṣalaḥ Al-Deen, which is devoid of significant details, like whether or not Copts were allowed to return to Jerusalem for pilgrimage, the chronicler timidly attempts to mention what the Copts experienced in the beginning of Ṣalaḥ Al-Deen's reign.

Abba Morcos Ibn Zar'ah suffered from difficulties and faced hardships in the beginning of the reign of Ṣalaḥ Al-Deen, when he decreed that crosses be taken down from the domes of all churches in Egypt. Whenever he saw a church painted white, he had it covered with black mud to cover the white paint. He also prohibited Christians from displaying palm branches [on Palm Sunday] anywhere, and from ringing church bells, just as before. In addition, he made Christians dress differently, in order to be identified from Muslims. They had to tighten their sashes around their waists and lift their turbans, and they were prohibited from wearing shawls in public. No longer could they ride horses or mules, only donkeys. They were prohibited from consuming alcohol in public and forced to pray in hushed voices.

Some of the greedy Muslim riffraff took advantage of the Copts at the time and abused them. They also arranged to tear down some churches in towns and villages, and the people faced great hardships, to the point where some scribes in Misr and Cairo renounced their faith and abjured their Christ [..]. As the Patriarch was fervently praying for his people, God softened the heart of their Sultan, who drew them close and used them in his Divân to manage the finances of his state. So, they were exalted even more than before, and they could now ride horses and mules. They were allowed to wear sandals and joyful clothes. They also joined [the Sultan] in his conquests, as scribes for his Divân, his family, relatives, and soldiers [..]. Through their patience, the prayers of their Patriarch, their repentance, and obedience to their chief, God transformed their abasement into exaltation, their insults to honor, their abomination to love, and their weakness to strength. They became more charitable, faithful in prayer, and they outdid each other in doing good deeds. So, their livelihoods were blessed, their bodies were healed, their children increased, their circumstances improved, their hearts were healed, and they were at ease [..].

It is strange that the chronicler does not refer to what other sources mentioned regarding the severe punishments, such as executions and crucifixions, that Ṣalaḥ Al-Deen handed down against the Copts (in the years 1168–1173), despite their loyalty and full support of him and their antagonism toward the Franks.[81]

***

At any rate, the Copts reconciled themselves to their *Dhimmitude* by counting obedience to their ruler and mere survival as the epitomes of achievement. They also faced the insults and greed of the Muslim riffraff. This is how the years of demise started, as is observed in the days of the Ayyubids, after Ṣalaḥ Al-Deen's demise.

The Copts in the Ayyubid Mill

With the death of Ṣalaḥ Al-Deen (1193), the sovereign left a vast kingdom and many heirs (sixteen sons).

In the days of Abba Yoannes VI (1189–1216), the 74th Patriarch, the chronicler, Abu Al-Makarem Ibn Barakat Ibn Abu Al-'Ela, who wrote this section of *History of the Patriarchs*, recounts,

After the death of Ṣalaḥ Al-Deen, his son, Al-Aziz Othman, took the reins and ran the affairs of Egypt and Jerusalem. The Franks honored the truce they made with Ṣalaḥ Al-Deen, even after his death [..].

The soldiers had no [work] during the two-year period of the truce, so they withheld the supply of grain, causing the price of wheat to soar to 170 dinars for 100 *Ardabb*, and even then, the prices were constantly fluctuating [..]. The people suffered for three years.

Then 'King' Al-Aziz marched with his army [in 1194], in an attempt to take Damascus [from his brother], Al-Afḍal, but he failed and went back to Cairo. Then, he was pursued by 'King' Al-Adel, [Ṣalaḥ Al-Deen's brother who ruled the kingdom of Al-Karak[i]]. Al-Adel besieged Cairo for months, but then reconciled with Al-Aziz, formed a united front, and returned to Damascus and took it from Al-Afḍal.

In [1197], the Frankish ships arrived in Acre, so Al-Adel preemptively marched to Jaffa, and took it after a three-day scrimmage, completed the *fat'h*, and killed many, but the number of captives he took was greater still. Then, more Frankish ships arrived and many [soldiers] disembarked on the coast [..]. Al-Aziz then went to the Levant to support his uncle [..]. Then, Al-Adel formed with the Franks a six-year armistice over the land, not the sea [..].

---

[i] North of modern-day Homs, Syria.

'King' Al-Aziz died [in 1198, during a hunting accident], and his son, Yusuf, took his place. Since he was young, [his uncle], Al-Afḍal, came and took the reins. He then assembled soldiers and marched to Damascus in an attempt to reclaim it from his uncle, Al-Adel, [Ṣalaḥ Al-Deen's brother], [but failed], and returned to Egypt [..]. Then, Al-Adel pursued Al-Afḍal, besieged Cairo, and took power [in 1200]. He also brought his own son, Al-Kamel, from Damascus, made him Sultan over Egypt, coined his name on [the currency coins], and forbade Imams in Egypt from mentioning [in prayers] Ṣalaḥ Al-Deen, or any of his other children. Instead, they were ordered to mention the [Abbasid] Caliph first, 'King' Al-Adel second, and then [the Sultan] Al-Kamel third [..].[i]

Then God withheld [the Nile flood] that year, and the land of Egypt dried up. The country was ruined, the parish perished, and the people dispersed. Many left Egypt for Damascus, taking their money and children, but they died [on the way] as a result of the cold, hunger, and being looted and slain by the Arab Bedouins. The carcasses of people, livestock, and cattle spread all the way from the outskirts of Bilbeis[ii] to those of Gaza. God, thus, struck the Egyptians with three blows: price hikes, exodus, and plague [..]. A quarter *Ardabb*[iii] of sifted wheat sold for one dinar, and a cup of prepared lupine beans sold for a dirham[iv]. People sold their furniture, belongings, houses, and male and female slaves for a small fraction[v] of their value. Many sold their children like *Mamluks* into servitude [..]. Sons stole bread from their fathers to survive, and people ate the meat of [animal] carcasses. Unable to breastfeed, women discarded their children in mosques and roadways,

---

[i] Notice the problems of 'inheritance' that ensued after the departure of Salah Al-Deen, and how the countries came to represent nothing more than feudal plots. Notice also, that sultans were openly adopting the title 'king,' further emphasizing the hereditary nature of the system, as well as the glory of the office.

[ii] A town 60 km northeast of Cairo, on the route to Palestine.

[iii] An ancient Egyptian unit for measuring volume, equivalent, in the case of wheat, to about 150 liters or 39 gallons.

[iv] One-dirham coin is about three grams of silver. One dinar is about four grams of gold.

[v] Literally, it says, "What is worth a dinar was sold for a dirham." One dinar = 37 dirhams.

where others would pick them up. The police arrested many women with cooked pots of both young and old human flesh [..]. The mighty lorded it over and devoured the weak, death became commonplace, compassion diminished, hope was lost, despair ruled, and the cities and villages were ruined [..]. Generous and prominent Muslim and Christian men acted charitably toward the poor, to the extent they were able to. These circumstances lasted for two years, until God, exalted be His power, had mercy on the people [..].

'King' Al-Adel ruled Egypt, Jerusalem, Damascus, Harran, areas beyond the Euphrates, and several other places and towns whose names we do not know. He was a just, indomitable, and powerful king, with many conquests in [the lands] of the Franks and the Muslims.

The King of Abyssinia sent messengers to request the ordination of a metropolitan by the Patriarch. The messengers carried a golden crown for the Patriarch, and a lavish gift to the Sultan [comprised of] an elephant, seven giraffes, and a zebra. The Patriarch took the messengers and all the gifts to Sultan Al-Kamel, who was delighted by the crown, and said, "I was unaware that they could fabricate such [wonders]." One of the messengers responded, "My Lord, we know the humility of the Patriarch, and that he would not wear the crown, otherwise we would have arrayed it with enough jewels worth the entire *Kharaj* of Egypt." The Sultan marveled and inquired about the King [of Abyssinia], his soldiers, and his wars. The messenger read a letter from the King [of Abyssinia] to the Sultan, and a particular section read, *"Your kingdom, O King [Sultan], is preserved by the prayers of the august, honorable, and great Patriarch. So, preserve and honor him, and allow him to ordain a metropolitan for us."* [..] The Sultan ordered that the gifts be accepted, but the Patriarch left also the crown to him; swore by the life of [the Sultan's] father, Al-Adel, that he should accept the crown, so he accepted. He also ordered that the messengers be allowed to return, and that a metropolitan be ordained.

Notice that the allegiance of the Abyssinian (and Nubian) Churches to the Coptic Church was one of the most important factors assuring peace along the southern borders of Egypt. It is for this reason that the Muslim rulers were inclined not to destroy the Coptic Church; some rulers perceived its populous strength at the time to be one of their own sources of power and influence, including by utilizing the Church in their power games with their southern neighbors.[i]

> Then a monk from the Monastery of Abba Maqar, named Yohanna, converted to Islam at the hands of Sultan Al-Kamel, who then put him in charge of Menyet Ghamr [town, in Delta]. Yohanna resided there for three years, working as a *muhtaseb*[ii]. Afterward, he remembered his religion and his monkhood. So, he took [a piece of cloth] and a shred of linen and stood up before Sultan Al-Kamel, saying, "This is my cerement, either kill me or allow me to return to my religion." So, Al-Kamel signed a letter, to all the *Walis*, allowing him to revert to his religion. He then put on the garments of a monk [and appeared to follow] the Christian religion. He remained this way for a while, until it happened that a Christian man from Upper Egypt converted to Islam and then regretted it. So, he took his cerement to Sultan Al-Adel[iii], before his departure to Damascus, and said to him, "Allow me to return to my religion in the same way your son, Al-Kamel, allowed that monk to revert to his religion." When he heard of this, [he summoned the monk], who reconverted to Islam at the hands of Al-Adel, and went back to being a *muhtaseb* in Menyet Ghamr [..].

Notice how 'freedom of religion' is always 'one directional.' In the above story, allowing for the reverting to one's former faith is a rare exception—even though the 'happy' ending was that the former monk ended up, through the encouragement of King Al-Adel ('the Just'), remaining a Muslim.

---

[i] This can be seen through multiple examples in this book of interactions between rulers of Egypt and Abyssinia.

[ii] A person assigned to ensure that the rules of Islamic *Sharia* are enforced, and polices public conduct. This includes tasks like inspecting commercial market dealings.

[iii] Whenever Sultan Al-Adel went to Syria, Egypt was governed by his son, Al-Kamel.

Then, [that former monk] came and told Sultan Al-Kamel that the monks dug a well in the Monastery of Abba Maqar and discovered [a treasure going back to the days of the Roum], made up of utensils and many [jewels] [..]. So, Al-Kamel dispatched three Mamluk representatives to accompany the former monk, along with witnesses, and they went to the monastery [..]. They took everything they could find, [including] liturgy vessels [chalice, paten] and sanctuary veils of the altar, and the witnesses documented everything on paper and carried all the items to the Sultan [..]. The Sultan brought expert jewelers and [metal experts?], and they appraised all jewelry, silk curtains, and utensils [..]. They also brought a man from Alexandria named Botros Ibn Yohanna, who was a deacon at the Church of Al-Sayedah [The Lady; St. Mary], but then converted to Islam. He read to the Sultan the Coptic writing on the cups, utensils, crosses, and spoons, indicating the names of the people who made each of the items [meaning that the items were not from the time of the Roum]. Sultan Al-Kamel was bewildered and ordered that three elderly monks take an oath that these utensils were not found in the well. They also summoned the worker who dug the well for them, and he happened to be Muslim. He testified before the Sultan that he was the one who dug the well, and that the well was empty when he dug it, and the Sultan believed him. Al-Hakîm[i] Abu Shaker told the Sultan, "My Lord, a [complaint] was raised to Sultan Al-Nasser Salah Al-Deen, may God rest his soul, about these utensils, and when he brought them in and discovered the dishonesty of the one making the complaint, he returned them to the monastery." Upon hearing these words, Sultan Al-Kamel ordered that everything be returned to the Patriarch.

The Patriarch in turn went out and bought many candles and walked the streets of Cairo and its markets, followed by Christians who were loudly praying for the Sultan. This was a memorable day, and the bitter [Muslims] in Misr disliked the sight of crosses in their streets and in their markets. However, none of them dared speak a word or lay a hand, because of the fear of Sultan Al-Kamel, may God extend his days.

---

[i] Denotes 'Wiseman' or 'physician.' The caliphs' and sultans' physician was a post usually held by Christians, because of their competence and trustworthiness.

Some observations can be made after reading the above story. First, notice how Al-Kamel ('the Perfect'), and Al-Adel, ('the Just'), wasted much of their precious time and obsessed over the matter of the alleged 'treasure.' Second, notice the naiveté and desperation of the Copts, who took to the streets to holler for the Sultan because he returned to them their church utensils that he had seized. Third, the Copts were happy that no one interfered as they publicly prayed for the Sultan on the streets. All this demonstrates the reality of the Copts' situation, and how low they set the bar of their expectations and ambitions, just to adapt with the circumstances of their lowly *Dhimmitude* status in the Islamic State…

> Afterward, another monk, named Abd Al-Masîḥ Al-Mosawar, from the Monastery of Abba Maqar, stood before the Sultan and wrote a complaint against the Patriarch, claiming, "Every year, the bishops pay him great sums of money, and the previous Patriarchs used to finance the fleet ships [of the Sultanate] from their own money." The Divân judge, Al-Aaz, presented the complaint to the Sultan [who upon verifying its falsehood] said, "If others were unjust, we shall not be like them, let this monk go back to his monastery until we summon him." [..] So the monk returned, embarrassed, and God protected the Patriarch from the monk's spite [..].

> This [Patriarch's] days were filled with trying circumstances, some of which we have mentioned earlier, but we would fail if we attempt to be exhaustive in retelling everything that took place in the land of Egypt during his term [..]. He died on [January 7, 1216], which is the day of Holy Epiphany [i].

After the death of Abba Yoannes, the Patriarch's chair remained vacant for about 20 years due to extenuating factors.

Al-Hakîm (the Wiseman/Physician) Abu Shaker was with the Sultan when he heard the news of the Patriarch's death. So, the Sultan asked him

---

[i] The dates of the Christian Feasts were synchronized all over the world until 1582, when the West adjusted their calendar through the Gregorian reform. Notice, as well, that around that time, the Western world began its journey toward democracy through the issuing of 'The Magna Carta' in England in 1215.

how a Patriarch is chosen. He replied, "My Lord, we choose three worthy, devout, and scholarly men on whom everyone is in agreement. We then write their names on three pieces of paper, and we write the name of Christ, our Lord, on another piece of paper. All the papers are then left on the altar, while we pray for three days, making supplications, and a litany of invocations. On the third day, we bring a small child to select one of the pieces of paper in the presence of the congregation. If one of the three men's names is drawn, that person becomes our Patriarch, but if Christ's name is drawn, then we know that He does not approve of any of the three. At this point, we go back to choosing three new men, and we continue repeating this process until one of the men's names is chosen, and then we nominate him."[i] The Sultan reacted fondly to the process.

Then, he asked about (the deceased) Abba Yoannes' profession prior to his ordination,

[..] So two priests [leaders among their peers] answered: "He was a merchant." The Sultan then asked, "Who of his heirs took his inheritance?" They replied, "His sister." The Sultan asked again, "What was her share of the inheritance?" They replied, "Half," but they erred, because they applied the Islamic law, whereas the Christian law allows the sister the entire inheritance if she is the only heiress. So, the Sultan asked, "To whom does the other half go?" They said, "To you, our Lord." Immediately, he asked for his share. But they said, "Ask his nephews," so the Sultan summoned the last surviving heir, whose name was Makarem, and he was brought in chains...

The Copts then split into different factions and groups, each favoring its own candidate (for Patriarch). The Sultan, his aids, and some of his *Walis* would also interfere by favoring this or that candidate. The Sultan also asked for a 'royalty,' and some attempted to pay bribes...

As circumstances were being sorted out, the *History* records,

---

[i] Notice that the process of a 'Sacred Casting Lot' used today, was the norm at that time to choose a new Patriarch.

In [September, 1217] news was received of the arrival of one of the Frankish kings, referred to as Al-Hankar [the Hungarian][i], by sea to Acre [..]. So, Sultan Al-Adel assembled his soldiers and marched to Nablus, near the Franks [..]. He also requested help from his nephews [the sons of Ṣalaḥ Al-Deen] and other Muslim rulers, but they ignored his requests. So, he went to Damascus [..]. He then found out that some of the Franks, aided by Arabs from Bani Oqba [their allies], headed to Al-Tor to take its fort located atop a high mountain. Then King, Al-Moazzam ['the glorified'] [Eisa Ibn Al-Adel, Sultan of Damascus], corresponded with Bani Oqba and turned them against the Franks [telling them that Allah will not approve helping the *Kuffar* shed the blood of the believers]. He swore to pay them a sum of money they agreed on, and to give them lands in a feudalistic arrangement [..]. So, they obeyed and swore allegiance to him [..]. They also informed him that since the Franks sleep at night, he should attack them by midnight [..], which he did, defeating and killing many of them [..].

When the Frankish king returned from Al-Tor to Acre, he passed by one of the towns in the valley. In this town resided Melkite and Syriac Christians, as well as Muslims. The king left in their care four injured knights to tend to and departed. The town Muslims rose up against the Christians, took [the knights], and killed them [..]. When the king heard of this, he dispatched his soldiers and killed all the town residents, because when he had asked the Christians [prior to entrusting the four knights to them] if there were any Muslims in town, they denied it. For this reason, the king refused their after-the-fact apology and excuse, claiming that it was the Muslims who killed the knights. He even killed the church priest, because he had sworn to him that no Muslim resided in this town.

[Many] people and cows died that year all over Egypt [because of a plague], similar to what took place prior to the end of the state of the Fatimid Caliphs.

---

[i] The Fifth Crusade, led by King Andrew II of Hungary and Leopold VI from Austria. Note that the chronicler continues to call them 'Franks,' the term ('eFrang') which started (and continues) to be used in general reference to 'white foreigners.'

In 1218, Sultan Al-Adel persecuted the Copts and destroyed several coastal towns, such as Tanîs, Damietta, and others. The residents of these towns fled, and many Copts sought refuge in Abyssinia, and they were welcomed by the king.[82]

Yohanna Ibn Waheb continues writing the chronicles of *History of the Patriarchs*, which were compiled by Elm Al-Malek Ibn Shams Al-Reyasat:

On one occasion, a Christian young man from Upper Egypt, who worked at an oil manufactory, was accused by a Muslim man [of raping] his young son [..]. The young Christian man was imprisoned for days and was offered to convert to Islam, but he refused. So, the *faqihs* [religious jurists] sentenced him to be stoned to death in public. They ruled that he be encircled by [the stoning] people, and if he converts to Islam in front of them, then he is to be let go, but if he [did not, then was stoned and] dies, then he deserved it. And so, they did. The slave of the Muslim boy's father cast the first stone, which hit the young Christian man on the jaw. At this point, he fell to the ground and succumbed to death under a hail of stones. A moment later, the Muslim boy [admitted] that the young Christian man was innocent, and that it was the slave [who cast the first stone] who had committed this abominable act...

In those days, the Sultan, may his victory be glorious, ordered that all prisoners be brought before him. Among the prisoners was a [Coptic] man called Assad, a weaver by trade. Assad had a dispute with his wife, who took him to the *Sharia* court. He uttered something there that was construed as his profession of the Islamic faith, but he denied that he did. He was imprisoned for one year. Then, they brought him before the Sultan, who enticed him [to convert to Islam] with money and clothes, but he still refused, saying, "I am Christian, and I will die a Christian" [..]. As the case kept being discussed until the day of Holy Epiphany, the Sultan ordered the beheading of Assad. The Cairo *Wali* brought him in front of Bab [gate of] Zwailah, called forth the witnesses, and offered him the religion of Islam in front of all present, but Assad refused to convert to Islam. One of the Mamluks approached and thrust his sword into Assad, penetrating his flesh the depth of four fingers. Then, he said to Assad, "Extend your neck," and when he did, the Mamluk struck his head clean off his body. Assad's corpse was hung on Bab Zwailah and remained there for three days. The people were praising God for Assad's perseverance and the strength of his faith. A group of godly Christians took and buried his body.

How many meek men, like Assad, sacrificed their own lives as a price for 'justice and freedom of religion' in the Islamic State? On the other hand, how many converted to Islam out of fear and have been forgotten by history?

In [June 1218], many ships arrived, and a large number of [Frankish soldiers] landed in front of Damietta [and exchanged mangonel (catapult) projectiles with the Muslims]. Many were injured and many died on both sides [..], but eventually, [the Franks] took the tower of Damietta. On the same day, Sultan Al-Adel died, as a result of indigestion, in Damascus, and was buried next to his brother, Ṣalaḥ Al-Deen [..].

A series of dire circumstances overwhelmed the people that year: the death of the Sultan, the enemies' attacks, the scarcity of the Nile's water, and the church not having a Patriarch. Furthermore, the Muslims decided to march against the Franks in a great battle [in which the Muslims were defeated] [..]. The people were increasingly terrified and anxious. They also became more fearful of the Franks and hesitant about confronting them.

Then winter came [..]. A man called Emad Al-Deen Ibn Al-Mashṭoub [drove a wedge between] the sultans, Al-Kamel, and his brother, Al-Faez. [Al-Kamel] feared being killed by the Kurdish soldiers, who would later install Al-Faez in his place. So, he escaped by night with all his belongings and his Mamluks to Ashmun [..]. [But] the powerful army commanders supported him.

As for the Maghrebis and the eunuchs, they spread all over the country, and the people were floundering. Atrocities continued to multiply against the Christians, and some began to treat them harshly [..].

The people of Menyet Bani Salsil [located between Ashmun and Al Manzalah] rose up against the Christians, killing many of them. With the passing of time, things got worse, and after each tumult, life became even more difficult.

Then, it was decreed that Christians prepay the *Jizya* for the coming year. [..] The Sultan decreed that, willingly or under compulsion, half of the people of Misr and Cairo had to join and fight in his army. Many people were drafted, but [the rich], for whom it was inappropriate to fight, saved themselves through the payment of gold, each according to his means. As for the Christians of Cairo, they exacted payment from them, as well as from those who could barely live within their means [..].

The *Wali* brought the Coptic and Melkite priests and said to them, "[If] you go to fight alongside the Muslims, then they will surely kill you before you reach the gates of the city, and no one will be able to fault them." This talk was primarily targeting the Melkites, because people slandered them by claiming that they were Frank-lovers, who follow their customs of growing out their hair, avoiding circumcision, etc. When they [Melkites] were thus struck with fear, one of them exclaimed, "We have a thousand dinars." The *Wali* responded, "Great," and to the Coptic priests, he said, "Now, you owe ten times as much," but eventually, he settled for three-thousand dinars [..].

And a torture stand[i] was hung in the Al-Muallaqa Church, another in the Melkite Church, and another in the Jewish Synagogue [..], and immediately, the hanging, flogging, and humiliation of people ensued [..]. This took place during Lent. Those days were difficult, and the persecution was great. As for the Melkites, they collected money from their people, but still came up short. So, they brought out the [altar] utensils and pawned them to a Muslim man, *Al-Faqih* [jurist] Naṣr, for 200 dinars, which were to be [paid off] for 250 dinars.[ii] Only a rare few got away without paying heavy penalties. All that [the Copts] could collect was 1100 dinars [..], and what remained was the responsibility of the churches, each one according to its ability. They kept seeking collections everywhere. They went to the outskirts and asked the Monastery of Tummwah and the Monastery of Sham' [Wax; Candles] for contributions to satisfy the imposed heavy penalties. They then went to Cairo, seeking donations [..] Those were difficult days, and many churches shut their doors for many days.

---

[i] A wooden beam with ropes on which a person was hung and lashed, if he failed to pay the *Jizya* or other penalties.

[ii] Meaning that the '*Sharia* Jurist' charged 25% interest.

The [Sultan] used ten-thousand infantrymen from Cairo [to fight the Franks], who were mostly Maghrebis. So, these men tore down every church they passed on their way to camp [..]. But they did not win, because the Franks created a trench and other fortifications [..]. The Sultan then tore down the walls of Jerusalem after he evacuated all its residents [..]. He also tore down the homes and the inns [..].

The Muslims rioted against the Church of Mar Morcos [St. Mark] in Alexandria, and the Sultan ordered its destruction [..]. [The Copts tried to save it, but] most of it was torn down, with only one frame left standing. The following Friday, after the Muslims finished their Friday prayers, they went and leveled to the ground what remained of the church.[i] There was great sadness, ongoing depression, and tangible hardships.

The Franks marched by land and by sea [..], but they retreated upon reaching the Muslim trench. So, the Muslims pursued and defeated them [..].

The Muslims rejoiced greatly, set birds free [in celebration], and decorated the city of Cairo [..] The captives were taken [on September 11th, 1219] to Cairo, Al-Maḥrousa ['the guarded'][ii], and there was discussion over a potential truce. It was almost decided that they take Jerusalem and keep all that they possessed at the time from what had been conquered by Ṣalaḥ Al-Deen. But the truce talks failed, and the Sultan ordered that everyone in Cairo be sent out to [fight] the invaders. The bells rung, signifying this decree, and the people went out en mass [..].

Then, the *Wali* of Cairo rounded up the Christians and hung some of them on the doors of their houses, and others, he tortured by tying to mills [like beasts]. He extorted money from them beyond their means, to the point where Christian [tailors] in Cairo had to raise 1300 dinars. People's conditions kept deteriorating [..]. The *Wali* of Misr [Al-Fustat] summoned the priests and demanded the payment of one-thousand

---

[i] A Mosque was built in place of the torn-down church. Footnotes, Part four, P. 131.
[ii] This is almost like a nickname, used mostly to refer to Egypt, but it may, at times, refer to Cairo, as is the case here.

dinars [..]. The priests went out and began [collecting the money], and those were hard times...

The Franks took Damietta[i] after a sixteen-month long siege.[ii]

[The notable] Muslims left [Damietta], and the commoners remained to fend for themselves [..]. The Sultan arrived and stayed across from Talkha.[iii] Accounts vary, concerning the invasion of Damietta [..]. Some said that there were six-thousand men [inhabitants] present, others eleven-thousand men. But Muslims claimed that there were only 600 souls left. Investigators claim that forty-six-thousand men were present, in addition to women and children [..].

The Sultan [Al-Kamel] summoned Ṣafey Al-Deen Abdullah Ibn Ali, who was his father's Vizier, and handed him the helm of his kingdom's governorship. Ṣafey assembled Muslim, Christian, and Jewish scribes, and set forth the penalties before them. He demanded money from them, and as a result [of being unable to pay], they filled the prisons. Some even abandoned their faith because of the hardship caused by the penalties [..]. These were tough times for the people, and as soon as they cleared one trap, they encountered a more sinister one.

Markets and inns, where goods were sold, ceased to function. It was decreed that trade was only permissible at the Sultan's market, to secure a sales commission. Circumstances became dismal, and if people had the ability to flee, the country would have been left uninhabited. Conversely, news about how the Franks [in Damietta] treated the people showed indescribable justice, luxury, and kindness toward the people [..].

The invasion of the Latin Christians had roused all the Muslim fanaticism from which the Copts suffered. The army, which marched to the relief of Damietta, destroyed every church by which they passed; even the church of St. Mark in the suburbs of Alexandria was leveled to the ground, in case the

---

[i] Part of the Fifth Crusade, led by Louis IX.

[ii] In 1219, St. Francis of Assisi, who had come to Damietta with the Fifth Crusade, met Sultan Al-Kamil, carrying a message of peace.

[iii] This was the location of 'El-Mansoura' (the victorious) army camp, which eventually became the modern-day city of El-Mansoura, in central Delta.

Crusading army should occupy it as a point from which to attack Alexandria.[83]

A Maghrebi Amir arrived in Misr, and Christians were the foremost object of his hate. His subordinates rounded up Christians and Jews by tying them with ropes, shamed and imposed on them penalties. He went so far as to take [forced deeds against them], showing that each person owed eleven-thousand dinars. Then, he sent these deeds to the Sultan, who thought that he went too far and rejected them [because of the exaggerated demands] [..]. This Amir then went to Upper Egypt to tax the homes, crops, and palm trees. These circumstances continued, and the hardships intensified to the point where some lynched themselves and others left the faith, which still did not benefit them.

The enemy[i] remained in a constant state of [skirmishing] [..]. Then, news arrived of the emergence of a king from the East, called the King of China [Genghis Khan], accompanied by many Turks [Tatars]. It was also reported that he vanquished the King of Persia and arrived in Babylon [Iraq] [..].

Then, King Al-Moazzam ['the glorified,' Sultan of the Levant] arrived with King Al-Ashraf [the Sultan of the East, Harran and Sinjar], the rulers of Homs and Hama, along with armies, to lend support to their brother, Sultan Al-Kamel. They launched land and sea attacks against Damietta [lengthy details of the battles are not included here], and finally, everyone agreed to a truce: Franks ceding Damietta, and exchanging captives.

The Franks took hostage some of the senior army leaders, fearing betrayal, then left them behind on a boat in the Mediterranean Sea [..]. The Sultan returned to Cairo, and it was a memorable and joyous day for the people [..]. The Sultan and the King of Acre and Jerusalem [Jean de Brienne] formed a great and genuine friendship, with gifts going back and forth between the two...

---

[i] Notice the recurrent reference to the Franks as an *enemy*.

A group of *Archons* discussed the ordination of a Patriarch with the Vizier, who asked that 500 dinars be paid to *Bayt al-mal*[i]. They began to collect the amount and divided the total sum among the churches, but no one had enough to pay, so the matter and the discussions came to a halt [..][ii]

Confiscations [of property] continued, and prisons were filled with scribes. The Vizier's primary mission was to exact money for the Sultan, whichever way he could [..]. In [1226], the Sultan ordered the creation of a minting house in the citadel. The freshly minted dirhams were released, and the Sultan decided that 37 of the new dirhams would be sold for one dinar, and that 42 of the old dirhams would be sold for one dinar.[iii] The ratchet kept tightening, and the people were floundering because the Sultan demanded and collected as much money, in whichever way he could.

During these days, a monk, from the Monastery of Abba Maqar, converted to Islam. He slandered the monks to the Sultan, [claiming that there are some who become monks in order to avoid paying the *Jizya*]. The Sultan ordered that an Amir [commander] go out with this man to investigate the matter. They went to the monasteries [of Wadi Al-Natroun], but no investigation took place. Instead, this Amir beat, hung, and punished the monks, and even imposed a 600-dinar penalty. He left with 400 dinars, and expected to collect the remainder during his next visit [..]. Some of the elders of the monks went before the Sultan, God cherish his victory, to plead their case. So, he ordered that the money be returned to them. In response, they lit candles and walked all over Cairo. This matter [of the Sultan returning the money] bewildered people and [was considered to be] a miracle [thanks to] the monastery fathers.

---

[i] *Lit.* 'House of Money.' A central treasury for the Islamic State, managing its finances and expenditures, according to *Sharia* rules (to the extent the rulers could separate personal from 'public' finances).

[ii] Notice the extent to which circumstances had deteriorated, to the point where the church was unable to come up with 500 dinars.

[iii] Notice the Sultan's currency manipulation.

Friends of Priest Dawood [Ibn Laqlaq] endeavored to nominate him as
Patriarch. They met with an individual who was close to the Sultan, God
cherish his victory, and they pledged to the Sultan, may God prolong his
rule, two-thousand dinars. He asked for one-thousand dinars
immediately, and for the rest of the money when the ordination was done
[..]. So, they took a loan for one-thousand dinars, that was to be repaid
1200 dinars in two months [..]. However, the infights and disputes
[among Copts] were fierce, so they returned the borrowed one-thousand
dinars with interest [..].

The *Jizya* for that year imposed on the *Dhimmis* was 100 dirhams per
person in Cairo and Misr, and 120 dirhams on all the [outside] cities.[i]

The Sultanate designated a group, called *Al-Ṣaqaoun* and *Al-Kushaf*[ii], to
go and demand money from the people[iii] for the use of cemeteries,
tombs, as well as the rocks and stones that were used for building their
homes. They claimed the ownership [deeds] of all the houses, and said,
"The whole country belongs to the Sultan, how else can all of you own
these things? Either you legally prove your ownership of these places,
or pay your rent arrears, going back to when you first settled in these
places." [..] The people were greatly oppressed by the man who was
charged with collecting the Cairo and Misr imposts [*Jizya* and
otherwise, and he committed grave acts of injustice against them.]

By the end of the month of *Kiyahk*,[iv] the Sultan returned from
Alexandria, intentionally taking a route that passes by the Monastery of
Abba Maqar. The monks hosted the Sultan and those with him, and
offered them from what they had. The Sultan donated to them 500
Ardabb of grain, and wrote a proclamation, stating that monks are to be
exempt from paying the *Jizya*[v], and that when a monk dies, his

---

[i] Meaning that the *Jizya* went up 33% factoring in the 'change of currency.' Note the
amount ranged between 2.7 and 3.2 dinars.
[ii] Surveyors and inspectors.
[iii] Presumably Copts and Muslims.
[iv] Fourth month in the Coptic calendar, lies between December 10th and January 8th.
[v] This indicates that, previously, the *Jizya* was levied on monks.

inheritance was to go to [the monastery], not to [his relatives, or the Sultan]. They discussed with him the matter of the vacant Patriarch seat and said, "Our Lord, our circumstances have deteriorated. There used to be 80 monks in this monastery, but today, only four remain." So, he replied, "Choose whomever you please [for the office of Patriarch], and I will nominate him for you." [..]

In [1228], Emperor Fredrick arrived in Acre from Sicily, by invitation from King Al-Kamel, who was seeking his help against his brother, Al-Moazzam. However, Al-Moazzam died prior to Fredrick's arrival. Gifts were exchanged [between Frederick and Al-Kamel] and their friendship deepened. In [1229],

[..] it was rumored that the Sultan, God cherish his victory, agreed to give Jerusalem[i] to the Emperor, along with the towns on the way to Acre, including Bethlehem [..]. And the matter was settled between the Emperor and the Sultan, may God prolong his rule [..].

In [1232], the sister-in-law of a priest, whose name was Ibn Saeed, purchased a Roum female slave from a Frankish man, but later on, sold her to one of the Frankish merchants who travelled back and forth frequently. When news of this reached the Sultan, he denounced the act and ordered that the priest, his sister-in-law, and her sister, [a nun], be sold in the slave market, and they were.[ii] This was an ordeal unlike any other. A godly Levantine man, a Maronite who converted to Islam, purchased them for sixty dinars [..] and immediately set them free.

---

[i] This was part of a ten-year armistice agreement, on the condition that no walls be built around the city, and that Franks were to not to damage the Dome of the Rock or Al-Aqsa Mosque. Furthermore, the *wali* of the Muslims was to have rule over the rustics (appurtenant towns and fields).

[ii] Considering that the enslavement of Byzantine women was a constant for the caliphate, it is unclear why the Sultan was provoked. Furthermore, even if the sister-in-law erred, what was the offense of the priest and the woman's sister in this story? Such discrepancies only serve to highlight the moodiness and whimsicality of the rulers...

Because a group of young men dressed in wool garments while in the cities, pretending to be monks, in order to avoid the *Jizya*, the Sultan decreed the collection of *Jizya* from any monk not residing in a monastery or devoted to the wilderness, as confirmed by witnesses. That was all the officials needed to hear, and they began seizing monks, not even sparing the elderly ones who had spent 50 years in the wilderness, [and they imposed the *Jizya* on them]. Circumstances were particularly severe in Al-Gharbeyah, where an overseer called Ibn Al-Qormsini detested Christians. He unleashed his spite against the monks, and they suffered greatly at his hands [..]. A group of monks brought a gift, according to their means, to the gates of the Sultan, God cherish his victory [..]. Then an order went out [from the Sultan] for things to return to their former ways, on the condition that monks not hide anyone on whom the *Jizya* is imposed. Another condition was that monks no longer be allowed to take the vows of the monastery, even those worthy of monkhood, before first being registered in the [Sultanate] Divân. They took the written proclamation to Al-Gharbeyah, but it changed nothing.

***

Thus, the Copts continued to experience the pressures of the Ayyubid mill, with a steady deterioration of conditions—and lowering the bar of expectations. But that is not the end of the story.

Harassed from All Directions

Going down the path of deterioration, we will see, in this chapter, that the intense pressures that the Copts succumbed to, produced more unfavorable outcomes, such as internal divisions and splintering, not to mention conversions to Islam. It will also become apparent that these pressures (from the rulers and riffraff) are surprisingly similar to what the Copts are experiencing nowadays.

Finally, after the Patriarchal seat was left vacant for 20 years, Abba Kyrillos III (Ibn Laqlaq) was ordained (1235–1243) as the 75th Patriarch. Regarding him, Yohanna Ibn Waheb, the chronicler of this section of *History of the Patriarchs*[i], says that he was learned and virtuous. However, he accepted simony and as a result, experienced many hardships (..). In fact, the Sultan had approved his consecration only on the promise of three-thousand dinars payment; something the community had to do, given the critical situation of the Church after 20 years of vacancy.

At the time of his ordination, only five bishops remained: three from the south [Tahta, Armant, and Esna] and two from the north (Melig and Damanhur). [..] After his ordination, he met with Sultan Al-Kamel, God cherish his victory, in a place called Abu Qir, and his [ordination to the patriarchal] office was confirmed. He took a loan for a thousand dinars, which he deposited in [the treasury of] *Bayt al-mal*, and wrote a promissory note for two-thousand dinars due in two months.[ii] [..] The Sultan sent the Patriarch an elegant outfit composed of a blue Etabi [?]

---

[i] It was collected by Elm Al-Malek Ibn Shams Al-Reyasat.

[ii] It is obvious that the Patriarch's disposition toward simony (the buying or selling of ecclesiastical privileges or positions) was in order to meet the financial demands imposed on him by the Sultan at the time of his ordination. Bear in mind that three-thousand dinars then is equivalent to twelve kilos of gold, worth $127,000 today.

vestment embroidered with gold and a mantilla. Attendants claim that it was a memorable day, and that most of the Sultan's [slave?] boys and servants were present [..].

The people were overjoyed because of the ordination of the Patriarch, after waiting 20 years.

Sunday morning, he [the Patriarch] left the Church of Mikhail in Ras El-Khalig, Misr, and headed to Al-Muallaqa [the Hanging Church]. Countless people from Cairo, Misr, and the surrounding areas came to see him, including Muslims, Jews, and many others, to the point where the road was filled. Crosses were raised on sticks before him, and Gospels were wrapped in [protective wrap?], while the deacons and priests read the hymns, and *Archons* rode on mules and horses [..]. Afterward, a group of Muslims got together and denounced what took place, finding especially atrocious the lifting of crosses before those in attendance [..]. They assigned a distinguished *faqih* [scholar] to write a complaint to the Sultan, concerning what happened. Our Lord, the Sultan, signed the complaint and sent it to the *Wali* of Misr, ordering that he summon the Patriarch to demand that he not transgress the *Sharia*. While the *Wali* sat with a teacher who taught at one of the mosques that the Patriarch's [procession] passed by, he summoned the Patriarch. He chastised him about the raising of crosses and other things [..]. [The Patriarch] then returned to Al-Muallaqa [Church]. This happened at the night of the Feast of Saint Mercurius.

Now, the Patriarch [intended] to go to his church on the [Nile] bank, but he was prevented when he was informed that a crowd gathered in front of the church door and mistreated the Christians going into the church, stoning some and defiling the clothes of others [..]. The *Wali* of Misr was brought before the Sultan, who said, "I was informed that the people of Misr harassed the Patriarch and his churches." He then swore [to hand down punishments] if such incidents were repeated. When the [Copts] heard what the Sultan said, they breathed a sigh of relief, and the Patriarch was invigorated. Even though the notable Muslims, without exception, helped and worked at peacemaking, these were the acts of commoners and the *fuqahaa*.[i]

People assumed that [the Patriarch] practiced simony indiscriminately with whomever he ordained; however, ordinations were not ordered around or conditioned by simony. Rather, he took from people [from people to be ordained] as they were able to give, without oppressing anyone. He began to ordain bishops over the empty seats [..], and he ordained over 40 [in his first year].

The Sultan, God cherish his victory, was informed of a mutiny of some of the soldiers, [who had taken] the outskirts of his eastern countries. So, he marched to the Levant with a great army. As for the rebel soldiers, they had burnt farmlands [around Damascus] and took Al-Suwayda [which was sold to them by its owner]. They also conquered Al-Raha (Edessa) by the edge of the sword. They killed the majority of its citizens and the rest; they took captive and enslaved. The majority of those citizens were Syriac and Roum Christians [..].

A great plague hit the land of Egypt, to the point where over 200 dead bodies went out of [Cairo] daily. This lasted from mid *Bābah* to the end of *Amshīr*.[ii]

Beside Al-Muallaqa Church was a mosque with a high minaret, which was also next door to the Patriarch's residence. Part of the Patriarch's residence included an unfenced yard. When the Patriarch tried to put a fence around his yard, he was prevented by the *muezzin*[iii]. When the Patriarch put up a fence anyway, the *muezzin* tore it down [..]. While the Patriarch was away, the person entrusted with the keys to his residence discovered that it was broken into from the direction of the mosque. When the *Wali* was informed of the break-in, he put the *muezzin* in

---

[i] Pl. *faqih*. When one reads about these early years, one is somewhat struck by what seems (occasional) lenient Muslim behavior — until one remembers that in these centuries, Copts still outnumbered Muslims, and so the latter could not attack willy-nilly as they do now.

[ii] That is over a five-month period.

[iii] Prayer caller.

prison. In response, the *muezzins* of the Ancient Mosque in Misr got irate and began sending groups to that mosque to make the prayer call in groups, in order to aggravate the residents of the alleyway. A complaint was made to the judge of the incarcerations *Divân*, who decreed that only one *muezzin* be allowed to call for prayer [..]. So, the Muslims gathered in great numbers and went up to the minaret, yelling and praying the *Talbiyah*.[i] Countless [Muslim] people swarmed in front of the Al-Muallaqa Church, causing the church congregants to feel angst, as the Patriarch was praying [..]. The *Wali* arrived, dispersed the crowds, and the situation was resolved peacefully. But the majority of the crowd still appeared before the Sultan's deputy, complaining that mosques are being shut down, while churches are being opened. He replied, "He who wants a mosque is free to go to a mosque, and he who wants a church is free to go to a church. However, no party [has the right] to impose on the other, for they [the Christians] are the subjects of the Sultan [just like you are]." [..] Thus, the interactions between Christians and Muslims were greatly equitable, gloriously honorable, and abundantly amiable [..].

Here is the lesson learned from this incident: when the ruler tries to (occasionally) act equitably, the troublemakers can be deterred. But this lesson has not been learned by most rulers, even the current ones in Egypt...

The Patriarch ordained a metropolitan over Gaza, Jerusalem, and the Levant [..]. This displeased some of the *Archons* who felt that this action was impermissible, since these countries are under the Antioch Seat [Patriarchate][ii] [..]. As for the metropolitan, he sought the Franks, befriended some of them, and he and his parish had authority over the affairs of Coptic churches. It is said that the Franks took [a letter from him], stating that 'his confession is their confession, and that his belief is their belief'[iii], and that this is their custom to prevent foreigners

---

[i] A Muslim prayer to Allah, declaring '*O my Lord, here I am, at your service and orders.*'

[ii] This indeed offended the Syriac Patriarch in Antioch.

[iii] This statement is unclear. Did the Metropolitan declare that the theological disputes that caused the fifth-century schism were, after all, of little significance?

[Christians from other denominations] from having authority, until they have first done that [write letters to the same effect] [..].'

In those days, news came that the [Tatars] descended upon Erbil [in Iraq] and took it by the sword [..]. The news from east and west revealed turbulent circumstances [..]. Then, our Lord, the Sultan [Al-Kamel], marched, desiring to take Damascus [from his brother, Al-Malek Al-Ṣaleḥ] [..]. He stayed in Damascus for 100 days, but then he fell ill and died [in April 1238]. His death was kept a secret, and they claimed that he was sick. They also claimed that he had planned to have all the high-ranking officials pledge allegiance to his younger son, [Al-Adel II], in Egypt, and for the sultanate to pass to him, but then they revealed the news of his death [..].

Disagreements among the Copts returned. Emad Al-Akhmemi, a monk who opposed the selection of the Patriarch, went looking for reasons to try and depose him. An old monk, Al-Saney, prepared documents for the Patriarch to sign and put into effect regarding simony, the distribution of building rent revenue, the administration of monasteries, etc. Then, the northern bishops [fourteen] assembled in the church located in the alleyway of Zwailah [in September, 1238] and drafted a list of doctrinal and church laws that would cause anyone who broke them to be excommunicated, and the Patriarch approved and signed these canons.

A group of Muslims who stayed at the mosque adjacent to the Al-Muallaqa Church rose up and tore down the wall separating the two structures, claiming that [part of the church plot] belongs to the mosque. This caused chaos among the churches, and church services ceased in Al-Muallaqa Church for many days during Lent. Muslims used to climb the stairs leading to the roof of the Patriarch's residence, to call for [Muslim] prayers, call for *Takbīr*[i], and recite [the Quran], which led to numerous disputes. Although the *Wali* of Misr imprisoned some of these

---

[i] The Arabic phrase *Allāhu Akbar*, usually translated as 'Allah is greatest.' It is a common expression, used in various contexts by Muslims; in formal prayer, in the call for prayer (*adhān*), as an expression of faith, or to express resolute determination or defiance.

culprits, it was still in vain, and things continued that way for a while
[..].

Two Arab tribes, *Jadham* and *Thalabah*, in Al-Sharqiyah province, who
had a long history of bad blood and feuding, rose up against each other
many times, and several were killed from both tribes [..]. *Thalabah*
sought the tribe of *Sinbes*, who arrived from Arabia. *Jadham* then sought
the two tribes of *Zanatah* and *Zanarah*, who arrived from Al-Beheira
[province]. During these days of war, the people were anxious and
highway robbery was rampant. The Sultan eventually sent a group of
[army commanders] and soldiers in an attempt to reconcile them [..].[i]

A man surnamed Shibl Al-Dawlah Khadem Al-Nabi[ii] began claiming
that he saw their prophet in a dream, and the prophet told him, "Make
the *Dhimmis* wear identifying clothes, because they have gone too far."
So Shibl began to beat the Christians and Jews and publicly slander
them. He forced the Christians to pull their hair up and tighten their
sashes, and the Jews to have a yellow identifying mark [on their dress]
[..]. This was announced all over Cairo and Misr, and the people were
severely troubled and burdened, because it had been 20 years since they
had to do these things. Shibl [insulted] whomever he came across [..],
and as a result of these actions, one of the fine Christians named Ibn
Shams converted to Islam. His conversion came about in this way. He
was in charge of the *Divân* of requirements, buildings, and stables, and
the servants ganged up against him and ordered him to tighten his sash,
and he did. They then asked him to pull up his tassel, but he refused, so
they overpowered him. Thus, he discarded his sash. They hence pushed
him to convert to Islam, which he did, and they became witnesses[iii] of
his conversion to Islam.

---

[i] This quote is meant to highlight the atmosphere of insecurity due to tribal infights.

[ii] *Lit.* 'the (Lion) Cub of the State, the Servant of the Prophet.'

[iii] It is enough that a person is heard saying the *Shihada* (that 'there is no god but
Allah, and that Mohamed is Allah's prophet') to be considered a convert. As a
'Muslim,' then, he/she is subjected to the rules of *riddah* (apostasy), should he want
to go back to his original faith.

The Christians at that time were under great duress and faced painful humiliation. They were insulted with vulgarities from the [Muslim] mob of commoners wherever they were found [..]. When the *faqihs* were consulted about how the Christians should dress, they decided that it was enough that Christians tighten their sashes in order to stand out among Muslims [..]. When the time came for the annual celebration of the Nile Flooding, a group of Christians went on a boat [for an outing]; some of them wore sashes, and others did not. So, when the servant of Shams Al-Dawlah saw them, he brought them before Al-Amir Gamal Al-Din, who handed them over to the *muhtaseb* in Misr, who beat them and publicly slandered them all over Misr. This frenzy took its toll on Christians, and the [Muslim] commoners abused them.

The Sultan found out that the soldiers had rebelled against him, and that they were three factions, so he arrested three [senior] army commanders and imprisoned them in the Citadel. These circumstances, along with the rumors surrounding them, left the people fearfully anxious [..]. Furthermore, the Bedouins became greedy and began taking turns looting, killing, and taking captives from Al-Gharbeyah[i] provinces [..]. In response, the Sultan dispatched an army commander called Khatlaba, accompanied by one-thousand cavalries [..], who arrived after the Bedouins had already fled to the desert. So, the [soldiers] began to take the people's money, women, and children, and disaster struck the same place for the second time [..].

When the days of the truce[ii] came to an end, the Franks left Jerusalem, leaving behind only one knight and 70 men living in the tower of David [..]. So, Al-Malek [King] Al-Naser, of Al-Karak, travelled to and took charge of Jerusalem, killing all the remaining Franks, and giving a great speech about the rule of the Quran.[iii]

---

[i] Western Delta.

[ii] This is the ten-year truce that Al-Malek Al-Kamel had signed with them.

[iii] Notice the assassination of those Franks left behind, despite the departure of the Frankish army, as per the agreement.

The aforementioned monk (Emad Al-Akhmemi) resumed making accusations against the Patriarch and attempting to trap him in his words. He succeeded in getting an order sent from the Sultan, to an Amir called Al-Ṣarem Al-Masoudy, to investigate the Patriarch. This was to be done before prominent Muslims, their judges, rulers, and [fourteen of their] Certified Witnesses [..]. The session was conducted in the presence of prominent Christians [..], [and the monk listed his accusations, and the Patriarch defended himself]. The meeting ended, with the Muslims showing no regard for the Christians or their leader: As for their leader [the Patriarch], how did he lack the wisdom to rein on their minds and win over their hearts? As for the Christians, how did they reach that point with their leader? The levelheaded [among the Copts] saw that the bishops and *Archons* should have met privately with the Patriarch and depose him, if he had violated their laws [..]. Then, all talk stopped, and nothing came of [this session].

The Patriarch decided on some reforms, such as choosing a trustworthy man to handle the affairs of endowments, to have two bishops accompany him when making judgments or taking action on certain matters, and not to have the final say without first consulting them. These reforms notwithstanding, disagreements continued among some of the bishops and monks...

A group of Christians signed a petition, [requesting] that Al-Muallaqa Church return to its formal status.[i] After they went and consulted with the *Wali*, they went by night and locked the doors, which the Muslims had opened. Then, *muezzin* Ibn Ḥawlah came and reopened the doors, went to the *faqih* [scholar] Abbas, the Citadel's preacher, and charged him with the matter, claiming that the Christians have annexed the mosque to their church. So, Abbas took the commander of the guards and went to the church, accompanied by Muslim commoners and countless mobs. With them were also engineers, but they were not allowed to speak the truth regarding what they saw. This took place on a Thursday. During the Friday prayer, Abbas, the preacher, stood up and said, "O, Muslims, he who is a Muslim and commended in the faith must

---

[i] Before the changes made by the Muslims of the neighboring mosque, as explained earlier.

come to the Al-Muallaqa tomorrow." The following day, they went to the church, broke its lamps, and the icon holder of the altar, and stole all the church utensils [..]. And so, they controlled the entirety of the western side, and the church remained closed and no one prayed in it [..]. The Patriarch remained in the alleyway of Zwailah Church.

As for the Sultan, Al-Malek [King] Al-Adel II, he was taken up by his uncle, Al-Malek Al-Ṣaleḥ Ayoub, to the Citadel, and no one saw him again [..].

Then, news came that the Franks arrived in Gaza [in 1241] and took Jerusalem [which was under the control of Egypt's Sultan] by agreement with Al-Malek Al-Ṣaleḥ Ghazi of Damascus, the Sultan's uncle...

Christians went back to contending with the Patriarch and [some complained about him to the Sultan, who] summoned the northern and southern bishops [..], and they assembled in front of the Sultan's assistant, the Vizier. An old monk, Al-Saney, along with the bishops of Fuwwah, Samannoud, and others, was the one bringing the complaint [against] the Patriarch. They had many arguments and disputes, and finally, they said, "We have for the Sultan three-thousand dinars to allow us to get a different Patriarch instead of this one." However, others said, "It is not permissible [to depose the Patriarch while he was alive]." The Vizier responded by saying, "We do not agree to what is not permissible, but [..] I want this money from the Patriarch." [..] After talking, [they brought the sum down] to 1500 dinars[i], which the Patriarch's relatives wrote deeds for. From that point on, the Patriarch's heart was hardened against the bishops, and their hearts were hardened against him...

The Sultan, may God prolong his rule, set up a place called Dar Al-Adl ['House of Justice'] with three individuals [acting as judges] [..], and people took their complains to them. This allowed the Sultan to rest and focus on his pleasures, riding, and hunting. [..] Then, the Sultan, may God prolong his rule, decided to tear down all the houses in the [Nile] island of [Al-Rawda] to build a castle [..]. He moved all the captive

---

[i] About six kilos of gold. Irrespective of the dispute, the Vizier took the opportunity to get money anyway.

Franks to Misr in order to work on the castle, and he made them lodge in the Church of Abu Marqoura on the riverbank, for proximity. Thus, the Christians were in a quandary because of what happened to Al-Muallaqa Church and what was about to happen to the Church of Al-Rawda [which would be torn down].

In those days, the bishop of Sandafa [in Delta town Al-Mahalah Al-Kubra] converted to Islam. The *Wali* put fur and *Sherbouch*[i] on him and paraded around Al-Mahalah on a horse. This was a novelty, the likes of which were never seen. This is because he had committed the sin of adultery [..]. There was a deacon whom the bishop had prevented from service. So, this deacon was watching the bishop, and he saw the adulterous woman, who was Muslim, visiting the bishop. He then went to the *Wali* and told him what he saw. So, the *Wali* brought the bishop and the woman, and beat the bishop so severely that he renounced his faith.

The Sultan, may God prolong his rule, became privy to a [conspiracy] by the Turkish soldiers in Alexandria and Bilbeis, so he captured and imprisoned [the masterminds]. [..] Then, a group of Ashrafeya Turks allied together to rob the Kurdish soldiers who were preparing for a [campaign] to Yemen, but the Kurds discovered this plot [..]. The Ashrafeya soldiers arrived in Cairo at night, so its gates were closed. The *Wali* of Cairo, many leaders, low-ranking officials, and soldiers, mostly from the Turkish Mamluks, were arrested. [..] The Yemen campaign was cancelled, and only 400 Turkish horsemen were sent away to Mecca [..], but when they reached the wilderness, they headed, instead, to the Levant [..]. Then, the Sultan, God cherish his victory, prepared soldiers to head to the Levant [in pursuit of the other soldiers], so they went to Gaza [..].

There are lengthy accounts of stories of conspiracies, the wars of the different Mamluk factions, and the Bedouin's looting attacks, which will not be included here...

A messenger arrived from the Emperor [Fredrick II] with plenty of goods and precious antiques, and he was brought to Cairo and given a tour, including the Pyramids [..]. The day of his arrival was great, and

---

[i] Distinctive crown-like triangular headcover, worn only by Emirs and dignitaries.

both cities [Cairo and Misr] were decorated. All the soldiers were mounted, and the people went out [to watch]. The messenger [and his assistant] rode two Nubian horses that belonged to our Lord, the Sultan, God cherish his victory [..]. They were generously hosted in the country until the winter.

Then news arrived that the Turkish soldiers in Qous[i] [revolted] and made their leader, Ṭgharabl Al-Gaḥafy, Sultan [..]. The Sultan prepared two-thousand horsemen on the eastern side and dispatched the Asharaf Arabs[ii] on the western side. They marched, [reaching Minya]. A man from Upper Egypt came [to plead on behalf of the rebellious soldiers], so the Sultan granted him safety, and everyone returned to Cairo El-Maḥrousa [the guarded]. But when they arrived [in Cairo], they did not see the face of our Lord, the Sultan. Days later, some of them were arrested, and the rest were ordered to go to the countryside [to work other jobs], so they dispersed...

On the Feast of the Great Angel Michael [June, 1241], a man, who was from the Qalandariyyah *Sufis[iii]*, stood up in the mosque in Misr after the Friday prayer and yelled at the top of his lungs, "O Muslims, he who seeks *Jihad* in the cause of Allah, go and attack Al-Muallaqa Church." Everyone at the mosque, countless myriads, came to the church, and the *Wali* of Misr was present in the mosque as well, so he dispatched his Mamluks and ten officers to preserve the church. Upon arrival, the *Wali* found countless people in front of the church, and some went on top of the adjacent mosque. He dispersed the crowds by using bludgeoning sticks and hammers. Then, the doors of the [nearby] Wax Palace[iv] were closed shut, and he arrested the leaders of this unrest and took them, tied [with ropes], to the *Wali*'s house, where they were tortured, and then imprisoned. Things calmed down in the city and the rioters were suppressed. Levelheaded notable Muslims, Christian, and Jewish

---

[i] A town in Upper Egypt, 40 km north of Luxor. It used to be important, being located next to 'Qoft' (Gebtu) which lies at the start of the road crossing the Eastern Desert, linking the Nile Valley to the Red Sea port of Qusair.

[ii] 'Honorable' or 'noble' usually denotes being a descendent of the Prophet.

[iii] Muslim mystics.

[iv] Qasr Al-Sham', or the Castel of Candle, in Old Cairo.

commoners prayed for the *Wali*, because he controlled a bad situation that had the potential to get out of control…

On the blessed lunar New Year, the Sultan ordered that the *Jizya* be collected [in advance] for the coming year, and it was exacted violently. The person in charge of collecting the *Jizya* was a man called Ibn Garadah. He did things no one else did. He incited the riffraff against the people, made the heads of artisan guilds collect money from those under them, and made the owners of building quarters collect money from those who live in their alleyways. A penalty was imposed on people. It was announced in Misr that, as per *Sharia*, Christians had to tighten their sashes on their waists. This was because Ibn Garadah complained to the judge that it had become hard to identify the Christians from the Muslims, and that his enforcers have, possibly, mistakenly arrested Muslims over the *Jizya*. So, the people went back to tightening their sashes, and the commoners went back to their usual domineering ways.

Then, some Muslims [..] singled out the Church of Abba Serga [St. Sergios] in Misr. They came to two of its ancillary adjacent buildings and claimed that each building used to be a mosque, and that they have known about this for about 40 years. They complained to the judge and brought the old monk who resided in the church and oversaw its affairs before him. When the monk denied the claims, the judge said to him, "Would you swear to it?" The monk replied, "Yes," so the judge replied, "Say: 'By Him who revealed the Gospel to the heart of Isa[i].'" The monk answered, "This is not in accordance with my faith, and everyone swears according to his faith." The judge said, "If you do not swear as I have told you [to swear], then I will puncture your skin," and the monk replied, "Do what you want." So, the judge sent him to jail [..]. They called the monk back on the third day and repeated the claims [about the two buildings], but he again denied their claims. They then brought a record in which eight Muslim men testified that the Christians violated the mosque. Some of those witnesses were not yet 40 years old,

---

[i] Isa (or Issa) is how Jesus (Yasou', in Arabic, or Yeshu, in Hebrew) is referred to in the Quran.

nonetheless, they testified [about events] that are over 40 years old. After discussions, the judge returned the monk to jail, and after three days, he set him free, based on some vouching for him, so he would search for [evidence]. [..] They provided one-hundred-and-thirty-year-old documents as proof, but the judge paid no attention [..]. Then the judge came to the church with the *Wali* of Misr and some witnesses and said to the monk, "It has been proven to me that this building was a mosque for the Muslims, and you must pay for the thirteen years you have lived here." The monk had no money to pay, so he was taken back to jail [..], where he remained for months. Even when the Sultan wrote a directive to release the monk from jail, the judge refused, saying, "This (monk) is in the jail of Allah according to *Sharia*. He is not in my jail that I may release him." [..]

The following year, the judge met with our Lord, the Sultan, God cherish his victory, and said to him, "These places which Christians call ancillary [endowment] buildings [used to be] mosques." The Sultan responded, "Do according to whatever you can prove by *Sharia*." So, the judge went to Misr and asked for the *Wali's* help to tear down the buildings and turn them into mosques. When the *Wali* sent a letter to our Lord, the Sultan, God cherish his victory, [to inquire about this matter], no reply was made.[i] So, the judge himself came and ordered that it be torn down, and it was [..]. A group of Christians tried to meet the Sultan, but he refused, which emboldened the judge, who ordered that three more buildings be torn down in the alleyway. Then, a man called Abu Al-Ḥassan Ibn Makin, a Moslemani [a Copt who converted to Islam], took a stone from the rubble and wrote on it the *Shihada*[ii]. Then, he buried it back under the rubble, but a woman who lived in the area saw him. The following morning, he went to the judge and said, "My Lord, the truth has been revealed, and we found the old *miḥrāb*[iii] containing

---

[i] It appears as if the rulers, like those of our times, used double standards to assure that the extremists and troublemakers are kept happy, even at the expense of justice.

[ii] The Muslim profession of faith ('there is no god but Allah, and Muhammad is the messenger of Allah').

[iii] A semicircular niche in the wall of a mosque that indicates the *qibla*; that is, the direction of the *Kaaba* in Mecca and hence the direction that Muslims should face when praying.

the *Shihada.*" So, the judge came with countless Muslims and saw the place, documented the incident, got the testimony of Certified Witnesses, and sent his documentation to our Lord, the Sultan. It is said that when the Sultan, God cherish his victory, saw that, he said that this man [the Moslemani] is one of Allah's devout ones[i]. A stranger case could not be found anywhere else, and any sane elderly Muslim must have known that it was impossible for this to be true [..]. However, all this happened because the Creator abandoned and punished that church, of which I [the writer of this chronicle] am a part.

The judge came to the church, and upon entering it, he took a sledgehammer in his hand and began to tear down the walls with his own hands. They also tore down the surrounding wall [..], which ended at a lateral cylindrical pillar [in the Babylon Fortress] containing three altars [..]. The above-mentioned church was behind that cylindrical pillar, so they tore down the other church, the ladder, and the ramp [..]. Only the three cylindrical pillars remained, and even the oven and [the place of service] were gone. And it was no longer possible to get on top of the two cylindrical pillars on the side. In all, four [internal] churches, seven altars, and five buildings were lost, and the Christians remained in agony and depression like they had not experienced in a while...

A Christian man [maker of confectionaries], named Makram, from Menyet Ghamr, was with his son, and was in the kitchen, working without a sash [because of heat]. Then, a *Ḥalfawy*[ii] man walked in [..] and saw him [without sash]. He then ordered his valet to bring that poor man from the kitchen, in his undergarments, uncovered head, and shabby clothes. Many ganged up on him, all striking and insulting him, and he remained patient. The *Wali* ordered that he be imprisoned [..], and then sent him to the judge's house, parading him as he walked in humiliation [..]. He was imprisoned for days and was only released after the *Wali* issued a letter, stipulating that the man is never to leave his home without wearing a sash.

---

[i] Because he 'uncovered' the hidden evidence.
[ii] Probably an influential person.

Notice in this story that the original 'legal' justification for the sash was to distinguish between Christians and Muslims in public; however, this man was working with his son indoors in a hot kitchen, suggesting that the real reason behind the sash was the sadistic and humiliating treatment of non-Muslims.

Then, the Patriarch fell ill and died [in 1243, in the Monastery of Sham']. Immediately, certain Christians arrived, such as the aforementioned Emad the monk, [and others]. They notified [the authorities], and the room was stamp sealed as he laid, dead. On the second day, the *Wali*, the Sultan's representative, and witnesses brought the deceased out, after he had spent one night in the dark without a light. They documented the assets [clothes and valuable books, etc.] and then said to his nephew and safekeeper, "Where is the money, or I will squeeze your skull?" [..] So, they found one-thousand dinars and some change under a tile. They took the money, sealed the place, and left away with the Patriarch's nephew [..]. The funeral was then conducted as per tradition [..]. The Patriarch's nephew and the safekeeper were delivered to the *Wali* who imprisoned them until they could pay twenty-thousand dinars. The *Wali* also brought the monks [from the Monastery of Sham'] and kept them there, leaving the monastery without mass or prayer [..]. The Patriarch's nephew and safekeeper had their heads squeezed several times, but they confessed nothing [regarding what money the Patriarch may have left behind]. So, they remained imprisoned [..], and the Patriarch's estate was sold.

The Patriarch's chair remained vacant for seven years.

***

In (1244), allied Ayyubid and Khwarizmi[i] forces dispossessed Jerusalem from the Franks. Then they employed various methods of persecution and torture, beheaded all the Christians, and took captive their women and children. They also targeted churches and synagogues. They entered the Al-Qeyamah (Resurrection) Church, destroyed the tomb of Christ, set the

---

[i] From Khorezm, in present-day Uzbekistan, near the borders of Turkmenistan.

church on fire, vandalized the graves of Christians and Frankish kings, and burned the bones of the dead. Later, Al-Malek (King) Al-Saleh Ayoub expelled Khwarizmis from Jerusalem, in 1245. [84]

> Then, the *Qadi* [judge] decreed that a grandson follows the grandfather if the grandfather converts to Islam, even [if the father is a Christian, since he was of age at the time of the grandfather's conversion to Islam].

A certain Christian was accused of being the grandson of a man who converted to Islam. So, the judge decreed that this Christian convert to Islam, and imprisoned him to force him to acquiesce. All the Christians went to meet the governor and managed to release the man in the dead of night. On the following day, mobs headed to the judge's house (who had been summoned by the governor to be admonished for his decision) in support of his decision. Shops were shut down, and stones were thrown at the local governor, who was forced to leave town. Then, the mobs went to the closest church and began to destroy it, burning crosses and pictures. They also vandalized the graves, exhumed corpses and threw them in the fire, and attacked the Christian residents of this area.[85]

The local *Wali* wrote to Cairo's Divân, complaining that the *Qadi*, by his unprovoked measures against the Christians, had excited an insurrection. The Christians themselves wrote to one of the Amirs to complain of the *Qadi*, and to demand that their church should be rebuilt. Both the *Qadi* and the *Wali* were summoned to Cairo, and an inquiry held before four of the magistrates, the *Wali* (of Cairo), and several of the principal officials. It seemed clear that the *Qadi* had been to blame, but the four magistrates sided with him against the Christians; and though the Amirs supported the *(local) Wali*, they stood almost alone, as the Sheikh of the *Wali*'s mosque inflamed the passions of the council by declaring that under no circumstances could it be right to take the part of a Christian against a Muslim, and ended with a bitter denunciation of the Amir, accusing him of blasphemy because he 'espoused the cause of the Christians.' Eventually, a sort of compromise was agreed to, both the local *Wali* and *Qadi* were dismissed, but no compensation was made to the Christians.[86]

> A Christian man, known as Abi Al-Magd Ibn Abi Al-Badr, had, 28 years prior, fought with some people while drunk and verbalized [what sounded like conversion *Shihada*] to Islam. So, these people held his

words against him and took him to the school of the *faqih* Al-Ṭousy, and left him overnight. When he came back to his senses, he escaped and hid with some Christians and then headed to [the Levant]. He lived there, got married, and was blessed with children and money. As time passed, he lost his money and some of his children and returned to Egypt, hoping that his matter would have been forgotten, and to be able to live as a Christian, [but his family warned him against doing that]. So, he hid in his brother's place, who sought to gather some money to give him in order to travel. But [Al-Badr] got sick and died, and he was buried in the Monastery of Shahran [in Helwan] as per his will. His poor brother was torn and fearful, so he went to the Citadel, and it was advised to bury him as a Muslim. So, he went, exhumed his brother's body, and gave him a Muslim burial [..]

***

Finally, after seven years, Athanasius III (1250–1261) was ordained as the 76th Patriarch. This was a critical period, as the Ayyubid State began to fall apart, and after many troubles and adversities, the Mamluks ended up taking over the power.

In (1250), Al-Malek (King) Al-Ṣaleḥ Ayoub died, and his female slave, Shajarat Al-Durr (whom he had married and had a son with), arranged with Amir Fakhr-Eddin and the chief eunuch to keep the matter a secret and to bring Ghayath Al-Din Turanshah, the son of Al-Malek Al-Ṣaleḥ, from the Levant. Meanwhile, she secured the support of the commanders, high officials, and the notables in authority (all being Kurdish and Turkish Mamluks). Two months later, Turanshah was killed at the hands of Baibars, and Shajarat Al-Durr took the reins with the help of the Mamluks, who benefited from the power vacuum. Sermons were given in her honor in the mosques and she was surnamed 'Al-Mustasemeyah Al-Saleheyah Malikat Al-Moslemeen Waledat Khalil Amir Al-Momenin' (meaning *The Refuge, The Righteous, Queen of the Muslims, Mother of Khalil, Commander of the Faithful*). But riots broke out, denouncing the rule of a woman over the country's throne. (Religious) scholars were decidedly against the rule of a woman, as being in opposition to *Sharia*. The Ayyubids in the Levant also revolted because of the murder of Turanshah. The Abbasid caliphate refused to recognize the Mamluks' deeds (supporting Shajarat Al-Durr). 80 days later, Shajarat Al-Durr gave up her office to Ezz al-Din Aybak, the Turkman (whom she married), and he was surnamed Al-Malek Al-Muezz. He became the first Mamluk sultan in Egypt...

In those days, the Arab Bedouins rioted, blocked the roadways, and said, "We are more entitled to rule than they are (meaning the slave Mamluks)." The mob was led by a man called Ḥesn Al-Din Thalabah. Bedouins joined him from all places, and he had one-hundred-thousand people following him. Sultan Aybak went out against them in battle with his Mamluks, and he defeated them near Dairut... Although the Arab Bedouins surrendered to the Mamluks, they, nonetheless, continued to burn everything in sight, creating violent disturbances that lasted a long time. This was made easier for them because of the constant replacements of the Mamluk sultans.[87]

One day, in the year 1257, while the Sultan (Aybak) was walking the secret hallway connected to the house of his harem, he was ambushed by white[i] eunuchs and strangled. They did this at the behest of his wife, Shajarat Al-Durr. His son (from another wife), Nour Al-Din, took his place, and he was surnamed Al-Mansour (the 'Victorious'). Several days later, Shajarat Al-Durr was murdered by the female slaves of Al-Mansour's mother, and her body was thrown off the castle wall... The conspiracies, conflicts, slaughtering, and murders continued...

***

Thus, Egypt, and the Copts, entered into a new tunnel—one even much darker than those before it.

---

[i] Either European or Circassian slaves.

The Slaves' State and Its Dark Days

In the middle of the 13th century, the Mamluks took over the rule of Egypt. It thus became the only country in the world (and a first in its history) to be ruled by slaves[i]. Only a few small Islamic states in the Indian subcontinent share this honor with Egypt.

The Mamluks were slaves that were either kidnapped, or sometimes purchased, at a very young age from non-Muslim countries on the outskirts of the Islamic Empire, especially in the mountainous countries of Southern and Eastern Europe[ii]. Ignorant of their parentage, in some cases even of their nationality, they were then reared in a strict militaristic and religious (Islamic) fashion. They were subject to no laws except the will of their commanding Amir. They resided in barracks secluded from the outside world to ensure complete loyalty. When a Mamluk was set free and became an Amir (commander or warlord), he had the right to own a certain number of Mamluks in accordance with his rank and status. The Mamluk depended

---

[i] The Muslims have been the great slave traders of the world ever since they overran and destroyed the ancient civilizations of the East. Slavery, of course, has been known since the earliest dawn of history; it was the recognized fate of captives taken in war, and slaves have always been bought and sold for domestic servants since the world began. But in these earlier forms of slavery, there always seems to have been one humanizing influence, a sense of responsibility. In most cases, a slave's ultimate freedom depended on conduct, and not on the arbitrary caprice of his master. But under the Muslims, the slave was with no rights beyond those of a beast of burden. It was the Arab slave-trade which sapped the strength and morality of the Christian kingdoms of the Sudan, and eventually rendered them an easy prey to the Muslims; it was the Turkish slave-trade which created that terrible tyranny of the Mamluks under which Egypt groaned for centuries. (Butcher, V-2, P. 160).

[ii] Salah Al-Deen could not obtain blacks in sufficient numbers for his purpose without conquering the Sudan. His descendants had followed his example, so that almost the whole army of Egypt was composed of these European slaves.

on feudal lands given to him by the Sultan, which would amount to the control of a town, city, or a greater area. Thus, the farmers of the land were left with nothing but hard work, drudgery, and paying taxes and levies.

When the number of Mamluks increased, and they became evermore powerful, they usurped the power from the Ayyubids. However, they always suffered from an inferiority complex as a result of their slave origin. To compensate for this feeling of inferiority, they covered it up by extremes of religiosity (religion being one of the two pillars of their upbringing, especially that they were not Muslims when they were kidnapped). They became keen to host the Abbasid Caliphs in Cairo (moving from Baghdad) in order to add a semblance of religious legitimacy to their rule.

Egypt continued to be ruled by these slaves for over two-and-a-half centuries. Their state was marked by tyranny, oppression, viciousness, despotism, and turmoil. Dominance went to the bloodier swordsmen and the good conspirators. Succession in rule was not primarily hereditary; rather, when the Sultan died (or rather, killed, as was usually the case), the next most powerful Amir took his place. 24 'Bahriyya' [i] Mamluk Sultans came to power between 1250 and 1382. The last of these, Sultan Al-Mansur Qalawūn, wanted to create a new faction of Mamluks that were loyal and dedicated to him alone and none of his other competitors. The Circassians[ii] were the most abundant faction in the slave markets after the Mongols displaced them from their countries north of the Caspian Sea and east of the Black Sea. But Qalawūn used too many of them, so they took power immediately after his murder, and 22 Circassian Mamluk Sultans ruled until the Ottoman invasion (in 1517). The Mamluks continued to exert influence, even after the Ottoman invasion in the provinces, until they were wiped out by Mohammed Ali in the beginning of the 19th century.

Conditions continued to deteriorate during the days of the Mamluks; the lack of general security became worse, and chaos, looting, and robbery became rampant. In his days, the Arabic chronicler, Al-Maqrizi (d. 1441), described them by saying, "Each one of them fornicates more than a monkey, steals more than a rat, and is more harmful than a wolf." He also said elsewhere, "Great trouble came upon the people (because of the Mamluks);

---

[i] Meaning 'of the river.' They were of Turkish origin and resided in Al-Rodah citadel on a Nile island, hence the name.

[ii] In Arabic 'Sharkasian,' which comes from 'Sharq' (east) 'Asia.'

things like killing, looting, captive-taking, to the point where if the Franks ruled Egypt, they would not have done worse (than the Mamluks)."[88] Considering that Maqrizi was Muslim, this is saying much.

Sabotage by Arab Bedouins exacerbated the already-deteriorating circumstances. They contended with the Mamluks to gain control of the country through their subversive efforts, especially exploiting the provinces, by looting them, killing the farmers, and committing acts of highway robbery. These tribes began immigrating (to Egypt) since the Arab invasion, and some rulers tried, in vain, to get rid of them. In fact, Al-Mustanṣir's Vizier, Badr Al-Gamaly, tried to eradicate them, as he likened them to monsters, not humans.[89]

As if the agony of the former centuries was not enough, Egypt entered a cultural coma that lasted five-and-a-half centuries, and was only awakened by the sound of Napoleon knocking on its door in 1798.

***

As we try to go back to the *History of the Patriarchs*, we find that the chronicles have turned, over periods sometimes stretching over two centuries, into nothing more than pithy statements. This, in and of itself, is proof of the dark days that Copts went through, because it appears that they did not even have anyone—and those they had were too scared—to record the events in detail. Thus, we will refer more to other sources to complete the picture.

***

After the casting of lots (1262), Abba Ghobrial III was chosen, but some of Misr's *Archons* had agreed on another, named Yoannes VII, so they made him Patriarch for about seven years. Then, the Sultan's Vizier had a stupendous fine of fifty-thousand dinars imposed on the Coptic community in 1265. When Yoannes was unable to produce the money, he was deposed in 1268, and Ghobrial recalled to try to raise the requested funds. As he was no more successful, for two years, he was deposed, and Yoannes was reinstated (1271), and continued to serve as Patriarch until his death (1293).

This situation indicates a most blatant and unparalleled intervention by the governing authorities. Yet, the story is also emblematic of the circumscribed role and exposed position of the Coptic Patriarchs throughout the Mamluk period in Egypt (1250–1517): the governing authorities often saw the Patriarchate merely as a point of financial transfer from the Coptic community to those in power. The Patriarchs, for their part, were hard-pressed to fulfill the role that was thrust on them, sometimes with threats (or actual exercise) of violence, and played a sharply delimited role.[90]

***

The *History*'s chronicler writes:

In [1264], the Sultan, [Al-Zaher Baibars], ordered that a large pit be dug, and that Christians be thrown into it and burned. He summoned the Patriarch and commanded him to pay fifty-thousand [?] dinars, and then they let the Christians go. For two years, they collected [the money]. The Christians and bishops experienced many troubles that would take too long to explain.

The above pithy statement about the burning of Christians deserves clarification based on other sources:

'One day, a Coptic scribe, who worked for a Haseki (?) Amir by the name of Ain Al-Ghazal, asked a broker about money owed to the Amir for whom he worked that was past due. He (the scribe) then ordered his servant to take the broker toward the house of the Amir. Then, the broker started yelling, the people gathered, and ruckus ensued. When the scribe was nearing the house of his master (the Amir), he was surrounded by the crowds, who threw him off the animal on which he was riding and released the broker. When the Amir's servants came to help, the crowds rushed to the mountain Citadel, and kept yelling. When the Sultan heard of this incident, he became angry and ordered Amir Bayder and Amir Sanjar Al-Shojai to gather all the Christians in front of him that he may kill them.

The two Amirs talked the Sultan out of this, and he settled on making a public announcement in Cairo and Misr, prohibiting any Christians or Jews from working for an Amir. All the Amirs were ordered to offer their Christian scribes to convert to Islam; those who rejected were to be beheaded, and those who converted to Islam were to remain employed in their current jobs. The Sultan's lieutenant was ordered to do the same thing with the administrators of the Sultanate *Divân*. When this edict reached all the scribes, the commoners and riffraff rushed to loot their houses. Looting became widespread, to the point where the homes of all Christians and Jews were looted. Moreover, their women were taken captive, and some were killed. Al-Muallaqa Church was also looted and some of its worshippers were killed. Then, Amir Bayder acted to stop the commoners, so they stopped.

These were some of the toughest circumstances, as many people died, including children and old men. Then, the Sultan's lieutenant gathered a group of the Sultan's scribes and Amirs, and brought them before the Sultan. Al-Shogai and Amir Jandar were ordered to have their servants go to the horse market under the mountain Citadel, dig a large pit, throw in the gathered scribes, and cover them with firewood. However, Amir Bayder mediated on their behalf, but the Sultan refused, saying, "I do not want any Christian in a *Divân* in my state." As Bayder continued to plead their case, the Sultan allowed those who converted to Islam to remain employed in his service, but that those who refused to convert to Islam be beheaded. So, Amir Bayder went outside to the scribes and told them (the Sultan's words), so they all surrendered (converted to Islam), and he took their written *Shihadas* and gave them to the Sultan…"[91]

In (1273), the King of Abyssinia requested the ordination of a metropolitan[i]. In his message, he was careful to emphasize to Sultan Baibars that he treated Muslims well in his country, and that there are one-hundred-thousand Muslim cavalry in his army. He also said, "All the Muslims who come to my country are kept safe and allowed to travel as they please." But Baibars rejected his request.[92]

In (1274), the Muslims defeated the Tatars in the Levant near 'Birat.' From there, they went to Armenia and performed a forceful *fat'h*, and Baibars sanctioned killing and bloodshed for days, and many lives were lost. Then, Sultan Baibars aspired to perform a *fat'h* of Nubia and Upper Egypt. So, he sent Amir Aq Sunqur with a great army to Aswan, which he fought and conquered. Then, he went to Upper Egypt conquering, performing *fat'h*, burning, destroying, and shedding blood, until he controlled all of Upper

---

[i] He starts his message by saying, "I address my request to the Patriarch of Alexandria, our Father John, whom I salute with all the reverence due to the successor of Mark and Inianos. (..) Listen to my words and grant me my request. Send me a virtuous Metropolitan who will be able to instruct me in all things good and useful…"

Egypt and made it submit to the ruler of Sultan Al-Ẓaher Baibars. At the end, Sunqur returned with an abundance of booty made up of gold, silver, ivory, feathers, male and female slaves, eunuchs, horses, and livestock.[93]

Sunqur made prisoners of several Nubian nobles—among others, of the viceroy of the northern province—and on Baibars' return to Cairo (from Syria), they were presented to him as trophies. Baibars, with the barbarity of his kind, had them all cut asunder in the middle of the body. After another war against Nubia, the king was to cede to the Sultan of Egypt, the northernmost province (which was a fourth part, and that the most fertile part, of the whole kingdom). He was also to revive the ancient tribute of 400 slaves, from which Nubia had been free for more than two centuries. From this date, the ruin and downfall of the Christian kingdoms of Sudan became a mere question of time.

Once more, the collection of slaves for tribute necessitated perpetual fighting and anarchy, so that all good government became impossible, and the kingdoms of Sudan were set one against another, instead of making common cause against the Muslim invaders. The richest province of the Nubian kingdom had been lost, and it was no longer possible to keep the Muslims out of the interior. In their new province, the Amirs of Baibars offered the inhabitants the usual choice: the faith of Islam, tribute, or death. As generally happened, the inhabitants chose the tribute, and every male Christian paid annually the *jizya* of one dinar.[94]

***

After the Patriarchal Seat was vacant for a year, Abba Theodosios (Tawadrous) (1294–1300) was ordained as the 79th Patriarch. He was from the Monastery of Saint Fana.

> [..] and it is said that he took his seat in a manner contrary to the law [*nomos*], and that he loved taking bribes[i]. In his days, people died, prices rose sharply, and many ate the dead [..].

---

[i] Meaning simony, which is considered a heinous crime as per the church laws. This was usually to pay the exuberant sums of money imposed by the Sultans on the church in the form of *Jizya*, or to pay the transferred *Jizya* of anyone who converted to Islam to the rest of the Copts who held to the faith. Footnotes, Part four, P. 6.

***

Then Abba Yoannes VIII (1300–1320) was ordained as the 80th Patriarch.

In his days, the blue turbans were worn, and the rest is well known.

A great earthquake took place [in August, 1303][i] [..]

One of the attendants of the Patriarch's funeral was the saintly Abba Barsoum Al-Eryan.

That is all the chronicler of *History of the Patriarchs* said about this Patriarch's period of 20 years. He did not even explain who 'Barsoum' was. However, we can find some details elsewhere. Toward the end of the Sultanate of Khalil Ibn Qalawūn (1290–1292), churches were shut down all over the country with the exception of Alexandria. An edict was issued forcing all the Copts to wear blue turbans. As for this Barsoum Al-Eryan (Parsoma), the *Wali* had ordered his lashing and imprisonment because he was found praying without permission, in one of the churches that was shut down. After his release, he went and lived on the roof of that church. He was lashed with the whip and imprisoned a second time, because he refused to wear the blue turban. [ii]

In 1299, a man named Abu Abdullah Mohammed rose up in Abyssinia, calling people to Islam. He assembled around two-hundred-thousand Arabs and fought the King (of Abyssinia). When the battles intensified, the *faqih* (scholar), Abdullah Al-Zeli, asked the Sultan to aid the Arab invaders in Abyssinia. The Sultan, in turn, mediated the Coptic Patriarch in this matter, who wrote to the King of Abyssinia, asking him to stop fighting the Arabs in his country, but the wars continued for a long time.[95]

The first three years of the new century were particularly hard. The principal Muslims clamored for the destruction of all the Christian churches, as well as for the enforcement of all the penal (*Sharia*) laws against them; and though the *Wali* of Cairo refused to grant the former demand, he did not dare to refuse the latter. He sent, however, for Abba Yoannes VIII and the

---

[i] It resulted in toppling the famous lighthouse of Alexandria.

[ii] St. Parsoma, a renowned Saint of the Coptic Church. A monastery in Helwan, south of Cairo, carries his name. https://st-takla.org/Saints/Coptic-Orthodox-Saints-Biography/Coptic-Saints-Story_513.html

principal men of both the Jewish and Christian communities and warned
them that he could not answer for the consequences if they did not oblige
their people to obey the laws against them. The Patriarch, at once, wrote
letters to all the dioceses, ordering that the Christians should wear blue
turbans and girdles, and refrain from riding on horses or mules on pain of
excommunication, since, in such matters, the powers that were to be obeyed.
The churches were ordered to be shut in Cairo for a time (during popular
riots).

Once more, the whole army of Coptic clerks was dismissed from
government service; once more, the mob hooted and stoned inoffensive
Christians daily in the street, or pulled down and savagely beat anyone who
ventured to ride even on the permitted ass. In Alexandria and the Fayoum,
the popular riots against the Christians were particularly fierce, and the
government did not attempt to restrain them. The festival of the Nile was
forbidden, and the lives and property of the Christian and Jewish populations
were in hourly danger all through the country.[96]

In 1312, the King of Abyssinia sent a gift to Sultan Al-Naṣer Muhammad
Ibn Qalawūn worth one-hundred-thousand dinars (?), which was considered
a rarity, requesting the ordination of a metropolitan for his country. The
Sultan approved…

***

Then, Abba Yoannes IX (1320–1327) became the 81st Patriarch.
During his days, the Christians experienced many difficulties. Some of
them were killed, others burned, and others were nailed [to crosses?] and
were paraded on horses. They were also forced to wear blue turbans.
Then [God] eased the people's burdens by His mercy.

These abridged and enigmatic statements do not quench a reader's thirst
for more details. Other historical sources tell the story of what took place on
Friday, (May 16th, 1320).

Many churches were set on fire simultaneously in Cairo, Misr,
Alexandria, and other places. There was also looting and killing taking place.
A month later, several fires were started in alleyways, buildings, and
mosques (*see below). Some Christians were [falsely] accused of doing
these things and were arrested, and as punishment, they were burned and

killed (**see below). Then, Christians were forced to wear blue turbans, and it was announced that if a Christian was found wearing a white turban, or riding a horse or a mule, then his blood and money were lawful. If Christians rode on donkeys, they had to ride facing backward. Christians had to wear bells around their necks when entering (public) bathrooms, and they were prohibited from dressing like Muslims. The Amirs prohibited their employment, and Muslims increasingly plotted against Christians.[97]

(*) Sultan Al-Naṣer Muhammad Ibn Qalawūn (1309–1340) ordered the building of a corral in the Tall Al-A'zam (great hill) area, near the Al-Ṭaybersi Mosque. When the digging was completed beside the Al-Zahri Church, the laborers kept digging around the church until it was suspended, but it did not fall. Then, the servants of the Amirs who worked on the digging, as well as others, kept screaming, demanding that the church be torn down. When it was Friday, the Sultan was in the mosque located in the mountain Citadel, and a poor man[i] loudly proclaimed, "Tear down the church located in the Citadel." His incessant yelling bothered the people. But the Sultan was intrigued by his words, so he sent an army commander to investigate the matter. So, they found, amid the ruins of the Tatars, close to the Citadel, a church, which they tore down. When the commoners heard of this, a group of Muslim riffraff gathered together and yelled loudly, "Allah Akbar," and they tore down Al-Zahri Church (close to the digging site) until only rubble remained. They also killed those who were inside the church and stole anything of value.

They then stretched their hands against other churches, tearing down the Church of Abba Mina in Al-Ḥamra which had long been highly esteemed. Then they attacked two more churches near the Seven Watering site. One of those churches is known as the Church of Girls, and many devoted nuns lived there. So, they broke down the doors of both churches, took over sixty (nuns) captive, stole all they could get their hands on, and finally burned and tore down these churches.

Al-Maqrizi adds, "When the people walked out of the mosques, they witnessed great horror because of all the dust, smoke, and people running everywhere with looted items, and it was like Judgment Day. When the Sultan was notified, he was disturbed and bothered, because the people dared

---

[i] Probably considered to be a 'pious friend of Allah' or an Islamic saintly man.

to do these things without his permission. So, he ordered Aydghamesh Amir Khour to ride with a group of Al-Washqeyah and handle the situation. Meanwhile, news broke that the mobs had destroyed a church in the alleyway of the Roum and a church in the alleyway of Zwailah. The mobs had also marched to Al-Muallaqa Church, but its doors were shut by those in charge of it, while they were inside, surrounded, and about to be taken. Then, four Amirs came down from the Citadel with an abundant force, so the looters escaped, and only those who were unable to move were captured. Then, the *Wali* went to Al-Muallaqa Church, but the looters bombarded him with a hail of stones, until he fled from them. While the mobs were on the verge of burning the church door, Aydghamesh and those with him took out their swords and were about to start killing the people. But when they saw the great numbers present, they feared the repercussions (..). Finally, the mobs dispersed. Then news came that the mobs destroyed a number of churches: four in Alexandria, two in Damanhur, four in Al-Gharbeyah, three in Al-Sharqiyah, six in Bahnasia, Assiut, and Manfalut, eight in Menyet Ibn Khasib, six in Qous, five in Aswan, one in Atifihhia, one in the Wardan market, and eight in the Qasr Al-Sham' [i]. News continued to travel about the many churches and homes that were torn down, and this was a great adversity.'"[98]

(**) A fire broke out in the alleyway of Al-Shawa'en (the grillers) in Cairo. On that day, the wind was so severe that palm trees were uprooted, and boats sank. So, the fire spread everywhere, and the people were unable to put the fire down until days later. Some Christians were accused of starting the fire, so, after they were (tortured), they confessed to starting the fires in retaliation against the destruction of churches. Therefore, (the accused) were burned on Friday and many gathered to watch them die. The commoners were emboldened against the Christians as of that day, and they utterly decimated them.

When the Sultan rode to the square, as was his custom, he found that many of the commoners had dyed rags in blue, and painted white crosses in the middle of the rags, and loudly exclaimed, "There is no religion but the religion of Mohammed Ibn Abdullah, O King Al-Naṣer, O Sultan of Islam, grant us victory over the people of *Kufr*." So, the Sultan ordered his janitor

---

[i] 'Wax Palace,' or 'Candle (Beacon) Castle,' in Old Cairo.

to go and announce publicly, "Whoever finds a Christian, it is lawful for him to take his money and his livelihood." The crowds cheered, "May Allah grant you victory," and they prayed for him loudly.

The Muslims increasingly then plotted against Christians, and things stayed that way for days. Then it was announced publicly that peace was to return, and this was because of all that befell the Christians, and because the (Muslim) people had gone beyond what was permissible. Then, an edict was issued, mandating Christians to wear blue turbans (etc.), and the Amirs were prohibited from employing Christians, thus Christians were taken out of the Sultan's *Divân*. The rest of the offices were also ordered to get rid of all Christian overseers.[99]

Apparently, the repercussions of these events were so large that in (1326), the King of Abyssinia sent messengers to Qalawūn, asking him to rebuild all the (Coptic) churches that were destroyed and to treat Christians honorably and respectfully. He also threatened to destroy the mosques in his country and to block the Nile to prevent it from flowing to Egypt. So, the Sultan mocked (the message) and sent the messengers back. The same thing took place the following year.[100]

In 1327, there was a fresh outbreak of attacks, and the church of St. Barbara was destroyed. The only reason given for this is the fact that the Copts—with the permission of the Sultan—had ventured to repair this church, and in so doing, had slightly enlarged the building.

***

Then, Abba Benyamin II (1327–1339) became the 82nd Patriarch.
In his days, Sharaf Al-Din Al-Nashou Ibn Tag became *Wali*, and hardships abounded. They humiliated women, children, monks, nuns, and bishops. Then Al-Nashou died, and God's vengeance was unleashed against all the evildoers.

The Mamluk Sultanate continued to persecute Copts and fired any who worked in the States' *Divân*s. So, some (Copts) fled to Abyssinia, led by Fakhr Al-Dawlah, the scribe, who was welcomed by the King of Abyssinia. (Fakhr reorganized the King's *Divân*, and set rules for taxation).[101]

The (Roman Catholic) Pope[i] interfered personally after these events in 1328, and a papal delegation was sent to Egypt, carrying a message from the Pope, asking the government to protect Christians. On behalf of the Catholic world, the Pope announced that Europeans might treat Muslims, hired in their countries, in the same way that Christians in Egypt and Syria were being treated.[ii]

***

Several Patriarchs were ordained, including Botros V (1340–1348), Morcos IV (1348–1363), Yoannes X (1363–1369), and Ghobrial IV (1370–1378); however, the chroniclers of *History of the Patriarchs* did not mention any events during their days.

But other historical sources refer to the conditions that the Copts faced, saying for example, that in (1354), Amirs Shaykho, Ṣarghtamsh, and Ṭaz, who ran the affairs of the state, decided to seize the endowed monastery and church lands (twenty-five-thousand *feddans*[iii]). The purpose of doing this was to bestow these lands to the Amirs. They also tore down several churches. And the commoners went back to destroying churches and tearing down homes as they did during the days of Sultan Qalawūn. Jews and Christians were prohibited from administrative positions in the *Divâns*. It was also decided that the cloth making up the Christians' turbans not exceed ten arms (in length), that they not enter a (public) bathroom unless they have a cross around their necks, and that their women not enter bathrooms with Muslim women. It was required that Christian women wear blue skirts, Jewish women wear yellow skirts, and the Samaritan women wear red skirts. Women had to wear sandals of two different colors.

Then Amir Alaa Al-Din, the *Wali* of Cairo, went to Shubra El-Kheima and tore down a church there, taking the finger of a martyr that was kept in a box. He brought it to the king (Sultan?) who burned it and spread the ashes. Thus, the feast held in honor of that martyr was discontinued ever since. The

---

[i] Pope John XXII (1316–1334), then based in Avignon.

[ii] Tagher, P. 258. Not clear if there was any Muslim response.

[iii] Acre; a unit of area, equivalent to 4200 square meters. A *feddan* is divided into 24 *kirat*, in which one *kirat* equals 175 square meters. (One sq. meter = 10.7 sq. feet)

commoners intensified their harsh treatment of the Christians, even robbing, looting, and committing other evil acts against them. As for the Sultan, he never disagreed with the commoners nor did he deter them (from acting wickedly). Then the commotion died down, and the Sultan intended to make Mūafaq Al-Din, who was a Copt who renounced his faith, a high-ranking official in his government. However, the Amirs objected and requested that Elm Al-Din, another Copt who renounced his faith, take that position instead.[102]

A decree was then sent in writing from the Sultan to the provinces (and to Syria), that no Jew nor any Christian should be taken into (government) service, and that whosoever embraced Islam should not be allowed to return to his house nor to the bosom of his family, unless they also become Muslims too. Also, that if any poor Christian embraced Islam, he should be made to attend the five prayers and the congregation (on Fridays) at the mosques. And that when a Christian died, the Muslims should undertake the management of his property among his heirs, if he had any; but if not, it was to be confiscated to the public treasury. The Patriarch was charged with the duty of seeing to it, and wrote an order, which was read before the Amirs, and then was taken down by the warden of the palace gates on a Friday, and read in the mosques of Cairo and of Misr—and that day was a high day. [..]

During this persecution, the Patriarch, Abba Morcos, was thrown into prison for torture and eventual death. The King of Nubia heard of it in time, and seized all the Muslim merchants in his kingdom as hostages for the life of the Patriarch, who was released in consequence. The Patriarch died in 1363.[103]

***

Then, Abba Mettaous I (1378–1408) became the 87th Patriarch. Before that, he was a monk in Mount Antonius (monastery in the eastern desert) who refused and escaped from the call to become Patriarch, but he was compelled to take the position. He was spiritual, charitable, humble, and performed good deeds,

[..] working with the laborers mixing mud, draining [cleaning] toilets, and lifting grain with the stackers [..]; despite these things, his reverence and dignity were not diminished in the eyes of the people.

A Syriac monk named Ibrahim abjured his faith before the King [Sultan] and became a soldier. He spoke against the Patriarch and against a group of wounded [?] monks in the wilderness. He then arrested some of them, bound them in chains, and transported them to Misr [..]. He persisted in going against the Patriarch and opposing him to the point where the people were annoyed with him and asked the Patriarch to pray against him, but he refused. He then said to them, "My children, do not pray against him, for I pray for him." [..] After some time, that former monk repented, [converted back to his faith, and was killed for leaving Islam].

When Amir Minṭash fought against Sultan Barqouq and defeated him, [a slanderer] told him that the Patriarch possesses money and [treasures], which Barqouq [supposedly] had entrusted to him before his departure. The Amir summoned the Patriarch and tortured him, but he was unable to find anything in his possession [..]. In another incident, an Amir named Yalbugha Al-Samly acted tyrannically and tried to [impose harsh measures on the people], but the Patriarch did not assent. So, the Amir drew his sword in anger to behead the Patriarch, who then stretched out his neck [..]. When the Amir witnessed the Patriarch's courage, he retreated [..]. A restive group attempted to demolish the Al-Adhra [Virgin] Church in Al-Muallaqa [..]. They took a large bowl filled with fire and placed it under the foundation of the church in order to burn it, [but the rain put out the fire] [..].

A group of [Muslims] overpowered the Shahran Monastery [desiring] to tear it down. They gave the Sultan a false report regarding the monks of that monastery, and he gave them permission. They gathered to tear it down, and their great number was beyond count. But the Patriarch was not afraid of them, rather, he confronted them and said, "The one among you who has authority, let him draw his sword and kill me, because as long as I am alive, I will not allow you to remove one stone from this monastery until I stand next to you before the Sultan and prove to him the falsity of your reports." [..] Then, he went to the Citadel and appealed to Sultan Barqouq. When the Sultan heard the Patriarch's screams, he sent four judges to inspect the monastery, but they could not prove anything that was [claimed] by the restive group.

Amir Sūdūn summoned the Patriarch and informed him of the changes he planned to enact, which, in part, included imposing that [Coptic] women wear blue skirts, among other things. The Patriarch decried the defaming of the daughters of his people in such a way that brought disgrace to them, making them the laughingstock of the simplest commoners. He said, "Truly, I say to you, O Amir, if you defame one of the daughters of my people, I will not stop [complaining across] your country from the edges of (Sudan) to the ends of Egypt. And I want to inform you, O Amir, that Christians are not without kings on earth (nor are they weak) as you deem them to be." [..] So, the Amir let the Patriarch go and stopped talking to him about anything [regarding this matter].[i]

Then one of the Amirs spoke to the Sultan [Barqouq] and the judges, suggesting the annihilation of Christians from the face of the earth, [but shortly afterward, he died].

Many Copts became involved in and stained with several types of sin. The Patriarch sighed and cried because of the misery that had befallen the Egyptians [..]. He continually warned the Copts, saying, "Wake up, my children, and be careful of the day of vengeance that will come against the Egyptians." [..] But the more he spoke to us about these things, the less careful we became. We became more rebellious and insolent and less fearful of God [..].

Because of the unbearable immensity and weight of the hardships that befell the people, which were even beyond reason, the Copts sought refuge in religious feelings. They began to interpret their reality as being a result of their own sins and of moving away from fearing God...

The *Wali* of Aswan at the time was an Amir who surpassed all Muslim traditions in his barbarity, particularly toward the children of (the Nubian tribe) Kenz. He sent the Sultan twelve heads and 200 living men of the Kenouz[ii] loaded with chains as an acceptable present. The tribe of Kenz rose against the Amir at last, pillaged the town of Aswan, killed a number of the inhabitants, and made themselves masters of the whole province, which, for many years, ceased to belong to the kingdom of Egypt.[104]

---

[i] A rare case of bravery, where the Patriarch stood up to the unjust *Wali*, leading him to relent from his injustice...

[ii] *Pl.* of Kenz.

In (1382), the King of Abyssinia sent gifts on 21 camels to Sultan Al-Zaher Barqouq, requesting the ordination of a metropolitan for his country.[105]

The terrible persecution had led to an unprecedented number of Copts renouncing their faith. One renegade, Michael Sabaan, was led in triumph about the city, clothed in royal robes, and mounted on one of the Sultan's mules, after which he was rewarded with an important post under government. However, in the year 1389, a strange procession entered Cairo: a great multitude of men and women, who cried aloud as they marched, that they were Christians, and that they renounced the faith of the false prophet, which they confessed with shame that they had adopted for fear of persecution. Their object in calling attention to themselves thus publicly, was to expiate their former fault by voluntarily seeking that martyrdom, the fear of which, had made them traitors to their Lord. They were surrounded, and the authorities, in vain, demanded their instant return to Islam. They constantly exclaimed with one voice, "We come here to be purified from our sin, and by the sacrifice of our lives, to earn the pardon of our Savior." As it was found that not one could be terrified into yielding, it was resolved to make an example of the men first. They were marched to the open place under the windows of the College of Saleh, separated from the women, and beheaded one after the other. The terrible sight had no effect on the determination of the women, but rather, confirmed them in their desire for death. Finding them obstinate, one of the chief *Qadi* ordered his guards to take the women without further delay to the foot of the citadel and behead them all. The example was not lost on the Copts.[106]

Within a few days, a monk, his friend, and three women connected with them, were beheaded and burnt — the first, for preaching against the faith of Islam, the others, for standing by him and encouraging him through his martyrdom. Toward the end of the year, both the Patriarch Mettaous and the Chief Rabbi of the Jews were thrown into prison; and the former had to be ransomed at the cost of 100,000 dirhams, the Rabbi at 50,000.[107]

In (1396), the Ahmadiyya Arabs made an alliance with Al-Knouz and Al-Hawarah Arabs and rose up against the ruler of Aswan. They looted the city and took captive its citizens, and the city remained, for years, without a ruler.[108]

Al-Nagashi[i] Dawood wrote a long letter in response to two letters that he received. One of those letters was from the Sultan Barqouq and was carried to him by Judge Borhan Al-Din. The other letter was from the Patriarch, Abba Mettaous, and it was delivered by Bishop Abraham. Al-Nagashi pointed out that the kings of Abyssinia desired 'good for all people, evenhanded justice, compassion, deterrence of the unjust, prevention of the corrupt, and the guarantee of rights to those deserving of them.' He almost implied that this was not how things were in Egypt. Then, he responded to what was said in those letters he received from the Sultan and the Patriarch. *"Regarding those who reported to you that we abuse the Muslims residing in our country by killing, insulting, and compelling them to convert to our religion,"* these are ridiculous claims worthy of the punishment reserved for liars. *"Because they (Muslims) willingly reside in our country, not under compulsion, and those who were poor have become wealthy merchants, traveling east and west without having to pay Jizya or any other levies (..). As for compelling anyone to convert to our faith, this is not part of our Book's teachings (..)."* (Possibly implying *'like it is in your Book.'*) He also referred to the efforts exerted in securing the roadways, assuring that those who have been fought were the Arab marauders which was the very group that the Sultan himself resisted in Egypt. He also implied that there were several Muslim kings (provincial governors) overseeing areas inhabited by Christians who paid the *Kharaj* as subjects. He then pointed out that, *"Muslims (in Abyssinia) enjoy peace and security, (whereas) you treat the Dhimmis (in Egypt) in a way that is contrary to that..."* He also brought up what was happening with the Copts and recommended, *"Taking care of them, treating them honorably, and returning their churches and monasteries, which you have seized and converted into mosques, which goes against the teachings of your Sharia regarding the protection of Dhimmis."* He then used veiled threatening language, saying, *"If you agree to maintain to them (Christians), as they were (used to) in the past, their churches, livelihoods, money, cattle, and livestock, then our covenant with you stands. We will show greater kindness to the Muslims among us than the kindness you show them. Likewise, whatever you do to our Patriarch and Christians brothers, good or evil, we shall also do to our Muslim subjects (..)."* Then, he added, *"The number of your Christian subjects in Egypt is equivalent to the number of*

---

[i] Negus. King, or emperor, of Abyssinia.

Muslims in only one of the provinces under our rule (..)." Then, Al-Nagashi criticized how Abyssinian traders and pilgrims, traveling via Egypt to Jerusalem, were being mistreated, "*And heavy-handedly forced to convert to Islam, and how this is against the Sharia and even against the traditions of former Muslim leaders[i]*."

Messages like this one clearly reveal, even if indirectly, what was happening to the Copts during the days of the Mamluks. They show that the persecution, if not the annihilation, of Copts, was a general ongoing policy, in accordance with the Sultan's desires, or under pressure of 'the Islamic street,' commoners and riffraff... O, how today looks so much like yesterday!

Not long after Barquq's death in 1399[ii], Abba Mettaous was again arrested for funds by Mamluk *Amir* Yalbougha.[iii] In 1408, the Abba was accused—and arrested—by another *Amir*, Jamal al-Din, of 'treacherous dealings with the kings of Abyssinia,' hoping thereby to get a big ransom from the Coptic community. He then prayed to be released from this oppression in such a way that the community not be harmed, and days later, he died peacefully.

***

Several Patriarchs served from 1409–1675, but the chroniclers of *History of the Patriarchs* did not record much of what took place in their days, with a few exceptions.

In 1412, during the time of Abba Ghobrial V (1409–1427), Sheikh Al-Mahmoudi became Grand Vizier (and reigned under the name Al-Malek Al-Moayed). The first care was to despoil the Jews and Christians. Three commissioners were employed to inquire into their number and resources,

---

[i] *History of the Patriarchs*, Part three, Appendix nine, P. 1808 from a manuscript in the Coptic Patriarchal library dated *Kiyahk*, 1179, Coptic Martyrs, i.e. December, 1463. But it appears that there is a dating error, because Sultan Al-Ẓaher Saif Al-Din Barqouq died in 1399, and Abba Mettaous I died in 1408. Perhaps the letter is from the time of Abba Mettaous II (1452–1465), in which case, it would have been addressed to Al-Ẓaher Saif Al-Din Khashqadm...

[ii] Sultan Barqouq had over 100 children, and five of them ruled after him.

[iii] Yalbougha is celebrated by having his name on a street in (ironically) the predominantly Coptic neighborhood of Shubra, in Cairo.

and a registry office to receive their names was opened in the building adjoining the mosque of Hakim. Eventually, the Jews and Christians were divided into three classes; the richest were to pay four dinars a year, the second class, two, and the poor, one dinar a year. He oppressed the Copts, and permitted his Mamluks to indulge in open violence and persecution. All the old oppressive laws were put in force against the Christians, and in 1418[i], Abba Ghobrail was summoned and threatened with death because the Abyssinians, who were supposed to be 'under his authority,' were oppressing the Muslims settled in their country. After stormy discussions, it was decided, as usual in times of persecution, that no Copt should be employed any longer in government. They began by making an example of Fadail, the secretary of the Grand Vizier. By the Sultan's order, he was imprisoned and tortured, and then paraded naked through the streets of Cairo, followed by an official who cried aloud, "Thus, shall it be done to every Christian in the employ of the Sultan." The Christian officials barricaded themselves in their houses, and waited till the Muslim rulers should again discover that the government's affairs could not be carried on without them. Some of them apostatized at a later date, under the continued stress of persecution.[109]

In the days of Abba Yoannes XI (1427–1452), many Copts were burned and killed, while others were nailed to wooden planks and paraded on the backs of camels on the streets of Cairo.[110] This took place during the days of Sultan Al-Zaher Jaqmaq (1438–1453), 'who was known to be moderate in his rule when compared to Barsbay, his predecessor. He was also known for his devout religiosity, so he forbade lewdness and the imbibing of wine.'[111]

It seems that there was no contradiction perceived by rulers between 'piety' and burning, killing and annihilating innocent people, just because they were not Muslims.

Between 1437 and 1439, there were renewed assaults: a church in Shubra was burnt, part of Al-Muallaqah was destroyed, and churches in Damietta were pillaged. The greatest shock was the destruction of the Monastery *al-Maghtas* ('Baptismal') in northern Delta, which was an important pilgrimage site (Virgin Mary Apparition).

---

[i] In that year, the head of St. Mark was stolen from Alexandria by a Venetian privateer, and this seems to have been regarded as a national calamity by the Copts.

In 1448, Jaqmaq had the Abba arrested, beaten, imprisoned, and fined. Then, he was forced to take an oath that he would henceforth have no contact with the king of Abyssinia in anyway whatsoever, except by the explicit permission of the Sultan. Any infraction of this oath would merit death.[112]

***

Abba Yoannes XII (1478–1483), the 93rd Patriarch, received
> a message from the Pope in the city of Rome, and he [responded to him] with a message written on three codices. The main points of his message were reconciliation, peace among all the Christian sects, and abandoning obstinacy.

Other history books shed some light. The persecution and fleeing of some Copts to Abyssinia continued. During the 15th century, several controversies broke out between Egypt and Abyssinia, and the Sultans refused to send Coptic metropolitans, and worked to sever the ties between the two churches. So, the King of Abyssinia turned his gaze to Rome, and the Coptic Church did not object, in order to ensure the continuation of the Abyssinian Church (in 1440).[113]

In (1443), the King of Abyssinia sent a letter to Sultan Jaqmaq (accompanied by gifts, which included 70 female slaves), to restore a good relationship with Egypt, and he directed the Sultan's attention to the treatment of Copts. He says, (..) "*You know that a ruler needs to take care of his subjects, and that God demands this of him. The Patriarch and Christians who live under your exalted rule and honorable kingdom are few, meek, and submissive in all things, and, by any reckoning, they cannot be more than the number of Muslims residing in one of the provinces of our country. And you, may God preserve you, surely know the vast numbers of Muslims living under our rule, and how we always treat them with kindness (..). It is also not hidden from you that the Nile flows to your country from our country, and we are capable of preventing the increase (the flooding) that waters your country. What prevents us from doing so is our fear of God and the hardships that would befall the servants of God (..).*"

The Sultan responded by refusing to acquiesce to the king's request to better treat the Copts, even though he sent appropriate gifts (..) and it appears that the response displeased the King of Abyssinia, who held the letter courier in custody and threatened to kill (one of the Muslim provincial governors). When Sultan Jaqmaq heard of this, he summoned the Coptic Patriarch, beat him, and threatened to kill him. The Patriarch, in turn, rushed to write a letter to the King of Abyssinia (..).[114]

In 1453, the Greek Empire of Byzantium finally perished, and the reigning Ottoman Sultan, Mohamed II, took possession of the ancient stronghold of Christendom.

In 1458, the Mamluk Amirs repeatedly set fire to various parts of the cities—probably those quarters inhabited chiefly by Jews and Christians—in order to create opportunities for plunder.

***

In the days of Sultan Qaitbay (1468–1496) and of Patriarch Yoannes XII (1478–1484), the commoners rose up against the Christians in Cairo. All their churches were shut down and they were prevented from performing any of their religious practices. Then, this spread south and north, and the tumult intensified, leading to the killing, taking of captives, looting, destruction, and bloodshed in the side streets and alleyways. The *Walis* in charge failed to deter the commoners. This lasted for many days until the sectarian strife died down, and the fallout was great.

This Patriarch's tenure was approximately six years, and they were spent in great misery because of the hardships of Christians being taken captive and enslaved. In his days, the Christians experienced all sorts of calamities and tribulations.[115] Moreover, in 1484, the monks of the monasteries of St. Antonius and St. Paulus (in the Eastern Desert) were all massacred, and the monasteries abandoned for 80 years. During this time, the greater part of the ancient library was used for fuel by wandering Bedouins.

Sultan Al-Ashraf Qansuh Al-Ghuri (1501–1516) intensified his mistreatment of Christians. He seized great sums of money from them and acted with greater severity in order to spite them, going as far as lashing some (Christian) women to punish them.[116]

***

During the period of Mamluk slave dynasties (1249–1517), the term 'Muslim Copts' was used to describe converts. Several writers of that era claimed that a Muslim convert of Coptic descent was potentially a false Muslim. Even worse, he was suspected of converting to the majority faith, admittedly often under duress, in order to aggrandize his own position at the expense of his 'genuine' Muslim colleagues. Indeed, such a person was frequently accused of converting in order to blaspheme against Islam and to lead true believers astray. Such a 'false Muslim' was always, it was alleged, on the verge of retrogressing to Christian practices.[i]

The Mamluks appointed 'Muslim Copts' to several of the highest executive offices of the state…but they do not seem to have gained access to offices endowed with authority to make decisions affecting the spiritual lives of the legitimate Muslims. They were not well-accepted, however, and the range of activities they pursued implies the limited extent to which their contemporaries were disposed to allow their penetration into the power structure.[117]

This indicates the existence of multiple strata in the society, starting with the rulers at the top, followed by 'true believers,' then suspect believers. *Dhimmis* would come last.

Worth noting, finally, is that under the rule of the Mamluks, the Copts were somewhat protected by their skill in handling taxation and state finances. Another factor in the survival of the Copts and their churches was the relationship with Ethiopia; the emperors interceded on behalf of the Copts at the Sultan's court.

***

In summation, the era of the state of the slave Mamluks constituted one of the darkest and most vicious eras for the Copts. The bloody rulers were united with, and in fact competed against, the riffraff and dregs of society, in abusing Copts.

At that time, the Ottoman Sultan Selim was preparing a *fat'h* against Egypt, after he had taken over and ravaged Aleppo and Damascus. This was the start of a new nightmare.

---

[i] This predates the Spanish Inquisition…

An Ottoman Paradise

Egypt experienced yet another *fat'h* — or conquest in the name of Islam — in January, 1517, by the Ottoman Sultan Selim I, who was known for his love of bloodshed. In order to rule, he fought his father, Sultan Bayezid, and poisoned him to death. He also killed his brothers, Ahmed and Karkoud, and then desecrated their bodies.

Selim sent a great army, like locusts carrying banners with quotes from the Quran, 'Indeed, We have given you a clear conquest'[118] and 'Help from Allah, and speedy victory.'[119] Prior to his conquest of Egypt, Selim sent a letter to Tuman Bay (*Bek*), the last of the Mamluk Sultans, filled with obscene insults and threats, saying, "Allah has inspired me to rule over all the countries, east and west, (..) and for there not to be a word above mine, nor a hand above mine. But you are only a Mamluk, [who may be] bought and sold, so it is not appropriate for you to rule, nor is it permissible for you to govern the free..." He ended his letter with the Quran verse, "And never would We punish until We sent a messenger."[120]

After fierce battles that ended with the defeat of the Mamluk army and the slaughtering of thousands of them, the Ottoman soldiers went around, looting anything that appealed to them in Cairo, for three consecutive days. They were abominable in their killing, plundering, and burning. They ravaged houses and mosques, with particularly improper actions committed in Al-Azhar Mosque. The Ottoman conquest of Cairo was likened to the conquest of Baghdad by the Mongolian warrior, Hulagu. Yet, the following Friday, the Imams of Misr and Cairo preached in honor of Sultan Selim, saying, "O Allah, give victory to the Sultan who is a son of a Sultan, the ruler of the two coasts and the two seas, destroyer of the two armies, Sultan of the two Iraqs[i], custodian of the two holy mosques, the triumphant, King Selim Shah."

---

[i] An older name of current day Iraq, referring to its two main centers, Kufa and Basra.

Then the looting campaign began; even worse than what took place during the reigns of the previous rulers, starting with Amr Ibn Al-Aas. Selim took anything of value from Egypt and nothing worthy was left behind in the Citadel. He took the pillars from the large palace halls; even Pharaonic stones from Upper Egypt were taken. All the booty was carried to Constantinople (Istanbul)[i] atop thousands of camels and aboard ships beyond number. He also took many highly skilled laborers, tradesmen, and farmers, in order to build his country. Thus, the people of Egypt faced hardships unlike any before or any recorded in ancient history. Ibn Iyas mentions the names of these miserable people, who came from all over Egypt, including Muslims, Copts, and Jews. Without doubt, they were the ones who built the Ottomans' finest structures of which they boast greatly, whether mosques, minarets, bazaars, or anything else.

When the rule over Egypt became sufficiently stable, Sultan Selim decided to bring back the Circassian Mamluk Amirs to rule over Egypt under control of the Ottomans, perhaps because he found that this setup would make it easier to control the country. As for the Arab Bedouins who had helped the Ottomans come to power in Egypt (to spite the Mamluks), they continued to exert influence as well. They were also sent the ordinances for feudal lands and garments (silk caftans); nonetheless, they continued to cause disturbances and commit acts of destruction and highway robbery against passing caravans.[121]

Since the start of their rule, the Ottomans acted harshly as the following droll story indicates. In 1521, an Ottoman judge strictly enforced the implementation of *Sharia*, and it was announced in all the streets of Cairo, that women were forbidden from going to the markets, unless they were elderly. If any woman disobeyed, she would be beaten, tied up with a horse's tail, and paraded in the streets. Every donkey renter who let a woman sit on

---

[i] Sultan Mehmed, the Conqueror, captured Constantinople in 1453, and his soldiers put its inhabitants to the edge of the sword. They went inside the Hagia Sophia (Church) where the Patriarch of the Roum (Byzantines) was praying in the midst of great masses. They killed everyone present by the sword, leaving no one alive. They proceeded to loot, take captive, and burn the city. They burned all the libraries, destroying over one-hundred-and twenty-thousand codices. Then, Sultan Mehmed moved his throne to Constantinople, which was officially named 'Istanbul' (*Gk.* from 'Stimboli' for 'in the city,' or possibly just a colloquial deformation of 'Constantinople') in March of 1930.

his donkey would be lynched. Several months later, the judge travelled to perform *Hajj*, and the people rejoiced. Women were the happiest of all, and some (women) singers began to sing, "Rise, let us act immorally and get drunk...for the military judge has left us," which became the people's favorite ditty, sung by young and old alike.[i]

***

As we have mentioned earlier, the chronicles of *History of the Patriarchs* are almost completely silent regarding the events that took place during the critical period between 1400 and 1675. This demonstrates that the Copts were rather occupied with something vastly more important: fighting to stay alive. Therefore, we will turn to other sources that help clarify the picture.

The concept of *Taifa* (denomination, or confessional community) was the framework that suited the Ottoman rule in Egypt, with the natural consequence that the Patriarch and his assembly of bishops became the legal representatives of the community before the government. One of the expressions of this structure was the Patriarch's responsibility to ensure the collection the *Jizya* from the Copts on behalf of the government. In this context, Pope Youhanna XIII (1484–1524), for instance, sent a letter to the Copts of Lower Egypt (the Delta), urging them to pay the *Jizya*, and to consider it a duty, which is consistent with the Gospel injunction, 'render unto Cesar the things that are Cesar's.' This was a heavy burden borne by the popes. An illustration of this occurred a century-and-a-half later, when the *Dîvan* (chancellery) of *al-Jawali*[ii] confiscated the inheritance of Pope Morcos VI (1646–56), because there was an outstanding sum due from the *Jizya* set on the Copts. His possessions were sold to make the payment.[122]

Generally speaking, *Dhimmis* bore heavy financial burdens, in addition to the *Jizya*, during the rule of the Ottomans, who exacted these levies in order to finance their wars. When Sultan Suleiman Al-Qanunî needed funds to accomplish the *fat'h* of Yemen, he gave orders that money was to be collected from the Copts, and he also imposed royalties on merchants. In 1631, Khalil *Pasha*summoned Abba Mettaous III (1631–1646) because he

---

[i] *Al-Kafi*, Part three, P. 64. This almost suggests that previous period of Mamluk rule may have been, in comparison, morally lenient and sexually liberal...

[ii] Responsible for the collection of taxes, such as *Jizya*, imposed on *Dhimmis*.

had not paid the usual ordination fees, so the Patriarch borrowed money from a Jew, and the *Archons* committed to raising funds in order to repay the loan. The rulers would resort to any means in order to exact money (from Copts); (for example) in 1672, the Ottoman soldiers slaughtered a loose woman and dumped her body in the Azbakeya lake. Then, the *Wali* of Cairo, unjustly and with animosity, shut down all the Copts' houses adjacent to the area where the body was found. He imposed on the people a penalty of one-thousand piasters [i] as restitution for the dead woman, in exchange for reopening their houses and returning to their livelihoods.

The testimony of *Dhimmis* was void in civil or criminal courts if it involved a Muslim; however, the head of police could still question a *Dhimmi* regarding any subject that was within his purview. The *Dhimmis'* houses of worship were routinely inspected every year. A comprehensive and detailed report was then prepared, specifying the validity of these places, assuring that the buildings were not renovated (implementing the Pact of Omar[ii]), making certain that state approval was secured prior to any building repairs, and that the variety of levied imposts have been collected. Copts could hold funerals and bury their dead only when permission was granted.[123]

In 1562, monk Yuhanna El-Numrusi was beheaded. He had been abducted as a child and sold to a rich Arab, who 'converted' him to Islam. The child's father, Youssef, succeeded to find and sneak him out and took him to St. Paula's desert monastery, where father and son hid and then became monks. At age of 21, Yuhanna announced himself in Cairo in front of a judge who ruled him to be a *murtad* (apostate), and after the approval of the Vizier (Shahin *Pasha*), he was tortured and killed.[124]

During the Sultanate of Soliman I (1520–1566), who succeeded Selim, the *Walis* treated the Copts with greater harshness, harassing and forcing them to leave their own lands. They succeeded in driving out many prominent (Christians), and proceeded to abuse those who remained, by destroying their homes and livelihoods, and the people faced great hardship. In 1582, the Ottoman *Wali*, Hassan *Pasha* Al-Khadem, ordered that Jews wear red, pointed hats (fool's caps), and that Christians wear black hats. The

---

[i] Equivalent to ten golden dinars.
[ii] Whereby *Dhimmis* may keep their houses of worship, but cannot renovate or build new ones.

following year, the new *Wali*, Ibrahim *Pasha*, walked around the cities to observe the people's activities, and upon seeing a great (historical) and luxurious Church building in Al-Mahalla Al-Kubra, with many native (Coptic) priests present, he decided that such a church ought not stand, because he thought it was too great to be in the hands of Copts. So, he ordered that the church be torn down and then built a (Islamic) school called Al-Mostawzeryah in its place.[125]

***

As soon as Sultan Murad III (1574–1595) came to power, he assassinated his brothers in order to secure his position. After his death, his son, Mohammed III, took his place. As per the tradition of the Ottoman Sultans, he, too, killed his brothers to secure his position. He then gave himself to hedonism and left the affairs of the kingdom to the Viziers who ravaged and destroyed (the people).

The *Wali* of Egypt (1597), Mohammed *Pasha* Al-Sharif, ordered that the pointed hats (fool's caps) worn by Jews no longer be red, but black. During his days, the soldiers' revolts multiplied, and they divided the country between themselves, ravaging the earth and destroying crops and lives, and committing acts of highway robbery. So, the *Pasha* assembled the Arab clansmen and their chiefs, and created a great army to fight the deserters. In the course of fighting, they would dump the bodies of the dead in the Nile River.[126]

***

In 1583, the Pope of Rome made fresh attempts[i] to get the Coptic Church to acknowledge his authority. The Coptic Patriarch, Yoannes XIV, summoned a council of bishops at Babylon, to hear the arguments of the Papal Legates and consider their proposals. The deliberations were stormy, for, as usual, the feeling of the whole church, was against any such

---

[i] A previous attempt was at the Florence Council (1431), where the Coptic Church's delegate is said to have arrived too late to join the discussions.

'surrender.' But the personal influence of the aged Patriarch,[i] who longed for peace and was ready to sacrifice his own dignity, prevailed so far upon the council that decrees in conformity with the suggestions of the Papal Legates were drawn up. They were, however, never signed, for in the night the Patriarch died suddenly, and the council broke up in confusion. The government arrested the Papal Legates as foreign spies and threw them into a dungeon. Between them, the richer Copts raised a ransom of five-thousand pieces of gold, which was afterward repaid by the Pope, and the Papal Legates were set free to return to their own country.[127]

In 1597, Patriarch Ghobrial VIII sent (according to Roman historians) two messengers to the Pope of Rome (Clement VIII) asking him, "To bless us with a yearly charitable offering, because we are experiencing severe hardships and troubles because of the many needs of our churches, monasteries, poor and needy, widows, orphans, and those in iron chains imprisoned because of the (*Jizya*) and other reasons…" The Pope responded by sending aid. And out of desperation — both moral and financial — the Coptic Church sent emissaries, in 1597, asking for inclusion under the umbrella of the Roman Catholic Church.[ii]

---

[i] He was most likely actuated by the belief that if he submitted to the Roman Pope on the easy terms demanded, the Copts would secure an efficient protector. In other words, he was driven by the dire situation of the Copts.

[ii] Tagher, P. 199. Tagher claims that this 'unity' with Rome lasted for one-and-a-half centuries. The Coptic Encyclopedia (Vol. Two, P. 610) provides this account: "On January 15, 1595, Clement VIII, in the presence of 24 cardinals, received in audience five representatives of (Ghobrial) Gabriel VIII. In his name, they made a profession of faith (the formula of Gregory XIII) professing obedience to the Pope of Rome and abjuring 'all they held until now which was opposed to the rite of the holy Roman church.' On 28 June, 1597, the representatives of Gabriel VIII returned with ratified documents of reunion (between the two churches) and were granted an audience with the Clement. The documents of this reunion did not grant the Coptic Church sufficient autonomy and demanded of the Coptic Patriarch a promise of obedience to the Pope of Rome. In a letter of October 7, 1602, to Gabriel (who had died on 14 May, 1601) Clement demanded due obedience, 'for the Alexandrian Church of St. Mark was of Petrine origin' and therefore, had to be especially closely tied to Rome. The union of 1595–1597 remained ineffective. Subsequent encounters between the two churches in the 17th century were not successful.

***

During the rule of *Wali* Ahmed *Pasha* Al-Daftardar (in 1616), the plague spread everywhere and all the markets, with the exception of the cerements' markets, were shut down in Misr and Cairo for a period of two months. It also happened that winds drove one of the Frankish ships to the seaport of Damietta where it ran aground. While some drowned, the 80 who remained alive were taken captive. They converted to Islam out of fear of being killed. So, the *Pasha* paraded them over horses and then circumcised them.

During the Sultanate of Osman II (1618–1622), Patriarch (Morcos V) died. In his 'days the Copts experienced hardships, sufferings, troubles, trials, and death as a result of the injustice and despotism of the *Walis*.'[128] After the (Ottoman) Sultan was assassinated by the Janissaries, Murad IV came to power, and the fuddle in the state increased. Then, Abbas Shah, the king of the Persians, attacked Baghdad and captured it by force. He then beheaded all the Ottoman Sultanate soldiers and the high-state executives.

***

During the Sultanate of Ibrahim I (1640–1648), Patriarch (Mettaous III) died. His days saw, 'plagues, soaring prices, ongoing trials, people's money being confiscated, the overreach of soldiers, the increase of troublemakers and rumormongers, the trying of the innocent, the levying of heavy financial penalties, and other forms of extortion.' Then, the Sultan was removed and assassinated, and because his son, Mohammed IV, was seven years old, the Viziers and high-ranking Janissaries ran the affairs of the country, and things continued to deteriorate and destabilize even further.[129]

***

Owing to the terrible oppression and calamities, a number of the Egyptians, and particularly of the Christians, who were always the worst off, had been reduced to slavery. A number of Christian slaves had also been acquired in the constant wars of the Sultans, and these were employed in forced labor for the government. Much excitement was caused in Egypt, in January, 1644, by the daring escape of a number of these Christians. They were employed in shipbuilding at Alexandria, and, wishing to launch 110 newly built vessels, the governor called up all the slaves, to the number of 600, to work, and was compelled to order their chains to be taken off. Instantly, about 150 of them, probably Europeans, sprang together and turned upon the Muslim guards, who did not venture to oppose them. They forced the door of the arsenal, secured arms, marched deliberately into Alexandria. They seized one of the vessels in port and sailed away, without the loss of a man. The rest of the 600 appear to have escaped into the country.[130]

In January, 1649, it was announced all over Egypt, that Christians were forbidden from riding horses, and wearing red coverings or red cloth hats or shoes. When Patriarch Mettaous IV (1660–1675) died, the clergy gathered and went to ask for the Ottoman *Pasha's* permission to bury him. He granted his request after receiving a large sum of money.[131]

***

A 1674 document entitled *The Record of Inspecting Existing Mosques and Churches in the Castle of Candle[i] and the Alleyway of Shenouda Located in Old Misr*, speaks loudly about the meticulous harassment of churches. In it we find written:

By permission of our Lord, the Sheikh of all the Muslim Sheikhs, chief among the scholars, the judge with the revocation and final word, the authoritative resource of all the honorable notables (..) upholder of the Sharia of the Lord of mankind[ii], on whom be the best prayers and abundance of peace (..) to look into the case brought by Sheikh Shams Al-Din Al-Sha'rani, which, in summary, claims that in Old Misr (..), where there are churches adjacent to mosques, the church caretakers have taken most of the stones and rocks of the adjacent mosques, thus vandalizing them, in order to put up their churches (..). After investigation, a mosque was found located between the Christian Church of Saint Barbara and a Jewish synagogue, and the mosque's walls were found to be dwarfed by the walls of the church and the synagogue. (..). Furthermore, another church, known as Al-Muallaqa, is located near a rundown and dilapidated mosque, with only stones and dust inside, while the aforementioned church is fully operational and stands

---

[i] *Qasr Al-Sham,'* located in the remains of the Babylon fortress in Old Cairo.

[ii] In reference to the prophet of Islam.

elegantly built. The Church of Abu Serga was inspected, and a nearby mosque, known as the Mortmain of Ibrahim Al-Nomani, was found, (with its ceiling) about to fall on the inside, and the church wall towering over it. Also inspected, was the Church of Al-Sayedah (the Lady) and a (ruined) mosque was found next to it, and all that could be seen from all the dust was the mosque's minaret and Miḥrāb. The church of Mercurius and the hermitage in the Alleyway of Shenouda were also inspected, and found their doors closed and no mosque near them. At that point, our Lord, the commander, ordered that the doors of all the above-mentioned churches be nailed shut, and it came to pass. This is the report from the scene. This report was written in Old Misr on that date.[132]

This document puts tyranny on display, because the presence of a functioning church beside a neglected or dilapidated mosque does not mean that the church is the reason behind these conditions, or that stones from mosques were used in building churches that were, at any rate, not allowed to be renovated.

In 1683, the Ottoman Grand Vizier, Kara Mustafa *Pasha*, marched with a great army and besieged Vienna, the capital of Austria, capturing all its fortified Citadels and tearing down some of its walls. However, the Kings of Poland, Bologna, Saxe, and Bavaria, came to Austria's aid and defeated the Muslim army after fierce fighting, causing Kara *Pasha* to retreat. News of this retreat enraged the Sultan, who sent one of his cronies to kill Kara *Pasha*, and after beheading him, he sent his decapitated head to Constantinople. Then, the Sultan (Mehmed IV) was ousted, in 1687, by his brother, Khan II, who took his place (ironically, Khan was the only brother who had not been killed by Mehmed). The wars continued in Europe and Asia, but these wars did not distract the men of the Sultanate from installing and deposing *Walis* over Egypt.[133]

***

We now return to a section of *History of the Patriarchs* where events were succinctly recorded, beginning in 1676:

Abba Yoannes XVI (1676–1718) became Patriarch. He was a scribe (land-tax assessor) prior to becoming a monk in Mount Antonius.

Before he became Patriarch, all the church caretakers were workers [craftsmen]. When he became Patriarch, all these positions were transferred to the *Moallem*[i] *Archons*, who fixed what needed patching up, [and they outdid] each other in doing good deeds, showing mercy to the needy, and clothing the poor on every religious feast [..].

Then, prices soared to the point where the poor were forced to eat dead donkeys, horses, and cats. We take refuge in God against those days, when people were laid out on the streets and alleyways, because God had struck the Egyptians with soaring prices and the plague [..].

In 1678, the Ottoman authorities became stricter in dealing with the *Dhimmis*, publicly announcing that Christians had to wear one bell around their necks, while the Jews had to wear two, when entering (public) bathrooms. They were forbidden from wearing finely woven cotton cloth or wool clothes, and Christian women were forbidden from wearing any white garments. In fact, Christians had to wear mostly black clothes.[134]

By the turn of the century, Copts were the most educated ('the least ignorant') and represented the majority of the following trades-goldsmiths, jewelers, shoemakers, smiths, tailors, sculptors, and architects.[ii]

In July of 1701, a group of Muslims filed an official complaint, claiming that some Coptic Christians renovated some of their church buildings. So, the *Pasha* appointed an Agha[iii], along with some architects and *Sharia* judges, to investigate the matter. Upon investigating, they were able to prove that (there were) some churches with recently renovated buildings. However, a group of Mamluks pleaded[iv] with the *Pasha* (to not tear down the churches), so the *Pasha* imposed a severe financial penalty on the Copts. As a result, the Patriarch went to the alleyways of the Christians to collect money for the penalty imposed.[135]

---

[i] *Lit.* teacher, educator, denoting 'erudite,' 'principal,' 'knowledgeable,' or 'doctor.' Used as a title for leading Coptic *Archons*, especially those occupying highlevel state positions: First or highest in rank or importance.

[ii] According to the French diplomat and historian, M. de Maillet; Butcher, V2, P. 288

[iii] Chief officer in the Ottoman system.

[iv] Most-likely they had some Coptic scribes working for them, who pushed them to do so.

In [1707], an individual by the name of Qurra Mohammed *Pasha* became *Wali* over Egypt for five years. He harmed the Christians over church issues, but by God's mercy and help, and through the prayers of the Patriarch, there was no real damage. This was also [thanks to] the presence of the Principal *Archons* taking care of the churches under the supervision of the notables of Misr [..].

In [1708], the Patriarch went to visit the Church of the Resurrection, in Jerusalem, with the *Moallem* Gerges Al-Ṭoukhi, priests, other *Archons*, and lay Christians. They travelled on land, not by sea. They experienced great joy, unmatched by any joy in the world.

This is the first mention, since the Arab invasion, in *History of the Patriarchs*, of a Coptic Patriarch visiting Jerusalem. As for the pilgrimage of the laity, it appears to be the first time since the start of the Frankish wars— but it will also be one of the last for a long time (see below, related to the year, 1753).

In [1711], a factional strife broke out between the soldiers [followers] of two Ṣanjaqs[i], one called Ayoub *Bek*[ii], in Bab Al-Inkeshareya ['Gate of the Janissaries'], and the other, Ghiṭas *Bek*, in Bab Alazb. Markets were shut down and trade ceased for 70 days, while the artillery kept firing [..]. Many of the people's houses were burnt, and the hardship was unbearable. The distress was palpable for everyone, especially the poor, who were forced to drink water from wells, since the roadways were blocked, and water deliverers ceased, because they were unable to draw water from Bulaq (lake) as a result of the many Arabs and enemies [..]. Then God had mercy on the people through the fleeing of Ayoub *Bek* to Roum territories [..], and in [1715], another strife arose in Misr [..], and many were killed [..]. In [1716], a plague ravished Misr.

Most of the days of this Patriarch were filled with 'hardships and compounded problems that almost brought religious rites to a halt, if it were not for God's mercy.'[136]

***

---

[i] Head of an administrative unit, such as district, part of a province, or a governorate.
[ii] A title of Turku-Mongol origin, lower than *Pasha*, denoting chief, lord, or dignitary.

Then, Abba Botros VI (1718–1726) became the 104th Patriarch. He was
from the area surrounding Syut (Assiut). He became a monk in the
Monastery of Abba Pola (Saint Paul), eventually becoming its abbot.

He ordained a bishop for the Jerusalem seat [..] and a metropolitan for
Abyssinia, who traveled, accompanied by the messengers [of the King
of Abyssinia], by sea, from the port of Suez via the city of Jeddah [..].
Then the Patriarch went to and toured the Delta provinces. He desired to
visit the Church of Saint Mark, the evangelist in Alexandria, but due to
strife [among the Ṣanjaqs], he was forced to return to Misr.

A group of [Muslims] [complained against] the *Moallem*, Loṭf Allah, to
the *Wali*, Rajab *Pasha*, accusing him of building the Church of Al-
Malak Mikhail [the Angel Michael] in the south [of Cairo] and the
Church of Abba Mina in Misr [..]. So, a group of prominent people, who
liked *Moallem* Loṭf Allah, went and appeased [Rajab *Pasha*] through the
payment of 40 bags [of money] [..]. However, the devil raised those who
killed [Loṭf Allah] as he was returning home one day [..].

During a power struggle in 1719, the riffraff seized the opportunity to
loot and pillage the people and start fires. This was the start of a series of
disturbances and conflicts that lasted until the arrival of the French
Expedition. The sectarian violence targeted the Copts, especially those of
Upper Egypt, intensifying their distress and imposing excessive financial
penalties that virtually nobody could escape. As a result, jewels were sold
for a fraction of their worth. Even priests, monks, boys, and the poor were
forced to pay these penalties. The Patriarch was compelled to pay the
penalties on behalf of the clergy.[137]

In October of 1723, Agha Mostaḥfezan (head officer of security forces)
went to Cairo and declared publicly to all Christians and Jews that they are
prohibited from going to (public) bathrooms unless they wore bells around
their necks to distinguish between the *Kafir* and the (Muslim) believer. So,
the owners of the public bathrooms (73 in all) held a meeting to discuss this
edict, which caused them considerable financial losses, especially because
the majority of those who frequented these public bathrooms were *Dhimmis*.
They collected a sum of money with which they bribed the Agha.

In 1726, the *Pasha* issued an edict, delivered by Ahmed Agha Lahloubah,
mandating that Jews wear blue fool caps or hats, Christians wear sashes, and
foreigners wear sashes and hats. All these groups were prohibited from

wearing anything with red cloth, or (certain outfits).[i] The (Muslim) subjects were entitled to take away whatever outfits which went against the edict. Also, any foreigner who stayed (without permission?) beyond three days was to be killed, and his blood was lawful.[138]

In 1729, the Sultan issued a *firman* (edict) where it was mentioned that 'some of the monasteries of Old Misr (..) have taken over some of the Muslim (cemetery land), and some have built and renovated tall buildings that stand higher than what was indicated in their original designs, and that they have created new buildings. These buildings are so tall that they overlook the houses of the Nation of Mohammed (Muslims), and (all these things) are disgraceful.' It was later revealed that these allegations were false, and thus, the monasteries were spared from being torn down as intended.[139]

***

Then, Abba Yoannes XVII (1727–1745) became the 105th Patriarch. He was from the area of Mallawi.

In his days, the *Jizya* was raised on Christians and Jews. The [upper class] had to pay 460 half-silver coins, the middle-class, 230, [and the lower class] 115. Bishops, monks, and priests had to pay *Jizya* (*see below). A group of *Bashtalis* would arrive every year from the honorable (Ottoman) Sultanate to collect the *Jizya* [..]. These days were filled with trouble and sadness for the poor, as well as for the crafts owners.

Furthermore, in [1740], prices rose sharply [..] and the people experienced great hardships, particularly the poor Christians. They worried about price increases and the *Jizya* [collected] mercilessly. In those days, there were in Misr some *Archons* who paid for the poor, who were in prison for failing to pay *Jizya* in order to set them free.

(*) From the beginning, the Ottoman government adopted the *Hanafi*[ii] interpretation with regards to the *Jizya*. Thus, considering the *fat'h* of Egypt to have been accomplished by force meant that (the *Jizya*) would vary

---

[i] Impossible to translate names, of Turkish origin, of these outfits, which fell totally out of use.

[ii] One of the four religious Sunni Islamic schools of jurisprudence.

according to the financial situation of the individuals, and that it may increase over time. Any *Dhimmi* would be stopped on the roadway and asked to present a card, indicating that he had paid the *Jizya*.[140]

In 1734, a Sultanate decree was issued to *Wali*, Osman *Pasha*, ordering him to take a census of the Jews and Christians and increase their *Jizya*. It was also decreed that monks were to pay the *Jizya*. 'So the *Pasha* paid close attention to this matter and sent tax collectors, who went around the country and took a census of all the people and began to commit (numerous) acts of tyranny and injustice to the point where the people began to groan, but in vain.'[141]

British anthropologist, Dr. Richard Pococke, came in 1737 and toured Egypt. Most of the Copts, he found, knew how to read and write, but hardly any other class of natives could do so. He mentions that the Turkish Janissaries used to be entrusted with the collection of the *Jizya* from the native Christians; but that now they were even worse off, as a Turk from Constantinople obtained this privilege by heavy bribes to the Sultan, and managed to squeeze even more out of the Copts than the Janissaries could do. Already, in 1733, the *Kashef* of each district had been ordered, in consequence of a *firman* received from the Sultan, to inflict a fine on every Christian or Jew in his district. They were roughly divided into three classes, according to their supposed means of payment. [142]

A report prepared in 1737 reveals that there were one-hundred-and-twenty-thousand *Dhimmis* in Misr who paid the *Jizya* (i.e. excluding women, children, and the elderly), which was estimated to be around two-hundred-thousand *Sharifi* gold pounds.[143]

Then, it was rumored among the people, that Judgment Day was coming on (May 9, 1735), so hedonists took to the gardens to bid the world farewell, while others went to wash in the Nile River as an act of repentance[i], and the affairs of the country came to a grinding halt. When nothing happened on that Friday, the people said that the Sidi Ahmed Al-Badawi, Al-Dessouki and Al-Shafei (popular Islamic 'saintly persons') interceded on the people's behalf before Allah, (thus postponing Judgment Day).

---

[i] Notice the resorting to an action resembling the rite of 'baptism.'

In June of 1736, while 'Osman *Katkhoda*[i] Al-Qazdghali' passed by the entrance of Al-Godareya (alley), the Patriarch of the Melkites was approaching from the opposite direction. *Katakhda's* archer ordered the Patriarch to dismount his donkey, but *Katkhoda* ordered that the Patriarch be beaten. So, he was beaten with clubs, and the monks who accompanied him interposed themselves to receive the beating in the Patriarch's place. Afterward, they picked up the bruised Patriarch (and went on their way).[144]

***

Then, Abba Morcos VII (1745–1769) became the 106th Patriarch. He was from the region of Qlosna.

In [1748], a great strife arose among the soldiers in Misr, and [a number of army commanders] were killed, while some of the [leading] Ṣanjaqs fled to Upper Egypt [..]. After that, the Arab tribe—*Sheikh* Hammam looked after them, made preparations for them, and sent them to the land of the Hijaz in boats from the sublime port of Al-Qoseir.

Then, the Patriarch passed away in the Monastery of Al-Adaweyah [..], after he had suffered countless atrocities, some at the hands [of rulers] and some by the devious and crooked [Coptic] people, and it would take a long time to explain everything [..]. The [funeral] was attended by the metropolitan of Abyssinia and the metropolitan of Upper Egypt[ii], who was chosen [by the Patriarch] out of fear for his good flock to shepherd them [..].

In the days of this Patriarch, 'Ali *Bek* Balaṭ' severely intensified his mistreatment of the Copts, imprisoning many of them, and levying a one-hundred-thousand-riyal penalty. He then dispatched his cronies to collect the money, and they ravaged, destroyed, and did nothing but evil.[145]

In 1753, an edict was issued, from Al-Bab Al-Aali[iii], forbidding Levantine Christians in Misr from entering the foreigners' Catholic churches. Any who entered had to pay the state one-thousand bags (of

---

[i] *Katkhoda*, is a deputy of the *Wali*.

[ii] Apparently, the church deteriorated to the point where only one metropolitan was overseeing the entire Upper Egypt (?)

[iii] The Ottoman 'Sublime Porte,' or the Sultan's governing offices.

money). Ibrahim *Katkhoda* arrested four priests from the monastery of the Catholics, imprisoned them, and took a large sum of money from them.[146]

It then came about that the Copts in Misr requested to go on pilgrimage in Jerusalem. Their leader was the *Moallem* Nayrouz, the scribe of Raḍwan *Katkhoda*, who spoke to *Sheikh* Al-Shabrawi concerning this matter and presented him with a splendid gift. So, the *Sheikh* wrote a *fatwa*[i] indicating that *Dhimmis* should not be prevented from practicing their religious rites. So, they went out in sedan chairs (palanquins) for their women and children, and they brought along Arabs to guard them along the way. After they went out, the matter displeased the Muslims, who denounced what took place. Then *Sheikh* Al-Bakri told *Sheikh* Al-Shabrawi, "O, *Sheikh of Islam*[ii], what is this that you have allowed them to do? Now you have made it legal (accepted habit) for them to go out next year in greater numbers, making for themselves howdah (*hawdaj*) caravans. And then people will speak of the pilgrimage of the Christians like they do about the pilgrimage of Muslims, and this sin will be counted against you on Judgment Day." Then, *Sheikh* Al-Shabrawi resented the situation and gave permission to the commoners to go out against (the Copts on their way to the pilgrimage) and pillage them. Another group, from the students of Al-Azhar, also went out against the Copts, joining forces with the others who had been incited by the *Sheikh*, and they began to stone the Copts and beat them with clubs and whipping rods (used on animals). They also looted their possessions, as well as a nearby church close to Al-Demerdash.[147]

***

Then, Abba Yoannes XVIII (1770–1796) became the 107th Patriarch. Do not ask about how much the Patriarch and his people suffered. Suffice it to say that so severe was the scourge, that it led him to go into hiding to escape the injustice of the rulers and governors. They oppressively burdened the Christians with a heavy yoke, especially by increasing taxes, and we are only mentioning a brief summary of their troubles.

---

[i] A legal opinion or decree handed down by an Islamic religious authoritative scholar.

[ii] Sheikh Al-Islam is the title given to the most senior sheikh of Al-Azhar mosque.

In 1774, a group of (inspectors) were designated to investigate the monasteries, among those was the Monastery of Abba Ruwais[i], based on a complaint from some Muslims. They claimed that the monastery church, which is near the shrine of *Sheikh* Al-Demerdash, had surpassed the limits of a restoration, and instead, was renewed. But upon investigating, it was discovered that the church has remained unchanged for many years.

Then, Ibrahim *Bek* and Mourad *Bek*, the leading Mamluks of Egypt, intended to have a government independent of Al-Bab Al-Ali, the Ottoman State, and they expelled the Vizier. Aware that the Ottoman State will not remain silent, but that it will declare war against them, they began to impose extremely excessive taxes on Egyptians, bordering on robbery and plundering. The Egyptians complained and sought help, but no one gave it. But all the injustice of the Mamluks paled [in comparison] to what the Hassan *Pasha* [the ottoman Sultanate's Vizier] did when he fought and defeated them and marched into Cairo. His soldiers committed unspeakable and blood-curdling acts. They went into the houses of Christians, and besides violating the sanctity of decency and abrogating the natural law of humanity as they mistreated the Christians, they also [took] all their belongings and sold them by orders from the *Pasha* before the people's eyes. O, how many homes and houses were deserted because people were leaving? Among other things, the soldiers arrested the wife of the honorable *Moallem* Ibrahim Al-Gohary, the chief assessor of taxes in Egypt, and forced her to confess to the location of the money and other assets hidden by her husband. So, she told them under compulsion, and they robbed his house [..].

Making matters worse was the [plague] that overtook Egypt [in 1791]. In Cairo alone, about one-thousand people died per day [..]. The plague also infected Ishmael *Bek*, who was made *Wali* by the Grand Vizier[ii], and he died. His replacement also died on the very same day [..]. So, Ibrahim *Bek* and Mourad *Bek* seized the opportunity (*see below), regained power, and went back to their tyranny and began to treat the Christians unjustly, just as they had done before.

---

[i] With urban expansion, this monastery became within Cairo, and is where the Coptic Patriarchate became located since 1968.

[ii] The highest-ranking official in the Ottoman State under the Sultan.

(*) After the death of Ali *Bek* Al-Kabir[i] (in 1773), the power struggle
continued between Mamluk factions and their Amirs. Mamluk Amirs would
go around the country, looting, robbing, stealing, and imposing royalties on
Copts, which forced some of them to flee. The Arab chronicler, Al-Jabarti,
mentions in his accounts (for the month of January, 1786) that Mourad *Bek*—
who was then at the helm of power—went around with a group of his *Kashifs*
(district governors or prefects) and Mamluks, touring the cities and towns in
the Delta, demanding the levied sums of money in addition to the 'Right of
Way' fee. If any town delayed in paying its dues, it was destined to
destruction and looting. He ordered one of his Alexandria *Kashifs* to tear
down churches if the levied sums were not paid, and so he destroyed many
churches.[148] Al-Jabarti also mentions in his chronicles (for the month of
September, 1786) 'that the Commander, Hassan *Pasha*[ii], arrested the
Moallem Waṣef, imprisoning and beating him, to coerce him to pay a certain
sum of money.' Waṣef was one of the well-known overseeing (senior)
scribes who knew the particulars of the (state) revenues and expenditures,
and had a copy of the financial records.[149]

At the behest of Hassan *Pasha*, a public announcement was made,
forbidding Christians from riding ornate animals, telling them not to employ
Muslims, and to abide by their former way of dress, tightening their sashes
and belts. So, the commoners domineered over the Christians, continually
harassing and stoning those who were found not wearing sashes. Hassan
Pasha went farther with his despotism and tyranny (..), to the point where
people moaned, and fear prevailed (..). This hardship afflicted all the
Christians; for they were financially penalized and were demanded to pay
seventy-five-thousand riyals at once. He also took a census of all their homes
and possessions, and decided on a certain sum of money ('rent') that must be
paid to the Sultan's treasury. He then levied another financial penalty of five-

---

[i] Originally called Ali *Bek* Balaṭ, he rose the ranks of Mamluks and taking advantage
of the fact that the Ottomans were preoccupied with their war against Russia, he
succeeded in being decreed as acting *Wali*. He then controlled the country and
prevented new *Walis* from being installed. He even went on (victorious, but very
expensive) wars against the Ottoman State in Yemen and the Levant. Yet, his own
army commander (Mohamed Abul-Dhahab) turned on him, after a *fatwa* by the
Ottoman Grand Mufti, and fought him to death.

[ii] A marine commander, who appears to have been assigned other administrative
responsibilities.

thousand bags (of money). So, life got even harder, and many people sold all their possessions, including their clothes and their children's clothes. He also imposed a new one-dinar *Jizya* on them without differentiation (between the rich and poor), which was on top of the *Jizya* imposed by the *Divân* on each of them. He also surveilled homes and seized any money deposits.[150]

In addition to the old oppressions, new insults were put upon them by Hassan Pasha. It was announced by heralds in the street that no Christian should be permitted to ride any animal at all, or own a single slave. Henceforth, moreover, no Christian or Jew was permitted to bear the name of any prophet or patriarch mentioned in the Old Testament. All those already known by such names were to change them at once. This order was obeyed only so far as their communication with the Muslims was concerned, so that from henceforth, many Copts were known by one name to the Muslims and by another among their fellow Christians.[151]

Hassan *Pasha* Al-Gazaearly left the country (1787) in the hands of Ismael *Bek* and Abedy *Pasha*, commander of the Ottoman army in Egypt. Al-Jabarti writes, "Ismail *Bek* and Abedy *Pasha* arrived at the house of *Sheikh* Al-Bakri for the observance of *Mawlid Al-Nabi*[i]. When they had settled down, the *Pasha* looked toward the Christians' alleyway and inquired about it. He was informed that these were Christians' homes, so he ordered that they be torn down, and that a public announcement be made to that effect. So, (the Christians) sought appeasement, and it was determined that a sum of thirty-five-thousand riyals be paid, seventeen-thousand was to be paid by the Levantines and the remainder was to be paid by the Coptic scribes."[152]

***

This was how the corrupt and tyrannical Ottoman Caliphate ruled Egypt. In addition, it was constantly engaged in wars (against the Persians, Russians, Austrians, Serbs, Bulgarians, Greeks, etc.) and constantly attempting to combat internal plots, intrigues, and revolts. On the other hand, Mamluk Amirs like Ibrahim, Mourad, and others, became increasingly influential in Egypt, but caring about the country's interests only to the extent these affected how much they could exact from its people through any means. They only cared about building their own palaces and buying their

---

[i] The celebration of the birthday of the prophet of Islam.

own Mamluks and female slaves. Traveler James Bruce (who visited Egypt in 1768 and 1773) says, "There cannot exist on the face of the earth a more cruel, unjust, aggressive, and tyrannical government than the government of those evil men." (..). Adding to the sum total of all these atrocities were the Arabs who competed against everyone with their warring, aggression and corruption.

Many similarities can be observed between the Mamluk State and the Ottoman State: both were originally feudal 'militarily theocratic' states, operating under the banner of Sunni Islam. [153] This also explains the competition and then the alliance between the Ottomans and the Mamluks during the point of their joint rule over Egypt.

Even though all Egyptians suffered and paid a price, nonetheless, it was the Copts who, as *Kuffar* were always on the lowest and most vulnerable rung of society, paid an exponentially higher price, because they faced the four-pronged attacks of the Ottomans, Mamluks, Arabs, and the riffraff, and they were defenseless against their barbaric subjugation.

On the other hand, (Muslim) Egyptians were content with the fact that the Ottoman Sultan was 'Caliph of the Muslims, protector of Islam against the *Kuffar* in the west and against the *Shia*[i] in the east.'[154]

***

It is worth noting that 136 Viziers (*Walis*) ruled Egypt between the years of 1517 and 1805. That represents on average one new *Wali* every 25 months, leaving enough time for each of them to plunder and create wealth.

Finally, as the 18th century was drawing to a close, Egypt and the Ottoman State entered a new phase, as Napoleon came knocking on the door.

---

[i] One of the two main branches of Islam, followed especially in modern day Iran, that rejects the first three Sunni caliphs and regards Ali, the fourth caliph, as Muhammad's first true successor.

Bonaparte Knocks at the Door

As the circumstances in Egypt during the bloody 'Ottoman's Paradise' had reached an ultimate low, someone was getting ready to knock on Egypt's door.

The French State after the Revolution expanded its influence at the hands of its army commander, Bonaparte, especially following his victorious Italian campaign. Since he never ceased to devise strategies to undermine England, his last standing and hostile enemy, he plotted to supplant their dominion over the Indian kingdom. To accomplish his goal, he decided that it was necessary to make Egypt the headquarters of his military movements and political maneuvers, by removing it from the grip of the Mamluks.

Bonaparte went out in a fleet of 550 ships, in addition to an army made up of twenty-eight-thousand soldiers and horsemen, seventeen-thousand assisting crew, 40 choice commanders, 160 engineers, city planners, chemists, and physicists. He also carried a printing-press capable of printing in Arabic and French, and brought scribes, translators, physicians, surgeons, ophthalmologists, and laborers of all sorts: diggers, etchers, etc.

On the night of July 2nd, 1798, Bonaparte and his army arrived in Abu Qir.[i] By morning, he made it to Alexandria, where he met the prominent people of the coastal city.

He wrote a statement that was to be announced in Arabic to the people wherever his army marched. This statement was intended to comfort and reassure them, and it began with, "In the name of Allah, the compassionate, the merciful, there is no deity but Allah, who has no son and has no partner. From the French, based on (in the name of) freedom and equality, General of the French Army, Bonaparte." He then informs the people of Egypt about the reasons for his expedition, which was to destroy the unjust Mamluks. He

---

[i] A port at the outskirts of Alexandria, about 20 km to its east.

continued, "I worship Allah, respect his prophet and the great Quran more than the Mamluks." He then announces the principles of the French Revolution, "All people are equal before God, and nothing differentiates them but their wisdom, virtues, and knowledge." Assuring everyone about his intentions, he says, "O, *Sheikhs*, judges, *Imams*, Çorbaçis[i], and prominent people of the country, tell your countrymen that the French are also faithful Muslims, evidenced by their attack on Great Rome and the destruction of the Pope's seat (..). Also, they have always been warm and devoted to his highness, the Ottoman Sultan, and antagonistic to his enemies." Finally, he warns against supporting the Mamluks and stressed the need to remain calm.[ii]

Mourad *Bek*, then leader of the Mamluks, began to prepare his army to fight the French. The (Islamic) scholars and *Sheikhs* of the poor [iii] Ahmadiyya, Rifaiyyah, Ibraheemiyya, Qadriya, and others, recited the *Dhikrs*[iv] at Al-Azhar, while the children (students in Muslim schools) loudly proclaimed, "O Gentle One."[v] The poor (Sufis) also went out with drums, horns, and banners, screaming, yelling, and loudly reciting different *Dhikrs*. Then, Al-Sayed[vi] Omar Makram, head of the *Ashraf* (decedents of the prophet), went up the mountain Citadel, and brought down with him the prophet's flag[vii]. He raised it, surrounded by thousands of people holding clubs and sticks, cheering and crying out *Takbīr* ('Allahu Akbar'). The scholars and *Sheikhs* sat in Bulaq, Cairo, praying and imploring Allah to

---

[i] *Lit.* 'soup maker' (Turkish) but refers to some notable descendants of Mamluks.

[ii] Notice how far Napoleon goes in covering himself with an Islamic cloak in order to assure the success of his campaign; however, this is all in vain, as the following events will demonstrate.

[iii] Sufi groups.

[iv] A form of devotion, associated chiefly with Sufism, in which the worshiper is absorbed in the rhythmic repetition of the name of Allah or His attributes.

[v] One of the names of Allah in Islam, but is also a statement that is usually spoken in fear, attempting to persuade Allah to forestall seemingly impending trouble.

[vi] *Lit.* Sayed means master, but in certain religious context is attributed to 'Ashraf' (noble ones), or descendants of the prophet.

[vii] The Holy Banner, or Sacred Standard, said to be the banner of Muhammad himself, or at least, to originate from his era. The origin of the Ottoman's acquisition of the relic (which is currently kept in the Topkapi Museum, Istanbul) is disputed. Nor is it clear why this relic was in Egypt and not in the Ottoman capital. In any case, it was taken out in major battles as a token seeking heavenly favor and victory.

grant victory. Then, Ibrahim *Bek* sent to the Arabs (Bedouins) near Misr, requesting that they take the front, near Shubra (north of Cairo). He also rounded up the foreigners in Misr and Cairo and imprisoned them while their homes were searched, fearing that they might have weapons in their possession. They also searched all the homes of the Levantines, Copts, and Roum (Melkites), as well as all the churches and monasteries. The commoners were agitated, wanting that all Christians and Jews to be killed, but they were prevented by the ruler.

After barely an hour-long battle against the French near Shubra Khit[i] (on July 13th), Mourad *Bek* and his army fled in retreat. Then Bonaparte delivered his famous speech to his soldiers near the foot of the Pyramids ('*Forty Centuries...*' [ii]). A second short battle took place near Imbaba on July 21st, where he defeated Mourad, who then fled to Upper Egypt. Bonaparte marched into Cairo on July 24th.

He then met with *Sheiks* to manage the country's affairs. He ordered that jobs be given to those with merit. But they urged that one of the Mamluks be appointed *Wali* of the police, going against Bonaparte's suggestion, "...because Egypt's riffraff are only afraid of and can only be controlled by the Turks."

On August 1st, the French fleet was destroyed in Abu Qir at the hands of the British Rear-Admiral (Sir Horatio) Nelson. Thus, the French had no means to access reinforcements and had to be self-reliant. In mid-August, 'the Great Sultan Bonaparte' celebrated his 29th birthday, in his new headquarters, the palace of Al-Alfi *Bek* in Azbakeya.[155]

***

Bonaparte began implementing procedures to organize Egypt's affairs, most of which angered the populace who had been used to a different way of life for centuries. For example, he created or expanded roads in the cities, removed alleyway doors, and lit the streets, alleyways, and markets with lanterns. He also implemented general hygienic regulations relating to public cleanliness, fighting epidemics, and burying the dead. He regulated the issuing of permits for shops and private property. He then established a

---

[i] Town on the way from Alexandria, about 140 km north of Cairo.

[ii] "From the heights of these pyramids, 40 centuries look down on us."

Divân, called 'The Judiciary Court,' to arbitrate general trade disputes, inheritance cases, and lawsuits. For its functioning, he instituted principles and rules for arbitration, installed twelve members, both Muslims and Copts, and placed *Moallem* Malaṭy, a Copt, as its head. He also established *Divâns* in the provinces and a General *Divân* in Misr made up of people's representatives from all over the country, chiefly responsible for looking into the country's affairs and regulating building, property, and shop taxes.

Bonaparte also founded the Scientific Institute of Egypt and participated in its operation. He also founded hospitals in Rawda, Alexandria, Rshîd, and Damietta. He established two newspapers, one in French and the other in Arabic, and factories to make weapons, paper, textiles, and other items that the country needed. The house of Hassan Kashef was turned into a public library. 'They accomplished all these great works in a short period of time with astonishing enthusiasm.'

***

What was the situation of the Copts, as seen by Bonaparte, according to French sources[156]?

In his letter (No. 3872) dated December 7th, 1798, to *Moallem* Girgis El-Gohary[i], Napoleon says: "I received, citizen, the letter that the Coptic nation wrote to me. I will always be pleased to protect it. Henceforth, [the Coptic nation] will no longer be despised; when conditions permit, which I expect not to be far away, I will give it the right to publicly practice worship, as is common in Europe, between followers of every belief. I will severely punish the villages where Copts were assassinated during rebellions. From today, you can announce to them that I allow them to carry weapons, ride mules or horses, wear turbans and wear clothes the way they like (..)."

Answering a message that El-Gohary appears to have addressed to him, Napoleon only promised to give Copts their worship rights, 'when conditions permit,' not to upset the Muslim population, given that his most important goal is the success of the expedition, the stability of the government, and the establishment of security.

---

[i] *Correspondance générale.* Gohary was appointed by Napoleon on July 30th, 1798, as General Intendant of Taxes on Egypt (see Letter No. 2698). A special translator (M. Bracevich) was assigned to him (Letter 3747).

In the same letter, Napoleon adds: "If every day is marked by my favors, if I have to restore to the Coptic nation the dignity of rights inseparable from humans, which it had lost; I have the right, no doubt, to demand individuals who compose (the Coptic nation) a great deal of zeal and fidelity to the service of the (French) Republic." He finds fault with the Copts' attitude toward the French Expedition compared to other Egyptians: "(..) I cannot hide from you that I, in fact, complain of the lack of enthusiasm shown by many (Copts). When the *Sheikhs* come every day to reveal to me the treasures of the Mamluks, then how are those [Coptic scribes], who were their chief agents[i], doing nothing to help me discover them?"

Napoleon continued to impose special and additional taxes on the Copts as a group, as is evident, for example, from the letter 2753 dated August 3rd, 1798, to Gohary, asking him to instruct *Moallems* Malati, Anfourni, Hanin, and Faudus[ii] to, "Collect the amount I requested from the Coptic nation. I note with regret that there are still 50-thousand talaris[iii] in arrears; and I want this to be deposited within five days in the army treasury."

In letter no. 3294, dated September 21st to Poussielgue, the superintendent of administrative and financial affairs of the army (and Egypt), he recalls the arrears from various merchant groups, and from the Copts (1,000 talaris). In another situation, Napoleon asked that certain loans be requested from various professional groups (like silk traders), including 150,000 francs from the 'Coptic Intendants.' These loans, however, were made against a signed document, with preset payment date.

It is worth noting that Napoleon may not even have cancelled the *Jizya* imposed on the Copts. The summary of the state budget by the French

---

[i] Administrating the Mamluks' affairs being usually assigned to Coptic scribes.

[ii] It appears from these names that in his function as the 'General Intendant of Egypt,' Gohary was assisted by some Frenchmen, in addition to the Coptic scribes; all being called '*Moallem.*'

[iii] A silver coin from Venice, the use of which was widespread at the time, and was equal to 5.28 French francs.

administration shows a special item 'taxes on non-Muslims' in addition to land taxes, trade, industry, and customs[i].

Napoleon did not hesitate to describe the Copts inappropriately in one of his letters. The governor of Sharqiyah (eastern Delta) Province, General Raynier, complained about certain actions of the Coptic tax assessor in the province, called Faltheos. Napoleon replied (letter 3130, September 10th, 1798): "I informed the General Intendant of taxes (Gohary) that you were not satisfied at all with the Coptic (tax assessors/scribes). They are mischievous people, and hated in the country, but they must be treated considerately, because they are the ones who hold in their hands the entire administration of the country. I have obtained from them huge records about the amount of taxes."

Indeed, the value of the Copts' competence was indispensable, as seen in Napoleon's letter (No. 2875) to Poussielgue, instructing him to appoint a Coptic Intendant, accompanied by a French agent (assistant) in each of the provinces of Beni-Souef and Fayoum. In the same day, he ordered (Letter 2876) to review the names of Coptic Intendants and French agents in the various provinces of the country.

Egyptians were perplexed by certain acts by the French that they had not seen from invaders for a long time, if ever. Systematically paying, against a receipt, for materials needed by the army, rather than simply expropriating, was unheard of. When three (Turkish) women were found killed one night, an investigation was promptly conducted, and two French soldiers who confessed the crime were condemned to death.[157] Fairness and rule of (just) laws were new ideas. In dealing with the *Divân*, Bonaparte often used a pedagogic approach to win over its members to his policies and actions. Once he told them, "The *Divân* and the people of Egypt should, hence, see, in this conduct, a particular proof of the sentiments that nourish my heart for their happiness and prosperity; and if the Nile is the largest river of the Orient, the Egyptian people, under my government, should be the first among all peoples."[158]

At the same time, Bonaparte keenly maintained his 'Islamic policies' (to win over the people's hearts and minds) by respecting and observing

---

[i] An amount of 88,504 out of a total 16,499,935 Francs, as reported in the *Correspondence*, P. 1149.

(Islamic) religious festivals, such as *Mawlid Al-Nabi* and Ramadan celebrations. He also transferred the religious jobs from the Ottomans to the Egyptian *Sheikhs*. He did not hesitate to commence his letters addressed to the *Divân* or to regional leaders with the Islamic *Shihada*.[i] He was careful to prevent the 'provocation' of Muslims as a result of non-Muslims attaining some of their civil rights. When some non-Muslims freed themselves from some of the demeaning shackles that the Muslims considered to be essential conditions for Islam to remain supreme, Bonaparte realized that this freedom would offend Muslim sentiments. He wrote in his diaries, 'It is useless to display deep respect for the Islamic religion if we are going to allow Copt, Roum, and Western Christians to enjoy a modicum of freedom that elevates their status as compared to the past. So, I have desired that they be more submissive to and respectful of anything relating to Islam or Muslims, as they had been in the past.' Al-Jabarti substantiates this, when he records in his chronicle (for the month of February, 1799), 'Levantine Christians stopped wearing white hats, and colored cashmere shawls[ii], because they were prevented by the French. (The French) also publicly announced, on the first of Ramadan, that Christians must respect the customs in dealing with Muslims, as they had done in the past. They were forbidden from publicly eating, drinking, or smoking in the markets (during Ramadan) ...'[159]

According to *La Description de l'Égypte*, the monumental work accomplished by the French Expedition, Egypt's population was then 2.5 million, with Copts representing 15–20%. But as the census was performed for 'fiscal' reasons (counting adults), the real population is believed to have been about four million.[160]

***

We now return to observing the conditions from the perspective of the chronicles of the *History of the Patriarchs*,

---

[i] In a message to the *Divân* (*Correspondance*, L. 4633, of 21st July, 1799) he mentioned that some warships that threaten Alexandria have Russians onboard, "...who hate nothing more than people who believe in one God, since they, according to their lies, believe in three Gods! But they will soon realize that it is not the number of Gods that matter!"

[ii] Something that they could not have done before.

Then, Abba Morcos VIII (1796–1809) became the 108th Patriarch, after having been a monk in the Monastery of Saint Antonius. He was contemporaneous with the French Expedition and the arrival of Mohammed Ali.

This [Patriarch] witnessed some of the troubles that plagued his predecessor, and he shared with the believers the hardships of that ill-fated generation. The Patriarch experienced gut-wrenching sorrow, hearing and seeing all the adversities that have burdened the backs of Christians. Adding to the cruelty and bitterness was the occupation of the country by Napoleon Bonaparte's soldiers [in 1798], because as soon as the soldiers set foot in Abu Qir and Alexandria, the [Muslim] riffraff in Cairo began to embitter the Christians. This happened despite [efforts] by their Amirs, who were telling the people that Christians were subjects of the state, and therefore, to dishonor them was to dishonor the state itself. However, that did not deter the mobs, nor did they fear Bonaparte and his aggressive soldiers.

When the [French] fought and defeated the Mamluks, taking control of Cairo, the Christians thought that things had settled down. However, most of the *Sheiks* of the Al-Azhar Mosque gathered there and sent [those] who would cry in the markets, "Let all Muslims go to Al-Azhar Mosque, for today is the day of *Jihad;* to war against the *Kuffar* and take revenge." At the sound of these words, the city erupted, and Muslims shut down their shops, took their weapons, and gathered at Al-Azhar Mosque (*see below). They then went around looting the homes of Christians, irrespective of race, killing whomever they came across on the roadways, be it a man, woman, child, or senior. Things were not better in Upper Egypt, which had become a sanctuary for every rebel and criminal, because when the Mamluks fled southward, they ravaged the people with injustice and looted the Christian's money.

(*) The General *Divân* of Egypt assembled in October and elected *Sheikh* Al-Sharqawi as their president. They also assigned a group to undertake a census, but when the people found out, they were enraged. So, a great crowd gathered around a man called Al-Sayed Badr with his Al-Husseiniya riffraff, and alleyway gangs, who exclaimed, "Allah grant victory to the religion of Islam." The mob then went to the judge's house and stoned him, because he did not go along with them. Many of those commoners and rabble assembled in Al-Azhar Mosque; some French cavalry were killed, and barricades were set up in Cairo. No one from the inhabitants of Old Cairo (Misr) or Bulaq participated in these events. When the French soldiers came out to respond, the Mahgrebis fought them. The commoners went out in a destructive frenzy. They exceeded in perversion, taking women and girls captive and looting the homes of Roum and Levantine Christians, as well as the nearby Muslims homes. Bonaparte awaited the response of the *Sheikhs* to his request to (stop) the masses, but they gave him no response. So, in the afternoon of that day, he ordered the firing of his artillery into the heart of Cairo, bringing the sedition (Cairo's 'first uprising') to an end. The *Sheikhs* then sent fliers to the people in all the provinces, urging them to disregard the words of the corrupters, asking Allah to damn whoever reawakens the sedition.[161]

The Christians had no sooner thought they survived this disaster, than to find themselves confronted with a harsher one. This is because when the treaty[i] between the French commander, Kleber, and Al-Ṣadr Al-Azam, [Grand Vizier, or Prime Minister of the Ottoman State], was not honored, by orders from the Ottoman State, the two sides began to fight each other in Al-Matareya[ii]. Meanwhile, having seen the French soldiers leave Cairo, Muslims seized the opportunity and rose up against the Christians.

Then, Naṣif *Pasha*, one of the Ottoman army commanders, came to the city with his Mamluks and publicly announced defeating the 'Franks.' He then ordered the killing of the remaining Christians, so the people proceeded to butcher them without making distinctions between Copts, Syriacs, or Foreigners. When Osman *Bek*, one of the Turkish officers, became aware of the situation, he approached Naṣif *Pasha* and said to him, "It is not just to shed the blood of the state's subjects, because this violates the [Sultan's] sublime will." So, the *Pasha* gave orders to the Muslims to stop the killing.

---

[i] That put in place the conditions for the withdrawal of the French Army from Egypt.

[ii] A district, north of Cairo. Its name is thought to come from '*mater*' which means 'mother' in Latin, or *mitera* (μητέρα) in Greek, in reference to the passage of Mary (and the Holy Family), and the related presence of the 'tree of the Virgin Mary' in this district. The name does not seem to be rooted in Coptic (where 'mother' is μααυ or *maau)*. It is close to the area whose name is related to the 'House of Re' (or Raa), the Sun God; Heliopolis.

Bonaparte had left secretly, returning to France (August 22nd, 1799), because of developments in the affairs of France and Europe, leaving Kleber in charge with the army only half of its original size, and insufficient equipment. Under pressure from the Ottomans and the British, a treaty was agreed upon for the withdrawal of the French army; however, the treaty was not honored. After the (*Wali*) *Pasha* fought the French (March, 1800), Naṣif *Pasha* told the people, "Kill the Christians and wage a *Jihad* against them." Upon hearing these words, the commoners erupted and cheered, and in a haste, began killing any Christians they encountered, whether Coptic, Levantine, or otherwise. A faction went to the houses in the Alleyway of Christians, situated in the area of Bein Al-Sourein and Bab Al-Shariyah, and the area of Al-Muski, and began to break into their homes, killing men, women, and children, looting and taking people captive (..). Thus, the Christians became terrified, and each person gathered as many French soldiers and Roum as they could [seeking their protection]. So, a battle broke out between both sides, and the Christians fought and fired rifles, while the other side fired from below, broke into homes (jumping over their walls) until the following day (..). Osman *Katkhoda* stayed in (the adjacent district of) Al-Gamaliya, and whoever arrested a Christian, Jew, or Frenchman, would deliver that person to Osman *Bek* for a *Baksheesh*[i] (..).

A Maghrebi man came along, attracting a group of Maghrebis, and they did evil acts of looting, killing, and taking people captive. He also spied on the homes of French people and Christians. He broke into their homes with mobs of commoners and lowlifes, killing everyone in sight, looting, imprisoning women, and stealing whatever they had on them. They also beheaded children and young girls (..). A man, named *Haj* Mustafa Al-Bashtili, rose up and gathered mobs of criminals and riffraff from Al-Sabtiah, and marched toward the French camp located on the Saḥel (riverbank) of Boulaq and attacked it. They killed any of the Frenchmen they encountered, pillaged the camp, and went back to barricade around Boulaq. There, they mistreated all the residents, whether Copts or Levantines, killing and looting, leading to extremely trying circumstances for everyone (..). (The Ottoman *Pasha* fled from Misr, while Kleber attempted to gain the upper hand, and the people barricaded themselves. As for the prominent Copts, such as Gerges Al-Gowhary, Falthaos, and Malaty, they requested security from

---

[i] A tip, gratuity, perquisite.

(prominent) Muslims, because they had been entrapped (by the mobs) in their homes, which were located amidst Muslim homes. So, they provided for their safety and then [the prominent Copts] went to meet the *Pasha*, *Katkhoda*, and Amirs, and provided them with money and basic needs.

As for *Moallem* Yaqob, he shut himself in his house in Al-Darb Al-Wase', in Al-Rowaiei area, with many weapons and soldiers. He prepared a fortified position in the citadel, which he had constructed after the first incident, for Hassan *Bek* Al-Gadawi mostly fought against him, calling for *Jihad* daily in Arabic and Turkish. After several confrontations, a truce was reached between Kleber and the *Sheikhs*, but the Janissaries and the Turks refused to reconcile, so the French attacked the city and a new truce was agreed to with the *Sheiks*.[162]

(See below regarding *Moallem* Yaqob).

***

The last hardship experienced in the days of the Abba [Patriarch, Morcos VIII] was the dismissal of [Christians] employed in the government *Divâns*. This was because when General Menou[i] took charge of the French army after the assassination of Kleber, he converted to Islam and called himself Abdullah [..]. In that time, the Cairo *Divân* was made up of Copts [and Muslims], so the [Copts] were dismissed and the [Muslims] were assigned to exact the *Kharaj*.

All in all, the French stayed in Egypt for three years, and the commoners called them the 'Francis' [or al-Franj/al-Frang].

After the rest of the French army left Egypt (September, 1801, including Abdullah Menou, who returned to France and attained several positions), the Ottoman State regained power. So, the *Wali*, Mohammed *Pasha*, treated the people with greater harshness, terrorizing them, increasing killings, crucifixions, burnings, and increasing the penalties and imposts. He surveilled the town notables without distinction between Copt and Muslim, for to him they were one and the same prey. He ordered that three prominent Copts be arrested, and those were the *Moallem* Antoun Abu Taqeyah, *Moallem* Ibrahim Zidan, and *Moallem* Abdullah Barakat. He then killed

---

[i] Jacques-François de Menou, baron de Boussay.

them, placed an official seal on their houses and possessions, and moved everything to the house of Al-Daftardar[i] to be sold in an auction. The dominance of the Mamluks in Upper Egypt became even stronger, and many from Al-Hawwara[ii] and Arab (Bedouin) tribes joined them, taking fortified positions at Hou (Ha'w), at the foot of the mountain (near Nag Hammadi[iii]). Then, they demanded that the *Wali* give them control over the area from Assiut to the end of Upper Egypt in order to collect its *Kharaj*, and the Ottomans were unable to prevent them. Chaos ensued as a result of the repeated attacks by the (Mamluk) Amirs, and the Sultanate soldiers' abuse and excessive killing, looting, ravaging, and obscenity. The Arabs (Bedouins) also committed acts of looting and killing. The Mamluks and their allies attacked the Ottoman soldiers in Minya and conquered it by force. They then proceeded to burn and destroy the city, killing many people by the edge of the sword.[163]

Some researchers claim that the Copts were relieved from paying the *Jizya* for the three-year duration of the French Expedition against Egypt. However, after the French left, the *Jizya* was collected retroactively and the people had to pay the *Jizya* of three years in one installment.[164] On the other hand, as mentioned earlier, sources from the French Campaign reveal that Napoleon did not do away with the *Jizya*, as the balance sheet of the state included a section entitled *Taxes from non-Muslims*.

The Ottoman soldiers rose up in Cairo because their salaries had not been paid, since there was no money in the treasury. So, *Wali* Mohammed *Pasha* was removed, and his deputy, Ṭaher *Pasha*, took his place. Immediately, he began tightening the noose on those with financial means and levied a 50-bag penalty on Copts. Then, he imprisoned a group of Coptic scribes, killed many of the prominent Copts and Levantines, and robbed several houses. He was then killed by the Janissaries,[iv] leading to the corruption of the land by

---

[i] The most senior position in the Treasury in the Ottoman system.

[ii] Hawwara, or Houara; a tribe spread across North Africa, likely of Berber (Amazigh) origin.

[iii] Town situated 80 km north of Luxor.

[iv] In the Turkish Ottoman language, *yeñiçeri* means "new soldiers" or "new army." They were an infantry army division who formed their own special order. They were the strongest and most influential Ottoman army division. Usually made up of boys and young men taken captive in war, they were reared according to the teachings of

the Arnaouts (Albanians). Then appeared their rising star, 'Mohammed Ali,' (a colonel in the Ottoman army), and the Amirs and men of prominence sought him. Then, the new *Wali*, Ali *Pasha* Al-Ṭaraboulsi, arrived, and he was ill-mannered, tyrannical, obstinate, arrogant, and narcissistic. The (Mamluk), Al-Alfy *Bek*, returned from London after having spent a year there (where he befriended the British forces that forced the French to leave Egypt), and the *Wali* gave orders to have him killed. In order to pay back the unpaid salaries of Albanian soldiers, the Amirs imposed a two-hundred-thousand-riyal penalty on the Copts of Misr; of which fifty-thousand riyals had to be paid by the *Moallem* Ghali, Al-Alfy's scribe, and thirty-thousand riyals from the estate of the *Moallem* Boqtor, who was the scribe of Al-Bardisi. The Albanians became more extreme in their killing, looting, and raping. Then, Al-Ṭaraboulsi *Pasha* was murdered, and Ahmed Khorshid took his place. He immediately imposed a financial penalty of five-thousand bags[i] of silver (coins) in one installment on the people of Misr and Cairo, with 1500 being the responsibility of the prominent Copts. Then, the vanguard of the Mamluks and Arabs arrived from Upper Egypt, but the soldiers of Mohammed Ali fought and defeated them. A messenger arrived from the Sultanate palace, giving Mohammed Ali Jeddah's governorship, but he refrained from travel. A group of *Sheikhs* and commoners assembled at the judge's house, exclaiming, "O exalted Lord, destroy the Ottomans," and they also gave written requests with the demands of their people.[165]

***

The worst sufferers from the French Expedition were, as might be expected, the Copts. It is true that, in spite of their 'profession of Islam,' the French soon realized the necessity of employing the Copts for offices of trust, and that they were permitted an equality with the Muslims, which filled the latter with profound disgust (the historian, Al-Jabbarti, cannot contain his wrath when he speaks of their being allowed to ride horses and to bear arms,

---

Islam, in a way like the Mamluks but not considered as slaves. Then the Ottomans began to recruit Christian war captives on a regular basis according to the '*Devşirme*' method of recruitment to add new members to their numbers every year.

[i] One bag contains 500 silver piasters (*Kuruş*), the equivalent of five golden lire (livres, pounds). Hence, the total would amount to an astronomical sum of twenty-five-thousand golden pounds.

like the Muslims), but, in the struggles for the possession of Cairo which took place at the beginning of the end, and in the revolt which broke out against the French during the occupation, Copts were always the first to suffer; and by the end of the time, their quarter was plundered and ruined beyond repair.

After the French left, in particular, the unfortunate Copts suffered horribly. Turkish troops were quartered upon them, plundered and outraged them at their leisure. Three of the principal Copts were put to death by the *Pasha*, probably because they had assisted the French against the Turks, since no reason is stated. All their property was confiscated, and a little later, *Moallem* Malati, the Copt who had filled the office of judge under the French, was also beheaded. All those who could took flight from Cairo and went into hiding. Again, and again, enormous sums were demanded from the half-ruined community as fines or ransom.[166]

Hence, as usual, the Copts paid the price of the French's coming and that of their departure; the price of the return of Ottoman butchers and that of the Mamluki vandals.

However, the people's animosity intensified against the Ottomans because of the killing and looting campaigns that they initiated, to the point where the Al-Azhar *Sheikhs* welcomed (October, 1802) Bonaparte's designated ambassador, *Monsieur* Sébastiani[i]. They voiced their desire to see the return of the French rule once more. In his report to his government, Sébastiani expressed his surprise at the courage shown by the *Sheikhs* in verbalizing such desires.

As Al-Jabarti observes, it appears that a new understanding of justice began seeping into the minds of Egyptians: 'For the French who disregard religion call for freedom and equality, and they were more just than the Muslim Ottoman rulers.' With the exception of times of war and uprisings, Al-Jabarti is astonished (in *Ajaib Al-Athar*) at the fairness of the French when it comes to daily dealings, their cash payments for any goods or services acquired, and their opposition to merchants having monopolies over products. He fondly recounts the justice shown by the French authorities during the trial of Suleiman Al-Halabi, who assassinated General Kléber, "In contrast to the actions of the riffraff soldiers, which we witnessed, who claim

---

[i] Horace François Sébastiani, was the French Consulate's emissary to The Levant, notably drafting plans to re-conquer Ottoman Egypt.

to be Muslims and *Mojahedin*, only to kill and compete with one another to destroy humanity at the whims of their animal lusts."

The hardships furnished the elements for a national awakening, gradually dispelling the myth of a religion that unites all Egyptians and Ottomans.[167]

***

While Al-Azhar *Sheikhs* were ready to have Egypt come under the rule of the French once again for her deliverance, the *Moallem*, Yaqob, was proposing a different vision: the independence of Egypt as a homeland for Egyptians...

Without recounting the controversial story of the *Moallem* (sometimes referred to as *General*) Yaqob, a portrait of this time period will remain incomplete. In Egypt's 'official' history, he has been vilified and presented as a traitor. But there is another side to the story, and none is better than Mohammed Shafiq Ghorbal, dean of the modern Egyptian historians, to turn to, in order to get a summary of his important and unique study on Yaqob, which he published in 1932[i]:

***

Any accurate history of Egypt shows no evidence of any forethought or attempt to gain national independence. This is true whether examining the positions of the commoners, their leaders, or opinion-makers. Egyptian history speaks of only one Egyptian during that time who preferred to not think of the French occupation as an unfortunate period that ought to be done away with in order to return to what was before it. Rather, he saw it as commencing a new life of an 'Egypt for the Egyptians,' by ending Ottoman subordination and breaking the Mamluks' power. That Egyptian is the *Moallem* Yaqob Ḥanna.

I do not wish to exaggerate by claiming that Yaqob fully understood all the possibilities involved in destroying the existing systems and the rule of a

---

[i] *Al-General Yaqob wal Faris Lascaris – Mashrou' Istiqlal Misr fi 1801* ('General Yaqob and Knight Lascaris – Project for Egypt's Independence in 1801'), by Dr. Mohamed Shafik Ghorbal, Ed. Dar al-Shorouk 2009, pp 17-39.

foreign nation over Egypt. Neither do I claim that he was transformed, during the few short months that he spent mingling with the French, from a tax collector, who was raised and reared in one of the houses of the Mamluk Amirs in the second half of the eighth century, to a preacher of nationalistic movements that became known in the 19th century West. Instead, I see Yaqob, even after associating with the French, retaining some of the attributes of tax collectors and administrators from among his kin at that time. Al-Jabarti mentions that Yaqob supported the French rule during Cairo's second uprising, "While the other leading Copts, including their most prominent of all, Gerges Al-Gowhary, supported the [anti-French] seditionists, by providing them with money and covering their needs, not out of support for the movement per se, but out of fear of losing their lives." But Yaqob, as Al-Jabarti records, "Shut himself in his house in Al-Darb Al-Wase', in Al-Rowaiei area, with many weapons and soldiers. He took a fortified position in the citadel which he had constructed after the first incident [meaning the first uprising in the days of Bonaparte], for Hassan *Bek* Al-Gadawi mostly fought against him."

None of [the writings of] Al-Jabarti or others mention that Yaqob travelled and followed the French army back to France in 1801, when the French occupation was over, for the sake of a serious project: to secure the foreign states' recognition of Egypt's independence.

However, I found documents pertaining to this project in the archives of the British and French Ministries of Foreign Affairs, after I had almost lost hope of finding a single instance of thought, by an Egyptian or non-Egyptian, about resolving the 'Egyptian Question' through the recognition of Egypt's independence. These are the four documents: the first was written in English by Captain Edmonds, to the First Lord of the British Navy, written from the Island of Menorca on October 4th, 1801, which includes discussions with Yaqob on the way to France. The second is a draft of a memorandum regarding Egypt's independence, written in French and appended to the aforementioned letter, written by Knight Lascaris. The third is a letter from Lascaris (signed by Nemr *Effendi*) to France's First Consul [Bonaparte, who assumed that role in November, 1799] dated September 23rd, 1801. The fourth, with the same signature, was sent to Talleyrand, France's Minister of Foreign Affairs.

After finding these documents, I began forming a different opinion about Yaqob and the nature of his relationship with the French.

Yaqob provided two types of services to the French. The first was what Gerges Al-Gowhary, Malaṭy, Abu Ṭaqeyah, and other prominent Copts provided to the French. This type of service was based on seeking personal gain, as well as deliverance from the (Muslim) rulers' contempt that was never alleviated, regardless of how much money they owned, their high standing, or how much the rulers needed them. The other type of service was meant to pave the way for the country's political future by temporarily supporting the Western rule.

By supporting the Western interference, Yaqob hoped to gain two things. First, delivering his country from the (Ottoman and Mamluk) rule, which combined the disadvantages of chaos and violence, thus not benefiting the rulers or those ruled. Yaqob reasoned that any kind of rule cannot be worse than what Egypt had to tolerate prior to Bonaparte's arrival. Second, it afforded the opportunity to communicate with and learn from the West. This was no less important, in his view, than what this (French) occupation allowed in terms of establishing an Egyptian military force trained according to the systems of the Western military.

Thus, the presence of a Coptic Legion was, hence, the first and main condition to enable a man from the Egyptian nation, followed by many farmers and tradesmen, to have an impact on the affairs of this nation, if the French left and it went back to being controlled by the Ottomans and Mamluks, who would share and ravage it. This is despite him not belonging to the sword-wielding Mamluks or Ottomans. And without this force, Egyptians are to remain where they were yesterday: reluctantly patient, seeking the mediation of *Sheikhs*, or people's commotions, which yield no significant change, and for which they alone pay the price. This is the biggest difference between Yaqob and Omar Makram[i]. Yaqob chooses to depend on a trained force, whereas Al-Sayed Omar depends on a popular agitation, which is easy to excite but difficult to control. So, Yaqob does not want the Mamluks and Ottomans to return, but works toward having an Egyptian faction play a role in determining the fate of the country.

Al-Jabarti records (May, 1803) a clash that took place between the Albanian soldiers and Turkish soldiers of the Ottoman *Wali*, Khesro. They (the Albanians) used to say to the people of Cairo, "We (fight) one another and you are subjects…submissive to the victor." Yaqob did not want things

---

[i] Head of the *Ashraf* (decedents of the prophet), referred to earlier.

to be so, depending on what he hoped would be a new Egyptian military force trained in the systems of the Western military. So, he was first to learn the lesson of the French victory over the Mamluks, which is the lesson that Mohammed Ali learned a short while later.

Yaqob proceeded on a path with regards to the French rule according to a plan that opposed things his kin were used to, such as quiescence, patience, endurance, and the occasional propitiation of their lives and property with money and gifts. The Patriarch and the clergy were not pleased with Yaqob's actions, and he advised him many times to live like the rest of his (Coptic) brothers, but he refused. History has shown his tendency, even in his youth, toward fighting and cavalry according to the ways of the Mamluks. He participated in the days of Soliman *Bek,* the Aga, in some of the Mamluk wars against the soldiers of the Ottoman Captain (Commander) Hassan *Pasha.* When the French arrived, he accompanied the General Desaix in his conquest of Upper Egypt, and he refused to just oversee what he was hired to do, mainly manage the finances, food rations, and delivering messages, but he additionally observed the marches of war. In one occasion, he even fought in front of Desaix himself, leading a battalion of French cavalry against a group of Mamluks, and he did splendidly. This compelled his commander to give him a sword to carry, even though the Coptic *Moallem*s were never given swords; rather they were clothed in fur or granted money to the poor.

Yaqob also listened to the discussions of the French and observed their ways of thinking. The Italian knight, Noble Theodore Lascaris[i], helped him. (He had many ideas, like the building of the Cairo barrages and the need to advance toward the Nile sources; both of these ideas were carried out by Mohammed Ali). He also thought that the French government should work on making Egypt independent by empowering the Egyptian Legion under Yaqob's command, so that they could play a decisive role in a dispute between the Ottomans and the Mamluks.

One of the conditions of the agreement that the French insisted on prior to their withdrawal from Egypt was the guaranteeing of safety of Egyptians who served the French authority or allowing them to depart with the French army. Despite Captain *Pasha* Hussain's promises and attempts to persuade him to stay, Yaqob left (with his wife, some of his relatives, a group of

---

[i] He had arrived with Bonaparte and held different positions and learned Arabic.

translators, Muslims, many Christians, Levantines, and Roum) with the intention of approaching the European governments with regards to the issue of Egypt's independence. He made this decision once he realized that the Coptic soldiers have disbanded and that the French leadership had failed to make any plans, either specifically to support the Coptic faction or broadly for the future of Egypt. Knight Lascaris accompanied Yaqob on the British vessel, *Pallas*.

Yaqob, while on the '*Pallas*,' contracted a (mysterious) disease and died on August 16th, 1801. The ship's captain honored his high standing, and instead of throwing his body in the sea, as was customary, he preserved it until they reached Marseille, where the body was buried.

Yaqob's friend, Knight Lascaris, continued the task by preparing detailed memoranda, which he sent to the British and French governments, about the importance of supporting the independence of Egypt. However, these correspondences only made their way to the archives...

Ghorbal thus concludes his words, which need no further commentary, except for reminding those who accuse General Yaqob of treason, that he was, in fact, more patriotic than most, and that he was no less patriotic than the likes of 'Aziz *Pasha* Al-Masri' who corresponded (with the help of some of the 'Free Officers' who later initiated the 1952 'Revolution') with the Nazi Germans during World War II, to give them support and to rid Egypt of the British occupation...

***

Briefly stated, although the duration of the French Expedition was short (1130 days, of which Bonaparte barely spent 400 days), nonetheless, it represented a massive shock to Egypt. That expedition certainly helped revive Egypt from its comatose state and planted the seeds of a number of Western ideas that Egypt had not known from the time of the Arab invasion (across the 1160 prior years)—ideas like independence, freedom, and that 'destructive' notion of 'equality before the law,' among other things. In addition, this period opened Egypt's doors to be influenced by (Western) civilization, after long centuries of imprisonment in the tombs of darkness and backwardness.

After the French Expedition, it was impossible for Egypt to remain unchanged from its prior state. But is there someone who is capable of building on top of what took place before, to begin a new phase putting Egypt on the path of exiting the tunnel?

Mohammed Ali's Attempts to Exit the Dark Tunnel

As we saw in the previous chapter, the end of the French Expedition and the return of the tyrannical Ottoman rule marked the beginning of a period filled with instability, strife, and disorder. Now (Lieutenant Colonel) Mohammed Ali was an officer in the Ottoman army, and he had succeeded in winning over the prominent *Ulema*[i], businessmen, and the Arnaout (Albanian) soldiers. When conditions deteriorated during that period of time, several *Sheikhs* approached him, desiring to make him *Wali*, but he pretended to appear reluctant. So, they proceeded to the Sultanate, demanding that he be installed as *Wali*. Then, Al-Sayed Omar Al-Naqib[ii], along with *Sheikh* Al-Sharqawi, incited their followers to make a commotion and create unrest. Then, (the Mamluk Amir) Al-Alfi and his Arab followers committed abominable acts of killing, plundering, and destruction all over the country.

At last, on July 9th, 1805, an edict was issued, installing Mohammed Ali *Pasha* as *Wali* of Egypt.

Immediately afterward, Mohammed Ali inflicted a huge fine on the Copts, in order to obtain money to pay his troops. It was divided between *Moallem* Ghali, the chief steward of Alfi *Bek*; the inheritors of *Moallem* Boctor (Victor), the steward of El-Bardisi *Bek* who had just died; and the rest by other Copts.[168]

***

---

[i] Muslim scholars ('clergy') who are recognized as having specialist knowledge of Islamic *Sharia* and religious tenets.

[ii] Al-Sayed Omar Makram, *Naqib Al-Ashraf* (head of the Descendants of the Prophet) referred to earlier.

We now turn to the chroniclers of *History of the Patriarchs* for their perspectives on that period of time.

Abba Botros VII [1809–1852] became the 109th Patriarch. Prior to his ordination, he was a monk at the Monastery of Saint Antonius. He was also ordained as a 'General Metropolitan' of the Coptic Orthodox Church during the tenure of his predecessor.

During his tenure, Mohammed Ali accomplished the *fat'h* of Sudan, and many Sudanese people returned to Christianity [..]. At that time, Zohra *Pasha*, the daughter of Mohammed Ali and the wife of Ahmed *Bek* Al-Daftardar[i], became possessed with an evil spirit, and being an unnatural ailment, the doctors were unable to help her. Now Bishop Sarapamon of Al-Monufia was known all over Egypt for his spiritual gift of exorcism. [So, the *Pasha* asked the Patriarch to bring the bishop], and he went to her, and the palace was filled with people [..]. When he began to pray, the evil spirit caused her to have convulsions, and cast her to the ground as she foamed at the mouth [..]. Then, the princess stood up, sane and sound. When Mohammed Ali was told the good news, he wanted to reward the bishop with a bag of four-thousand pounds, but the bishop refused [..]. Instead, he asked him to act more sympathetically toward the Copts and to tend to their sons who were dismissed from their jobs, and his request was granted [..].

One year, the Nile River's flood did not rise to its expected level, [so the *Pasha* ordered] the religious leaders to pray and make supplications [..]. Then, Abba Botros and other clergy prayed [..], and the Nile overflowed [..]. Therefore, the status and regard of the Patriarch and his community were elevated in the *Pasha's* eyes.

The story became known that when Ibrahim *Pasha* [Mohammed Ali's son] ruled the Levantine countries and Jerusalem, he summoned Abba Botros to observe the light emitted from the tomb of Christ, the Lord, [the night of the celebration of the Resurrection][ii]. So, Abba Botros, the

---

[i] An in-law of Mohamed Ali and one of his most trusted friends, he was appointed *Daftardar* (senior financial administrator).

[ii] The Holy Light (or Holy Fire) event, which happens annually on the day preceding the Orthodox Easter Sunday at the St. Sepulcher Church. A blue light emanates within Christ's tomb (usually rising from the marble slab covering the stone bed believed to be that upon which Jesus' body was placed for burial). It eventually

Patriarch of the Roum, and Ibrahim *Pasha*, went inside the tomb. The *Pasha* had doubted the veracity of the phenomenon of the light [..], so when the light shone, he became terrified and repeatedly exclaimed in astonishment, "Oh! My father!" [..]

Mohammed Ali sought to unite the Coptic Church with the Church of Rome. This was because many of the new reforms that were implemented in Egypt took place through the aid of the French and their experts. When the *Pasha* perceived his indebtedness to them, he wanted to repay them. So, he attempted [..], based on the advice of one of the [French] army commanders, who was a 'Papist' [catholic] to bring Egypt's Christians under the umbrella of the Church of Rome, which would be pleasing to the Franks [i] [..]. So, he summoned the *Moallem* Ghali and his son, Baselios *Bek*, the finance chief [minister], and ordered them to acquiesce. Finding themselves in a difficult situation and fearing a [church] schism, they replied to the *Pasha*, "The conjoining of the entire denomination, at one time, to the Roman Church cannot happen without causing disturbances [..]. We see that it would be better that this be accomplished gradually and through habituation. We ourselves will first convert to Catholicism on the condition that we would not be forced to change our [religious] practices or our eastern traditions, and then we can gradually win over members of our denomination." The *Pasha* accepted their opinion and informed the Franks [of the plan] [..]. So, the *Moallem* Ghali and his son pretended to convert outwardly to Catholicism, along with a few of their relatives in Misr and Akhmim, while inwardly maintaining their loyalty to their own church[ii] [..].

***

---

forms a column, in a form of fire which doesn't burn when touched. From it, candles are lit and are then used to light the candles of the clergy and pilgrims in attendance.

[i] 'Frang' or 'eFrang,' a distortion of Franks, initially meaning French, but later used for (white) 'foreigners.'

[ii] Ghali, his sons Bassilios, Doss, and Tobia, his brother, Francis, and their families and their retinues converted to Catholicism in January, 1822; the Catholic Church thus found its first roots in Egypt. See: *Marcus Simaika: Father of Coptic Archeology* by Samir Simaika,

It is apparent from what preceded that the chroniclers of *History of the Patriarchs*, at the time, could not fully comprehend the changes and developments taking place in the country, for they mentioned nothing of significance, such as the following events, which are of general nature, but important to keep in mind in order to understand Egypt's and Copts' situation.

After becoming *Wali*, Mohammed Ali worked toward stabilizing conditions, bolstering his rule, and appeasing the soldiers by paying them their wages back. So, he forced the Copts to loan him a large sum of money, dividing the sum among their prominent leaders. He dispatched his cronies to collect the money, and they ravaged the Copts and did what was evil. Then, the *Pasha* arrested the *Moallem* Gerges Al-Gowhary, who was responsible for the *Kharaj* of Egypt, and a group of prominent Copts and imprisoned them in the arrest house of *Katkhoda*. He then asked Al-Gowhary to present an account for the previous years, summoned *Moallem* Ghali, the scribe of Al-Alfy *Bek* from Upper Egypt, and set him in Al-Gowhary's place. He continued to harass (Al-Gowhary) and imposed on him the payment of a large sum of money. So, he sold his furniture to pay a part of the money that was levied, and the *Pasha* kept him imprisoned for days.

Along his reign, Mohammed Ali surrounded himself with Europeans and Christians, because he perceived that they were better educated, more energetic, and as a general rule, more trustworthy. At the same time, he invariably chose, if possible, Armenian, Roman Catholic, or other European Christians, since he might have perceived the possible future danger of allowing the Copts to obtain any preponderance of influence in the country, which they never forgot was their own by inheritance.[169]

In February, 1809, the Ottoman Sultan asked Mohammed Ali to prepare to fight the *Wahhabis*[i] in Al-Hejaz, because they had fought and ravaged many people, committing acts of looting and murder, and prevented the people from performing *Hajj*. They were followers of Abdul-Wahab Al-

---

[i] Followers of Wahabism, a fundamentalist and ultraconservative Muslim doctrine and movement, founded in Arabia in the 18th century by Muhammad Ibn-Abdul Wahab, and later revived when Ibn-Saud formed an alliance with them in the early 20th century.

Dar'i, who learned the doctrine of Ibn Hanbal[i] and then went to Isfahan, Iran. There, he sought *Shia* scholars and learned from them, to the point where he mastered the study of the origins and branches of *Sharia*. Then, he returned to his hometown (Dara'a) and established his own doctrine (of Islam), and he became famous and was sought after by many people.

In March, 1811, Mohammed Ali committed the famous 'Citadel Massacre' to eradicate the Mamluks.[ii] Then, he attended to managing the affairs of the country and multiplied the important projects, such as digging canals, restoring bridges, and building great plants. He also built war equipment that he sent as reinforcements to his son, Amir Ṭusun, in Al-Hejaz. Then, he assembled a large army, which included many Arabs (Bedouins), under the leadership of his son, Ismail, in conquest of Sudan and Darfur, which he viewed as a valuable addition resource of territory, gold, and slaves.

Since the downfall of the Christian kingdoms by the end of the 15th century, there had been no settled government in the great zone lying between Egypt's southern borders and the northwestern frontier of Abyssinia. The Sudan was in the hands of a group of Arab slave traders who lived by the wholesale robbery and plunder of a dependent population, among whom the traces of (Coptic) Christianity were few and far between. Mohammed Ali sanctified his expedition in the eyes of his Muslim subjects by sending with the troops three *Ulema* to prevail upon the Sudanese to profess Islam. The expedition penetrated with little difficulty and found remains of the ancient civilization planted there by Copts. Though in great misery and secrecy, a remnant of the Christian faithful endured, still in certain districts, down to our own times.[170]

---

[i] Founder of one of the four main doctrines of Islamic jurisprudence, the Hanbali, which is the strictest of them.

[ii] On March 1st, 1811, Ali organized a grand ceremonial procession in the Citadel of Cairo to which he invited some 500 Mamluk notables. They were warmly welcomed, but when the time came for the procession, they had to go down a narrow, winding passageway between high walls in single file. Suddenly, the gates at each end were slammed shut and the *Wali*'s soldiers appeared on top of the walls and opened a murderous fire with muskets. All of the Mamluks were killed. More Mamluks were swiftly hunted down and killed in Cairo and elsewhere in Egypt, for a total of perhaps 3,000.

Mohamed Ali then decided to create an army made up of the 'people' (conscription) according to the system of the French army. He announced to his subjects that the only conditions for anyone to sign up to serve the country were to be twenty-five-years-old, white[i], and physically unblemished. So, the people rushed to volunteer. He also recruited a prominent French officer (Colonel Sève, who converted to Islam and became known as Suliman *Pasha*, the Frenchmen) to organize the army. He established schools for infantry, cavalry, artillery, and plants to build war machinery.

The Greeks rose up, demanding independence from the Ottoman rule, and they perceived that this could only be accomplished through the spreading of freedom and equality between all citizens, and ridding themselves of the yokes of captivity and slavery. They created associations to defend their political rights. Their members reached about twenty-thousand, who were trained to use a weapon. The Sultan dispatched a great army to subdue them, but it was defeated after its soldiers committed atrocious acts of killing and looting, and taking women and children as prisoners of war. Associations were formed across Europe, favoring the independence of nations, and they supported the Greek revolutionaries. Those who joined these associations included the French poet, Victor Hugo, the English poet, Lord Byron, and the son of George Washington, the liberator of America. The Sultan assigned Mohammed Ali to be the *Wali* of Morea and Crete, and ordered him to fight the Greeks. So, he assembled an army led by his son, Amir Ibrahim, and assisted by Suliman *Pasha*, the Frenchman. (In 1826), the Egyptian and Ottoman soldiers landed and forcefully conquered the country, ravaging and killing along the way, going as far as Athens. Then, the Czar of Russia, along with the Kings of England and France, pressured the Sultan to grant the Greeks their administrative independence, while still being obligated to pay the *Jizya*, but the Sultan refused. So, fighting broke out, and all the Egyptian and Ottoman battleships were destroyed. In response, the Sultan called all the forces of his kingdom to go to war and wage *Jihad* to defend Islam. But Ibrahim decided to withdraw, and the Greeks gained their independence.

One of the ironies of history is that Egyptians were drafted into a national army for the first time in many centuries, but their first mission was to fight

---

[i] Meaning to exclude 'black slaves.'

the Greeks to compel them to remain prisoners of the Ottoman State, the very state under which they themselves groaned.

In October of 1831, the Egyptian army, led by Amir Ibrahim and Suliman *Pasha* the Frenchman, marched to conquer the Levantine countries (under Ottoman rule). They were able to take Beirut, Homs, and Aleppo, and then rushed to Anatolia, desiring to conquer Constantinople. The Sultan threatened to resort to the Russians to fight back against him, and France and England advised Mohammed Ali to retreat, but he did not listen. Then, the Sultan made an offer (in 1833) to Mohammed Ali (and for his children after him), to rule over Egypt, Arabia, Sidon, and Tripoli, but he refused. So, the *Fatwa* Committee of the Sultanate issued an edict that he had disobeyed the Commander of the Faithful, and that he should be stripped off his office and punished by being put to death, but he still paid no attention to that. Then, the people of Hauran[i], Lebanon, and the Levant rebelled and called for deliverance from Amir Ibrahim's yoke of bondage and the oppression of his soldiers, but he put down the rebellion and tortured those who participated to make an example of them. In 1840, the Convention of London[ii] was signed, guaranteeing the rule of Mohammed Ali and his progeny over Egypt, and the rule, only during his lifetime, of half of the Levant, but he rejected the treaty. So, the British battleships besieged Beirut and bombarded it. Then, the Ottoman soldiers marched in, the people of the Levant rebelled (against Mohammed Ali's rule), and Alexandria was besieged. Finally, he succumbed, with only Egypt remaining under his rule. He also had to accept certain conditions, such as having to pay an annual *Kharaj* of (8000 bags of gold) to the Ottoman Sublime Porte, and limiting his army to eighteen-thousand soldiers, along with other stipulations.

Finally, Mohammed Ali ceased his conquering adventures and focused on mending the affairs of his kingdom. So, he established iron and linen plants, paved roadways, and founded schools taught by English and French

---

[i] Area located in the south of current day Syria, near and across the borders with Jordan.

[ii] The Convention of London of 1840, or *Convention for the Pacification of the Levant*, was signed between the great powers of U.K., Austria, Prussia, and Russia on the one hand, and the Ottoman Empire on the other, lending support to the latter, which was 'having difficulties with its Egyptian possessions.'

teachers. He also brought about 1500 French farmers and dispersed them all over the country to teach Egyptians their farming methods, as well as bringing a French expert to cultivate cotton. Medicine was a top priority for him, so he brought the famous French expert, Antoine Clot, who founded one school of medicine and another for midwives, as well as hospitals for the sick or wounded soldiers. He also brought *Monsieur* Linant de Bellefonds[i] to manage the Nile water by building many canals and bridges.

Then, Mohammed Ali became mentally disturbed and began to hallucinate. His son, Ibrahim, managed the affairs of the country (1848), before quickly deteriorating and dying, and Abbas (Ali's nephew) took his place. Mohammed Ali died in August 1849, around the age of 80.[171]

***

Thus, Mohammed Ali laid the foundations of a modern Egyptian State, but, for most of his rule, he squandered the country's resources on useless military campaigns. His grandiose project was essentially to establish a stable rule for himself and his dynasty after him. For that, he wanted to create a strong army, along with the industrial infrastructure it needed, to fend off the cupidity of the Ottoman state and foreign powers.

With regards to Copts, Mohammed Ali preliminarily ended their segregation when he decided to make use of and depend on Egyptians. He did not stop Christians from their religious rites, nor did he deny church building or restoration requests, evincing the cultural impact the Bonaparte adventure had. He also facilitated the pilgrimage process to Jerusalem under the supervision of authorities. Additionally, he was the first Muslim ruler to bestow on Copts the title of *Bek* [ii] and to have Christian advisers (but they

---

[i] To facilitate the construction of dam projects on the Nile, Muhammad Ali suggested — and fully expected Linant to achieve — the removal of some or all of the Great Pyramids as pre-cut building material. Linant realized that if he resisted, the *Pasha* would simply appoint another engineer, so he cleverly prepared an elaborate financial analysis that demonstrated that quarried stone would be more cost-effective and the plan to dismantle the pyramids was scrubbed. (https://en.wikipedia.org/wiki/Louis_Maurice_Adolphe_Linant_de_Bellefonds)

[ii] Bassilios, son of *Moallem* Ghali, was appointed by Mohammed Ali to his father's former position and given the title, *Bek*, (a conciliatory sign, after Ghali's killing in

were from the Levant, not Copts). In 1814, he appointed a Copt[i] as governor of the lands east of the Delta, and gave him the title, *agha*.

At times, Mohammed Ali supported the Copts without hesitation. One example was during the sedition of the Cairo garrison (1814), when Christians seized by terror, sheltered themselves in their neighborhoods. So (according to Al-Jabarti) the *Pasha* sent them reinforcements of gunpowder and weapons. Another example was when a fight broke out between a (Muslim) muleteer and a Coptic farmer in Damietta, in 1845. The muleteer complained to the authorities, accusing the farmer of swearing at him. The (local) governor ordered that the Copt be struck 500 lashes and that he be paraded around the Christian quarters to be insulted by everyone. When Mohammed Ali heard of this event, he fined the governor and ordered his imprisonment for five years in the Citadel of Abu Qir.

Mohammed Ali did not put an end to the *Jizya*, even though the *Firman* (Edict) of Gülhane[ii] was issued to that effect in (1839). However, he did allow for exemptions, such as for the Copts who served in Alexandria armory or those, "Who were taken for military service, since they were performing official duties, which necessitated taking care of their needs and pleasing them" (May, 1836). On the other hand, Mohammed Ali rewarded those who converted to Islam and gave them government positions. Thus, he encouraged Colonel Sève to convert to Islam, "Because it was impermissible for a non-Muslim to lead the army," and he never hesitated to punish apostates. No Christian could be a witness if one of the parties in the case were a Muslim. (A Christian could be witness for a Christian and a Jew for a Jew). This system was followed until late in the 19th century. Clot *Bek* (who founded the medicine school) mentions in his memoirs, that a student once assaulted him. The court listened to what the student and his colleagues had to say, and refused to listen to what Clot *Bek* wanted to say because he was a Christian and therefore, was not allowed to make a statement against a

---

1821, by Ibrahim *Pasha*, following a dispute on increasing taxation). In any case, this was the first time this title was granted to a Copt. Samir Simaika *op. cit.*

[i] Rizk Ghobrial.

[ii] The Gülhane Hatt-i Şerif (Supreme Edict of the Rosehouse) or Tanzimât Fermâni (Imperial Edict of Reorganization) was a proclamation by the Ottoman Sultan in 1839 that launched the Tanzimât period of reforms and reorganization in the Ottoman Empire.

Muslim. Mohammed Ali did not care to recruit Copts for the regular army.[172]
Also, the educational missions to France did not include a single Copt (even
if it did include a few Levanite Christians) [i]

It is worth mentioning what the Swiss traveler, Johann Ludwig
Burckhardt, observed in Upper Egypt, where the Arab Bedouin tribes were
dominant. He describes the relationship between Coptic families and the
tribal *Sheikhs* as resembling that of 'hereditary slaves.' This is because some
Coptic families were under the control and protection of a certain *Sheikh* and
were considered his property, working on his land only. It was also lawful
for Coptic families to be inherited by and sold among the *Sheikhs*.[173]

***

After Mohammed Ali's death, his grandson, Abbas *Pasha* (the son of
Ṭusun), became *Wali,* and his days saw regressions from the reforms of his
grandfather. He associated with slanderers and snitches, despised foreigners
(for example, he gave three-thousand Greek residents two weeks to leave the
country) and purchased many Mamluks and black female slaves. He was
indignant at the Copts, so he removed many of them from the service of the
state and prohibited their employment. He excessively demeaned them; for
example, he replaced the (Coptic) administrators with a group of arrogant
(Muslim) youths, and compelled the administrators to teach and train them
before a certain deadline. Thus, the *Divân* affairs fell into disarray. His hatred
of Christians intensified, and he summoned *Sheikh* Al-Bagoury, the *Sheikh*
of Islam[ii] at the time, and asked him, "I have made plans to drive away all
the Christians out of my country and away from my government to the
outermost region of Sudan, what do you think?" It is reported that the *Sheikh*
disapproved of his idea regarding the *Dhimmis,* "Who are the natives of the
country and its owners," because they are the responsibility of the Muslims.
He also warned him about the Foreign Christians, saying, "If you mistreat
them, it will be done to your country, as the French did to Algeria."[iii]

---

[i] The first Copt sent abroad to study was Wassef Azmi, in 1855, under Said *Pasha.*
He studied law and after his return in 1860, worked in the judiciary.

[ii] The most senior Sheikh of the country, usually the Grand Sheikh of Al-Azhar.

[iii] In reference to the argument between Hussein Dey, the Ottoman *Wali* of Algiers
(which had become a base of Barbary pirates and slave traders, who attacked

During his tenure, the words of the Arab Bedouins were domineering, and they were very influential. They, hence, ravaged the country and destroyed the crops and lives.

Abba Botros was God-fearing, ascetic, and virtuous, loving all that is good. He was slow to anger, reverent, dignified, and was a man of few words. He spent his day reading while sitting on the floor and slept only on straw mats. He never got involved in politics and never met with any government officials.[174]

***

Abba Kyrillos IV (1854–1861) became the 110th Patriarch. Before his ordination, he was the Abbot of the Monastery of Saint Antonius. After he was selected to the Patriarchate, Abbas *Pasha* refused to officially recognize him, because he was warned by fortunetellers that this would bring him misfortune and death. Thus, Kyrillos was ordained as a Patriarchal Vicar and a General Metropolitan for fourteen months prior to assuming his role as Patriarch.[175]

The chronicles of *History of the Patriarchs* say,
This Patriarch is credited with the modernization and successful cultural elevation of the Copts, because he expended utmost efforts to refine their youth and teach them the sciences. He founded the Great Coptic School at the Patriarchate, and another school in the Alleyway of Al-Saqqayeen where he revived the instruction of the Coptic language after almost becoming [extinct], since, at that time, Coptic was used only in Egyptian churches [..]. He also introduced foreign languages [besides] Arabic, and brought expert Arabic, French, English, and Italian teachers. He acquired teaching tools and systematic books to aid in teaching. He established a printing press and delegated its operation to some of the school graduates who printed many books in the fields of theology, history, and literature. He tended to teach and mentor girls [and faced many forms of resistance for doing so].

European ships and settlements in the Mediterranean and elsewhere), and the French consul, which lead to a naval blockade followed by the invasion of Algiers in 1830.

He also restored the Church of the Alleyway of Al-Saqqayeen and, toward the end of his life, began building a new, larger church, after tearing down the old church [in Al-Azbakeya, which was established by Ibrahim Al-Gowhary (*see below)]. He had intended to see the building project through to the end, but he was prevented due to his incarceration, where he encountered many dangers that almost cost him his life. This took place because when he traveled to Abyssinia (**see below), some Englishmen maligned him before Al-Nagashi Tawadoros [King of Abyssinia], accusing him of [wanting] to make Abyssinia subject to Egyptian governance and claiming that the soldiers of Egypt followed him as he traveled to Abyssinia. So, Al-Nagashi became irate and ordered that the Patriarch be burned alive, but he was prevented by the Queen who safely sent the Patriarch back to Egypt.

(*) Ibrahim Al-Gowhary was the head of the scribes ('senior minister') during the early days of Mohammed Ali's reign and during the period of Patriarch Morcos VIII. At that time, it was extremely difficult for Copts to get church-building permits from the government. Then, it so happened that a lady from the Sultanate family came to Egypt as she was heading for *Hajj*, and since Ibrahim was highly placed in the Egyptian government, he himself oversaw all her services and presented her with a valuable gift. Desiring to reward him (..), she asked him about what he wanted, and he requested her assistance to have an edict be issued to build the church in Al-Azbakeya, and she agreed (..). But he [was imprisoned at the hands of Mohammed Ali, and then] died before the church began to be built, so his brother, Gerges *Effendi* [i], along with Abba Morcos and other prominent Copts, oversaw the building of the church, and moved the Patriarchal headquarters.

(**) When Said *Pasha* (Mohammed Ali's son and the uncle of Abbas *Pasha*) became *Wali* in July, 1854, Al-Nagashi, (king) of Abyssinia, was attempting to unify his country, and he tried to expand into some of the territories belonging to Egypt [ii] on his borders with Sudan. So, Said prepared to war against him, but he was counseled to send a delegation headed by Abba Kyrillos to mediate instead. He was then a Metropolitan and the

---

[i] A title of nobility meaning master, comes lower than *Bek*.

[ii] Territories acquired by Mohamed Ali's army, led by his son, Ismail, starting 1820.

Patriarchal Vicar [i] after the death of Abba Botros. So, they were sent on a Nile ship to Upper Egypt and then rode on camels until they reached the borders of Abyssinia. Al-Nagashi rushed to meet them, treated them with utmost generosity, and asked Kyrillos to anoint him King of kings (emperor) of Abyssinia, since he had not been anointed yet. Kyrillos obliged and presented him with a golden vestment, a gift from the *Pasha*. He also asked him to relent from what he was doing on the border to prevent bloodshed, and Al-Nagashi agreed. Then, (based on a complaint by the Metropolitan of Abyssinia), he requested from (Al-Nagashi) to stop the English missionaries, who had accompanied those who trained soldiers and manufactured weapons, from evangelizing according to the teachings (of Protestantism). And instead of having these (army-related) services provided by the English, he promised Al-Nagashi that he would ask Said *Pasha* to provide them instead. Al-Nagashi agreed and cast them out of the country. Kyrillos was happy (with his accomplishment) and wrote to Said *Pasha* to inform him about what took place. In the meantime, the British Consul in Egypt became privy to these events and was determined to exact revenge. So, he approached Said *Pasha* and filled his head with lies, saying, "The Copts believe in a book that tells them that Abyssinia will march against Egypt and forcefully capture it on a particular day known to them." Said told him that he thought this was nonsense. However, the consul told him to be on guard against Kyrillos, and he kept influencing him until doubts got the better of him. So Said *Pasha* wrote to Kyrillos, berating him about what happened and summoned him. Then, he went out with a great army to war against Al-Nagashi and arrived in Khartoum in (January, 1857). Then, the English planted someone who told Al-Nagashi, "The only purpose behind Kyrillos's visit was to prevent you from preparing your soldiers to defend your kingdom against the attack of the *Wali* of Egypt who sent you a poisoned vestment with Kyrillos." These

---

[i] Kyrillos had been, for some years, the head of the famous monastery of St. Anthony when he was called by popular support to fill the Patriarchal throne. Apart from the previously mentioned superstitious objections by the *Pasha*, it is also said that the bishops were old and timid, and hesitated to give supreme power to a young enthusiast who had been 'educated under foreign influences.' Under pressure, a compromise was agreed upon: No Patriarch was to be immediately elected; Kyrillos was to be consecrated Metropolitan of Babylon (Cairo) and a Vicar on the understanding that if he proved himself worthy as a bishop, he should be shortly afterward elected to the Patriarchate.

words alarmed Al-Nagashi, and upon hearing that Said *Pasha* arrived in Khartoum, he placed Kyrillos, who was oblivious to what was happening, under house arrest. Then Al-Nagashi went out with his army to meet Said. Meanwhile, Kyrillos managed to meet with Al-Nagashi's mother and complained to her. Then, Al-Nagashi confronted him, but he vehemently denied the accusations and wrote to Said *Pasha*, asking him to withdraw from Khartoum. Said *Pasha* agreed and pledged to Al-Nagashi that he would not attack his country. When Kyrillos returned to Egypt, he felt the coldness of Said *Pasha*, so he attempted to meet with him many times to discern the truth, but he was unsuccessful. So, he secluded himself in the monastery until the truth would be revealed. However, the British Consul increased his false messaging, deluding the *Pasha* to believe that Kyrillos intended to place the Coptic Church under the protection of Russia.[176]

On the other hand, while he was *Wali* of Egypt, Said *Pasha* reformed what his predecessor left in disrepair. His soldiers fought the Arab Bedouins in the eastern and western mountains, and those who remained were dispersed to Hejaz and the Levant. But some hid in the villages (of Egypt); these dressed and spoke like the farmers and not like Arab Bedouins, while in the past, Bedouins, even those who were poor, disdained the thought of mingling with the natives and considered that to be shameful and humiliating. Safety returned and the people were unafraid. Said *Pasha* also restored what Abbas *Pasha* had abolished, including factories and schools, even bringing back the expert Rifaa *Bek* [i] from Sudan, where he was exiled by Abbas, and gave him control of the schools. Schools were also established by the (French and Italian) communities, as well as the Franciscans, the Frères (Jésuites), the Good Shepherd, the Sacred Heart, and the Protestant missionaries. Said had installed the telegraph lines, as well as the railways. He devoted resources to the military and made military service mandatory, while shortening its duration. The famous Ferdinand de Lesseps approached Said *Pasha* with regards to digging a canal to join the Mediterranean with

---

[i] Rifaa al-Tahtawy: writer, teacher, translator, and renaissance intellectual. He was among the first (Muslim) Egyptian scholars to write about Western cultures following his stay in Paris as the chaplain of the groups of 44 students sent by Mohammed Ali, in 1826, to acquire modern knowledge. Among other things, he translated and commented on the *Déclaration des droits de l'homme et du citoyen* adopted, in 1789, after the French Revolution.

the Red Sea, but he was skeptical, thinking this was impossible to accomplish. After persistence and explanation, the *Pasha* approved the project, after the Commander of the Faithful (the Sultan) gave his approval. He decreed the utilization of about twenty-thousand citizens taking turns, working as forced labor on this project.[177]

Said *Pasha* did not favor nor was he partial to any one religion.[i] Thus, he was loved by his subjects. In December, 1855, he put an end to the *Jizya*[ii] 'desiring to act more leniently with the *Dhimmis* included among his subjects.' He also worked toward removing stumbling blocks in the way of incorporating the Copts as an integral part of the country's fabric; thus, he decided to accept them in the army. The decree (January, 1856) stipulated that 'the sons of prominent Copts will be called to carry arms just like the prominent Muslims in accordance with the principle of equality.' That was an important change because ever since the Arab conquest in 642, no Copt had been allowed by their Muslim rulers to bear arms; and after the suppression of the last great Coptic revolt in the ninth century, it had become almost impossible for any Copt to obtain them even for self-defense. However, Said *Pasha*'s decree was used as an instrument of persecution against the Copts. In Assiut, all the males in some of the Coptic homes were seized, not one being left to support the women and children. Once in the army, they were exposed to a regular system of bullying and persecution, in order to force them to change their religion. So great was the misery inflicted on the Copts by that decree that the Patriarch appealed so that the Copts once more be exempted from military service.[iii]

Said commended the governor of Girga because 'he broke up the crowds that had gathered to celebrate the conversion of a Copt from Sohag to Islam by publicly parading him in the markets. He then removed the mayor of the area for indulging and tolerating this behavior.' He also installed a Christian ruler in Sudan. However, Copts were still not allowed to advance in the army,

---

[i] He had been educated in France.

[ii] Before its abolition by the Ottoman Sultan in 1856.

[iii] However, they uniformly joined the military during the reign of Ismael *Pasha*. Also, one wonders about a historical connection between these incidents and the modern-day incidents of murdering enlisted Coptic soldiers by their comrades, who are typically reported as 'committing suicide' or 'self-inflicted.'

or to enter military, medicine, and engineering schools that were forbidden to them.

In 1856, the European Powers secured a verbal promise from Sultan Abdul Mejid, later recorded in the *Hamayuni* Edict[i] (or Restrict, made on February 18th), regarding non-Muslim communities. It was based on the principle that religions other than Islam might be permitted to exist, but not to expand. It still proclaimed the 'equality of all citizens' under the law (thus allowing non-Muslims to become civil servants) and granted civil and political rights to the Christian subjects. It covered the regulations pertaining to installing the Patriarchs (of various denominations), regulating the building and restoration of houses of worship, and establishing Communal Councils for the various religious communities. Regarding the houses of worship, the edict states, "The plans of these different buildings, in case of their new erection, must, after having been approved by the Patriarchs or heads of communities, be submitted to my Sublime Porte, which will approve of them by my Imperial order, or make known its observations upon them within a certain time."

The edict, which was presumably a 'progressive' stance, thus had a built-in discriminatory mechanism that continues to be a source of huge problems till nowadays. The necessity to have church-building permits approved by the Sublime Porte was inherited by subsequent regimes long after the demise of the Ottoman State itself. In Egypt, kings followed by presidents had to issue the decrees related to repair or building of churches, schools, or cemeteries.

***

Pope Kyrillos IV died in January, 1861, but his short reign[ii] of six-and-half years earned him the justified title of 'Father of Reform.' In all, he established five schools which continued to flourish after him, becoming a real engine for progress. Many of its graduates created a new elite for the Copts and for Egypt in general, since the schools were open to Copts and

---

[i] *Khatt-i Hamayuni* (lit. *'Imperial handwriting'*), a document or handwritten note of an official nature composed and/or signed by an Ottoman Sultan.
[ii] It is said that because of his activism and for his attempts to help his people, he was poisoned by order of the government.

Muslims. Five of Egypt's prime ministers and numerous ministers and leaders in the following decades graduated from these schools. He imported a printing press, only the second in the country after that left behind by Napoleon, and set up—amid big celebrations—a print shop which produced a variety of books beyond religious ones.

He paid special attention to elevating the status of women. Two of the five schools were for girls (the first governmental school for girls was opened years later by *Khedive* Ismail). He set fourteen years as a minimum age for girls to marry, and made marriage conditional upon a girl's approval. He set equality in heritage between (Christian) men and women, after centuries of applying *Sharia* rules of inequality. In sum, during his short reign, he inaugurated a movement of reform from within, which never quite ceased afterward.

***

Then, Abba Demetrios II (1861–1870) became the 111th Patriarch, and he was formerly in charge of the Monastery of Saint Maqar.

He continued where his predecessor left off and continued to build the church [Saint Mark's Church in Al-Azbakeya] [..], which became the Copt's best, largest, highest, and greatest church in the Egyptian territory [..]. He also revived the schools [and *kuttabs*[i]]. He had the privilege of appearing before his royal highness, Sultan Abdul Aziz, when he graced the land of Egypt. He also attended the celebration of the inauguration of the Suez Canal [in November, 1869], where he received a great deal of attention from the Sultan,[ii] who bestowed on him

---

[i] Elementary schools attached to churches, where Coptic and Arabic alphabet, arithmetic and basic religious education is given.

[ii] Abdul Aziz was the first Ottoman Sultan to visit Egypt since Selim I (350 years prior). Although the Sultanate was then struggling on two fronts: externally, from the provinces that demanded independence and internally, from the 'Young Turks,' who violently attacked the rulers' corruption; and despite the barbaric destructions committed by the Ottomans against Egypt across the previous centuries; nonetheless, the Egyptian crowds received him with overwhelming hospitality. When he 'looked at them, as if greeting them, they would increase their crying and do so more loudly, which was a reception that the Sultan never experienced in his own country.'

several plots of farmlands for the expenditures of the Patriarchate and the community's schools.

In this Patriarch's days, Ismael *Pasha* became the first to be given the title of *Khedive*[i] by the Ottoman State.

Ismael (Ibrahim's son and Mohammed Ali's grandson) became *Wali* in January, 1863, then promoted to *Khedive* in 1867, and resumed the reforms. He cancelled an agreement that Said *Pasha* made with de Lesseps, refusing to utilize Egypt's citizens in forced labor in the digging of the Suez Canal. He also ordered that the canal and surrounding lands be under the control of Egypt's government without granting any privileges or rights to any other nation. Then, he desired to imitate the major European kings with constitutional governments, so he decreed (December, 1866) the forming of the country's *Shura* (Consultative) Council which included two Copts (out of a total of 75 elected members). Afterward, he organized the army and built citadels, and plants for gunpowder, blank (bullet), and alcohol distilleries. He brought in high-ranking American militaries and engineers to teach his soldiers.

At the invitation of Napoleon III, he visited Paris for the inauguration of the *Exposition Universelle* (1867) and stayed there for a month-and-a-half. Upon returning to Egypt, he ordered the establishing of two theaters, one for comedy and another for opera, and brought actors and actresses from Europe for these theaters, as well as art professors. For the inauguration of the Suez Canal (1869), he held a great celebration, which was attended by the French Empress Eugenie, the Emperor of Austria-Hungary, the Princes of Italy and Prussia, and others. Then, he sent scientific and military missions to the heart of Sudan and Abyssinia for the sake of exploration and road-planning. He also annexed parts of Somalia, Suakin, and Massawa[ii] in exchange for increased tribute payments to the Ottoman Sultanate. He desired to make Cairo like the capitals of the civilized nations, so he spent large sums of money to expand the roadways, build structures, plant trees, light streets, and extend railway tracks. Primary schools spread all over the country, and several preparatory schools were founded, including for girls. Then, the treasury was depleted, and he was forced to borrow at very high interest rates.

---

[i] A title largely equivalent to the English word viceroy.

[ii] Respectively, on the coasts of current day Sudan and Eretria.

As debts multiplied, he began to sell the Suez Canal Company shares to England, and many of the country's resources were seized to repay the debt.[178]

Egypt and Britain signed (in 1877) the 'Anglo-Egyptian (Anti-) Slave Trade Convention' in Sudan. But this caused the Sudanese to be outraged at the Egyptian rule, because slave trade was linked to the economic and social composition of their society.[179]

> Going back to the *History of the Patriarchs*, we read:
> One of [the Patriarch's] remarkable deeds was that he toured the southern territory of Egypt on a ship provided by the government, [to confront the increased foreign missionary campaigns to the Copts] [..]. When he died, his seat was left vacant for four years and nine months, because the government had delayed issuing an edict, approving the ordination of a new Patriarch. Abba Morcos, the Alexandria Metropolitan, managed the affairs of the Patriarchate [with the help of a Community Council made up of twelve from the laity].

Ismael (who was educated in Vienna and then Paris) expanded the policy of religious tolerance by ordering that the children of both Christians and Muslims must be accepted into the public (government) schools without discrimination. He also provided financial aid and an endowment of one thousand *feddans* to the Coptic schools.[i] He established equality by nominating Copts to the elections of the Shura (Consultative) Council and by appointing Coptic judges to the courts. In (1863), a Copt came forward, desiring to convert to Islam, so (Ismael) ordered the officials to summon a priest and a number of Coptic mayors to have this person sign a statement confirming before them that he is intent on converting with his own free will which would be followed by their endorsement of the statement that would be kept with the authorities.[ii] When the streets of Cairo were being redrawn and Clot *Bek* Street was being established, the project required the removal

---

[i] Compare this to the state's confiscation of Coptic endowments in the latter part of the 20th century.

[ii] These procedures, later on, became known as 'advisory sessions,' which were in effect until the Ministry of Interior ordered their repeal at the end of 2004, opening the door wide for uncontrolled and difficult-to-prove coercion and manipulation.

of a Coptic Church. So, the government offered to Abba Demetrios to build, instead, a more luxurious church and Patriarchal residence at the government's own expense. However, the Patriarch declined, regarding the tearing down of a church, for the sake of opening a public roadway, as an evil portent, so the *Khedive* ordered that his wishes be respected.[i]

Ismael was the first to request the title of *Pasha* for a Christian (Nubar, an Armenian), and many among the Copts held high offices, for example, Waşef *Pasha* Azmy was the Senior Protocols Officer.[ii] He was the first to appoint a Christian, Nubar *Pasha*, prime minster, and Copts, as judges. He approved building churches in some new cities [iii] where they were not allowed to do for centuries. Ismael summarized the matter by saying, "In Turkey, Christians live in an atmosphere of tolerance mixed with contempt, while in Egypt, they live in an atmosphere of tolerance coupled with respect."[iv] Owing to these policies, the people's mentality began to gradually change, relationships between 'the two elements of the Nation' improved, and the principle of equality grew increasingly familiar. Thus, it became possible for the people of the city of 'Biba,' in which only thirteen Coptic families resided, to elect 'Gerges' *Effendi* as mayor. Christian Prime Ministers, like Nubar *Pasha* (and later, Boutros Ghali *Pasha*) would preside — on behalf the *Khedive* — over the annual celebration of the *Hajj* caravan where a newly fabricated Kaaba cloth cover is paraded ahead of departure to Mecca.[v]

***

---

[i] Compare this to the decree issued by the Egyptian government in the days of president Sadat, to remove the Church of All Saints, near the Nile *Corniche*, in Wekalet Al-Balah area, to make room for the sixth of October Bridge, while alternatives were not only available, but easier to implement.

[ii] Compare this to the non-existence of a single Copt, even in the role of office boy (pager), in Egypt's Presidential Cabinet.

[iii] Al-Mansoura, Kafr Al-Sheikh, Belqas, and (New) Nabaruh.

[iv] This statement perhaps reflects Ismael's feeling more than it does reality.

[v] Tagher, P. 242. It is interesting to note the impact of top-to-bottom policies on people's mentality. One and half centuries later, such a presence of Copts in highly visible posts is almost non-existent, because the political leadership (especially the presidents) do not apply such policies.

Abba Kyrillos V (1875–1927) became the 112th Patriarch.

He was a monk at the Paromeos[i] Monastery at a time when that monastery was experiencing extreme financial and moral poverty, bringing in meager revenues incapable of supporting the monks. Its farmland was under the control of others, exploiting it for the benefit of others. The monks could only obtain a scanty sustenance with great difficulty. In fact, at times, days would go by with the monks having nothing but lupini beans for their sustenance [..]. For this reason, the number of monks in that monetary decreased to four. Some have even reported that at one point, only one monk resided in the monastery for three years all by himself [..].

After he was ordained, he turned his attention toward the ordering and organizing of schools. Therefore, he increased the number of teachers to keep up with the fast rates of enrollment; he introduced Arabic studies, mathematical studies like arithmetic, algebra, and geometry [..]. He founded schools in the Patriarchate and in the alleyway of Zwailah and Bulaq, and focused his attention on the monasteries near Cairo [..]. Then, he ordered that religious books be published, encouraging the monks to study and read, and establishing schools within the monasteries [..]. In his days, many books on preaching, theology, science, and history were published [..]. During his tenure, the [spiritual and intellectual] quality of clergy improved somewhat. Science and other forms of knowledge, and mastery of the Coptic language increased, to the point where many were able to converse in Coptic. Teaching books were even published in Coptic [..].[ii]

In the days of Tawfiq *Pasha*, one metropolitan and three bishops were ordained and sent to Abyssinia [..].

Khedive Tawfiq began his reign in June, 1879, after deposing his father, Ismael, and he was concerned with reigning in the spending to deal with the debt problems. He thus decreased the size of the army. The Egyptian officers,

---

[i] Located in Wadi Al-Natroun; dates back to early Fourth Century. *Pa Romeos*, or 'that of the Romans' refers to two sons of the Roman Emperor Valentinian I, who had their cells at that place.

[ii] Publishing books in Copts had dwindled since the 12th century.

led by Brigadier Ahmed Urabi, complained that they were dismissed while favoritism was shown to the Circassians. The *Khedive* responded (under threat) to their complaints by removing the defense minister. Urabi then lead the 'revolt' which culminated in presenting a list of the soldiers' demands to the *Khedive:* dismissing Riyad *Pasha* (the prime minister), increasing the number of soldiers, and reinstating the *Shura* Council. These demands were gradually granted. He went around with soldiers and many religious scholars, urging 'the stipulation to support religion (Islam), disobedience to the (religiously) incorrect Ottoman Caliphate, and obedience to an Arabic Caliphate based on the *Sunna*[i] of Allah and his prophet.' He also sent a message to Sharif of Mecca, Al-Senussi in Tripoli, and others to the same effect. It is said that his heart desired the position of *Khedive*. Then, he became the defense minister in the cabinet of (prime minister) El Baroudy *Pasha*. However, contentions continued to grow between the *Khedive* and El Baroudy *Pasha*, who set his heart on the position of *Khedive*. The *Khedive* attempted to remove him from office, but chaos spread in the country and British and French battleships arrived in Alexandria. In June 11, 1881, the riffraff in Alexandria rose up and began to beat and kill the foreigners, committing atrocities of looting, plundering, and destruction of shops and homes. Some (foreigners) sought protection from the police who killed every last one of them by the spearheads on their guns. On July 11th, the British bombed and destroyed the forts of Alexandria. Arabs spread like locusts and, acting like wild beasts, they and the soldiers looted shops and homes, and raped virgins and mothers, and set towns on fire, leaving a horrendous scene filled with indescribable hardships. When the *Khedive* heard of these things, he wept and ordered the ending of the looting and burning, and he remained in Ras Al-Tin (palace, west of Alexandria). Meanwhile, Urabi called a council of *Sheikhs* to remove the *Khedive*. The Ottoman State was in discussions with other countries regarding the possibility of sending Ottoman, or a coalition of, soldiers to Egypt to restore order. The Sultan decreed that Urabi was mutinous who disobeyed the Commander of the Faithful. The British seized the opportunity by going to Alexandria and then Port Said, and they fought Urabi at Kafr El Dawwar. The mosque *Imams* urged the people to wage a *Jihad* to fight the *Kuffar*.

---

[i] *Lit.* 'tradition'; the bodies of Islamic custom and practice based on Muhammad's words and deeds.

In Tanta, Damanhour, and Al-Mahalla Al-Kubra, the Muslims rose up against the Christians, slaughtering them, looting their homes, and taking their women and children captive. The murdered (Christians) were dragged on the ground from their feet, like cattle taken to be skinned after being slaughtered. The riffraff along with the *Divân* sentinel guards seized every Christian who passed by them, letting go of their victim only when he was no longer alive. After such a gruesome death, another group would receive the body, some would drag the person by the legs, and others would beat the head with a bludgeon until the limbs would come apart.

Urabi was defeated in the Battle of Tell El Kebir against the English. The chronicler then says,

[..] The [British] armies marched to Cairo and captured it without the slightest resistance, but they did not harm anyone, nor did they transgress anyone's rights, which was peculiar for us [..].

Then, Urabi and his cronies were arrested and tried according to the Ottoman law, charged with disobeying the *Khedive*. Urabi chose three English lawyers to defend him. The *Khedive* mitigated the sentence to exile (instead of death). Urabi and those with him departed with their women and female servants to Ceylon.[180]

Thus, Egypt came under British occupation. However, from a legal standpoint, Egypt was not 'Property of the British Crown' (like India and other countries). Rather, the Ottoman rule continued through the office of '*Khedive*' and remained as such until it was declared a 'British Protectorate,' at the beginning of World War I (1914). The ruler became a 'Sultan,' then a 'King,' with the issuing of the Constitution of 1922 and the (partial) independence.

Under the British influence[i], especially following the policies of Baring, Earl of Cromer[ii], Copts saw themselves being gradually excluded from certain key jobs in the administration, which they traditionally held for

---

[i] In their eyes, Coptic Orthodoxy lacked 'the true and spiritual part of Christianity,' and therefore, bore no resemblance to European Christianity.

[ii] Evelyn Baring, 1st Earl of Cromer. As of 1879, he was the British controller-general in Egypt, part of the international control which oversaw Egyptian finances after the 1876 Egyptian bankruptcy. He became the counsel-general in Egypt (1883–1907), holding de-facto control on Egypt's finances and governance.

generations because of the special competencies required. Known for his dislike of the Copts, Baring denounced 'their habits of servitude,' and resented their resistance to his administrative modernization, which lessened the Copts' traditional control of the state's administrative apparatus. He also made the point clearly (as he put it in a letter to his superiors in 1889) that he would rely on Muslims for administering the country, as any appearance of 'preference' toward the Copts would lead to problems for the British. On the positive side, starting 1886, Copts were allowed, for the first time, admittance to the various schools (of Engineering, Medicine, Law, etc.) established by Mohammed Ali.

Back to the *History of the Patriarchs*:

While the Urabi revolt was taking place in Egypt, an Arab man from southern Africa, named Mohammed Ahmed, rose, [purporting to be the awaited] Mahdi[i]. He assembled an army of men and marched toward the Sudanese lands under the rule of the *Khedive* of Egypt and ruled these parts. But he was resisted by the Egyptian army, [after he killed hundreds of them and committed acts of looting] that defeated his army, taking many of his soldiers as prisoners, thus keeping Suwaken [port on Red Sea] in the hands of Egypt.

This Patriarch was wearied as a result of contentions within the [Community] Council,[ii] because its leaders[iii] requested an investigation of church affairs relating to schools, endowments, priest ordinations, and other matters of impropriety [..]. However, the Patriarch, along with the bishops, monks, and others, did not approve. The dispute continued between the two parties, but the council heads were supported by and influenced the government to exile (the Patriarch) to the Paromeos Monastery [September, 1892],[iv] but he was brought back [in February,

---

[i] The expected end-of-days 'messiah' of Muslim tradition.

[ii] Was made up of twelve non-clergy members to assist with the handling of Church affairs while the Patriarch's Seat remained empty. This council continued to function, intermittently, even after the ordination of Abba Kyrillos. Later on, this council came to be known as the 'General *Melli* (Community) Council.'

[iii] Headed by Boutros Ghali *Pasha*.

[iv] Regardless of which side was correct in the dispute between the '*Archons*' and the Church clergy, the intent of the former to exile the Patriarch, a rarity in the history

1893]. Then, all the denominations and the government knew that the Patriarch was in the right [..].

With regards to monasteries, we can say that during the first generations of monasticism, hundreds of flourishing monasteries existed in Egypt, but then they fell in ruins [..]. During the tenure of this Patriarch, there was a total of seven monasteries: four in Wadi Shehit [Wadi El-Natroun] [..], two in the eastern mountain [the Red Sea], and the seventh was El-Muharraq Monastery [..]. Between 400 and 500 monks reside in these monasteries.[i] Each monastery had its own farmed lands that were either donated to them, or purchased, in addition to endowment lands. As for the convents, they were five in total, with three being in Cairo and two in Old Cairo. There was a total of nineteen metropolitan and bishop seats [..], including the Metropolitan of Jerusalem, the Bishop of Khartoum and Nubia, the Metropolitan of Abyssinia and his three bishops. However, the number of these seats was susceptible to increase or decrease [..].

Khedive Tawfiq awarded the Patriarch the First Majidi Medal[ii], and the beloved *Effendina* [iii], Abbas Helmy *Pasha* II[iv], awarded him the same medal. The Majestic Sultan Abd Al-Hamid Khan awarded him the First-Class Ottoman Medal[v]; the Czar of Russia, Nicholas II, awarded him a First-Class Medal [..], and the Egyptian government appointed him as a member of the Shura Council, as one of the state's representatives.

Overall, we can say that during the days of this Patriarch, the Egyptian government had reached the highest levels of justice and administration, ended sectarianism, approximated equality between its Christian and Muslim subjects, and lifted most injustices. The government also performed many worthy projects that benefited citizens. These included the establishing of railway tracks, telegraph lines, post offices, water

---

of the Church despite all the woes it has gone through, is nonetheless a matter worth pondering...

[i] Though relative, notice the tremendous boom in the affairs of the monasteries as compared with years prior, even during the first days of this Patriarch's tenure.

[ii] Created by the Ottoman Sultan Abdel-Majid in 1851.

[iii] *Effendina*; our master.

[iv] Ruled 1892–1914.

[v] These high decorations, his critics say, were in return for his effort to discourage reform and the growth of national aspirations among his own people.

canals, bridges, barrages, and built paper and sugar factories, as well as
expanding the use of steam engine machines. Laws were also enacted,
and security was heightened without infringing on personal and
religious freedoms. Schools were founded and knowledge of the arts and
sciences spread. The city of Cairo saw great improvements as well, such
as the increased number of buildings, improved road infrastructure, and
the lighting of streets by gas [lamps]. Water pipes were also laid under
roadways. The number of schools and print shops increased. Also, the
city of Alexandria [saw many improvements]. Also, in these days,
relations and exchanges flourished between the countries of the world,
since travel became easier, thanks to steam trains and steam ships, and
it also became easier for news to travel. The number of newspapers and
published books increased, and so did the number of scientists,
particularly in Europe. Many Europeans lived in Egypt, and through
them engineering, scientific, and political projects were undertaken to
improve Egypt [..]. In totality, Egypt almost resembled the European
kingdoms.

***

With these positive and very optimistic words—which were written in
the second decade of the 20th century—and which appear to clearly steer
away from some troublesome events (as we shall see in the next chapter), the
chroniclers of *History of the Patriarchs* sealed their chronicles which are no
longer being updated to record current events.

At the end of the 19th century, the estimated number of Coptic churches
in the country was 418, served by 837 priests. There were several active
monasteries and three convents for nuns. There was a total of 21 bishops,
including three for Abyssinia, and one each for Sudan and Jerusalem; of the
remainder, there were four abbots, two for the Delta, and ten for Upper
Egypt. Social norms were changing fast. For example, while 20 years earlier,
a Copt would have been as much ashamed of being seen with his wife or
other female relations as if he were a Muslim, the younger men were
becoming aware that in ancient times, the Egyptian women were as free and
as much respected as their Western sisters are now, and became anxious to
do away with the draconian customs borrowed from the Muslims in this

respect. To do away with 'arranged marriages,' the Patriarch issued, in 1895, an encyclical letter to all his clergy, reminding them that, in accordance with the Canons of the Church, young people intending to marry should not only see, but mix with each other, so as to know one another well, and calling upon the priests to ascertain whether there was mutual knowledge and consent to the marriage on the part of both man and woman before the ceremony was performed.[181]

***

In short, it may be said that one century after the shock delivered by Bonaparte, and thanks to the efforts of Mohammed Ali and his progeny after him, especially Said and Ishmael, rays of hope began to break through, foreshadowing Egypt's exit from the dark tunnel of religious discrimination, humiliation, and coercion in which it and the Copts had languished over the prior twelve centuries of occupation. The makings of a modern state began to form on the horizon, where 'citizens' could live with a certain level of legal 'equality,' irrespective of religion. Despite the setbacks and massacres of that era, because of the impossibility of easily disposing of the effects of deep-rooted religious discrimination, Egypt began facing new questions regarding the formation of an Egyptian nation, and the nature of that new state.

But, was a final answer proffered? And if so, favoring which side?

Fake Liberals, Real Fascists

Egypt started the 20th century questioning its own identity. The answer on one side was unambiguous: 'Pan-Islamism,' which was promoted by Mustafa Kamel, Mohammad Farid, Gamal Al-Afghani, Abdel-Aziz Gawîsh, Rshîd Rida, and others. Egypt, for them, needed to get rid of the British and return to its natural place within the (Ottoman) Caliphate. Rashîd Rida's journal, al-Manar, consistently called for a return to an 'earlier Islam,'[i] and a society in which the connection between religion and government was closer than it was in 19th-century Egypt. The answer, which came timidly on the other side, was an Egyptian nation-state where all citizens are equal. Copts were, naturally, the most vocal about this answer, visibly encouraged by progress made over the prior few decades.

The influx of Western ideas into Egypt in the 19th century began to change both the theory and practice of government and communal organization. These ideas opened up new opportunities to the Copts to improve their community's status and to make an active contribution to the politics. The Copts had long been excluded from this arena; for the first time, new ways of thinking gave them a chance to play a serious role in determining their own destiny.

The first mention of the existence of a 'Coptic Problem' and the attempt of some Copts to find a solution to it was in 1897. That year, a Coptic delegation consisting of Wissa Boctor, Andraws Bishara, and Akhnokh Fanus went to Prime Minister, Mustapha Fahmi, and to Earl of Cromer[ii] with some demands: equality of Copts and Muslims in appointment to administrative positions, suspending court sessions on Sunday, appointing a third Coptic member in the Consultative Council, and teaching the Christian

---

[i] In other words, "Salafism." Although Rida's journal failed to survive his death in 1935, some of his views found new champions in the Muslim Brotherhood.

[ii] British consul-general (1883–1907), during the British occupation.

religion to Coptic students in public schools. Earl of Cromer agreed to the second and third demands and ignored the rest.

The Copts had two main newspapers: *Al Watan* ('Fatherland,' established in 1877) and *Misr* ('Egypt,' est. in 1895), which were rather vocal about the Copts' rights. Such articles angered Sheikh Abdel-Aziz Gawîsh, a leader in the National Party. On 17 June, 1908, he launched a series of articles in the party's newspaper, Al-Liwaa (the 'Standard'), starting with a famous (rather infamous) one, titled, "Islam is strange in its home." Examples of the kind of language he used in it are: "The Copts' cheek-skins are good to make shoe-soles," "The Copts must be beaten to death," "(Copts) have faces and bodies similar to those of the demons and monkeys, whose presence in the world is proof of Darwin's theory that man's origin is a monkey." Other mouthpiece papers of the Islamic camp joined these hate-filled attacks.

This 'controversy' resulted in the resignation of the few Coptic members of the National Party, led by Wissa Wasef. At the same time, the Copts had concerns about the real position of the other party, the *Umma* ('Nation') Party, despite its adoption of the Egyptian identity, as its leader, Ahmed Lutfi al-Sayyid[i] refrained from publishing any article responding to the attack by Sheikh Gawîsh. This led the Copts to say that, "when it comes to Coptic matters, there is no difference between Lutfi al-Sayyid and Gawîsh."[182]

In November, 1908, Boutros Ghali *Pasha* became Prime Minister[ii] after having been the Minister of Foreign Affairs (1899) and an Interim Minister of Justice (1906). He was the first Copt[iii] to occupy this post, and his appointment was rejected by the National Party 'on political grounds,' but Abbas Al-Akkad, a writer in the party's paper, was clearer: he wrote that a Christian choice for the post was an affront to Muslims, portraying the absence of an efficient Muslim.

On their part, the Copts were comforted by his appointment. But when one of them approached him and said, "*Pasha*, God willing, you will look into our old requests and help us gain equality during your tenure—" he

---

[i] He would later become a 'Liberal' intellectual, and the first rector of Cairo University.

[ii] In the days of the *Khedive* Abbas Helmy II (1892–1914).

[iii] He was not the first Christian, as Nubar *Pasha,* an Armenian-Egyptian, was appointed to the same post from 1884 to 1888.

interrupted him, saying, "I do not intend to get involved in this matter,[i] so do not get your hopes up for now."

In 1909, questions were raised about the teaching of the Christian religion, the non-acceptance of Copts in female teachers' institutes, the absence of representation of Copts from the boards of governorates, and their inadequate participation in the Consultative Council. (A delegation consisting of some leading Copts[ii] had met in June, 1908, with the *Khedive* carrying the Coptic demands).

The Copts then complained that Prime Minister, Boutros-Ghali, had not intervened to resolve their problems because he was embarrassed, being a Copt. The only positive step toward the Coptic demands was made by Minister of Education, Saad Zaghloul, which the Copts would later remember for agreeing to teach the Christian religion to Christian students. However, this gesture was only partial, as he stipulated that there should be a large enough number of students in the class (to justify a teacher) and that the Copts would pay teachers' salaries, both of which instantly hampered the ability to enact this reform.

On the other hand, that period (1908–1909) witnessed incidents of mob attacks on Copts in Assiut, Cairo, Qena and Sohag. Attempts were also made to threaten Coptic newspapers, such as *Al-Watan*, by the state.[183]

In February, 1910, Boutros-Ghali was assassinated at the hands of Ibrahim Al-Wardani, a youth from the National Party, on the charge of being a 'traitor.'[iii] When a court sentenced the assassin to death, the Mufti refused to approve the sentence[iv]. An elite group of Egyptian lawyers from the *Umma*

---

[i] This is exactly what his grandson, Dr. Boutros Boutros-Ghali, said and did every time he was petitioned to use his (national and international) prestigious status to appeal the Egyptian Government to seriously work on remedying the issue of Coptic equality in citizenship.

[ii] Akhnokh Fanus, Tadros Shenouda El-Manqabdi, and Habashi Moftah.

[iii] 'Political' reasons given were Ghali's role in signing a treaty with the British on Sudan, his role in extending the concession of the Suez Canal Co., and his role in the trial of Denshway, where four peasants accused of killing British officers were sentenced to death by a court composed of Egyptian and British judges.

[iv] All death penalties in Egypt, until now, need to be are viewed by the Mufti. Note that *Sharia*, in general, does not allow the death penalty for a Muslim killer of a Christian: 'A Muslim cannot be killed for (killing) a kafir' (*Al-Bukhari, Hadith #* 6517 by Ali).

Party stood up to defend him, led by Ahmed Lutfi Al-Sayed. The National Party considered the killer a 'martyr.' On the day of his execution, the Egyptian masses went out, exclaiming, "Well done, al-Wardani…he killed Boutros, the *Nosrani*[i]."

***

In the absence of any alternatives before them, the Copts held on March 6th, 1911[ii], a conference in Assiut under the title of, *The Coptic Conference.* The agenda included raising certain demands concerning the problems the Copts face, as well as a number of internal issues of concern to the community. The conference was completely rejected by the (Muslim) majority and was strongly attacked at the time of holding it. The British consul in Egypt, Gorst (who replaced Earl of Cromer in 1907), led a campaign that rejected the conference. The Coptic Pope, Kyrillos V, expressed his concerns in a statement published on March 4th, but the Metropolitan of Assiut, Makarios, reassured the Pope and supported the conference.

Soon it was followed by another conference on 29 April, under the title of the *Islamic Conference,* and then amended to the *Egyptian Conference,* to counter to the Coptic demands.

The *Coptic Conference* was attended by 1150 delegates. Each of these had to carry a procuration from another ten Copts; figures suggesting that there was a real movement with a popular backing that supports it. The leadership of the conference, all of which elected, were well-known names in the Egyptian political arena before and after the conference. The Chairman of the Conference was George Wissa (member of the parliament thereafter), Vice-Chairmen were Akhnokh Fansus (president of the Protestant Community), Khalil Ibrahim (member of the Coptic *Milli* Council in 1883–1892).

The conference came out with five demands: 1) Sunday as an official holiday for Christian government employees and students, 2) Appointments and promotions in government posts should be in accordance with

---

[i] Nazarene, a derogatory label of 'Christian.'

[ii] It was originally planned for February, 1910, but had to be delayed because of the assassination of Boutros Ghali, which took place just days before it was set to start.

competency and not religion, 3) Adopting a proportionate electoral system that ensures representation of minorities (the Belgian system proposed), 4) Equivalence of Coptic and Islamic (private) schools in government-education subventions, 5) The equality of Coptic charitable organizations with Islamic ones in government support.

Except perhaps for the first (Sunday's), none of these claims can be described as sectarian. On the contrary, these demands came with a speech demanding equality between citizens. The same spirit prevailed in the speeches delivered at the conference, emphasizing national unity, warning against the message by some who were telling the Muslim that 'the Copt is not his brother, but rather, the Muslim who lives in other countries.' Some other speeches emphasized that the Coptic problems are the product of the British divisive policies.[184]

During the conference, the slogan, 'Religion is for God (alone), and the Fatherland for all (its people)' seems to have been coined by the Coptic leader, Tawfiq Doss. This formulation, which expresses the conviction that there was a fundamental separation between religion and state, was the only statement to come out of the Coptic Congress that was not only accepted by many Muslims, but was raised by many of them to the level of political cant. It became a favorite slogan of nationalists and politicians. Although cheapened by frequent repetition and increasingly irrelevant with time, it neatly summarized the main political hope of the best-educated and most vocal segment of the Coptic community; a segment which wanted to institute a state free from religious bias and a religion free from state interference. With the creation of a new political system came new opportunities to realize that hope. It was to this end, an escape from the uncertainty of marginality, that the Copts' advocacy of democratic government, secularism, civil equality, and integration in its widest sense were aimed. Many worked to develop a new collective identity with new ways of interacting for Muslims and Copts.[185]

The counter-conference, the Islamic (renamed the 'Egyptian') Conference was held, with discrete government sponsorship, and chaired by ex-prime minister, Mustapha Fahmy *Pasha*. The organizing committee reported its conclusion that the Copts were planning to form 'a separate nation for themselves,' and that they were relying on fabricated grievances to enable them, with British help, to gain precedence over the Muslim majority.

The body of the report, read out by Lutfi al-Sayyid, deserves quotation: "...the principle is founded that every country should have an established church and that such a religion will be that of the government or the majority...that a state should have more than one religion is perfectly unthinkable and it would be absurd to admit that religious minorities can exist animated by political ambitions toward the exercising of public rights other than those of an essentially religious nature that are guaranteed by freedom of worship. The religion of the Egyptian people is Islam. For Islam is both the religion of the government and that of the majority."

Delegates agreed that Islam must continue to be the official religion of Egypt. They insisted that certain administrative posts, like that of the governor of a province, should be held only by Muslims.[186]

The Coptic demands were refuted and rejected, and government's policy of allocating some seats for Copts in the Shura (Consultative) Council was criticized, as well as allowing Copts to have their own newspapers and clubs. Delegates voted to oppose the teaching of Christianity (to Coptic students) in government schools.[187]

It is rather telling, from the above, to notice that many of the minority's demands and the majority's rejections have remained unchanged since then.

***

In December, 1914, the *Khedive* of Egypt was elevated to the level of Sultan, and the country declared as a British protectorate, thus terminating definitively the Ottoman sovereignty which was, for three decades, a mere legality. Shortly after the WW-I armistice in November, 1918, a delegation of Egyptian nationalists led by Saad Zaghloul made a request to High Commissioner, Reginald Wingate, to end the British Protectorate and gain representation at the planned Paris Peace Conference. The delegation included eleven other members, of which two were Copts (Sinut Hanna *Bek* and George Khayat *Bek*). This move was accompanied by large popular demonstrations. The British decided in March, 1919, to exile Zaghloul and three other members of the *Wafd* ('Delegation') party to Malte.

So, after eleven centuries[i] during which the Egyptians did not revolt against invaders or oppressors—and God knows how many of these came

---

[i] The last serious revolt was in 832 by the Peshmurians against the Abbasids.

and stayed or left—the British succeeded in uniting the Egyptians, from all walks of like, including Muslims and Copts, men and women, in rising against them in 1919. Shortly after news of Zaghloul's deportation spread, Morcos Sergius led a huge demonstration to Al-Azhar and was the first Coptic priest to speak from its pulpit and became one of the fieriest speakers of the revolution. During the revolution, slogans such as 'Crescent and Cross unity,' and 'Religion is for God, and the Fatherland for all,' were raised.

The Coptic role in the revolution was highly visible and substantial, and Copts were involved in all its facets. Nationalist committees in many provinces included Copts, and the one in Assiut contained a majority of Copts. After Zaghloul's release in April, Sinut, Khayat, and Wissa Wasif travelled with the *Wafd* to Paris for the Peace Conference. Wasif Ghali, who was already in Paris, and Wissa, were put in charge of propaganda, an activity that required good French.[188] The Central Committee of the Wafd Party soon had several wealthy and mainly landowning Coptic members[i].

This highlighted a rare moment of what would be affectionately called 'National Unity,' even though this would be later voided of its significance.

Egypt gained a limited independence[ii] in 1922[iii] (keeping in the British hand the issues of security of the communications of the British Empire in Egypt; the defense of Egypt against foreign aggression; and the protection of foreign interests and 'minorities'[iv]), and the *Sultan* Fouad became King. A constitution based on a British-like parliamentary representative system was adopted in 1923[v], and Zaghloul became the first popularly elected prime

---

[i] Morcos Hanna, leader of the Egyptian Bar since 1914; Tawfiq Doss, a renowned lawyer; Kamil Botrus; Dr. Habib Khayat; Fahmi Wissa, another Protestant; and Sarufim Mina Ebeid. Makram Ebeid joined later.

[ii] Through a unilateral declaration by the U.K. that, however, refused to recognize full Egyptian sovereignty over Sudan, or to withdraw its forces from the Suez Canal Zone; issues that were later agreed upon in the 1936 Treaty.

[iii] In the same year, Howard Carter discovered Tut-Ankh-Amun's tomb, thus awakening a sense of pride in past history. Interest in the Pharaonic past became an intellectual infatuation of the 1920s.

[iv] The mention of 'minorities' was motivated by the then-recent massacres of the Armenians. The vague term was thought to refer to foreign communities in Egypt, and was never raised concerning native Copts.

[v] It was suspended and replaced by another, more 'autocratic' constitution in 1930, but was restored in 1935.

minister in January, 1924. He included in his cabinet two Coptic ministers instead of one, as it used to be the custom in prior cabinets. Five weeks later, in March, the (Ottoman) caliphate was abolished.

***

The 1923 Constitution deserves some particular attention, given that it was the first document of its kind in Egypt's history, and that it represented a reference point of comparison for all the subsequent constitutions or amendments till the present time—and indeed there were many. Two issues are of importance.

The first issue relates to setting a religion of state. Many Egyptians argued for a separation between religion and politics. The incorporation of an article (149) naming Islam the religion of state made this impossible from the outset. The (constituent) Commission, without demur from its non-Muslim members and with no discussion, agreed to its inclusion. The Commission's members either failed to see, or felt unable to correct, the contradiction inherent in the special obligations this article imposed on the government and the promise of equality to all Egyptians, regardless of their religion.[i]

The second issue was about the representation of minorities in parliament. Dr. Mahmud Azmi, a lawyer, writer, and strong secularist, wrote[ii], that national solidarity demanded minority representation, backed proportional representation, but stipulated that only Copts participate in electing Coptic representatives. The Egyptians, he wrote, were still motivated by religion and, it was only fair, when a state religion had been fixed, to regard religious groups as political groups and to have those groups represented in parliament. Azmi also wished to eliminate the importance religious expressions had in social and political life. Until this could be done

---

[i] Carter, P. 130. Indeed, the guarantee of equal rights and duties stipulated in the constitution was a radical departure and went well beyond what the old system had afforded non-Muslims.

[ii] In a letter to the Head of the Royal *Diwan*, the *ulema* (Islamic 'clergy') complained about an article written by Mahmud Azmi, advocating both secularism and minority representation, and asked for an injunction to prevent Azmi from publishing articles 'against Islam.'

across the board, there would still be a majority and a minority; nationalism was not enough to unite the two as long as family, education, the court system, and other factors prevented a full blending of the different ethnic groups. He insisted that as long as the constitution did not abolish outmoded special principles and institutions, the minorities needed special representation.

On its part, the Coptic Community (*Melli*, Lay) Council sent a message, supporting minority representation to the Constitutional Commission. Doss, Coptic leader, and member of the Commission, suggested a weighting of the electorate which would give 20% of the seats to minorities. Yusuf Qattawi, representing the Jewish community, and Metropolitan Yoannes (also members), agreed with these views. A vote was taken by the Commission, and Doss's proposal was defeated by a vote of fifteen to seven.[189]

So effectively, the founding elites of the Egyptian nation-state opted for a unitary political and cultural formula that tried to repress the significance of religious differences as far as possible. They promoted a homogenizing nationalist ideology that eschewed the recognition of Coptic distinctiveness and adopted a non-sectarian political system that made no special provisions (e.g. quotas, constitutional minority status, etc.) for the integration of the Coptic minority.[190]

***

Despite the limitations of the constitution, a new era was supposed to have started, which was based on liberal and egalitarian beliefs, and the revolution it sponsored, in 1919. Past grievances were forgotten in this attempt to acquire independence and build a new and just society.

However, setbacks very quickly started to show in the new democratic experience. One such setback was the introduction of Islamic religious principles and sentiments into political discourse. All parties fell prey to the temptation to use this handy weapon against opponents, since it was one which was readily understood and responded to by the masses. What began to appear was a more concerted and organized attempt to gain and keep power by relying partly on traditional prejudices, and it, therefore, threatened to upset the new and fragile political system. By the late 1930s, the Copts were already longing for the golden days of the revolution. Almost all political parties, however originally intended to be secular, capitulation to the strong religious feelings was evident in the 1940s. By the late 1940s, intercommunal relations again showed a serious deterioration and were perhaps worse than they had been in 1907.[191]

The effects of Article 149 started to be felt, but the more serious problem than the naming of a religion of state, was the fact that the much-vaunted guarantees of freedom of worship and equality were not taken seriously. When a Coptic convert to Islam wished to return to Christianity, the court denied him permission on the grounds that the state's religion did not recognize the right of apostasy. Ultimately, Article 149's reinforcement of the traditional relationship between Islam and government prevented the full political integration of the Copts and made a secular polity legally impossible. How could the Copts be part of a national community which undertook as one of its tenets the necessity of defending and promoting Islam?

Article 149 did oblige the government to build mosques, teach religion, train Imams, celebrate Muslim holidays and adhere, at least in part, to religious law. In addition, the king was charged in the constitution with various religious responsibilities; he was, for example, the head of religious institutions. Public funds collected from Muslims and Copts, were distributed inequitably, and certain benefits accrued to one sector of the population alone. Al-Azhar's budget increased between 1923 and 1937 by more than six times.[192]

The problem of religious instruction in government schools started to poison the atmosphere. It was one new to the 20th century; before this, education was largely private. Copts educated their own children and taught them what they liked.

Now, the state dictated what Coptic children would be taught, first in state-owned schools and later in private Christian schools. In the former, Islamic religious instruction formed a larger part of the curriculum, particularly for the younger, more impressionable children. Not only were the Copts upset at the exposure of their children to lectures on Islam, but they were angry at the state's failure to use public revenue to provide equal Christian religious instruction.

In 1931, the Minister of Education, in announcing plans for compulsory elementary education legislation, stated that religious education would be mandatory for Muslims. It would not be provided for Christian students, but they could make their own arrangements for instruction to be given during the periods Islam was taught. In 1933, when a Coptic senator asked that Christian education be provided, the Minister of Education objected, claiming that it was impossible for a state with a constitutionally established religion to teach a second religion in its schools.

In the same year, the government passed a law that the Coptic Museum (which was founded by Morocs Simaika in 1908) should be supervised by the state and thus, nationalized. This was a thorny issue; not only did the museum belong to the church's properties and endowments, it also housed liturgical artifacts that could be used in the celebration of the Mass. Furthermore, adjoining the museum's campus was the Muallaqa Church where regular worship took place. The Pope and the Melli (Communal) Council protested vehemently, but to no avail.[193]

In 1936, a Quranic examination was made mandatory for all students in the first two years of secondary school. The Patriarch, under some pressure from his flock, finally requested an exemption for Coptic students; and the *Wafd*, in power, in 1937, agreed.

Azharis, others of similar religious ilk and the *Wafd*'s political opponents objected to the exemption; one petition, from the Central Committee of Young Muslim Societies, is typical: "The Arabic language is the official language of the state and the Quran is the noblest expression of this language. It is truly astonishing that a group of the sons of the nation is to be deprived from tasting the literature of the official language of the country..."

Political pressure pushed the *Wafd* into showing some support for Islamic religious instruction. It developed a list of recommendations which were supported by the Muslim brotherhood and included the following: (1) setting a religious examination for students in the final two years of secondary school; (2) building a mosque in every school and appointing one of the teachers to lead prayers; (3) requiring a sermon every day before the noon prayer, and (4) establishing a religious library in every school.

From 1946, the Copts were particularly vehement about the need for Christian religious education, an unsurprising response to the increased degree of Muslim pressure. The Coptic Community (Lay) Council was particularly vigorous in this debate.[194]

***

The Copts complained repeatedly that all important civil service posts were reserved for Muslims. The better-educated Copts had long occupied a greater proportion of bureaucratic posts than their percentage of the population. However, by the turn of the 19th century, Muslims were beginning to compete for these positions. The 1937 census recorded a decline in the Coptic share by one-third in 27 years, to 9.1 percent.

Few Copts were employed in Defense and Foreign Affairs ministries, or in ministries and departments that had considerable power over the Copts, like the police and the ministries of Education and Social Affairs. Furthermore, their access to positions of influence in other ministries was limited. Very rarely was a Copt made undersecretary. Few Copts reached the top posts in any ministry. Few directors of departments or sub-departments were Copts. In the Ministry of the Interior, there was never a Coptic governor or deputy governor of a province; nor (since 1924) a Coptic district officer (*Ma'mûr Markaz*).

There were some Coptic army officers, but their influence seems to have been slight. The appointment of a Muslim as Director of the Coptic Museum, in 1950, in defiance of the law was a blow, which seemed to symbolize the mounting discrimination Copts felt they met with in all walks of Egyptian life.

It was traditional, even for cabinets in the period before independence, to include one Copt. Only the *Wafd* broke with this custom by appointing two Copts. The Ministries of the Interior, Justice, and Education were never entrusted to a Copt. The *Wafd*, again, was more willing to appoint a Copt to Foreign Affairs than other parties. Salib Sami, a Copt who had served as Royal Adviser to the ministry of Foreign Affairs, was, to his considerable surprise, appointed Minister of War in 1933. A decade later, when Prime Minister, Husain Sirri, tried to move Sami from Foreign Affairs to the Ministry of Defense, senior army officers objected.

Although the number of portfolios expanded from ten in 1925 to sixteen in 1951, Coptic representation did not increase. From February, 1946, those Copts, who were appointed, were relegated to uninfluential ministries.[195]

***

As long as the constitution and Islam imposed certain duties on the state, many Copts believed that the community had a right to protect its religion and culture, in absence of any guarantee that the government would establish an appropriate secular alternative for both Muslims and Copts. The Copts were particularly sensitive on two subjects, personal status jurisdiction and government restrictions on their freedom of worship.

In 1944, the Copts were already alarmed due to the enactment of a law formally obliging non-Muslims to follow Islamic inheritance laws. The law passed, seemingly without Coptic opposition to the substance of the bill.[196]

Churches could be built only with the permission of the government; the government, however, was often loth to grant this permission. The restrictions were manifold[i]: churches could not be built near a mosque or in a Muslim area if the inhabitants objected, nor could they be built if the government decided that an adequate number of churches already existed in the area. If the church was too near a public building, a bank of the Nile, or an irrigation canal, the appropriate ministry had first to approve the proposed construction. Sometimes Copts waited as long as ten years only to be denied a permit. What often seems to have happened was that no sooner was a site chosen and a permit requested than a mosque was built nearby in order to defeat the petition. In 1951, *Misr* newspaper expressed dismay because, at a time when many mosques were being built in heavily Coptic Shubra, it was so difficult to build churches in such quarters. Contrary to popular belief, it was also difficult to obtain permits to repair existing churches.[197]

***

By the mid-1940s, the Copts felt that they no longer had an adequate representation in parliament. Added to that was a realization that their constitutionally guaranteed religious freedom was not safe from the government or the mob. Mounting hostility toward the Copts persuaded several of them to call for the disestablishment of Islam as the state religion.

They increasingly saw the state apparatus as biased against them; their access to it was restricted and its interference in their cultural and religious affairs was intolerable. By the late 1940s, the Copts could feel the state's

---

[i] In February, 1934, Mohamed Al-Izabi *Pasha*, undersecretary of the Ministry of Interior, issued a ministerial decree, referring to the Ottoman *Khatt-i-Hamayuni* (of 1856), and detailing the conditions necessary to build a new church. https://www.masress.com/shorouk/369948

chains tightening. There were more theoretical objections to equality than there had been in the 1920s; if anything, Egypt seemed to be moving farther and farther away from her ideal. The state could offer the Copts some protection and a degree of religious tolerance; anything more than this could and would be construed as catering to them.

Furthermore, Copts, who had new ambitions raised by the spread of Western ideas, could opt for nothing else other than secularism, and they understandably saw the confusion of Islam and politics as something that threatened both liberty and tolerance. From the mid-1940s, the (Coptic) secularist, Salama Musa, and others writing in the pages of *Misr,* called for a constitutional amendment disestablishing Islam as the state religion. In 1948, (Coptic priest) Morcos Sergius circulated a petition for signature among Copts, calling for the separation of religion and state, and for complete equality.[198]

**

Arabism started to flourish in Egypt in the early 1940s. There were two sorts of theorists here: those who saw Egypt as Arab because she was Muslim and for whom, therefore, religion and national identity were inextricably entwined; and those who wished to build a foundation for including Egypt in a secular pan-Arab union. The first tended to see Arab unity as a step toward the ultimate aim of Islamic unity. For the second, religion was incidental, a fact which was witnessed by the important contributions Syrian Christians made to pan-Arab thinking.

The connection between the language and the religion could only be ignored by the most obtuse. It was precisely because of this connection that the Copts were barred from study at the faculty of Dar al-Ulum, which trained language instructors, and from teaching Arabic in schools. In 1951, the Ministry of Education, noting this connection between language and the Quran and Hadith, and voicing its dismay, ordered an investigation into rumors that private schools were employing non-Muslims to teach Arabic.

As the 1940s progressed, the Copts became increasingly worried about pan-Arab sentiment. They saw themselves as potential, if not actual, victims of this dangerous idea.[199]

**

The rise of the Muslim Brotherhood had a key role in communal violence in Egypt. The Society of the Muslim Brothers was founded by a schoolteacher, Hassan Al-Banna, in 1928, as a religious, political, and social movement, with a goal to instill the Quran and the Sunna as the 'sole reference point for...ordering the life of the Muslim family, individual, community...and state.' Coming just a few years after the collapse of the Caliphate, the Brotherhood made it an ultimate objective to revive a global Caliphate state. Within a decade of its creation, the organization became a major political force in Egypt. In postwar Egypt, most political groups recognized the value of and competed for Brother's support.

From 1946, the Copts focused on the Muslim Brotherhood and related religious groups like the *Shabab Muhammad*[i] and the Young Men's Muslim Association as the greatest threat to both their safety and the concept of national unity. There were frequent reports in that year of the 'aggressive attitude' of the Brothers in the provinces that had taken toward the Copts... However, their religious and political beliefs, as well as their zeal in promoting them, played an important role in exacerbating tensions. The Coptic newspaper, *Misr*, saw the Brothers' activity as aimed at the creation of an Islamic state and abhorred their encouragement of anti-Coptic feeling. The Brothers used both mosques and leaflets to spread their anti-Coptic message. So worried were the Copts by Al-Banna's ambitions and so often did they hear themselves compared to the Jews in Europe, that they feared that they would meet a similar fate. The Brotherhood adhered to earlier Islamic beliefs; these confined non-Muslims to an inferior position (*Ahl-al-Dhimma*). All authority exercised by non-Muslims over Muslims was offensive and against the God-given order. The *Shabab Muhammad* announced that they would allow non-Muslims freedom of worship only if they paid the old jizya.[200]

The Muslim Brotherhood committed several acts of violence to terrorize the society at large and impose its presence. They killed two prime ministers (Ahmed Maher, in 1945, and Mahmoud Al-Nuqrashi, in 1948), a speaker of the parliament (Hamed Gouda, in 1949), and a senior judge (Ahmed Al-Khazendar, in 1948). They attacked several movie theatres in Cairo (in 1946–47). They set ablaze the Jewish Alley in Cairo's Al-Mousky

---

[i] 'Youth of Mohammed.'

commercial quarter (twice, in July and September, 1948) and attacked several Jewish-owned businesses.

During 1946, there were attacks on Christian churches in Cairo. In March, 1947, tensions in Zaqaziq flared when an angry Muslim mob burned a Coptic church. Communal relations there had been strained for at least two years, partly due to Brothers' activity.[201]

The Muslim Brothers and associated groups (*Misr al-Fatat*[i], *Shabab Muhammad*, and the Young Men's Muslim Association) which did the most to promote the Palestinian cause, until the late 1940s, were moved more by religious than pan-Arab sentiment. Palestine had so aggravated Egyptian Muslim sentiment that attacks on Egyptian Jews and foreign Christians were becoming common, and these did not inspire confidence. Already, in 1938, election campaign saw a group of Azhari demonstrators rather wildly demand that the Copts be expelled and sent to Palestine.[202]

In October, 1948, Morcos Sergius, the Coptic priest who had made anti-British orations from Al-Azhar's pulpit, drew up a petition, calling for the dissolution of the Brotherhood and all organizations which mixed religion and politics and were detrimental to equality, and then circulated it among Coptic notables. In the wake of a number of political assassinations and the discovery of the Brothers' secret paramilitary apparatus, the government finally acted by dissolving the society in December, 1948. The Copts were relieved, but the Brothers continued to operate underground and were implicated in the sacking of a Coptic church, in 1949.

There were anti-Coptic demonstrations in Cairo, with marchers shouting, 'Christianity is finished in Egypt,' 'One faith in Egypt — Islam,' and 'Today the Jews, tomorrow the Christians.' One activity of the Cairene Brothers at this time was to visit heavily Coptic quarters and paint crosses on the houses (as markers for targeting). On 4th January, 1952, a Coptic church, school, and Benevolent Society building were destroyed, and three Copts murdered by a mob in Suez. The government did nothing to stop the mob. The Patriarch and the Community (*Milli*) Council announced that Christmas[ii] would be a time of mourning and not celebration. The government tried to dissuade the church from making this very public gesture, but failed. Cairene Copts demonstrated outside the Patriarchate and one group shouted that although

---

[i] 'Young Egypt' later renamed the 'Islamic Party of Egypt.'

[ii] That would have been celebrated on the eve of January 7th.

the burning of the church was a great crime, silence was an even greater crime.[203]

The winds of liberal and democratic ideas coming from Europe brought also those of Communism, Fascism, and Nazism, among others. Each found fertile ground of its own, and with their dictatorial or even totalitarian tendencies, they will continue to play important roles in the coming decades.

***

The period that lasted barely three decades after the independence came to an end on a July day of 1952. Despite the Copts' huge disappointment with its outcome when compared with the expectations of 1919, it would be nostalgically remembered in the following decades as the 'Liberal Era.' By 'liberal,' it is meant to refer to 19th-century liberal ideas of personal liberties, free economy and free thoughts, associated with some form of representative democracy in a 'constitutional democracy'—give and take.[i]

So, what did the 'Free Officers' have in mind for Egypt —and the Copts?

---

[i] Obviously, this 'liberal' differs from the current use of the term in North America, where it mostly denotes left leaning 'progressive' ideas and ideologies.

Dhimmis in the Republican *Umma*-State

The 'Free Officers,' composed of fourteen mid-level officers[i], started their 'Blessed Movement' which would shortly afterward be labeled the '1952 Revolution.' They promised to go back to their barracks after implementing the six reformative principles they declared. This, of course, never happened, and Gamal Abdel Nasser emerged as the strong man who abolished the monarchy, and presided over the newly created republic till his death in September, 1970. Furthermore, the army became, and remains, the real—if not the sole—holder of power in the country.

Very soon, the 'Revolutionary Command Council' (R.C.C.) suspended the 1923 Constitution, disbanded all political parties and associations, except for…the Muslim Brotherhood. This exception highlights certain complicity, as in fact most, if not all, of the Free Officers were at one point, members of the Brotherhood. However, the realities of governance soon led to a clash of interests. As a result, the Brotherhood was banned in 1954, and its aspirations and designs had to be shelved—for now.[ii]

Worth to remember that as a result of the Anglo–Egyptian Treaty, signed in 1936, Egypt gained control over the military for the first time since 1882. The *Wafd* government decided to expand the entrance opportunities to the Royal Military Academy to a much more diverse pool of Egyptians, largely from middle and lower-middle classes. The leader and some members of the

---

[i] Colonel Nasser was the highest-ranking officer of the group, but one senior officer, Major General Mohammed Naguib, who joined the movement at the last minute, ensured the success of the coup. In addition to the fourteen leaders who did not include any Copts, there were some 30 junior officers, among whom there was one Copt, a first lieutenant by grade.

[ii] The Brotherhood, which was represented by two members in the cabinet, pressed Nasser to apply quickly some *Sharia*-compatible measures, which he rejected. Relations between them soured, and one of its members attempted to assassinate him in October, 1954.

Free Officers were among those admitted to the Academy in 1936 and
onwards, and (irony of History!), were the ones to disband the *Wafd* along
with other political parties.

Coming from a specific social milieu, they were culturally conservative
and internalized religious beliefs, which explains their initial openness to
collaborate with the Muslim Brothers.[204]

Nasser quickly announced his political orientation[205] when he identified
Egypt's priorities. At the top came, "*Pan-Arabism associated with Islam,*"
because, "*The Arab sphere is the most important and closely related sphere
to us. It has historically merged with us and we have suffered the same
ordeals and experienced the same crises [..]. This sphere has also religiously
merged with us, transposing the centers of religious radiation, within the
borders of its capitals, from Mecca to Kufa, and then to Cairo.*" The second
priority, or circle, was Islam, being, "*A sphere of the brothers of faith who
face with us, wherever they are under the sun, toward one Qiblah,[i] while
their lips whisper the same prayers [..]. Then, I return to the lost role, seeking
a hero to play it [..] and we alone (in Egypt) by virtue of our 'location' are
capable of playing it.*"

Sure enough, Nasser embarked on his populist campaign of Pan-
Arabism, to regain the glory of the 'Arab Nation.' He launched unity
projects, with Syria then with Iraq, in the course of which 'Egypt' lost its
historical and venerated name and was reduced in 1958 to be a 'southern
province' of a United Arab Republic. When the unity floundered in 1961,
Egypt still called itself, bizarrely, the U.A.R. (It was renamed the 'Arab
Republic of Egypt' under Sadat, as of 1971).

On the Islamic front, Nasser was no less energetic. He promoted Islam
as the religion of state, to become Article-3 in his new constitution of 1956[ii].
It is interesting to note that the constitution of the U.A.R., (1958) the state
that united Egypt with Syria, dropped the religion of state altogether, fearing
it would annoy the Syrian Christian minority (who were pro-Arabism, but
not pan-Islamism). However, after the collapse of the unity, Nasser issued a
'constitutional declaration' in 1962, reestablishing Islam. It was a clear
message to the Copts that their stand on such issues was of no importance.

---

[i] The direction that Muslims face when they pray. It is in the direction of the *Kaaba*.
[ii] Thus becoming part of the section on the 'foundations of the state,' instead of
Article 149, in the 'general rules' section, in the pre-Revolution constitution of 1923.

Nasser's long-time confidante and chief-of-cabinet, Sami Sharaf, enumerated[206] a long list of achievements in 'service of Islam,' which includes:

— He built ten-thousand new mosques in Egypt between 1954 and 1970; almost as many as the eleven-thousand that were built since Islam entered Egypt.

— Al-Azhar was transformed into a university in which natural and secular sciences are taught alongside religious subjects.[i] Branches of Al-Azhar University have been opened in many Islamic countries. Dozens of *Da'wa* (proselytizing) Azhari missions were sent across Africa and Asia to spread Islam (government financed).

— Hundreds of Azhar institutes (*madrasah*) for boys and (separately) for girls have been built in Egypt, for students from age six to 18.

— Established the Islamic Missions City, on an area of 30 acres, to house tens of thousands of Muslim students from 70 countries, to study at Al-Azhar and live in Egypt, at the government's expenses.

— Initiated the Organization of the Islamic Conference, based in Jeddah, whose first secretary-general was Anwar Sadat.

— The Quran was translated into several languages and (freely) distributed worldwide. A Quran Radio station was set-up, to broadcast throughout the day. The entire Quran recitation was recorded on C.D.s and tapes for the first time in history, and hundreds of thousands of copies distributed throughout the world. Quran memorization competitions were organized throughout the country, the Arab world, the Islamic world; President Abdel Nasser, personally distributed the prizes to the winners.

— Islamic heritage books were printed in the state printing press and widely distributed in order to be accessible to all.

— Religious instruction became compulsory in schools.

— Masonic lodges, Rotary clubs and Bahai temples, were closed. Gambling prohibited.

***

---

[i] Coptic students are not allowed to enroll in secular faculties, even though the university is financed by all taxpayers.

The Copts received a number of serious blows under Nasser's rule. By abolishing political parties (with a special animosity toward the liberal 'pro-secular' *Wafd*) and enforcing the agrarian land-reform law (whereby the upper limit of land ownership for a family was set at 200 *feddans*), the Copts' elite and leadership, made up of politicians and/or wealthy landlords, was virtually decapitated overnight.

This was followed by another hard blow in July, 1961, when Nasser nationalized businesses and confiscated assets belonging to hundreds of people. 'Egyptianized' foreigners[i] and Copts were particularly targeted. In a significant departure from their historical attachment to their homeland, the Copts started their first wave of large-scale immigration (to the U.S., Canada, and Australia), where persons with good professional qualifications found a ready welcome. Some wealthy Coptic families sought refuge in Europe.

The fact that no Copts[ii] were on the R.C.C., meant that the Copts were totally excluded from inner power circles. One Coptic minister would, as a matter of token representation, be member of the cabinet, even though the total number of ministers almost tripled from before 1952, and would typically be a loyal, and obedient technocrat, and never given an influential portfolio. Discrimination was significant in holding posts, especially at higher levels, in the administration and the huge 'Public Sector.'[iii] Copts were totally excluded from having jobs in the presidential offices and the various security apparatuses.

There was not a single Copt out of 350 members in the new National Assembly (parliament) of 1957. A stipulation was then added in the 1962 Constitutional Declaration allowing the president to appoint ten members. This was used to appoint five to six Coptic members, in addition to two (rarely three) elected, thus corresponding to a dismal percentage of the total membership. In average, there was a total of eight Copts in each of the parliaments of 1964, 1969, out of 360 members, at 2.2 percent, compared to

---

[i] These were mostly Greeks, Italians, Levantines, as well as the Jews, who were still in Egypt, after the expulsion in 1956 of the bulk of the community.

[ii] This fact in itself can be understood given the history of the Egyptian military. Nevertheless, it shaped the views of the Free Officers and set the pattern for subsequent exclusionary and discriminatory policies and practices. (See Note 204)

[iii] Composed of the nationalized, and the new government-funded, companies. It was quickly growing as Egypt adopted a socialist system of economy.

an overall average of 6.4 percent for the ten parliaments in the periods between 1924 and 1950.

In 1956, a family-status law was applied to all Egyptians. While considered part of the civil code, it still has considerable religious elements, referring to the *Sharia* as a basis for Muslims, and to the corresponding religious principles or regulations for each of the non-Muslim communities. Quite significant is the rule that in case the two parties of a marriage union were (or became) from different religions, or different denominations of the same religion (e.g. Orthodox and Catholic), *Sharia* rules would apply. Also, *Sharia* applies in matters of inheritance.[207]

In 1953, the church endowments, estimated at more than 2,500 *feddans*, were effectively confiscated and put under the Ministry of (Islamic) Endowments. It took over four decades of legal battles, until finally some 1400 *feddans* were returned in 1996.

After the 1956 crisis of Suez, the bulk of the Jewish community in Egypt (which numbered about 70,000 in 1950) were ordered to leave Egypt. Many of those had ancestors living in the country (especially in Alexandria) since the first century B.C., were so deracinated at short notice, departing—mostly to Europe—with only their personal belongings in hand.[i]

***

A new Pope, Kyrillos VI, the 116th, was ordained in May, 1959. Initially, he had tense relations with Nasser, but soon, the latter realized the importance of the Coptic Church, given his pan-African policy and the need for good relations with Ethiopia, where the church was influential. Nasser is said to have agreed that some 25 churches be authorized per year[208], and permits granted based on the Pope's proposals. Nasser also approved a financial subsidy[ii] to help build a new Cathedral, after being solicited by the

---

[i] It is quite astonishing that when these deportees are met in their new homelands (e.g. in France), they always show affectionate nostalgia rather than bitterness about what they unfairly faced. The 'People of Saturday' now gone, the fate of the 'People of Sunday' remained to be seen.

[ii] Nasser agreed to a contribution of L. E. 500,000, half paid in cash and half in the form of work done by contracting companies in the public sector. Ironically, it was

Pope; an unavoidable demand as there were no longer enough rich Coptic families ready to cover the cost.

The recognition of the unique place of the Coptic Church of Alexandria was made abundantly clear when Kyrillos VI welcomed 172 delegates from around the world, who came to participate in the celebration of the 1900th anniversary of the martyrdom of St. Mark, its founder and patron. On June 25th, 1968, Kyrillos, together with Nasser and Ethiopia's Emperor, Haile Selassie, inaugurated the new cathedral (for which the foundation stone was laid three years earlier). The rest of St. Mark's relics were brought from Venice and buried in the cathedral.[i] Nasser realized the benefits of such an event, not only as a matter of national pride, but an international affair highlighting Egypt's (and his personal) prestige as the leader of the Middle East.

With the virtual disappearance of the Coptic elite, the church suddenly became the *de facto* leader and sole representative of the community. The few gains achieved over the prior decades in making a Copt more of a citizen than a community-member just evaporated. On the other hand, the Pope, a hermit, mystic and traditionalist, embarked on sizeable efforts to modernize the church. In a move to empower a new generation of well-educated monks, he took the significant step of appointing, in 1962, three 'general' (at-large) bishops without territorial dioceses. Bishop Samuel was responsible for relations with other churches, as well as with the emerging Coptic churches abroad. Bishop Gregorius, with a doctorate in theology from Greece, was in charge of Coptic Studies. Bishop Shenouda, a journalist and a poet before becoming a solitary monk, was made responsible for education. The latter's weekly lectures at the cathedral became enormously popular, especially among the youth for whom he became an idol, and was normally attended by as many as ten-thousand people.[ii]

---

a nationalized company that had belonged to a Coptic contractor (Adly Ayoub) that did the construction.

[i] During Kyrillos' reign, beginning on April 2nd, 1968, repeated apparitions of the Virgin Mary were seen at the church of Zaytûn, north of Cairo.

[ii] This author, then following his engineering studies, can attest to this. Under pressure from the authorities, the Pope asked Abba Shenouda to stop his lectures and return to the monastery. But this provoked so much opposition, that he was allowed to return a few months later.

***

Anwar El-Sadat became president in October, 1970, after Nasser's unexpected death. Immediately, he started making his Islamic orientation even more ostentatious than in previous years. He instructed state media to label him the '*Pious* President'[i] and heavily infused his public speeches with Islamic references. He liberated Islamists (Muslim Brothers and others) who were prisoned under Nasser, and invited others who had left (mainly to Saudi Arabia) to return back.

Sadat then initiated what one could, in hindsight, term 'the Great Islamic Transformation' of Egypt, to reverse whatever 'symptoms of secularization' that might have developed over the prior century. The first step was to stipulate in the Second Article of his new Constitution, promulgated in 1971 (long before Khomeini embarked on his Islamic revolutionary campaign), that—in addition to establishing Islam as the religion of state—the principles of Islamic *Sharia* were 'a main source' of legislation. In May, 1981, the '*a*' was replaced with '*the*,' making Sharia *the* term of reference for the entire constitution, meaning all other articles were to be interpreted in light of *Sharia*. That change provided the legal, political, and 'psychological' basis for the Islamic transformation to proceed in an inexorable fashion. Sadat's famous slogan, "I am a Muslim president of a Muslim state," was a clear indication of this transformation.[209]

Under the direct supervision of Mohammed Othman Ismail, a local Muslim Brotherhood leader in Assiut, and upon orders of Sadat personally, the 'Islamic Group' was created in 1972, and a campaign of harassing and terrorizing the Copts began. The choice of the area was deliberate, because Assiut was the governorate with the highest concentration of Copts, exceeding a third of the population. After his initial success, Ismail was appointed governor of Assiut, and the Islamic Group expanded its activities to other parts of Egypt. Fouad Allam writes, "We have been reporting to the President Sadat the excesses that are taking place, and the complaints of Christians in Assiut from the actions of Islamic groups and the Muslim Brotherhood, and warned of the growing risks of sectarian strife which began with individual attacks on churches and culminated in incidents, like that of

---

[i] The word 'Pious' in Arabic is identical to 'Believer,' thus carrying an implicit insinuation directed at non-Muslim 'unbelievers.'

Zawya Hamra," [i] but to no avail.[210] Sheikh Omar Abdel-Rahman (the 'Blind Sheikh')[ii] became the group's 'spiritual' leader, and issued a *fatwa*, making it legitimate to rob Copts (especially goldsmiths) because 'they no more pay *Jizya*.'[iii] Little did Sadat know about the monster he created: the leaders of this group were the very same assassins who shot at and killed Sadat himself less than a decade later. Many of these Islamist terrorists left Egypt to engage in the international Jihadi terrorism, starting in Afghanistan, that still hounds the world. It is rather astounding how little attention is paid in the West, especially in the U.S., to Sadat's active role in developing the modern phenomenon of Jihadism.

***

On March 7th, 1971, Pope Kyrillos VI[iv] died, and on November 14th, Shenouda III became the 117th pope.

Barely six months later, church and state came into conflict. A prayer hall belonging to the Bible Friends Association was used as a church without a formal permit in the Cairo suburb of Khanka, and after 'unknown' people set it ablaze, the police moved in and knocked the building down. The day after, Pope Shenouda ordered bishops and monks to go to the ruins of the church and celebrate mass there, even if they risked being shot at and killed. The police tried to stop them, but they went on.[v] Sadat was dismayed—and no wonder! For the first time since the Arab-Islamic invasion, a Coptic Pope was prepared for such an open challenge. He determined to have a show down, considering that, "Shenouda has gone beyond everything," and was threatening, "I am not going to take anymore (..). I can't carry on with this time-bomb ticking away underneath me." Finally, he was advised to calm down and to ask the parliament to investigate the whole matter.

---

[i] A massacre that took place in June 1981, claiming the lives of over 80 Copts.

[ii] Omar Abdel Rahman served a life sentence (till his death in Feb. 2017) in a North Carolina prison for his role in the 1993 World Trade Center bombing. Ironically, he was the one to issue a *fatwa* in favor of 'killing the ruler who does not rule according to Allah's laws,' which was used by the Group to justify Sadat's assassination.

[iii] A wave of attacks on Coptic merchants and goldsmiths followed, using the proceeds of the thefts utilized to finance the terror groups.

[iv] He is highly venerated, and is already pronounced a Saint by the Coptic Church.

[v] In the evening, mobs attacked some Copts' houses in the area.

A committee, chaired by Deputy Speaker, Dr. Gamal Oteifi, investigated the issue and duly reported in November, 1972. Rather honestly, the committee concluded that, "Unless we address the roots of the problem, probe the factors that lead to it, and come up with a remedy, the follow-up efforts will stop when things calm down." It continued that there was a need to find a permanent solution in place of the temporary sedatives which threaten the recurrence of the hidden disease that will become more serious and fatal." Among other recommendations, the committee highlighted the need to abolish the *Khatt-i Hamayuni* and replace it with a simpler regulation that would not require a presidential decree for every church. Later, in 1973, Sadat met with the Pope and the Synod, and said that he would authorize 50 new churches a year.[211] (In retrospect, the promise was never kept[i], and he specifically refused to authorize a church in Khanka).

In 1976, Sadat ordered a review of all existing laws to ensure their compliance with *Sharia*. The committee, headed by speaker, Sufi Abu-Taleb, himself a strong proponent of applying *Sharia*, considered also to issue a law on *riddah*, whereby anyone who apostatize from Islam would be given one chance to repent and return, but if he persisted in his apostasy, he would be hanged, and only two witnesses would be needed to convict him. There was talk of putting into practice the strict *Sharia* punitive code (Hudud) which ordained that a thief should be punished by having his hand amputated. Some judges were so enthusiastic that they began to pass judgment according to *Sharia* rather than civil law[ii].

As was to be expected, all the talk about the necessity for all citizens, Muslims and Christians alike, to conform to *Sharia* had profound repercussions in the Coptic community. Other intimidating—to say the least—measures included persistent articles by senior Azhari Sheikhs, in the state-owned flagship newspaper *Al-Ahram*, depicting the Bible as 'adulterated,' accusing Christians of '*Shirk* and *Kufr*—the two worst crimes in Islam's eyes—and calling for decisive victory by Muslims over the

---

[i] The total number of permits issued in four years, including backlog, was 58.

[ii] At the beginning of 1982, one judge went as far as to punish a man who appeared before him on a charge of drunkenness to 80 lashes. He later published a lengthy explanation of his action, insisting that as a judge, his duty toward Allah was above his duty to human law.

Kuffar.[i] Another bit of 'information' *aggressively* diffused in the media was a government census giving the number of Copts to be slightly over two-million, out of a total population of thirty-seven-million.[ii] The new National Assembly (350 members) had only one, appointed, Copt.

On January 17th, 1977, a Coptic conference, echoing the one of 1911, was held in Alexandria and ended by producing a communiqué which was never openly published:

"Circumstances have made necessary the calling of a conference of the Coptic people in Alexandria (..). His Holiness, Pope Shenouda III, attended the opening meeting on 17th December, 1976, in the great Cathedral of Alexandria. The conference proceeded with a discussion of the problems on the agenda, and took into consideration the work of the preparatory committee, which met on fifth and sixth July. All members of the conference, clergy and laity alike, agreed on two propositions which, in their opinion, could not be separated from each other. The first is an unassailable belief in the eternal Egyptian Coptic Church, founded by Mark, the evangelist, and sanctified by the sacrifices of martyrs through the ages. The second is the sense of responsibility toward the Fatherland, for which we are ready to sacrifice our lives, and in which the Copts represent the most ancient, pure, and authentic element. No people are more attached do the soil all Egypt, or prouder of their country and their nationality, than the Copts."

The communiqué referred to the most serious issues of freedom of belief and stated that 'freedom of belief means that every human being is free to embrace the religious belief in which he believes and not to be harmed or to suffer because of this belief. However, some trends that are against the freedom of Christian faith, and regrettably, followed by some official bodies, such as the directorates of security, the administration of civil status registry, notary offices, and personal status public attorneys; in cases of conversion to Islam on the one hand, and the cases described as apostasy from Islam on the other hand.' It then called for the freedom of religious practice, the protection

---

[i] Respectively, by Sheikh Hussein Makhlouf, on 12.03.76; Sheikh Mohammed Al-Fahham, 22.10.76; and Sheikh Mohamed Bissar on 24.09.76.

[ii] A figure described by Mohammed Heikal (P. 165) as 'certainly too low' (thus admitting to the manipulation of the figures by the state), adding that the number attributed to President Carter, in 1977, during a meeting with Pope Shenouda at the White House, of seven million, or nineteen percent, was 'no less certainly too high.'

of the family and Christian marriage, equality and equal opportunity (in jobs), the (adequate) representation of Christians in parliamentary bodies, and 'warning against extremist religious trends.'

The conference called for abolishing the draft apostasy law, abandoning the thought of implementing laws derived from Islamic law on non-Muslims, the need for firm intervention by government authorities to eliminate extremist religious trends, and demanding the lifting of official or disguised censorship of Christian publications, putting an end to writings attacking Christian belief, and to include in the curricula of historical, literary, and cultural studies in the various stages of education and in the universities, regarding the Christian era in the history of Egypt for six whole centuries before the Islamic conquest.

The conference was the most serious gathering of its kind since 'The Coptic Conference' held in Assiut, in 1911—with one big difference: it was sponsored by the Pope, no less, whereas the then-pope had opposed the previous one. To conclude, it suggested that 31st January to 2nd February, 1977, should be a period of fasting for all the Copts, and that the conference would remain in session until its resolutions had been implemented. The conference had received messages of support from Copts abroad.[212]

For once, there was a courageous Patriarch willing to stand up for the rights of his suffering community.

In April, Shenouda was the first Pope to visit North America, where he spent 40 days in U.S. and Canada. He met with President Carter who greeted him as the spiritual leader of 'seven million' Copts[i] — a remark that enraged Sadat even more.

Sadat, meanwhile, stopped talking about the proposed *Sharia* laws. But as a counterblast to the Coptic Conference, the rector of Al-Azhar, Sheikh Abdul Halim Mahmoud, convened a conference of Islamic organizations in July. This conference issued a series of resolutions: any law or a regulation which runs counter the teachings of Islam should be treated as null and void, and should be a rejected by Muslims. The application of *Sharia* is mandatory and not the consequence of parliamentary legislation, for there can be no questioning Allah's law. The delay in enacting true Islamic legislation is due to appeasement of non-Muslims, and the parliament should, without any further delay, pass the legislation which has been already tabled. The

---

[i] A figure almost three times as much as Egypt's official census of 1976.

conference declared its appreciation of the recent speech by the president in which he spoke of his intention to purge the state machinery of atheists. The conference also appealed to the president to ensure that religion (Islam) should be made the basis of all education.

On the eve of the Coptic Christmas, January 6th, 1980, bombs exploded at a number of churches in Alexandria, and when the government did not move to apprehend the perpetrators, Pope Shenouda decided to take a public stance. On 26th March, 1980, the Pope held a session of the Holy Synod, after which a stern statement was issued: "Having studied the situation of the Copts and the numerous complaints that they made from all the governorates across Egypt, and complaints by the Coptic students inside and outside university cities (dorms); what the Copts are subjected to by way of insults and accusations of *Kufr*, as well as different kinds of incitation and attacks on their lives and churches, the kidnapping of Christian girls and converting some of them in various ways; the Holy Synod decided to cancel the official celebrations of the glorious Easter this year (to be celebrated on April 6th), limiting them to prayers in the churches, while not accepting the congratulations of the feast, as an expression of the sufferings by the Copts." The members of the Holy Synod also decided to retreat in monasteries during the feast. The statement was to be sent to the priests of the churches of Cairo, to read out to the congregation at the end of the Palm Sunday and of Good Friday prayers. The statement also noted: not to put decorations on the facade of the churches and not to accept congratulations on the eve, or the day, of Easter.

On May 14th, Sadat gave address to parliament, in which he said he had knowledge of a 'plot by Shenouda to become a political as well as religious leader of the Copts and set up a separate Coptic State with Assiut as its capital.' "But the Pope must understand," he said, "that I am the Muslim president of a Muslim country." He told one of his aides that he considered sacking the Pope by means of a plebiscite. Apart from the preposterous accusations, it is, to say the least, alarming to think what the repercussions would have been—based on the precedent of the preceding history—if a plebiscite had been held in a predominantly Muslim country to determine the fate of the head of the Christian church there.

June, 1981, saw the most serious 'clash' for many years. In the Zawya al-Hamra popular quarter of Cairo, what 'started as a quarrel between neighbors turned into an armed battle' (as the police reports put it). Once again, the origin of the dispute was to be found in the 'illegal' setting up of a church, with members of the president's National Party trying to prove their religious zeal by using force to stop its construction.[213] The government said that seventeen Copts were killed and 54 injured, but a few months later, it became widely known that the real number of victims was 81.[214]

During a visit by Sadat to the U.S. in August, the Coptic community took half-page advertisements in the *Washington Post* and the *New York Times*, listing their grievances, and staged two demonstrations in Washington. These took place in spite of the fact that Pope Shenouda had sent Bishop Samuel in advance of the visit, asking the community to lie low and not provoke him.

On September 3rd, Sadat arrested many of his political opponents[i]. He also arrested 170 Copts, both clergy (including eight bishops and 24 priests) and laymen, and ordered the closure of *Al-Kiraza,* a bi-weekly church publication, as well as *Watani*, the only Coptic newspaper in Egypt[ii]. Two days later, Sadat announced in a televised speech the 'annulment of the government's recognition of Pope Shenouda,' effectively suspending him from his administrative functions which were transferred to a Patriarchal committee of five bishops, including Bishop Samuel. The Committee declared (on September 22nd) that the, "Coptic Church, according to its sacred evangelical teachings and ecclesiastical laws, is committed to obedience to the ruling authorities, in accordance with the Holy Bible, 'every soul is subject to the superlatives.'"

The doors of the Monastery of Abba Bishoy, where the Pope was in retreat, were shut on September 5th, and troops surrounding it stopped all movements to or from it. A month later, on October 6th, 1981, Sadat was killed, (as well as Bishop Samuel, who was on the same parade tribune). For most Copts, this was a prompt divine judgment.[215]

***

Hosni Mubarak became president, but despite numerous demands, especially by Coptic diaspora, he left Pope Shenouda under confinement in the monastery for a total of 40 months. On January 5th, 1985, the Pope was

---

[i] About 1530, political figures, journalists, activists, etc.

[ii] Published weekly, on Sundays, since 1958. A new publication permit was later obtained, and it reappeared in 1984.

released after 1213 days, and a presidential decree formally reversed the one made by Sadat.

Following Sadat's assassination, the first period of Islamic Jihad's armed conflict in Egypt came to an end. By the 1990s, the second phase began, including a long series of terrorist operations against the Copts, the government, and tourists. This phase ended with a terrorist attack targeting tourists in Luxor in November, 1997.[i]

Then came the phase of the 'ordinary people' attacks against Copts. Mubarak's era was marred with homegrown violence that rather came from individuals not belonging to or acting on behalf of a particular terrorist group. It was common in these cases that no specific perpetrators are named, and the criminal charges thus become 'diffuse.' Thus, the aggressors have rarely been brought to justice, nor has any condemnation ever been issued. This was also the result of the security apparatus' failure to handle and process criminal evidence appropriately. Reason for mob attacks could be discovering a place where some Copts were 'praying without permit.' Another reason would be a case of a Coptic man accused of having a relationship with a Muslim girl. The opposite would, of course, be fine, and even encouraged; scores of Coptic girls every year, often underage, are lured and converted to Islam, with the full complicity of the police, and other authorities.

State-sponsored Islamization of the society continued and intensified. This strategy employed by the regime had attempted both to satisfy and keep the Islamists in check by offering them a formula in which the state continued to rule from the top while the radical Islamists determine and supervise social norms. Islamization penetrated the media, education, and the state infrastructure. Throughout the process, the regime took action only in cases that threatened its own stability, tolerating, if not encouraging, the oppression of Copts. The 'Islamic street' grew stronger and kept demanding greater Islamization, and the regime met these demands in order to increase its own legitimacy, power, and domination. In addition to the Muslim Brotherhood, Salafist groups became ever more present.[216]

In fact, fighting sectarian strife was not the political priority for the regime because it was not perceived as a threat to its survival; consequently, the crucial state agencies (local administration, police, state security, and so

---

[i] The attack claimed 61 lives, including 58 foreign tourists.

on) were never instructed to adopt a consistent strategy against it. The authorities' typical approach was to procrastinate and take the path of least resistance; logically, this usually consisted in appeasing the Muslim majority.[217]

Violence against the Copts was, and continues to be, only one facet of systematic discrimination they face. The situation has even been described as one of 'daily martyrdom.' In the words of a Copt whose brother was killed in one of the attacks, "We all envy those martyrs. They escaped the humiliation that we endure (..) the Lord saved him from the miserable treatment and loathing the rest of us get."[218]

In the judiciary, some judges ignored existing civil laws and ruled according to *Sharia* (referring directly to Article II of the constitution). In one typical incident, the Administrative Court rejected a lawsuit by a Copt, contesting the state changing his religion to Islam after his Christian father had converted when he was seven years old. The ruling rejected his demand (thus, the man was considered to be a Muslim because his father had converted), and stated that he could not 'convert' to Christianity since conversion was only permissible if it followed a certain order 'sanctioned by the Almighty Allah: he who believes in Judaism is called on to embrace Christianity, and he who believes in Christianity is called on to embrace Islam, the seal of all religions. In all these cases, the opposite is incorrect, as evidenced by Allah's ordering of the revelation of His religions, and in accordance with public order and morals in Egypt.'[i]

Mubarak's era saw numerous massacres against the Copts, the last of which took place in Alexandria[ii] less than a month before a popular uprising that ended with toppling his regime. Under Mubarak's watch, some 324 incidents of sectarian attacks[219] (i.e. excluding common law crimes) took place against Copts 'for who they are.' These resulted in 157 persons killed, over 800 wounded, and 103 churches attacked or burnt, as well as burning, looting, or ransacking of properties or businesses belonging to 1380

---

[i] Ruling on June, 30th, 2009, on case no. 4475/58 filed by Girgis Malak Wasif,

[ii] On 2011, New Year's eve, at the church of the Two-Saints, where 24 people were killed. The perpetrators were never identified, and the authorities stalled all attempts to reveal the facts, leading to speculations that in fact one of the country's multiple security apparatuses might have been behind it, as a part of inter-agency war.

individuals. Perpetrators have very rarely been prosecuted, let alone condemned by a court. Most significant among them were al-Kosheh massacre in January 2000 (20 killed).[i] In 2010 a number of incidents took place, in Nag-Hammadi (7 killed), Matruh, and Omraneya.

Other forms of discrimination against the Copts and their alienation continued with little improvement[ii]. At one time, the president's party, which typically holds the crushing majority of the parliament, did not even bother to propose a single Coptic candidate in the parliamentary election of 1995. The total number of Copts in Mubarak's seven parliaments averaged eight (including those appointed), at an average percentage of 1.7 from the total.

***

The Republican regime (since 1952) never tried to compensate for the initial under-representation caused by the low percentage of Copts in the upper ranks of the military. Thus, the situation was perpetuated through a mixture of tolerated individual discrimination, ceilings for Copts representation in certain areas, as well as career choices among the Copts themselves influenced in turn by the anticipation of discrimination. The fact is that the underrepresentation of the Copts was never addressed during the Mubarak era (in fact, the regime consistently denied the existence of discrimination).

The oft-bemoaned Coptic retreat to the community sphere and the political role of the Coptic Orthodox Church were a clear consequence of all this political marginalization.[220]

Signs of cultural exclusion, if not persecution, permeate the state's policies. One telling example was when renowned Coptlogist, Gawdat Gabra, planned to prepare a volume on Coptic cultural history in 2003, the Egyptian State Security Department, one of the fearful epitomes of the country's 'deep state' rejected a project for a book titled *Coptic Civilization.*

---

[i] https://www.copticsolidarity.org/2020/01/08/al-kosheh-massacre-how-did-it-turn-into-a-state-crime/

[ii] In a symbolic gesture, Mubarak decreed, in 2002, that the Coptic Nativity feast, celebrated on January 7th, becomes a national holiday. Also, in 1998, he delegated to the provincial governors the 'presidential authority of issuing repair permits' for churches.

It took ten years of relentless efforts, and publishing was only possible during the aftermath of the (ill-fated) 'Arab Spring,' when the grip of the security apparatuses was momentarily loosened.[221]

***

For at least one decade after the release of the Pope by Mubarak from his 'monastery confinement,' the President and the Pope maintained an arms-length distance, but without confrontations. Over the years, some kind of *entente* was established, and the Pope became more mellowed and even a supporter of Mubarak's regime in its last years. Some say that this was a mere window-dressing aimed at giving an impression of harmony, but devoid of any genuine ability to achieve structural changes.[222] It is certainly true, but the dilemma facing the Pope, and indeed the international community, was that Mubarak presented the political options in a binary way: "Either me, or the Islamists." The Pope probably preferred 'the devil we know.' He did, however, continue to relentlessly endorse Coptic civil and citizenship rights. When asked (even on state T.V.) why wouldn't he rein in Coptic activists abroad who criticize Mubarak, his answer would typically be two-folded: "They live in free countries where they enjoy their freedom of speech and hence (he) could not muzzle them," and, "The best way to avoid their critiques would be to resolve the problems so that there would be nothing to complain about."

The assertive adoption of Coptic demands by the church leadership and the activities of expatriate activists started in the 1970s. This was followed by an intermediate course steered by the church between the accommodation and assertiveness became the dominant form of Coptic public expression throughout the 80s and early 90s.

***

The tipping point came on 2011's New Year's Eve, when suicide bomber killed 23 worshipers and wounded 97 in the Two-Saints Church in Alexandria. The government was quick to blame the Mossad (the Israeli secret service) and Al-Qaida. This time, the public fury came from Copts, as well as from Muslims.

The breakdown of the Mubarak regime (February, 2011) immediately caused a state of insecurity and anxiety that deeply affected large parts of the Coptic community and made them more pessimistic than never before. On the other hand, Coptic activist circles achieved an unprecedented degree of mobilization that culminated in several large demonstrations and sit-ins in central Cairo. As a result, public and official reactions to incidents of sectarian violence were more sensitive to Coptic demands than ever before.

These openings did not last long. The growing Coptic rights movement on the streets by youth Copts was a significant development. But it was confronted and bloodily repressed by the army on October 9th, 2011, in the Maspero massacre where 28 Copts were massacred.

The political scene was dominated by bitter power struggles between the Military Council, the revolutionary street, and different political camps and the state bureaucracy and judiciary. The Muslim Brotherhood achieved their decades-old dream of taking over the rule, with the implicit but unmistakable support of the Military Council, when their candidate won the presidential election and their party the parliamentary. However, in their greediness, the Brothers overplayed their hand and thought that they could monopolize the rule, dismissing the understanding that the army would continue to hold the 'power' behind the rule. The *bras de fer* quickly ended with an army-backed street 'revolution' that toppled the Brotherhood's rule on July 3rd, 2013. The Brothers' revenge targeted the Copts, when massive simultaneous attacks on August 14th resulted in the burning of 43 churches and dozens of Christian religious institutions and schools, and Coptic-owned businesses and homes[223]. This was the largest and most widespread series of attacks since that of May 16th, 1320, under the Mamluks. It was also quite rightly called 'Egypt's *Kristallnacht.* '[224]

The army quickly imposed the upper hand, in a barely disguised alliance with Salafi Islamists, adopting the 'Pakistani model' of the turban-helmet alliance. The new regime lead by El-Sisi, president since June 2014, is hence by no means less Islamic than that of the Brotherhood, if not more.

***

On March 18th, 2012, Pope Shenouda III passed away, aged 89, after a reign of over 40 years. In an unprecedented scene, hundreds of thousands of Copts closed the streets around the Cathedral in Cairo where his funeral was held. He is remembered as probably being the most visible Pope in the history of the Coptic Church. Bold and critical, he knew when to be conciliatory and when to be outspoken, as he had no intention of suffering in silence.[225] The change of leadership of the Coptic Church from the towering figure of Shenouda III signaled a return to age-old accommodation, conciliation and submission habits, befitting the traditional *Dhimmi* syndrome. Coptic concerns all but disappeared from the country's public agenda.

Overview and Analysis:
The Copts Under Arab Islamic Rule

In the previous chapters, we let the events speak for themselves with minimal remarks. The purpose of doing this was to avoid starting with conclusions and then looking for supporting evidence.

Now is the time to offer some remarks and conclusions which will be presented under several subheads, pointing out the connections between each one. We hope by proffering such a reading of history to aid in understanding the present.

First: At the Time of the *Fat'h*

The Copts were surprised by the Arabs' unexpected advance. The defeat of the armies (some of which had Coptic soldiers, but were Byzantine led) was caused by the limp and weak fighting abilities, mismanagement (Egypt was divided into four separate provinces), and tactical floundering. Sensing impending defeat, the Romans (Cyrus and the generals of the armies) negotiated to relinquish control of the country to the invaders, but the people of Alexandria were angry because of the terms of the treaty that they were not privy to. They rose up against Cyrus and sought to stone him; however, it was too late, and the army generals refused to continue fighting. But the Copts (as a people) took a somewhat neutral stand during the time of the invasion. They were too bitter toward the Byzantines, following the schism, to actively help their army, but also quite wary toward the unknown invaders who followed another religion, all while underestimating their real intents.

When things settled down for the invaders, and when Amr realized Patriarch Benyamin's status, he granted him security to return from his hiding place, perhaps intending to make him partially responsible for the people's loyalty. As for the Arab historian, Ibn Al-Hakam's, claims that Benyamin sent a message to all the bishops ordering them to support the invaders, these have been debunked by the actual events and ignored by the other historians. Moreover, there is nothing to indicate that the Copts offered to Amr's army an aid of any significance—if at all—during his long siege of the Babylon Fortress.

Yohanna Al-Nakyousi (a contemporaneous witness) paints a bleak picture of the events of the invasion, recording acts of killing, looting, and destruction. He summarized, in his Chronicles, the conditions by saying, "For Amr had no mercy on the Egyptians, and did not observe the covenant they had made with him, for he was of a barbaric race."[226]

After things settled down militarily for the Arabs upon seizing full control of the country, a question was raised, "Was the *fat'h* (conquest) of Egypt peaceful or by force?" The answers given to the question were contradictory according to the category—Copts or Arabs—for whom one wanted to defend the 'acquired rights': rights inscribed in the peace treaties for the Copts, or 'right of conquest by force' for the Arabs.[227] The likely definitive answer was 'by force'; the presence of Copts in the Byzantine armies being evidence of the natives' resistance to the invaders. In addition, the army garrisons for Babylon and Alexandria requested the fighting to cease only when circumstances got out of control. In fact, Amr seems to deny his abiding by any treaty; while one day in the mosque, he said, "I sit in this position and none of Egypt's Copts can make demands of me with regards to treaty or pact (..); if I desire, I kill, if I desire, I (apply the rules of) the fifth, and if I desire, I sell."[i]

The 'fifths' referred to above require a bit of explaining: splitting the booties taken from the *Kuffar* in Islamic *ghazawat* is regulated according to Quran and Sunna rules. One-fifth goes to charitable destinations and the remaining four-fifths divided between those who took part in the war (unless decided differently by the Prophet or, later, by the Caliph). This reference clearly indicated that Amr considered the 'Conquest of Egypt' as a mere *ghazwa*, and that whatever the Muslims hands could claim from the *Kuffar* as war booties.

---

[i] Al-Balathury, P. 217. On the other hand, there are indications that, at the end of the military confrontations, Amr signed a covenant with Cyrus after the surrender of Babylon, but this did not cover Alexandria which was conquered by force.

Another telling incident was when a man who converted to Islam during the time of Omar Ibn Al-Khatab requested to be freed from his obligation to pay the *Jizya*, Omar said, "No, the *fat'h* of your land was by force." Later, *Wali* Ḥayan Ibn Sharîḥ wrote to Caliph Omar Ibn Abd Al-Aziz (r. 717-720), asking if he agreed that the living Copts had to pay the *Jizya* of the dead Copts. When the Caliph asked (Sheikh) Rak Ibn Malek (for his opinion), he responded by saying, "I have not heard of a covenant or a contract, for they were conquered by force, and thus of equal status to slaves," so Omar wrote back, agreeing with Ḥayan.[228]

The Muslim writers seem to have been aware that in Egypt, in particular, and especially with regard to the Copts, the ancient agricultural population of the Nile Valley, the problem of principle was posited immediately after the conquest. Thus, the following words are attributed to Urwa Ibn Al-Zubayr, whose father had been one of the Arab generals who had led the Egypt conquest along with Amr: "I lived in Egypt for seven years, I took a wife. I saw its inhabitants overwhelmed (*majâhîd*): they imposed on them what exceeded their possibilities. And yet, Amr had conquered it on the basis of a peace treaty in exchange for something (*Jizya*) they had to fulfill."[229]

Clearly, this issue was not merely a matter of theoretical or historical debate, but it was fundamentally one of '*Sharia*,' since much depended on the settling of this question. Things like the prohibition against building new churches or rebuilding ones that have been torn down. In fact, it is not impossible that it was the Copts themselves who propagated later on the idea of a 'peaceful *fat'h* (conquest)' to convince the rulers of their right to build and renovate their churches.

Altogether, the account of the sources from an Egyptian Christian milieu on the Arab conquests gives the impression that the Copts at that time did not recognize the nature of this conquest. Their reaction to this event would come later, at a time in which they are not allowed to express themselves freely.[230]

Second: The Raping of Egypt

Since the Arab invasion, because of it, and as a result of it, Egypt was raped many times, becoming everyone's proverbial doormat. Thus, Egypt became the subject of successive attacks, large and small, each one competing with the one preceding in terms of barbarism and destruction.

After around one century of the *fat'h* (640), a second Arab invasion took place at the hands of the Abbasids (751). Despite receiving help from the Copts to get rid of the Umayyads, they were still more barbaric and vicious (as proven, for example, by their bloody oppression of the Peshmurians). After another century, the rule of the Turkish *Walis* (Seljuks, in 856) emerged from under the cloak of the Abbasids, and they were eviler and more harmful than their predecessors. A century later, came the invasion of the Maghrebis (Fatimids, in 969) with its many inconsistencies and the atrocious persecutions of Al-Ḥakem bi-Amr Allah. Two centuries later, came the rule of the Kurds (Ayyubids, in 1171) with all its bigotry, whose impact was amplified by the Frankish wars and their consequences. After another century, the slave Mamluks emerged from under the Ayyubids' cloak, and took power, causing hellish tyranny and injustice. This lasted for over two-and-half centuries, ending with the invasion of the Turkish Ottomans (in 1517), who, for their part, matched the barbarianism and incivility of all their predecessors. Throughout these eras, and in tandem with the changes in governing clans, tens of Bedouin Arab tribes, and other fortune-seekers from all over the region, came to Egypt, ravaging, destroying, killing, and looting, and the peaceful unarmed natives paid the price.

After the shock that Bonaparte delivered in 1798 and the attempts that followed to exit the dark tunnel at the hands of Mohammed Ali and his progeny after him, the 20th century saw the vicious *Brotherhood-Wahhabi-Salafi* attacks, from which Egypt is still reeling. It would not be an exaggeration to make the claim that this is but a new link in the chain of oppressive and barbaric invasions (even if they are invasions from within), particularly since there are always those Islamists who call for Egypt's '*fat'h*' anew.

During all the periods of the invasion, the Caliphate's central authorities were only concerned with the exacting of taxes and sending the revenues back to the Caliphate. *Walis* were not left for long durations, to prevent them from having enough time to attempt becoming independent.

A quick survey that we did of the number of *Walis* and Sultans who reigned over Egypt between 640 and 1805 (with the exception of the Fatimid rule, when the Caliphs resided in Cairo) reveals that they were no less than 315, which is the equivalent to one *Wali* every three years. During the time of the Ottoman State alone, between 1517 and 1805, the number of *Walis* (Viziers) came to 136, meaning that the average Viziership lasted no more than 25 months. The *Walis'* foremost concern was becoming rich, and any means were considered lawful, so long as they were successful in exacting money and amassing wealth. The country's state of affairs was of secondary concern, if at all. Thus, it was not strange for a Bedouin Arab, such as Amr, and those who succeeded him, to hoard the money, finding himself overnight before great wealth that he never dreamt of.

There were no long-term, or even short-term, plans to grow the country's economic wealth. General reforms were completely neglected, with the exception of a minority of rulers who, seeking independence, sought to establish the foundations of their personal rule and legacy through the implementation of some projects—most of which were variations on the theme of 'religious architecture.'

While the total *Kharaj* and *Jizya* revenue amounted to about twelve-million dinars in the days of Amr Ibn Al-Aas, the amount decreased to one-and-a-half million dinars by the time the French arrived, which indicates the country's level of impoverishment. In fact, the area of cultivated farmlands decreased from six million *feddans* at the time of the '*fat'h*' to less than half as much barely 80 years later, during the reign of Hisham. This area of cultivated land remained roughly the same until the time of Mohammed Ali.

Egypt's population dwindled from about fifteen million people at the time of the *fat'h* to about three million people at the time of Bonaparte's arrival.

Regarding the rapidly deteriorating conditions in Egypt, Alfred Butler says, "One might also sketch the decline of those great and splendid cities which the Romans had left in Egypt: for Alexandria, though first among the cities of the East, if not of the world, was only one among many which reached from Syene (Aswan) to the Mediterranean. One would find that temples and palaces were suffered to fall into ruins; that precious marbles were quarried for building or burned for lime; that bronze statues were melted down and turned into coin or domestic vessels..."[231]

The Civilizational Jihad

How utterly atrocious was the civilizational devastation that Egypt experienced across the various eras of the occupation. Starting with Caliph Yazîd's (r. 680-683) directive to *Wali* Oqba Ibn Muslim, ordering him to smash Pharaonic 'idols and statues,' and him 'doing his best to oblige,' all the way to the looting campaign initiated by Selim I, after the Ottoman conquest, taking anything of value from Egypt and leaving behind nothing valuable in the Citadel. He took the pillars from the large palace halls; even Pharaonic stones from Upper Egypt were taken. All the booty was carried to Constantinople/Istanbul atop thousands of camels and ships beyond number. He also took many highly skilled craftsmen, tradesmen, and farmers in order to build his country. The churches experienced the same fate years earlier when Caliphs (like Al-Motaṣem) ordered that 'marble pillars in the churches everywhere be taken.'

As an example, the first mosque in Egypt was built on the site where the present mosque of Amr, though more than once rebuilt, it still stands; but all the columns needed for it were brought at a later date from the churches of Memphis—a precedent which has been followed ever since, the Arabs having no faculty for stone-carving. Many of the churches in Alexandria were ruined by the forcible removal of their pillars of porphyry and precious marbles which were coveted for the ornamentation of mosques.[i]

It may not be politically correct to put it this way, but Butcher bluntly says: "This may appear a startling assertion to make, but it will be borne out by anyone who will take the trouble to study the history of Egypt under the Muslims, and who will put aside popular prejudice in examining her condition at this day. The Arabs, and after them the Turks, were splendid soldiers, and had some virtues which the Egyptians would have done well to emulate; but at heart they were, and have remained, barbarian. Their idea of

---

[i] Butcher also says: "Amr was almost aghast at the wealth and splendor of Alexandria, and wrote to Omar in extravagant terms of his conquest. But though he writes much of the baths and the shops, he says nothing of the books or the works of art which still adorned that city, and everyone knows the story of the library." Butcher, V-1, P. 388. It is a common remark of the modern tourist that the Christians had done the same in their time, and stolen the pillars from the pagan temples for their churches. It is superfluous to assure anyone who has studied the history of Christian Egypt that this remark is untrue. The early Christians of Egypt were particularly careful to use nothing that had served for the worship of the old Egyptian gods. Even when necessity drove them to build their churches inside the strong walls of a deserted temple, they covered the hieroglyphs with plaster, and set up their own pillars in the enclosure. (Butcher V-1, P. 99).

government is personal aggrandizement, and their idea of civilization personal luxury."

Certainly, it was not the first or only time in world history for barbarians to attack civilized and settled peoples. As Ibn Khaldun says, "*Those who were more innate in nomadism and more vicious, were more apt to defeating others.*"[232] For how much damage was done by Germanic, Norman, Viking, and other tribes to Europe, and by the Tatar in the East. Yet in most cases, the barbarians, whether they remained or left, ended up becoming civilized. The Arab invaders were exceptional; they tried to impose their barbarism on the civilized nations which they subjugated.

On the 'soft' civilizational devastation front, the Arab-Islamic conquests were accompanied by arrogant and ignorant attempts to 'abrogate' any history prior to their arrival, considering Egypt's real history to have had its genesis with the rising sun of the Arab Islamic *fat'h*.

In modern times, and if it were not for the world's high interest in Egypt's ancient civilization, the cradle of world civilizations, (and for Egypt's dependence on income from tourism), perhaps Egypt's old heritage might have been abandoned for good.

But despite this (touristy) 'interest' in the artifacts of the ancients, the Egyptian government still rejects the establishing of a 'Coptic' studies department in any of its public universities, while such chairs or departments exist in over 50 universities around the world.

However, in hindsight, this might be a blessing! In the past few years, a new kind of persecution against the Coptic community has developed in the field of culture. It was noticed during local and international conferences on Egyptology or Coptology that some (Egyptian) individuals introducing themselves as 'scholars' give lectures based on false historical backgrounds, all aiming at destroying Coptic culture and Christian faith. Recently a 'professor' claimed that the words 'prayer' and 'fasting' didn't exist before Islam and were introduced by the Arabs.[233]

For what is it worth, we note that 40% of the curators of the Coptic Museum (in Old Cairo) are Muslims. One might welcome this as an indication of 'national unity,' or that 'science is science,' but then why Copts aren't allowed to work in a place like the Museum of Islamic Art? In fact, non-Muslims aren't even allowed to teach Arabic language at school!

Third: The Perpetual Violence Machine

The Arab (Bedouin) tribes were used to raiding and looting one another, as well as those groups living around the oases. These raids were means of 'redistributing wealth,' or rather of 'creating' wealth; instead of other means involving thinking, working, exertion, and the exchange of benefits. But when the spirit of 'brotherliness' had set in, as commanded by the new religion, ('Those whose hearts have been reconciled')[i], zealous tribes began to ally under the banner of the new Islamic State (particularly after the *Ridda* wars[ii]) and direct their bloody activities against the surrounding peoples. They began with those closest to them and then moved outwards in a series of *ghazawat*[iii] and *fat'h* wars, in which the 'spread of religion'—strictly speaking—appears to have played no major part.

When Omar Ibn Al Khatab was installed as Caliph, he began to incite the people to accomplish the *fat'h* of Iraq, saying, "Al-Hejaz is your home only in as far as it is a place of pasture. Those who dwell there have no power over it except in this respect. Where do emigrating reciters (of Quran) stand with regard to Allah's promise?, so travel in the land that Allah promised to you in His book for your inheritance."[234] Amr made his desire to conquer Egypt clear by telling Omar Ibn Al Khatab, "Its *fat'h* would strengthen and aid the Muslims, for it is the land with the most wealth and yet the least capable of fighting and engaging in war," without any mention of the propagation of the *Da'wa*. And when one of the Copts asked Amr, "Inform us of the value of the *Jizya* for each of us so that we may pay it accordingly," Amr replied, "Even if you paid me from the floor to the roof, I will not tell you exactly what you owe. All of you are our treasury, when we are asked to deliver more (money as requested by the Caliph), we impose more on you, and if less is demanded from us, we lighten your burden."

Caliph Sulayman Ibn Abdul Malek wrote to Osama, the *Wali* overseeing the *Kharaj* of Egypt, saying, "Milk the udder until it dries out, and milk it more till the blood runs dry."

---

[i] Quran 9–60, regarding those working, or doing *Jihad*, for the cause of Allah.

[ii] Many people left Islam after the death of the prophet, as Islam had been for them a 'politico-tribal' pact, rather than anything else, but the first Caliph, Abu-Bakr, fought them to force them back into Islam (*Riddah* wars).

[iii] Assaults or conquests, such as the 27 (or 29?) conducted during the life of Islam's prophet.

Thus, the invaders' first, and foremost, goal in the beginning was to acquire booty through looting and plundering. And since Egypt's '*fat'h* was by force,' then converting to the invaders' 'doctrine' (faith) to escape paying the *Jizya* did not lead—for an entire century after the invasion—to being exempt from paying it, even if it helped in getting closer to the invaders and eventually sharing the booty. Still, converts did not become part of the Arab community upon conversion; rather, they had to request to come under the umbrella of one of the Arab tribes *Waley* (custodian) by paying a certain price, and content themselves with a status of a *Muwali* (loyal, partisan).

For example, in the days of *Wali* Abdullah, son of the Umayyad Caliph Abdul Malek, they were running out of space in the treasuries because of the abundance of accumulated money. So, he ordered that mosques be built (to spend some of the excess money). This indicates that the grave injustice in the exacting of money was not due to a lack in finances, but was 'violence for the sake of violence.'

On the other hand, once the war machine began its revolutions, it never stopped for anything; for war is the natural activity. So, the Arabs did not need to find a reason to start their wars; rather, their social structure came to depend on war, and without victories, it would crumble. Here, we find the expansionist tendency unguided by any real objective; instead, it is vicious and arising from a historical need. And perhaps these conquests would have taken place even if 'Islam' did not exist.[i]

In fact, the account attributed to Amr Ibn Al-Aas (explaining why the conquests were launched)[ii], even if it were not authentic, is amazing in its straightforwardness, especially that it was written by a Sunni scholar, in the 12th century. It simply says that spreading the 'light of Islam' was never a motivation behind the conquests. Furthermore, it bluntly says that what Islam's prophet brought was a 'law' (*sharia*) which was imposed by force. This, later, 'empowered' the Arabs and made them feel entitled to conquer other countries to share their wealth.

---

[i] On the other hand, the *Da'wa* would have never succeeded if it had urged people to embrace humility and peacefulness. So, although religion was not the first reason for the conquests, it nonetheless helped their spread. In this author's book, *Al-Hurreyah fil Asr (Freedom in Captivity)* P. 276, we showcase an idea taken from Joseph Schumpeter's *History of Economic Analysis*.

[ii] Refer to the chapter above, titled, *Was It a Peaceful of Forceful Conquest?*

Examples of Gratuitous Violence:

We will deal later with matters pertaining to the *Jizya*, 'religious freedom,' religious conversion, etc. but in what follows, we will present samples of the violence machine practices against the Coptic people of Egypt throughout the centuries:

—During the Umayyad Caliphate of Hisham Ibn Abdul Malek, the *Wali* in charge of collecting the *Kharaj*, increased the harassment severely against the Copts. He added one carat for every dinar, and when the people asked for leniency, he refused. When the Copts in the eastern side revolted against him, he killed, took captives, looted, destroyed, and shed enough blood 'to fill a sea.'

—In the days of Caliph Abdullah Al-Mamun (the son of Harun Al-Rashîd), the *Wali* in charge of the *Kharaj* abused people (the overwhelming majority of whom at that time were Copts) everywhere. Many of the Christian Peshmurians were severely tortured, even being forced to sell their own children in order to pay the *Kharaj*. They were tied to mills, taking the place of beasts, and beaten in order to grind. Finally, they started to revolt. Mamun massacred them and sold those alive as slaves.

—The Abbasid Caliph Jafar Al-Mutawakkil imposed on Copts certain vestimentary rules aimed at humiliating non-Muslims, which became common practice across the subsequent twelve centuries. He also ordered that frightening wooden images of devils be nailed to doors of houses. He banned Copts from working for the Sultanate and prohibited them from teaching Muslims, although in that day, Copts were the ones with knowledge of the various disciplines and sciences.

—Copts were forced to work on war ships without receiving a single dirham to compensate their travel expenses and necessities. They were only given a daily ration of food. The *Wali* (Anbasah) did these things because of 'how much he hated the Christians.'

—Halfway through the ninth century, the *Walis,* who were Oguz (Turks and Kurds), used to neigh at the women like horses, kidnap and defile children without fear, steal the cattle, and do 'other despicable things.'

—The Fatimid Caliph, Al-Zāhir, and his Vizier, Al-Gergai, filled the prisons with people, men and women, to the point where women were giving birth in prison. The *Walis* committed innumerable acts of oppression and injustice against the Christians.

—Ṣalaḥ Al-Deen—long portrayed in the West as a 'chivalrous knight'—handed down severe punishments against the Copts, such as executions and crucifixions. When Copts in Qeft protested the excessive taxes, they were promptly suppressed by Al-Adel, brother of Salah Al-Deen, who inflicted upon the town the most terrible reprisals; 3,000 of the inhabitants were hanged on trees, using their own girdles and turbans for ropes.

—During the days of the Ayyubid Sultan Al-Kamel, a man appeared to the people, claiming that he saw their prophet in a dream, telling him, "Make the *Dhimmis* wear identifying clothes, because they have gone too far." So, he began to beat the Christians and Jews and publicly slander them. The Christians were under great duress and faced painful humiliation. They were insulted with vulgarities from the Muslim mobs wherever they were found.

—In the days of the Ayyubid Al-Malek Al-Saleh, a certain Christian was accused of being the grandson of a man who converted to Islam. So, the judge decreed that this Christian convert to Islam and imprisoned him to force him to acquiesce. Mobs headed to the judge's house in support of his decision, then went to the closest church and began to destroy it, burning crosses and pictures. They also vandalized the graves, exhumed corpses and threw them in the fire, and attacked the Christian residents of this area.

—In the days of the Mamluk Sultan Al-Zāhir Baibars, it was publicly announced in Cairo and Misr that Christians and Jews were not allowed to work for any Amir. The commoners and riffraff rushed to loot the homes of Christians and Jews, taking their women captive, and killing some with their own hands. Al-Muallaqa Church was also looted and some of its worshippers were killed. These were some of the toughest circumstances, as many people died, including children and old men.

—In the days of Mamluk Sultan Ibn Qalawūn, 54 churches were simultaneously burned in different parts of the country. A month later, a fire broke out in the alleyway of Al-Shawaen (the grillers) in Cairo. Severe winds caused the fire to spread. Some Christians were accused of starting the fire, and were burned on a Friday, and many gathered to watch them die. When the Sultan rode to the square, the commoners exclaimed, "There is no religion but the religion of Mohamed Ibn Abdullah; O King Al-Naṣer, O Sultan of Islam, grant us victory over the people of *Kufr*." So, the Sultan ordered to announce publicly, "Whoever finds a Christian, it is lawful for him to take his money and his livelihood." The crowds cheered, "May Allah grant you victory." Later, an edict was issued, mandating Christians to wear blue turbans (etc.), and the Amirs were prohibited from employing Christians.

—During the days of Sultan Al-Ẓaher Jaqmaq, 'who was known to be 'moderate' in his rule when compared to Barsbay, his predecessor, as well as for his devout religiosity (thus forbidding the imbibing of wine,'), many Copts were burned and killed, while others were nailed to wooden planks and paraded on the backs of camels on the streets of Cairo.

—Sultan Al-Ghuri intensified his mistreatment of Christians. He seized great sums of money from them and acted with greater severity in order to spite them, going as far as lashing some (Christian) women to punish them.

—In the days of Sultan Qaitbay, the commoners rose up against the Christians in Cairo. All their churches were shut down. Then, this spread south and north, and the tumult intensified, leading to the killing, taking of captives, looting, destruction, and bloodshed in the side streets and alleyways. The *Walis* in charge failed to deter the commoners.

—During the Ottoman Sultanate of Selim I, the *Walis* treated the Copts with greater harshness, harassing and forcing them to leave their own lands. They destroyed their homes, ended their livelihoods, and the people faced great hardship. Christianity experienced trials and troubles.

—In 1678, the Ottoman authorities enforced restrictions, as Christians had to wear a bell around their necks when using (public) bathrooms. They were forbidden from wearing *goukh* (smooth-woven) cloth or wool clothes, and Christian women were forbidden from wearing any white garments. Christians had to wear mostly black clothes.

—When Napoleon arrived, the Muslim rabble in Cairo began to embitter the Christians. When the French fought and defeated the Mamluks, Al-Azhar *Sheikhs* called for waging *Jihad* and fighting against the *Kuffar* and taking revenge. They then went around looting the homes of Christians, irrespective of race, killing whomever they came across on the roadways, be it a man, woman, child, or senior, (thus avenging themselves against the more powerful European infidel by abusing vulnerable local infidels).

—After Napoleon left Egypt, the Ottoman Naṣif *Pasha* told the people, "Kill the Christians and wage a *Jihad* against them." The commoners erupted and cheered, and in a haste, began killing any Christians they encountered, whether Coptic, Levantine, or otherwise. A faction went to the Alleyway of Christians and broke into t homes, killing men, women, and children, looting and taking people captive. Whoever arrested a Christian, Jew, or Frenchman got *Baksheesh* from *Katkhoda Bek*.

— In June July, 1881, under *Khedive* Tawfiq, Muslim mobs in In Tanta, Damanhour, and Al-Mahalla El Kubra rose up against the Christians, slaughtering them, looting their homes, and taking their women and children captive. The murdered (Christians) were dragged on the ground from their feet like cattle taken to be skinned after being slaughtered their guns.

—In 1949 (during the 'Palestine War'), anti-Coptic demonstrations erupted in Cairo, with marchers shouting: 'Christianity is finished in Egypt,' 'One faith in Egypt – Islam,' and 'Today the Jews, tomorrow the Christians.'

— In November 1972, under Sadat, the Holy Bible Society building Khankah, a suburb of Cairo, was burnt and demolished. Several Copt-owned homes and businesses were burnt or sacked.

— In June 1981, 81 Copts were killed in the Cairo suburb of Zawya al-Hamra, in a massacre organized with the complicity of the authorities in order to give Copts a lesson they won't forget.

— In January 2000, 20, under Mubarak, Copts were massacred in al-Kosheh village. Perpetrators, known to everybody, were never convicted.

— In October 2011, under the authority of the then-ruling Supreme Council of Armed Forces, Coptic peaceful demonstrators (protesting recent attacks on churches) were attacked by the army. Armored personnel carriers (APCs) proceeded to drive in zigzag patterns through the crowds in an effort to run over as many demonstrators as possible. The State-run television simultaneously aired an urgent message claiming that Christians were attacking Egyptian Army soldiers and urging "good Egyptian citizens" to defend the military. The brutal confrontation left 27 Coptic demonstrators dead (14 of them were crushed to death under the armored vehicles) and 327 injured.[i]

Some specialists speak about scapegoating mechanisms and how they led to anti-minority measures in Europe during outbreaks of plague. However, the anti-*Dhimmi* agitation in Egypt (especially in the middle ages)

---

[i] Account reported numerous times, e.g.:
https://www.copticsolidarity.org/2014/10/08/coptic-solidarity-maspero-massacre-victims-still-without-justice-in-egypt/, or
https://en.wikipedia.org/wiki/Maspero_demonstrations

does not appear to have been exacerbated by the usual pretexts—warfare, plague, earthquake, or famine—but was a constant regardless of any given situations which would typically lead to aggressing innocent minorities. One factor behind persecuting Copts that has been suggested is the intensification of a rigidly Sunni religious ethos. The ongoing process of restoring Sunni ascendency (after two centuries of Shiism under the Fatimids) continued apace under the Mamluks; visiting scholars such as Ibn Taymiyya (d. 1328) agitated and wrote enormous treaties against all that he saw as 'un-Islamic,' including Christians playing roles in Egyptian society.[235]

Fourth: the *Jizya* and Its Effects

The *Jizya* was a fact of life in the ancient world, imposed on vanquished nations for a certain period of time, and in accordance with a treaty, or until circumstances changed. However, they usually lasted for several years, or a few decades at the most. But what took place in Egypt (and the Levant) was perhaps the only instance in the history where the *Jizya* was imposed on entire populations, for twelve centuries, based on purely religious reasons and injunctions.

In countries conquered by Muslims, *Jizya* took a decisively religious connotation. In application of the Quran (Al-Tawba — 29)[i], it is imposed upon the non-Muslims as a badge of humiliation for their unbelief. Some *Fuqaha* consider this tax as punishment for their unbelief, because their continued stay in a Muslim land (*Dar al-Islam*), is a crime, hence they have no escape from being humiliated, degraded and submissive ('…until they pay Jizya readily being brought low').

Some of those who follow the schools of 'hagiographic history' and 'the pious and sinless *Salaf* (early predecessors)' like to claim that, "The *Jizya* was an inconsequential sum of money," or that, "The *Jizya* was imposed on *Dhimmis* as a substitute for being drafted into the Muslims armies." However, the truth is that it was an exorbitant sum of money that left the poor and many of the middle-class incapable of making payments.

---

[i] "Fight those who do not believe in Allah or in the Last Day, and who do not consider unlawful what Allah and His Messenger have made unlawful, and who do not adopt the religion of truth from those who were given the Scripture — [fight] until they give the jizyah willingly while they are humbled." (https://quran.com/9/29).

Furthermore, Copts were often drafted, and even exploited in corvee, while having to pay the *Jizya* and additional wartime taxes.

In fact, the ultimate objective of *Jizya* was not only financial, but to compel—or according to Islamic hagiography, 'guide'—the *Dhimmis* to embrace Islam[236].

The average *Jizya* amounted to two (gold) dinars for every male who reached puberty (with the exception of the idled elderly), but in the countryside, it was levied on entire villages and then collected from individuals, each according to his wealth. It usually meant that the poor had to pay one dinar, the middle-class, two, and the rich, four, in addition to about 30% 'exaction fee.' A report prepared in 1737, during the reign of the Ottomans, indicated that there were one-hundred-and-twenty-thousand *Dhimmis* (adult males, not counting the elderly) in Misr who paid the *Jizya*, which totaled two-hundred-thousand Sharifi gold pounds, amounting to an average of one-and-six-tenths golden pounds per person.

If accepted for the sake of argument that one gold dinar (= four grams) has the same 'purchasing power' today and assuming that the average income brackets at the time is equivalent to those of today, then the *Jizya* would be equivalent to about the third of a poor individual's income, and about one-eighth of a middle-income earner's income.

It is estimated[i] that the *Jizya* was equivalent to 20 weeks' worth of wages for a day-laborer (middle-class or poor), which confirms, and even exceeds, the aforementioned conclusion in our above calculations.

As recorded in the various historical sources, the rich along with the church jointly paid the *Jizya* on behalf of the poor (as well as the *Jizya* of the monks and clergy who were no longer exempt). If we assume that the 'poor' make up about half of the citizenry and that the rich make up three-to-five percent, and that every rich individual paid tithes, then a simple calculation reveals that between 40–70 percent, at the most, of the poor 'may' have had their *Jizya* paid on their behalf by the rich. As for the rest, they remained under the mercy of the sword, with no alternative but to convert to Islam.

---

[i] By Tamer El-Leithy, currently Assistant Professor at Johns Hopkins University (http://history.jhu.edu/directory/tamer-el-leithy/); from a lecture given in Cairo in August, 2008, sponsored by the Egyptians Against (Religious) Discrimination Association, MARED.

Furthermore, as the number of rich Copts declined, due to coercive conversions to Islam,[i] so did the number of the poor who could have been protected from coercive conversions. Thus, contrary to what is claimed by some, the *Jizya* did indeed have a decisive impact on the conversion of Copts to Islam and it further had an outsized impact on the *rate* of Coptic conversions.

For example, in the days of the Ottomans, around 1734, the *Jizya* was increased and collected from Patriarchs, bishops, monks, and priests. Any *Dhimmi* would be stopped on the roadway and asked to present a card, indicating that he had paid the *Jizya*. These days were filled with trouble and sadness for the poor, as well as for the crafts owners. The people, particularly the poor Christians, experienced great hardships. They constantly feared price increases and the merciless *Jizya* collection. In those days, there were in Misr some *Archons* who paid for the poor, who were in prison for failing to pay *Jizya*, in order to set them free.

Another factor was the way *Jizya* was collected, for, in fact, it was (along with *Kharaj*) put for auction on a regional basis, usually for a period of four years. The bidding 'winners' would do whatever it took to collect the sums committed plus, naturally, their own cuts. The senior Copt (*Archon*) in an area was made responsible to report changes in the population; movers in or out, boys who reached puberty, etc. Furthermore, in the countryside, *Jizya* was usually a collective responsibility. The total amount in a village, corresponding to the sum of individual dues, was to be collected no matter what. If an individual failed to pay for whatever reason (including death), the rest of the villagers would have to make up for the difference.[237]

In any case, even if the *Jizya* was the reason behind 'mass conversions in the Middle Ages,' (as Leithy puts it), it was not the only reason, since the cumulative effects of harassment, humiliation, compulsion, and persecution cannot be underestimated. Furthermore, the 'snowball effect' cannot be ignored, since when the percentage of Muslim citizens increased, the pressures on non-Muslims increased as well.

---

[i] This was done to avoid losing their livelihoods, as in the case of scribes and others, particularly in the days of the Mamluks.

Fifth: The Circumstances of the Coptic Church

1. The Rulers and the Church:

After Amr Ibn Al-Aas showed 'hospitality' to Patriarch Benyamin, the reality of the conquering rulers' ugly faces began to surface, for the Patriarchs suffered many insults, imprisonments, torture, and threats of death. The profound statement of the church's chronicles summing up a Patriarch's days at his death may eloquently serve as a general descriptive statement, for they would typically say that, "His days were filled with hardships, sufferings, troubles, trials, death, and evanescence for the Copts, as a result of the tyranny and despotism of the *Walis*."

In fact, out of the fifteen Patriarchs ordained from the time of the Arab invasion to the beginning of the time of the Turkish *Walis* (856), six were arrested, imprisoned, tortured, and humiliated. There are several recorded examples of such mistreatments, such as Abba Yoannes III (677–686), whose feet were placed in a copper bowl filled with burning coals, or Abba Khail, who was incarcerated, with his legs placed in wooden stocks and a metal ring around his neck. He was also placed in a windowless prison cell with no view of the sun, under the stress of iron chains for one month during the reign of the Umayyads.[i] He was later imprisoned twice during the Abbasid rule, at the hands of Abdul Malek Ibn Musa Ibn Nusair, who imposed on him to pay an exorbitant sum of money and 'subjected him to great hardship and assaulted the Christians with the sword (..), abducting many nuns, looting and destroying their convents...'

In later eras, four more Patriarchs were imprisoned. For example, Ahmed Ibn Al-Mudaber pursued Abba Shenouda I (859–880), registered the number of monks, imposing on them the *Jizya* and *Kharaj* for the palm and other trees, and imposed on the Patriarch to pay seven-thousand dinars. Then, following a snitch, he threw him in prison with thieves, murderers, and other evildoers, and he suffered greatly, since he was sick. Ahmed Ibn Ṭūlun 'imprisoned Abba Khail III (880–894) with thieves and murderers, and the jail was extremely crowded. After spending a year in prison, the (sick) Patriarch paid some money to the jailer in order to make him (a toilet).' Al-

---

[i] Abba Khail I (744–768). Refer to chapter above titled, *The Turkish Walis* to see more details of the incident, and how Abba Khail faced Ibn-Ṭūlun with the composure and courage of a martyr.

Ḥakem bi-Amr Allah left Abba Zakharyos (1003–1032) in prison for three months and during this time, 'they terrorized him daily, threatening to burn him alive or throw him to the lions if he did not convert to Islam. They told him, "If you convert, you will be greatly honored and made the chief judge," but he paid them no mind.' Al-Yazouri arrested 'Abba Khristodolos (1046–1077) and several bishops and asked them for money. Three of the bishops were tortured to death.'

In sum, eleven out of 25 Patriarchs were prisoned and tortured during a period of less than four centuries after the invasion. The same pattern took place in particular under the Mamluks.

The 'tradition' of humiliating the Patriarchs remained in effect until Anwar El-Sadat, who put Pope Shenouda III under house arrest in one of the monasteries in the desert (September, 1981), and whose successor, Hosni Mubarak, kept him banished for 40 months.

On the other hand, the rulers realized the moral and spiritual authority wielded by the Patriarchal position, so they kept the Patriarchs under close scrutiny, requesting that they submit to the authorities, even preventing them from making decisions regarding religious matters under their jurisdiction without first asking for permission from the rulers. They also sought to endorse the election of any Patriarch prior to him assuming his responsibilities. On many occasions, the church had to pay a certain sum of money before the ordination of a new Patriarch would be approved, which sometimes resulted in the seat remaining vacant for long periods of time when the church was unable to pay the demanded sums of money. The rulers always wanted to know what was said, particularly in the Patriarch's sphere, as well as in the books of prayer and teaching, to ensure that these were all free from any critiques of Islam.

Despite everything, the stance of the church remained consistent all its days, refusing to return violence for violence as a matter of principle, and submitting to all the rulers, whoever they were. The church opposed the acts of the Peshmurians and tried to turn them away from revolting, which was a reason for the people's diminishing support and the eventual failure of the Peshmurian attempts (and, one must add, the massacre that ensued). The Patriarchs employed gentleness, respect, and (excessive) reverence in dealing with the rulers, perhaps as one of the ways of 'taming' (the beasts), even though it could be argued that at times, they were too submissive.

It was rare occurrence for any of them to confront the ruler demanding the easing of persecution; instead, they resorted to praying, consoling the persecuted, and collecting alms to protect the poor. However, there were a few exceptions, such as Abba Khail III, who responded to Ibn Ṭūlūn's threats by saying, "I am in your hands, do as you please, for you have authority over my body, but my soul is in the hands of its Maker," (thus, he was imprisoned). There was also Abba Mettaous (1378–1408), who decried forcing women to wear blue skirts, among other things, saying, "If you defame one of the daughters of my people, I will not stop unleashing the defamation in your country (..). And I want to inform you, O Amir, that Christians are not weak as you deem them to be…" Or when Amir Yalbugha tried to impose harsh measures on the people and the Patriarch did not assent; so, the Amir drew his sword in anger to behead the Patriarch, who stretched out his neck, causing the Amir to retreat in face of the Patriarch's courage.'

Abba Shenouda III (1971–2012) stands out as a rare example since the Arab-Islamic invasion to stand up against the head of state (president Sadat) and firmly denounce the growing persecution of the Copts, all without any hint of calling for revenge or violence.

2. The Serial Assaults: Churches and Crosses:

In addition to the ban on building new churches, or the near impossible permission to rebuild ones that have been torn down, the Church also suffered from innumerable assaults. These are samples as reminders:

— The Umayyad *Wali* Abdul Aziz ordered that 'all crosses be destroyed, which unsettled the Christians in Egypt.' Then, he ordered 'the banning of holy masses (church services), and he called the Christians misguided for claiming that God has a wife and a child.' The Abbasid Caliph, Jafar Al-Mutawakkil, 'brought immeasurable trouble on the churches everywhere. He then ordered that the churches be torn down.' *Wali* Anbasah Ibn Isḥaq broke all the crosses in churches in bulk, and Christians could not pray in churches unless in a hushed voice that is inaudible from the outside. He then put an end to the ringing of church bells and prevented Christians from congregating in groups for mass.' *Wali* Ibn Al-Mudaber ordered that churches in Misr (Old Cairo) be shut down, with the exception of one church. His emissaries gathered the wardens of churches everywhere, locked them up, put them in iron chains, and carried them away to Misr.'

— Around 912, the great Church of the Resurrection in Alexandria was burned down. It was highly esteemed by Christians and yet, not one stone was left upon another.

— Al-Ḥakem bi-Amr Allah sent edicts to all the provinces of his entire kingdom ordering them 'to tear down churches, bringing all their gold and silver utensils to his palace, and to collect money from bishops everywhere.' He also ordered the *Wali* of Jerusalem to demolish the Church of the Resurrection (St. Sepulcher) and to 'level it to the ground.' The Fatimid Vizier, Ibn Al-Wakhshi, pillaged the churches in Cairo and Al-Khandaq, and Muslims burned the Armenians' monastery, known as Al-Zahri.'

— In the beginning of the reign of Ṣalaḥ Al-Deen, he decreed that crosses be taken down from the domes of all churches in Egypt. Whenever he saw a church painted white, he had it covered with black mud. He also prohibited the ringing of church bells and forced Christians to pray in hushed voices. At the time, Muslim riffraff seized the opportunity to humiliate and abuse Copts. They also arranged to tear down some churches in towns and villages, and the people faced great hardships, to the point where some scribes in Misr and Cairo renounced their faith and abjured their Christ.' In the days of the Ayyubid Sultan Al-Adel, 'the Muslims rioted against the Church of Saint Mark in Alexandria. The following Friday, after their prayers, they went and leveled to the ground what remained of the church. There was great sadness, ongoing depression, and tangible hardships.'

— During the days of the Ayyubid Sultan Al-Kamel, a group of Muslims at the mosque adjacent to the Al-Muallaqa Church tore down the wall separating the two structures, claiming that part of the church plot belongs to the mosque. They used to climb the stairs leading to the roof of the Patriarch's residence, to call for *Adhān* (Muslim prayers), cry out *Takbīr*, and recite (the Quran), which led to numerous disputes.

— In the days of Sultan Qalawūn, 'Muslim riffraff gathered together and yelled loudly, "Allah Akbar," and they tore down Al-Zahri Church until only rubble remained. They also killed those who were inside the church and stole anything of value. Then they tore down the Church of Abba Mina in Al-Ḥamra, which had long been highly esteemed. Afterward, they attacked two more churches near the Seven Waterwheels site, taking over sixty nuns as captive, stole all they could get their hands on, and finally burned and tore down these churches. The mobs destroyed a church in the alleyway of the Roum and a church in the alleyway of Zwailah. The mobs also marched to

Al-Muallaqa Church, but its doors were shut by those in charge of it, while they were inside, surrounded, and about to be taken. Then, the mobs destroyed a number of churches in Alexandria, Damanhur, Al-Gharbeyah, Al-Sharqiyah, Bahnasia, Assiut, Manfalut, Menyet Abi Khasib, Qous, Aswan, Atifihhia, Wardan market, and Castle of Candle. News continued to travel about the many churches and homes that were torn down, and this was an extremely great adversity. Al-Maqrizi reported that 54 churches, not counting the monasteries, were completely destroyed and that many people were killed.

— In 1354, the Mamluk Amirs decided to seize the endowed monastery and church lands (twenty-five-thousand *Feddan*) and destroyed several churches. The commoners went back to destroying churches and tearing down homes.

— In the days of Sultan Qaitbay, the commoners rose up against the Christians in Cairo. All their churches were shut down and they were prevented from performing any of their religious practices. Then, this spread south and north, and the tumult intensified, leading to the killing, taking of captives, looting, destruction, and bloodshed in the side streets and alleyways.

— In a 1674 document entitled, *The Record of Inspecting Existing Mosques and Churches in the Castle of Candle and the Alleyway of Shenouda Located in Old Misr*, we find the Ottoman ruler's order that the doors of several churches be nailed shut, because the walls of these churches were higher than the adjacent mosques.

— In January 1952, a Coptic church, school and a benevolent society building were destroyed, and three Copts murdered by a mob in Suez.

— On 2001 New-Year's eve, a massacre at the Two-Saints church in Alexandria claimed 23 lives.

— In May 2011, three churches in Imbaba, near Cairo, were attacked and burnt and many Christian-owned houses and businesses ransacked; 15 people were killed, and about 232 injured.

— In August 2013, after the dispersal of Muslim Brotherhood sit-ins in Cairo, over 43 churches were attacked across the country leading to burning or destruction of 37 churches, in addition to dozens of Christian religious institutions.[i]

---

[i] https://www.hrw.org/news/2013/08/21/egypt-mass-attacks-churches.

— In December 2016, an explosion in the St. Peter church, adjacent to the patriarchate in Cairo, claimed 29 lives.

— On Palm Sunday, 9 April 2017, twin suicide bombings took place at St. Mark Cathedral in Alexandria, and St. George church in Tnata. At least 45 people were reported killed and 126 injured.

3. The Church and the People:

The relationship between the Copts and their church is somewhat complicated. Despite rallying around her and their vehement defense of her and her doctrine, we still find a significant number of differences and divisions, or rather, internal backstabbing. While some of these cases were a result of overriding interests and personal considerations, psychologists may interpret some of the other cases as necessities to relieve the unbearable external pressures (similar to a child lashing out at his mother if he was insulted at school without being able to defend himself).

The office of Patriarch continued to weaken over time. Although the Patriarch was respected by his subjects, he, nonetheless, ranked second after any Copt who was trusted by those in power (usually the senior 'scribes' overseeing the country's finances). This is especially true since Patriarchs did not reside in Cairo until the 11th century. This dynamic may have caused the controversy over the moral seniority during the incident of the General Congregation (Community, or *Melli*) Council at the end of the 19th century.

The situation changed dramatically after 1952, with the decimation of the Coptic laymen elite. The *Melli* Council became a toothless (often useless) body and the church became the *de facto* leader of the Copts and the main—if not sole—interlocutor between the state and the people. This reality appears to have suited well the governments, as a convenient means to control and exert pressure indirectly on the Copts, leaving the church leadership obliged to do the rulers' 'dirty work.' On the other hand, this situation only emphasized the status of the Copts as mere *Dhimmis*, rather than citizens.

4. The Outcomes of the Siege:

With the arrival of the Arabs, the spread of Islam, the moral isolation of the Copts, and the burden of constant blows, the status of Egyptian Christianity waned over time. Jacques Tagher offers (in 1951) a harsh verdict upon the church that needs to be understood in the context of these pressures and outright persecutions: 'Making the problem (for Copts) worse was the ignorance of the clergy, their lack of interest in civil education, and their preoccupation with raising funds for the purchasing of (ecclesiastical) offices. It is true that some monks tried to reform both the system and the hearts (of the people). Some authored religious and scientific books, but they were a small minority. Moreover, their works were void of originality and novelty. The Patriarchs followed one after the other without adding any important chapters to (the church's) history. The peace or trouble of their eras depended on the rulers' satisfaction or dissatisfaction with them, and on the level of tranquility in the country. None of them made a real effort to imbue a new spirit into the church, which was gradually fading away. In certain instances, long periods of time would elapse before the election of a new Patriarch. Things became more serious after the Ottoman occupation: belief in Christianity seemed superficial and religious education was non-existent; the clergy became ignorant of the basics of religion. The Patriarch's first and only priority was to live in peace.'[238]

The consecutive blows led to the almost complete collapse of the institution of monasteries which had preserved the cultural and religious traditions of the Copts across the ages. In the first generations of monasticism, hundreds of monasteries populated with thousands of monks existed in Egypt, but then after the Arab conquest, they were gradually destroyed until the number of monks in the Middle Ages dwindled until they could be counted on one hand. The fatal blow came in the mid-14th century when the Mamluk Amirs decided to confiscate the remaining monastery and church endowment lands (twenty-five-thousand *feddans*). Monasteries made a comeback only at the turn of the 20th century.

5. The Church and the Outside World:

The Patriarch's attempts to establish or strengthen his relationship with those outside the country, who were united to the Coptic Church's doctrine (and/or were spiritually and hierarchically aligned with her), infuriated the rulers. Woe to him if he corresponded directly with those parties without the ruler's knowledge. On the other hand, the allegiance of the Abyssinian and Nubian (until Nubia's succumbing to Islam in the 15th–16th century) Churches to the Coptic Church was one of the most important factors assuring peace along the southern borders of Egypt.[i] This may have been one of the main reasons that the Muslim rulers were inclined not to utterly destroy the Coptic Church. Oftentimes, the rulers blackmailed the church to pressure the Kings of Abyssinia to spread the Islamic *Dawah* and build mosques in their country.[ii] Al-Nagashi (Negus) often sacrificed his pride by sending gifts to the ruler in Egypt requesting that a metropolitan be sent to his country. At times, Al-Nagashi also attempted to intervene to halt persecution in Egypt.

Amidst its isolation, the Coptic Church had some contacts with the Church of Rome. In 1440, the Roman Pope, Eugene[iii], sent to Pope Yoannes XI an invitation to join the union between Latin and Greek churches that had been proclaimed the previous year at the Council of Florence[iv]. The Coptic Pope had the letter read aloud during a liturgy[v] and responded with a letter marked by the greatest courtesy and flowery language, confessing the Orthodox faith and offering thanks and prayers for the Latin Pope. However, no practical or canonical issues were broached. Andrea, superior of the Monastery of St. Anthony, travelled to Florence and in February, 1442, the bull, *Cantate Domino*, announced the union of the Coptic and Roman churches. The union came too little, however, as the two churches seem to have had different understandings of the 'union.'[239] In 1583, the Pope of Rome made fresh attempts to get the Coptic Church to acknowledge his authority during the days of Yoannes XIV, but with no different outcome.

---

[i] Since the fourth century, the Ethiopian Orthodox Church was dependent on the Coptic Church for its ecclesiastical life, and a bishop (called *abun*), Egyptian by birth, was consecrated by the Coptic pope. In 1881, a metropolitan and three bishops (all Egyptians) would be appointed. In 1929, the bishops were to be Ethiopian. In 1951, the first Ethiopian *abun* was consecrated. In 1959, *abun* was elevated to the rank of catholicus, thus allowing him to consecrate other bishops. The Communist rule, in 1974, broke off the cords with the Coptic Church until a protocol was signed in 1994, organizing the relations between the two churches.

[ii] As an example, the Fatimid Vizier, Badr Al-Gamali, ordered Abba Kyrillos II to send to Abyssinia two bishops who were to assure the building of mosques and propagation of (Islamic) *Da'wa*.

[iii] A previous attempt was at the Florence Council (1431), where the Coptic Church's delegate is said to have arrived too late to join the discussions.

[iv] It was organized on the initiative of the Byzantine emperor for the sake of Christian unity, to face the escalating Turkish danger.

[v] At the Church of the Virgin in Harat Zwailah, in Old Cairo.

The situation of the church, and the Copts in general, deteriorated to the point that in 1597, Patriarch Ghobrial VIII sent to the Pope of Rome, asking him 'to bless us with a yearly charitable offering, because we are experiencing severe hardships and troubles, and because of the many needs of our churches, monasteries, poor and needy, widows, orphans, and those in iron chains imprisoned because of the (*Jizya*) and other reasons...' and the Pope responded by sending aid.

On the other hand, the Coptic Church tried to maintain relations with that of Antioch, with frequent synodical letters exchanged between the Patriarchs of the two churches. This 'Syrian connection' was important for the life of the Coptic Church, and perhaps also for Antioch's, in their isolation. Of particular importance was the presence of Syrian monks who, by the early ninth century, had established themselves at the Monastery of the Theotokos of St. Bishoi, which came to be known as Dair al-Suryan, or the Monastery of the Syrians (Syriacs), in Wadi Al-Natroun.[240]

6. Historical Responsibility:

Over the time, the Coptic Patriarchs' authority in many areas was eroded and they were left often unable to preserve—let alone promote—their faith. Forced into the role of political leaders and representatives of their people in addition to their religious roles, the Patriarchs had to answer to policing Muslim authorities while abiding by the curbing laws.

On the other hand, there can be no denial that the Copts, and their church, bear some responsibility in what befell them in Egypt. There is no denial that in adapting to the reality, Copts often mistook Christianity's sublime teachings about love and peacefulness and, instead (usually under guidance of the clergy), clung to *pacifism*, shunned (legitimate) resistance and opted for appeasing the rulers.[i]

That said, there are specific instrumental moments in the church's history that helped reaching the current sad situation. These are briefly examined in the Appendix three.

---

[i] Nations like Spain eventually repelled Arab-Islamic invasion whereas Egypt did not: the former fought tooth and nail for centuries to achieve such liberation, whereas the Copts apparently opted for submission.

Sixth: Religious Conversion

Reviewing the path of conversions reveals certain key turning points. Toward the end of reign of the Umayyads, Caliph Marwan came to Misr and ordered that, "Anyone who does not convert to my religion [Islam], pray the way I pray, and follow my (religious) views, I shall kill and crucify; but whoever converts to my religion I will favor, dignify, enrich, and fix his name in my *Divân*," and immediately, one-thousand people prayed as he prayed (converted to Islam).

In the beginning of the reign of the Abbasids, Caliph Abdullah ('*Al-Saffah*' or 'the Slaughterer') decreed that, "Anyone who adopted his religion and prayed the way he prayed was to be exempted from the *Jizya*. The excessiveness of the *Kharaj* and the inordinate financial burdens made many, rich and poor, abjure the faith of Christ." After the massacre that was later carried out against the Peshmurians, many Copts in the northern Delta area converted to Islam. The Abbasids further stressed the equality of Muslims regardless of ethnic background—they themselves were more Persianized (from Khurasan) than Arab—and the desirability of non-Muslims' conversion to Islam. This was done through encouraging this conversion by exempting converts from *Jizya*, as well as other means such as anti-*Dhimmi* writings and dismissal of non-Muslims from government service.[241]

To be noted is that conversions to Islam presented the rulers with financial problems, since the treasury would incur the losses of the unpaid *Jizya* of those who converted, so they often maintained the same *Jizya* amount levied on villages, irrespective of the conversions of some of its inhabitants. By default, this led to increasing the financial burdens on those who did not convert to Islam, which would therefore accelerate the rate of conversions to Islam. By the end of the ninth century, even a poor individual who was incapable (of securing) his daily wage was forced to pay (two dinars), to the point where the people of Egypt growled from this great torment. Therefore, many Christians abjured their faith (and converted to Islam).

Al-Ḥakem bi-Amr Allah, in the 11th century, decreed that nothing was to be sold to or purchased from Christians anywhere. In an attempt to coerce ten *Archons* to convert to Islam, he tortured one of them to death, and after his death, Al-Ḥakem still ordered that he be whipped with one thousand lashes. Another one of the ten was beheaded and his body burnt. As for the rest of the ten (*Archons*), he ordered that they be tortured and lashed. When the beatings increased, four of them converted to Islam, but the rest were tortured to death.

At the end of the 13th century, Sultan Al-Ẓaher Baibars ordered that a large pit be dug and that 'Christians be thrown into it and burned, because he did not want in his state a *Divân* (full of) Christians.' Finally, the Sultan allowed those who converted to Islam to remain employed in his service, but ordered that those who refused to convert to Islam be beheaded. So, they all converted to Islam, and their written *Shihadas* were given to the Sultan.

Especially during the periods of excessive persecution, Copts converted to Islam: it was becoming clear to them that it was in the Muslim community that opportunities of social and career advancement lay, both for themselves and for their children. Some of those conversions may have been purely formal at first, but eventually entire families were lost to the Coptic community.[242]

It is also certainly true across the ages that anyone who converted to Islam by mistake (i.e. by accidently saying words similar to the *Shihada*) or under compulsion and then tried to convert back was beheaded (with very rare exceptions).

In addition to the aforementioned factors, the circumstances of the church deteriorated under the burden of constant blows. These include the seizure of Church endowments and resources, the loss of benefits by those who had previously been exempted from paying the *Jizya,* through the collection of the *Jizya* from monks (and clergy), and the collapse of the institution of monasteries, the shortage of the number of churches due to the stumbling blocks that were in place to prevent renovating them, and the clergy's intellectual and spiritual decline and their inability to perform anything but the bare minimum of tasks pertaining to their religious roles.

It is doubtless that the spread of the Arabic language, beginning in the 11th century, helped increase the number of conversions. As Copts began dealing and praying in Arabic, the translations of their religious books used some Islamic terminology (such as considering *Allah* to be equivalent to *God* in their understanding); the factor that we believe to have facilitated the process of 'crossing over' to Islam by those whose faith had faded. This was especially true for those who were fatigued by constant humiliation and persecution, or who found converting to Islam to be the only pathway to bypass the stumbling blocks of discrimination and unlock the doors of upward social mobility.

Despite all that has been discussed above, Christians remained to form over half of the country's population all the way until the end of the Fatimid State. Afterward, the rate of conversions accelerated, turning into 'mass conversions' in the days of the Mamluks.

Seventh: The Coptic Language

At the time of the Arab invasion, the 'Egyptian language' was the language of all Egyptians. At its final stages, 'Demotic,'[i] it adopted the Greek alphabet in addition to six (or seven) special characters for its script, becoming what is known as Coptic writing of the Egyptian language—that is, the Coptic language. The elites and the rich also knew Greek, which was the language of the official documents. This remained the case even after the Arab invasion.

In 706, the *Wali* Abdullah Ibn Abdul Malek decreed that Arabic was to be the language employed to carry out the *Divân* dealings. But the matter was not implemented before at least another century, as the documents continued to be written in Greek, or Coptic, or (later on) in either one of those languages in addition to Arabic. The reason for this is quite simple, and is often overlooked by most historians: Arabic language at the time was rather primitive and inadequate for maintaining *Divân* records and dealings (or, for that matter, any other purpose). Arabic only started its journey of development through the efforts of the Persian linguist, Sibawayh (d. 796), who came up with 'dotted letters' and diacritical marks, as well as elaborating and systematizing the rules of grammar.

Although the Arab conquest was a hard blow to Coptic literature, it nevertheless blossomed in the second half of the seventh and the eighth centuries, probably as a sign of resistance. It was characterized by being popular (folkloric) and worldly more than before, possibly because the monastic system became less strict, whereby monks were allowed to read non-religious books inside the monasteries. This new literature was written in the *Sahidic* dialect and contained poetry and stories (fiction) in addition to religious writings.[243]

---

[i] From '*demos*,' i.e. the popular version of the formal hieroglyphic writing.

In the tenth century, there was a sharp increase in Coptic manuscripts in the various monasteries, thanks to the spread of the use of paper. These included republishing older texts, both literature and religious.[244] The *Divân* records continued to employ Coptic alongside Arabic for a long period of time after the Conquest, until Coptic was no longer used.[245]

The Copts began to gradually learn Arabic. Although reasons for this are not definitive, nonetheless, there are several factors behind this transition. For example, there was the increasing urgency to learn the language in order to maintain their *Divân* positions and to deal with the rulers and the increasing numbers of settling Arabs, and those who have become Arabized and Arabicized. This gradually took place after it became apparent that the Arab *fat'h* was an actual colonization and not only a conquest. Arabic words began to be written using Coptic letters.

The war of attrition against the Copts and their religious institutions, particularly the monasteries, forced them to neglect their language and heritage, which started the gradual demise of the Coptic language. By the tenth century, Arabic became widespread. Sawiris Ibn Al-Muqafa' (who died prior to 1000) was the first to compose a book employing the Arabic language, writing *History of the Patriarchs* (his language was flimsy at times, but the chroniclers who came after him had a better command of the language) where he said in the book's introduction that he requested help from 'those Christian brethren with whose fitness I was acquainted, and begged them to assist me in translating the histories that we found written in the Coptic and Greek languages into the Arabic tongue, (which is) current among the people of the present day in the region of Egypt, many of whom are ignorant of the Coptic and the Greek...'[246]

The Coptic language received a blow at the hands of Al-Ḥakem bi-Amr Allah, who issued strict orders completely prohibiting its use in homes, roadways, or schools (in Misr and Cairo). Those who failed to comply had their tongues cut off. He even ordered that if mothers spoke to their children in Coptic, they too were to have their tongues cut off. He personally walked the streets of Cairo and eavesdropped on Coptic homes to find out if anyone was using the Coptic language.

In the days of Abba Ghobrial II (1131–1145), who, prior to his ordination, was a distinguished scribe, 'an avid reader of books, and a capable Arabic and Coptic transcriber,' he prioritized the translation of the Gospel and the rest of the liturgical books (under pressure from the *Wali*?).

He also allowed the use of Arabic during the public reading of the Gospels and preaching in all churches, after they had previously been read in Coptic. By the end of the Fatimid State, the Coptic language wilted—even if it continued to be used in Upper Egypt until the 16th century. In the 18th century, the Coptic language written using Arabic letters appeared, as is the case today in some of the liturgical books.

The process of moving from Coptic to Arabic must have been agonizing, as attested by a text thought to be written in the tenth or 11th centuries, where the anonymous writer puts in the mouth of an earlier monk, St. Samuel of Qalamoun (d. 695), these 'prophetic' words about the future, when Copts would do something else,

'which if I were to tell you of, your hearts would be greatly pained: they are abandoning the beautiful Coptic language, in which the Holy Spirit has spoken many times through the mouths of their spiritual fathers, and they are teaching their children from infancy to speak the language of the Arabs, and to take pride in it! Even if the priests and monks—they as well!—dare to speak Arabic and to take pride in it, and that within the sanctuary! Woe upon woe!'

'O my beloved children, what shall I say in these times, when readers in the church do not understand what they are reading, or what they are saying, because they have forgotten their language? These truly are miserable people, deserving of being wept over, because they have forgotten their language and speak the language of the *hajarah!*' [i]

'But woe to every Christian who teaches his own the language of the *hajarah* from his infancy, and causes him to forget the language of his fathers.'

(Later, an elderly monk says to Samuel): "Understand what I tell you, Samuel, my son. At the time when the Christians shall have the audacity to speak the language of the *hajarah* inside the sanctuary…woe to the Christians at that time! Woe multiplied seven times!"

The text—composed in Coptic but preserved, ironically enough, only in Arabic translation—bears eloquent witness both to the phenomenon of Arabization of the Coptic community, as well the alarm that this phenomenon occasioned in conservative monastic circles.[247]

---

[i] *Hajarah*, descendants of Hajar, Abraham's maid who is supposed to be the mother of the Arabs.

In another place, pseudo Samuel says:

'Christians will give their children Arabic names and teach them from a young age to speak the language of the Arabs... Many books will fall into disuse... They will forget many of the martyrs because their biographies will disappear... Many churches will fall into ruin... Men will commit serious sins and there will be nobody to correct them.'

The writer makes the important connection between loss of language and loss of religious tradition and identity. These predictions came true. Tamer El-Leithy notes that, "The author considered cultural and linguistic assimilation as an urgent problem precisely because he saw them as conversion's dangerous precursor."[248]

The gradual move from Coptic to Arabic was responsible for a situation whereby churches were full of people who were religious, yet lacked the basic Christian formation necessary to sort out sense from nonsense. Many of them, almost by a process of osmosis, were becoming socialized into the specifically religious language of the mosque. The work entitled *Kitab al-Idâh* ('The Book of the Elucidation'), sums up the issue eloquently. There, the root of Christian confusion about the core doctrines of Trinity, Incarnation, and redemption is identified as the believers 'mingling with *hunafaa*' (Muslims), and 'the disappearance of their language, through which they know the truth of their religion.' The writer goes on:

'It has come to be the case that they do not hear any mention of 'the Trinity' among themselves except rarely; nor do they hear any mention of 'the Son of God' except in a metaphorical sense. Instead, most of what they hear is that God is 'unique (*fard*),' 'everlasting (*samad*),' and the rest of the language that the *hunafaa* use. The believers have become accustomed to this, and have been brought up with it, so that the mention of the 'Son of God' has come to be difficult for them; they do not know any interpretation or meaning for it.'[249]

The strongest pillar of Coptic identity was thus shaken when Copts abandoned their national and ancient language. In fact, this represented a form of cultural genocide—a 'soft jihad' — which had devastating effects on the very ethos of all Egyptians, especially in that adopting Arabic as one's language is not a condition for converting to Islam (for the Persians, Turks, and others maintained their languages after Islam).

Particularly striking is that until the present day, the Egyptian State adamantly decries the interest of some (Coptic and Muslim) Egyptians in studying the language of their forefathers—Coptic—just as Europeans are interested in studying Latin and (classical) Greek, even though both are also dead languages, and considers the matter as a threat to 'national security.'

Eighth: The Relationship of the Copts and the Invaders

There are several landmarks that may be observed as follows:

1. The Shock:

Egyptians, since ancient times (particularly when the central authority was weak), were used to raids from tribes coming from the Eastern and Western deserts that targeted Egypt for looting, pillaging, kidnapping, and taking people captive. Although those marauders eventually left, a short or long time after their raids (such as the Hyksos, the ancestors of the Peninsula Arabs[250], who were chased out of Egypt after three centuries), it appeared that those new invaders were no different from the previous marauders except for remaining in the country, like an unwanted guest, for an indefinite period of time... Thus, the *fat'h* morphed into a 'colonizing occupation.'

Becoming aware of their new and bitter reality, the Copts tried initially to ignore and 'escape' it by dedicating their attention to activities that are typical of stable and civilized citizenries; leaving to the invaders things that they know about and love...

2. Resistance:

In opposition to the greed of the new rulers, their imposition of different kinds of taxes, and their intransigence in the methods of collection, the Copts sought passive means of resistance, such as forsaking their farmlands and migrating en masse to other places in order to escape from tyranny. This was especially the case after resorting to monasteries no longer exempted them from their financial obligations. But the rulers responded viciously and harshly, so they no longer permitted anyone to travel or resettle in another area without a specific permit ('passport'). They also confiscated lands of those who did not return and gave them to Arab tribes. Then, Coptic farmers were forced to tend the land without wage. As for the land tended by the

Arabs, it was considered 'tithing land,' meaning that no *Kharaj* was owed on it; only the *Zakat*.

As a result of the increase in unjust taxes in various ways—which included forcing the living to pay the *Jizya* of their dead—and the increasing oppressive methods employed in their collection, the resistance began to take the form of 'revolts,' lasting for more than a century, covering the north and south, but they were forcefully put down. The first revolt was under the Umayyads in (706) in the Delta, the second occurred in Upper Egypt. A third revolt was in (738), the fourth was in (740), and the fifth was in (749) during the last days of the Umayyads, and it was violently put down, which led the Copts to support the Abbasids. Then there was the revolt of the Peshmurians (831), which ended in a bloody massacre and taking captive the remnant alive to be sold as slaves or to work in the swamps of Shatt Al-Arab, in southern Iraq. This took place at the hands of the Abbasid Caliph Abdullah Al-Mamoun, whose memory is immortalized by the Egyptian State, which has named one of the major streets of Heliopolis[i] — among others—after him.

This period was an exception after which the Copts never went back to standing up for violence, abiding by the peace (rather, pacifism) called for and encouraged by the church.

3. Attempts to Tame the Invaders:

The Copts accepted the de facto situation, and they attempted—according to their ways at the time—experimenting with the notion of 'land in exchange for peace,' where they would give up their country (and independence)—that is the land and governance—in exchange for resting assured that their lives and property were safe. But they ended up losing both sides of the trade, and the noose did not delay in gradually tightening until it chocked out their spirit of resistance.

Then they began experimenting with ways of courting and getting closer to the invaders—who had become settlers—by providing services, or by even imitating the customs of Muslims. They then went further by learning the language of the invaders to improve communication, which was the step that eventually led to neglecting their national language, ending with the

---

[i] An upscale suburb, north of Cairo.

weakening of their national identity. At any rate, these attempts ended with nothing more than further oppression, humiliation, and contempt.

4. Surrender:

The Copts tried to hold on to their livelihoods, and to a general role in the administration of the country, the role of the 'squatting Egyptian scribe.' The administrative system (i.e. the bureaucracy) was completely dependent on them, because of their skills in surveying the land, accounting, and bookkeeping, which the Arab invaders knew nothing about. So, the Arabs let things be run by the Copts, as they had in the past, and occupied themselves with the collection of taxes, *Jizya*, and *Kharaj*. Getting rid of the Copts meant the impossibility of evaluating (and therefore, collecting) the *Kharaj* and taxes, which was the foremost interest of the invaders-turned-settlers.

It was for this reason that the rulers were unable to get rid of the Copts, despite the legal Islamic texts and the strict orders of the Caliphs, such as what the Commander of the Faithful, Omar Ibn Al-Khatab, said to one of the *Walis* who employed a Copts, "Man, what is this you have done? Allah will punish you. Do you not understand the meaning of Allah's words, 'O ye who believe! Take not the Jews and the Christians for friends. They are friends one to another. He among you who taketh them for friends is (one) of them. Lo! Allah guideth not wrongdoing folk.'"[251] When a *Wali* responded by claiming that he used the Copt for scribal work only, leaving aside his doctrine, the Commander of the Faithful responded, "That is not an excuse, I will never honor those whom Allah has despised, I will never lift up those whom Allah has demeaned, and I will never get close to those whom Allah has separated from Himself."[i]

Seven centuries after the words of Omar, the *faqih*, Ibn Al-Naqqash (d. 1362), confirmed this view by saying, "Know that *Sharia* does not allow the employment of *Dhimmis*, and this is the view of all Muslims. As for the

---

[i] To show the 'fairness' of Omar Ibn Al-Khatab toward the 'Copts,' some recount the story in which Omar is said to have ordered one of the 'Egyptians' to beat the son of Amr Ibn Al-Aas (because he had struck that Egyptian when he lost a horse race). Omar said to Amr, "When did you enslave those whom were created free?" However, the events in the story refer without ambiguity to an Arab who came as part of Amr's army to settle in Egypt, and not a native Copt.

fuqahaa,[i] they opined (gave *fatwas*) that *Dhimmis* are not to be employed, completely forbidding the practice, or at least indicating their disapproval."

Ibn Al-Naqqash published an epic book whose title, *The Slander (or Slanderous Act) of Employing Dhimmis*[ii], says it all. He emphatically states that the *fuqahaa* are unanimous about *Kuffar*, even if peaceful and subject to *Dhimmitude* status: Their knowledge and experience may be sought and put in service of Muslims. They may be employed, on condition that they are never in a position of authority over Muslims, and never to have affection (amity, cordiality or friendliness) toward them. He laments that many Muslim rulers fail to observe these strict rules demanded by Quran and *Hadiths*.

Some of the rulers disregarded these orders; other times they got rid of the Copts and then quickly brought them back, since they knew that—ultimately—the most important thing for the Caliphs or Sultans was money and nothing else. However, others were careful to obey the commands of the *Sharia*. For example, Caliph Omar Ibn Abdul-Aziz (who was reputed for being 'just and tolerant') hated employing *Dhimmis* and told his governors, "The *Moshrekîn* (polytheists) are filth, and Allah made them the soldiers of Satan and made them the greatest losers as to their deeds; they are those whose efforts are in vain in this worldly life, while they think that they are doing good. I swear they are those upon whom the curses of Allah and the damnations of the cursers descend. In the past when Muslims went into a city populated with *Moshrekîn*, they made use of them only because they were knowledgeable in matters relating to tax exaction, writing (record keepers) and administration. They only remained for as long as Allah willed it. If (now) I knew of a scribe, or a tax collector, or any other worker who was not a Muslim, I will get rid of him and replace him with a Muslim man, for to destroy their work is to destroy their religion. It is more befitting to degrade them to the level of abasement and servility that Allah has degraded them to."[252]

Ṣalaḥ Al-Deen (who surnamed himself *Qame' Abadet Al-Solban* i.e. 'the Oppressor of the Cross Worshippers') is another example. He signaled that 'Christians should not be employed as administrators over the state's

---

[i] Plural of *faqih*.

[ii] '*Al-Madhamma fi Iste'mal Ahl Al-Dhimma*'
http://www.alukah.net/web/triqi/0/32123/#_ftn16.

finances or supervisors and therefore, during his rule and his progeny after him, Christians were not employed in administration or supervision.'

5. *The Battle for Survival:*

With time, the rulers easily blackmailed the Copts for money without fearing any revolts, and they set the Copt's fate as they, or the populace (riffraff), desired. The Copts reconciled themselves to their *Dhimmitude* and ultimately counted obedience to their rulers and their mere survival as the epitomes of achievement. Thus, the times of demise started with the end of the Fatimid era and the arrival of the Ayyubids. Then came the spread of the mentality of victims adopting the views of their executioners about their own selves,[i] in addition to viewing the disasters that befall people as a form of divine judgment, which made Copts blame themselves (their own impiety) for what was happening to them. They were also forced to lower their 'bar of expectations' and ambitions to rock bottom.

Copts adapted to the conditions of their lowly *Dhimmitude* status in the Islamic State, to the point that they even took to the streets to holler for the Sultan, because he returned to them their church utensils that he had illegitimately seized, and they were also happy that no one objected as they publicly prayed for the Sultan on the streets.

The sight of an influential Copt, who successfully held an important office, caused 'the Islamic street,' especially during the time of the Mamluks and afterward, to bare its fangs. In fact, they utterly rejected the thought of non-Muslims having any rights whatsoever. Most likely, the services that the Coptic *Archons* provided to the rulers were, as Mohammed Shafiq Ghorbal[ii] says, "Based on seeking personal gain, as well as deliverance from the rulers' contempt that was never alleviated, regardless of how much money they owned, their high standing, or how much the rulers needed them."

Thus, the Copts splendidly played the only role they were allowed to play (scribes) up until the early 20th century, and the spreading of education; thenceforth, there was no more 'need' for them. Therefore, it may indeed be

---

[i] As explained by the French sociologist, Pierre Bourdieu. It corresponds to the 'Stockholm Syndrome,' which is the label given by modern psychologists for the 'hostages that defend their kidnappers.'
[ii] Egyptian historian (1894–1961).

'normal' (in keeping with the letter and spirit of *Sharia*) that their inclusion today in the various state agencies is kept at a 'nominal' percentage, which never exceeds two percent? Does this not fit with an Islamic state that preserves its own religiosity and 'purity'?

On the other hand, a number of Copts betrayed their kin for personal gain, in addition to reconciling themselves to their lowly *Dhimmitude*; a disease that has remained with them. However, in fairness, one must stress that such ignoble behavior was often a byproduct of the nonstop and horrendous oppression they lived with continuously.

Many of the Muslims' do's and don'ts were imposed on the Copts, such as forcing their women to wear the veil, or the segregation of women and men in churches. The Copts even began to imitate many of their customs, such as child circumcision which Christianity had done away with, and it was not in effect prior to the Arab invasion, but in the beginning of the 12th century, the Patriarch made it compulsory. By the 13th century, the writings of the Copts were filled with Islamic religious expressions such as the *Basmalah*.[i] Church parishioners would, at times, also imitate some of the Muslim practices, such as the (partial) 'ablution' prior to prayer. Some even prohibited the eating of pork. Christian marriage contracts began to include the pre-marriage and post-divorce dowries. Many Copts disregarded the Gospel's teachings on divorce, and the Church was forced to indulge this trend in an effort to prevent people from leaving Christianity.

The only arm left for the Copts was education and proficiency in whatever they do. The Coptic Church had never in her darkest days entirely neglected the education of her children. In every parish there was a school, where they were taught to read and write, plus arithmetic if nothing more. The capacities of the ancient race were always valued, but they gradually became reduced to the level of mere government clerks.

Thanks to their abilities and proficiency, the Copts continued to occupy most of the administrative position of the government. At least until the end of the Fatimids' era, they represented the vast majority of artisans of all kinds, especially in towns. Some activities even carried their name, such as *qabati*, or weaving special tissues and dresses, made of wool, linen and silk.

---

[i] The words 'In the name of Allah, the Merciful, ...'

Architecture and building were—at least during the first centuries after the conquest—professions practiced by Copts exclusively. The same goes for manufacturing of paper (from papyrus), glass, metal crafts, and pottery.[253]

6. Neo-Dhimmitude

In the modern era, and after realizing their failure in changing their country's political system into one that treats them as equal citizens, many Copts seem to have abandoned efforts to regain their rights and, instead, revived a modern version of old submissiveness, but more elegantly clothed into a 'neo-*Dhimmitude*' attire that hides behind soothing but false excuses. These may be, 'realism,' 'pragmatism' or selectively picking—and misinterpreting (with the strong encouragement of the church)—some verses such as 'love your enemy' (as if demanding equality implies seeing other citizens as 'enemies,' let alone not loving them), 'be submissive to rulers and authorities, (and) be obedient,' 'the Lord will fight for you; you need only to be still.'[i]

Many members of the Copts' modern elite have thus turned into 'useful idiots' to the benefit of more Islamist[ii] hegemony and turned a blind eye to the endless sufferings of their poorer or more vulnerable kin. At times, it appears as if Copts in diaspora, people living in economic security and cultural and political freedom, chose to uphold the flaws created by a repressive society they left behind. [254]

Ninth: Between Awakening and Regressing

The awakening came with the French Expedition, with the new ideas and principles it brought, and despite the continued suffering of the Copts because of Bonaparte's 'Islamic policies.'[iii]

Real and serious efforts began, after Mohammed Ali's initial steps, through the modernization and Westernization policies carried out by Said

---

[i] Respectively, St Paul's Letter to Titus, 3–1 and Exodus 14–14.

[ii] Islamist, relates to the political ideology of Islamism which ultimately aims at imposing Islam and its *Sharia* as the system of governance.

[iii] Refer to above chapter titled 'Bonaparte Knocks at the Door.' It's Bonaparte's policy of winning the hearts and minds of the Muslim population by appearing as a Muslim, or even a better Muslim than the likes of the Mamluks.

Pasha and *Khedive* Ismail. Kyrillos IV ('Father of Reform') poured his efforts into the fields of education and publishing. He founded the Coptic schools, (which were open to everyone), revived the instruction of the Coptic language, after almost becoming extinct. He even introduced the education of girls, despite facing resistance for doing so. He also established a printing press that produced many books in the fields of theology, history, and literature. Kyrillos V followed suit in establishing more schools and attended to monasteries (in the beginning of the 20th century, seven monasteries became inhabited with over 400 monks) and the publishing of books. He encouraged the monks to read and established schools for them in the monasteries. During his tenure, the clergy's level of knowledge improved. Enlightened rulers (such as *Khedive* Ismail) helped by giving lands for schools in the form of endowments. In part, the revival was significantly helped by the foreign evangelistic missions' efforts in spreading schools to all parts of the country, and by creating 'competition' in preaching and doctrine, stimulating the Coptic Church to develop itself.

In an atmosphere of modernization, and by the help of enlightened rulers and political forces, the Copts, with astonishing speed, shook off the dust of isolation and became politically involved. Their involvement reached its peak during the Egyptian Revolution of 1919, which was followed by a short 'liberal era,' prior to the attack of the religious fascistic ideology of the Muslim Brotherhood. However, the Copts' political involvement practically came to an end after 1952.

Thus, the 100 year period, which some refer to as the 'golden era,' but we shall call instead the *'gold-plated* era,' between the mid-19th century and the mid-20th century, unfortunately appears to be—and we hope to be mistaken in making this assumption—just a historical exception, after which, Egypt and the Copts went back to their former status quo: a theocratic (Islamic) militaristic Egypt, with the Ottoman-Mamluks period being the closest example. In this 'status quo' the Copts, are viewed as a sect (or *Galiya*),[i] that could never have equality in citizenship (on the basis of

---

[i] The *Dhimmis* were labeled *'Galiya'* (driven out) because Omar Ibn Al-Khatab *Galahom* (drove them out) of Arabia. This designation remained with them wherever they went, and then it became attached to everyone who paid the *Jizya* from the 'People of the Book' (Jews and Christians in the Quran) in every country under the rule of Islam, even if they were not driven out from their countries. (Footnotes, Part

complete equality) in a state that is based on religion and only religious fraternity.

This 'gold-plated' era was tainted by the British occupation. No point in attempting to compare the different types of occupation, but a judicious consideration reveals that the harmful effects of the short-lived British occupation are incomparable to what the Arab-Islamic occupation brought over Egypt and its devastating repercussions. In fact, the British occupation of Egypt brought in several undeniable institutional and administrative improvements. On the other hand, it had the unintended effect of the unification of the various citizen factions around a pivotal 'nationalistic' cause in a way that had not been seen centuries before, or since.

***

At any rate, the revival efforts remain, above all, without any real political dividends. This is the result of the ruling powers, allied to the 'Islamic street,' shutting and locking the door to any real modernization which would, among other things, lead to the 'full citizenship of the Copts' and their political participation.

This brings us back to the question raised earlier, after referring to the period of vacillation between the calls of 'Pan-Islamism,' and the 'Pan-Egyptianism' (nationalism) that Egypt went through in the late 19th and early 20th centuries.

It is clear that after 1952, Nasser identified Egypt's priorities first as 'Arabism associated with Islam,' because 'the Arab sphere is the most important and closely related sphere to us.'

Sadat promptly emphasized that the role of Egypt revolves around Islam first and foremost ('the believing president,' and 'I am a Muslim president of an Islamic state,' etc.). There is little difference between this and the '*to hell with Egypt*'[i] statement, uttered by a leading Islamist; both emphasize a concept that has been engraved in the country's constitution.

---

two, P. 734). Notice as well that the *Jizya* was, at times, referred to as '*Gawali*,' which is derived from the same Arabic root. *Galiya* also designates 'a community of foreigners.'

[i] Interview with Mohamed Mahdi Akef, the Muslim Brotherhood's Supreme Guide with journalist, Said Shoueib, published in Rose Al-Yousef magazine, April 9th,

Thus, Egypt in the 21st century is not much more than a mere 'province' in the 'global Islamic state' in which the (virtual) '*Wahhabi* Caliphate'[i] plays the role of leadership through the Organization of the Islamic Conference and other institutions emanating from it or associated with it, and other groups seeking to restore the 'Caliphate.' In fact, Egypt often attempts to outdo everyone—all while pretending to call for 'moderate religious discourse.'

***

The nation building process in Egypt failed to lead to the formulation of a coherent and unified framework in dealing with the different religious groups. The institutional relationship between the state, Islam, and other religions in the country is partly a continuation of old and traditional models. The typical characteristics of this 'modern' version are the incorporation of Islamic institutions into the state (as official Islam or state Islam) and granting of a measure of autonomy to the non-Muslim religious institutions (e.g. in family laws). However, it has failed to develop mechanisms for the adequate representation of the Copts in and through the state (media, education, etc.); therefore, it has strengthened tendencies of Muslim domination over the state and Coptic alienation from the state. More problematic from the Copts' point of view, the system does not even provide collective equality because Islamic family law is a superordinate to all other legal codes. The perpetuation of legal flaws within the system has been used in the absence of political will to repair them, even though they have caused an increasing number of sectarian conflicts. (Child custody conflicts, involuntary conversions etc.)

2006. Akef said, "To hell with Egypt, to hell with Egypt's father, and Egypt's inhabitants...(..) Islam is the nationality (..). I wouldn't mind that a Muslim from Malaysia rule over us," and that, "The Ottoman Turks were a Caliphate state...and being corrupt does not make it an occupation."

[i] Saudi Arabia, the home of Wahabism, has seen some positive changes in the recent few years, driven by a young crown prince. However, their depth and durability remain to be seen. Another country that went through fundamental changes is Turkey, where the Kamalists installed a radical secular regime in the 1920s. Yet, a century later, the people 'Democratically' brought to power an Islamist, neo-Ottoman, regime.

The public discourse (as if in a preemptive effort to abort recognition of Copt's legitimate grievances) adopted a dual discourse of 'national unity' and 'religious patriotism' when addressing and defining the Coptic question. The national unity discourse is mainly based on the power of certain myths and rituals cultivating the ideas of essential harmony and unity in Muslim-Christian relations in Egypt. As any form of discord or any expression of particular interest was already perceived as an attack on national unity, this discourse effectively precluded the recognition of legitimate Coptic grievances. Consequently, the actions of Copts who have publicly raised complaints have been seen as the real cause for the deterioration of national unity. The religious patriotism approach fuses religion (Islam) with nationalism and allocates to religion a socially and politically integrating role. Looking at the Coptic question through the lens of religious patriotism means identifying religious extremism or fanaticism as the main challenge that is contradictory to both the message of the 'heavenly religions' and the patriotic spirit that seeks harmonious coexistence. However, Muslim authorities tended to be extremely sensitive to Christian critiques of Islam while hardly ever considering which forms of Muslim proselytizing had the potential to offend or alienate Christian compatriots.

As a consequence, 'accommodation' has long been a widespread attitude among Copts. The typical and most influential representatives of this trend were Coptic officials and regime politicians. The public discourse of the church has always sought religious conciliation with Islamic dignitaries and even praised the tolerant character of Islam. The readiness to seek accommodation and to make concessions to the majority's perspective has always been coupled with the implicit assumption that this would induce the majority to reciprocate by making concessions to the concerns of the minority. But when Muslim indulgence was not forthcoming, the accommodating trend was increasingly perceived among Copts as futile and self-defeating. A direct reaction to this was the rise of attitude that may be called alienation, expressed socially through a withdrawal to the community sphere. However, many who have embraced withdrawal and openly expressed it in the community sphere have remained publicly committed to accommodation.[255]

The state-run media have ready-made clichés: the 'Good Copt' is he who accepts Islamic hegemony and lauds the moderation of Islam and its institutions; the 'Bad Copt' is he who claims even the most elementary rights.

Tenth: Uprooting – Re-rooting

Even though profoundly attached to their fatherland, Copts started to emigrate from Egypt in the late 1950s and early 1960s. This was when the real face of the Nasser regime started to show itself. Successive waves followed with varying intensity in the subsequent decades, but their major exodus came following the 2011 uprising which resulted in empowering the Islamists.

The Coptic diaspora grew to represent currently about 15% of their total population. These are mostly in the U.S.A., Canada, and Australia, but also in Western Europe and even Eastern Europe. Tens of thousands of Copts also moved for temporary employment in Arab countries.

Wherever Copts went, churches followed them. In 1964, the first priest especially consecrated for serving Copts abroad, was sent to Toronto and another priest was sent to live in Germany for a year. A priest had already been sent, in 1961, to the Coptic community in Kuwait. In 1969, a priest was sent to Australia and, in 1973, to Los Angeles. The first churches were rented from Protestant and Catholic churches until Copts could collect enough money to build their own. The Coptic Church has about 600 churches outside Egypt.[256] These are (currently) supervised by 35 bishops, who represent over 25% of the total members of the church's Holy Synod.

The expatriate communities have proved vital for their kin and for the church in Egypt, and have left deep imprint on its international presence and self-image. Emigrants, often successful in their adopted countries, send generous donations to the mother church.

These waves of Coptic immigration have led to the emergence, starting as early as 1970, of a revivalist current that focused on human rights work in order to obtain full citizenship rights for their kin back in their fatherland. After the birth of this current at the hands of a small group of committed pioneers in Canada and the U.S., another generation of activists entered the scene in the years 2000, to face the challenges through professional work adhering to modern rights standards and terminologies as elaborated in the international law[i]. However, these efforts have yet to succeed in creating sizeable international pressure groups, as they remain curtailed by lack of a

---

[i] An example of such organizations is 'Coptic Solidarity,' established in 2010 in the U.S., with affiliated organisms in Canada and Europe.

'rights culture' among the Copts, as well as a prevailing counter-culture of 'neo *Dhimmitude,'* endorsed and promoted by the official church. That is to say nothing of the attempts at infiltration, enlistment, and recruitment by the state apparatus, which seem to be followed with a strange persistence (and with much success—one must admit) in order to suppress any work that might help the Copts reach their modest goal. So, the movement is expending much of its effort into clatter with limited impact.

On the other hand, the vast majority of Copts, both in Egypt and the Diaspora, have opted for shrinking back and withdrawing from public work, focusing their attention (perhaps motivated by their survival instinct based on history lessons that do not inspire a sense of encouragement) on matters related to living, protecting their families, and having successful careers on Earth, as well as securing their Afterlife. These are certainly laudable enterprises but remain individual, if not individualistic, with little bearing on the situation and status of the community at large.

Eleventh: A Reality Snapshot — Institutionalized *Dhimmitude*

We write these lines close to the end of the second decade of the 21st century. Yet, basic unalienable rights are still denied to the Copts. Worse, denial continues to be the position of the Egyptian authorities when the issue of discrimination and persecution of the Copts is raised. Rhetorical references are often made to absurd historical myths about how well Copts have been 'treated' ever since the Arab invasion, to avoid talking substantively about the present. This tactic further fails to hide that Copts are being viewed and treated as *Dhimmis* who may (or may not) be well treated. A strategy of denial and obfuscation and refusing to admit to the root problems, is relentlessly adhered to. Considerable energy and resources are consumed to conceal and silence the voice of anyone who dares to speak out or advocate for equality and human rights for Copts in Egypt. The 'Coptic Issue' is treated as a mere 'dossier' in the hands of 'National Security,' rather than being a high-priority citizenship issue under the responsibility of the president.

Violence against Copts is what may attract the public attention, when it is severe. But in all cases, it only represents the tip of the iceberg of what the

Copts live through on a daily basis in Egypt, by way of profound exclusion or even enforced Ghettoization. Such exclusion further reinforces the sense of second-class status of the Copts which, in a diabolical vicious circle, leads to more exclusion.

Here is a 'snapshot' of the current picture:

1. **The census of Copts**. It is still kept as a secret. Even though the national Civil Status Administration has records of all citizens (born after 1900), of which 'religion' is a mandatory identifying element, the government continues to deny that they know how many Copts there are.

2. **Justice denied**. Of the hundreds of assaults on the Copts over the past several years, few, if any, have been brought to justice. Major massacres, such as the attack on the Two Saints church (Alexandria, 2011, New Year's Eve), or the massacre of Maspero (October 10th, 2011) and many others have never been investigated, and justice never rendered. Whenever fanaticized mobs attack Copts (often with the complicity of the National Security department), authorities hold 'Reconciliation Meetings' to force the victims to forfeit their rights and submit to the tyrannical ruling of the fanatics, emboldened by the authorities. Such meetings, sometimes followed by forced relocation of innocent families are held, while fully knowing they are against law and justice.

3. **Government positions**. Of the 33 ministers and 15 deputy ministers[i] in the Egyptian government, there is (since September, 2015) only one junior Coptic minister, who is without a portfolio or a real job. Of the 27 appointed governors and 23 deputy governors, there are two Copts[ii]. Out of 524 (government appointed) heads of city, district, or town councils, there is barely a single Copt. The percentage of Copts in the various judiciary bodies is kept below two-percent, while there is not a single Copt in the Supreme Judiciary Council. Egypt has in its Foreign Service 167 diplomatic or consular missions around the world; among the heads of these missions there are never more than three Copts at any one time, and these can never be in a main western capital nor an international organism. No more than one

---

[i] As of December, 2019.

[ii] In September, 2018, two Copts, including a woman, were appointed as governors in a surprising positive move which proves, in itself, that if the political leadership has the will, many things could be done.

percent of high-level posts in the administration (general manager or undersecretary) are held by Copts.

4. **Army, police, and special services**. Copts accepted each year at the various military academies and the police academy are kept below two-percent.[i] No Copts among the members of the National Defense Council that oversees the Armed Forces, or the Supreme Council of the Police. Copts are prohibited from working for the National Security department or any of the intelligence services. No Copts at the presidential offices or the Republican Guards. Moreover, Copts have increasingly been killed in the military by their Muslim countrymen, with no credible investigation that goes beyond the systematic claim of 'suicidal case.'

5. **Parliament**. Of the 596 members of the current parliament[ii], there are 39 Copts (including 24 on restricted electoral lists, 12 elected individually, and three appointed). That represents barely six-percent and is linked to the Constitutional provision (Art. 244) of temporary (unspecified) measures to favor certain groups (women, Copts, farmers and workers) to be elected on restricted lists.

6. **Freedom of worship and belief**. A unified law to regulate the building of *all* houses of worship has been rejected, not to treat churches at the same footing as mosques. Instead, a special church law was adopted which codifies existing obstacles (since the Ottoman *Khatt-i-Hamayouni*) and leaves the entire process in the hands of the National Security Department. If a group of Copts are caught praying in a house, they are arrested and prosecuted for 'praying without permit.' Most villages have no churches and a majority of their Coptic inhabitants may never see a priest in their lifetime.

The religious affiliation is a requirement on national I.D. cards and on all official and private application forms, commercial contracts, notarized acts, and even club membership forms. One's religious affiliation can be instantly changed by the authorities in case of conversion *to* Islam, but the reverse is

---

[i] Official numbers of admissions are hard to get. However, in November 19, 2013, Esmat Murad, the commander of the Military Academy said that 2510 students were accepted for enrolment that year, including 32 Christians. See endnote (204), and: https://www.youm7.com/story/2013/11/19/-السيسى-يصدق-على-نتيجة-الكليات-والمعاهد
العسكرية-قبول-2510-طالبا/1352694

[ii] Elected in October 2015, according to the 2014 Constitution.

impossible. Over 50 cases of 'Derision of Religion'—'blasphemy'—were handled by the courts in the past few years alone. Rarely these concerned Christianity, even though it is attacked on a daily basis in mosques and even some talk shows. Several Copts were sentenced to prison on fabricated charges of deriding Islam, sometimes for things as trivial as a Facebook 'like,' while vociferous Islamic hatemongers remain free. Of the dozens of Imams who publicly incite hatred and violence against Christians, none have been brought to justice.

7. **Forced conversion**. Dozens of women are lured or coerced to convert to Islam, including several cases of underage girls, every year. This insidious activity is well-organized and is conducted under the watchful, and supportive, eyes of the authorities. On the other hand, a mere suspicion that a Christian man is having a romance with a Muslim woman leads to riots and collective punishment of relatives.

8. **Universities**. In the 23 public (state-run) universities in Egypt, there are over 90 leadership positions (president or vice president). None of these is occupied by a Copt. These universities include 450 faculties, with more than 1550 leadership positions (dean and vice-dean). Barely a hand full of these are occupied by Copts. Coptic students who have scored top grades in the anonymous High School Diploma exams become surprisingly 'too dumb' to be top students during the years of college, leading to (the desired) outcome of having fewer Copts in academic positions than normally expected if the system was unbiased. In the public universities in governorates of Assiut and Minya, Coptic students represent 25–30% of the total, yet the percentage of Copts among the teaching faculty (lecturers up to professors) is below five-percent. Coptic medical graduates are prohibited from specializing in gynecology.

9. **Education**. The official curriculum of the ministry of education ignores seven centuries of the Coptic-era history, while glorifying invading 'heroes' for having slaughtered thousands of Christians in Egypt and North Africa. The official curricula of the Arabic language include topics and texts that instill hatred of people of other faiths, entice violence, foster a sense of 'Islamic supremacy' and force non-Muslim students to learn and submit to Islamic percepts that denigrate their own faith.

10. **Al-Azhar**. Originally a religious institute, its role has been expanded from teaching Islamic studies to a complete portfolio of colleges teaching medicine, engineering, dentistry, etc., making it one of the top ten largest

universities in the world, with over half a million students in 87 faculties. Christian students are not allowed to study at Al-Azhar's non-religious faculties. Al-Azhar University (whose budget, in 2018, was more than four times larger than that of Cairo University and accepted 85,000 new students in September, 2018[257]) is funded by Egyptian taxpayers, including from Egyptian Christians. Over forty-thousand foreign students are given scholarships to study Islam, while no funding whatsoever goes toward any Christian educational institutions. Al-Azhar has been allowed to create a mammoth, state funded, parallel educational system, from kindergarten to high school (similar to the 'Madrassa' of Afghanistan and Pakistan), which covers every town and village in Egypt, and enrolls almost 2.1 million students. The curriculum of Al-Azhar schools and universities include material that teaches hatred and incites violence against Christians. Holders of Al-Azhar high-school diplomas are allowed to enroll in police and military academies, knowing that they would most likely become religiously—rather than patriotically—motivated officers who naturally despise non-Muslim colleagues or citizens.

11. **Sanctioned societal discrimination**. Of the 69 football clubs, with over two-thousand players in the Premier League, second and third division, players are rarely Copts, numerous complaints by Coptic athletes of being banned from joining sports' teams in most clubs are ignored. The national Olympic team in 2016 did not have a single Coptic athlete. Hundreds of private businesses of various sizes openly prohibit the hiring of Copts.

12. **Media**. National (state-run) audiovisual media devote about 15% of daily transmission time to Islamic religious programs, but only a few hours per *year* to transmit Nativity mass. T.V. dramas and soap operas often highlight and explicitly encourage cases of a Coptic girl falling in love with a Muslim man—but never the reverse! Coptic journalists in state-owned media (all kinds) are less than one-percent. Reporting on cases of discrimination against Copts is unthinkable.

***

Many of the above-mentioned grievances that defy the very basic principles of any modern nation-state are decades old, and yet receive from the country's political leadership little more than denial or—at best—void lip service. Moreover, they are so systematic that they point to a more fundamental, rather *systemic*, problem.

How sad to be at such a point, after two full centuries of attempts to right some of the numerous wrongs inflicted upon the Copts—the indigenous population of Egypt—over the prior twelve centuries since the Arab Islamic invasion and colonization.

One wonders if it is not already too late to save the founding myth of the Egyptian nation-state, the dream of a society in which Muslims and Christians live together in peace harmony[258] and equality, and jointly work to build a better future for their country.

Conclusion: Triumph of *'Islamocracy'*©

Vae victis! Woe to the conquered, the vanquished! Not only because of what they would go through after their defeat, but because history would be written by, and from the point of view of, the winners. Trying to understand the history of Egypt's Copts while keeping in mind their own viewpoint, as the defeated, summarizes the ultimate objective of this book.

This was also an attempt to examine history with an eye on the present. It could even be an attempt of writing about the present, with an eye on the past.

The reader is free to reach whatever conclusion he/she sees. But this author believes that the history of the Copts under Arab-Islamic rule is, overall, best summarized as a 'black book,' which includes a few 'gray' or 'bright' lines. Put differently, it is a history where, for every positive step taken forward, two or more were taken back.

This general conclusion may seem biased, pessimistic or even exaggerated. But those who read the excerpts that we presented from the pages of history (for which we find little reason to doubt their credibility—not least because they so mirror current realities) ought not, if they are unshackled from the excuses of 'political correctness,' reach a different conclusion.

This sad truth is hard to accept and will be rejected by many people. But, as Arthur Schopenhauer put it, "All truth passes through three stages. First, it is ridiculed. Second, it is violently opposed. Third, it is accepted as being self-evident."[259] So, hopefully this truth will be accepted one day and—better still—changed for the better.[i]

---

[i] A Latin proverb rightly says *'Errare humanum est, perseverare autem diabolicum;'* To err is human, but to persist [in error] is diabolical.

***

There are, of course, some counter arguments. There are those who like to boast about the 'good treatment of Copts under Arab-Islamic rule, which was tolerant of them' and give evidence of that by claiming that, "Copts still exist, and have not been completely annihilated by the sword or by forced conversion (as in North Africa and elsewhere)." In fact, many Islamists in Egypt claim that Copts are the 'happiest minority in the world,' meaning that, as *Dhimmis*, they must not get more than what they actually do. However, the 'survival' of the Copts as a minority is nothing but a living *evidence* of the historical crime perpetrated against them. In addition to the unusual resilience, if not stubbornness, of the Copts and their will to survive, and the existence of some residual cultural practices deeply embedded within the psyche of the Egyptians in general, perhaps one of the reasons for 'allowing' some of them (Copts) to survive would be the need to have them serve as a '*bouc émisaire*' (scapegoat, subject of common envy and hatred)[260] which is necessary to maintain the majority's own cohesion.

Some may reluctantly admit that there was injustice, but quickly add that 'the Copts and the Muslims together' suffered the injustice of the rulers. But they completely forget that the Copts were suffering long before there were 'Egyptian Muslims.' And since that time, they have always paid double the price, especially in cases of a collusion of rulers and rabble (sometimes driven by the instigation of the *Sheikhs*) competing to persecute and blackmail the Copts.

Some (as if to say, 'no one is better than the other') claim that Egyptian Christians 'persecuted the followers of the Pharaonic religions.' Their favorite evidence for this is the story of the murder of Hypatia[i] (in 415). It is enough to say that this incident, whatever its real circumstances and whoever committed it, is strongly condemned. It remains an exceptional matter, and its rarity affirms the general rule that Copts never forced anyone to convert to their religion. And, in any case, should this have exceptionally happened,

---

[i] She taught philosophy and mathematics at Alexandria and, toward the end of her life, she advised the Roman prefect. After accusations that she aroused him against Patriarch Cyril and the Copts, she is said to have been killed by a Coptic mob. There is no mention, however, that the Church knew, let alone instigated, the act.

it does not in any way negate nor justify what happened to the Copts under Arab-Islamic rule.

Some would also argue that the entire world, including the 'Christian West,' has experienced the persecution of followers of non-majority religions or sects. Let this point be granted for the sake of argument. But this, again, does not negate nor justify what happened in Egypt. What is important is that for a long time the modern world has seldom inflicted persecution and discrimination on the basis of religion—except for 'certain' (read 'Islamic') states, practicing, legitimizing and initiating discrimination and persecution with bold faces and without any sign of change.

***

The Arab-Islamic invasion in mid-seventh century, and the subsequent Islamic invasions, were waves of imperialist and dominant colonization that turned Egypt, the 'Saddle of Civilization,' into anything but that.

Genuine efforts have been made over the period starting from the chock of Napoleon to shed away the obscurantism and backwardness of the prior twelve centuries and establish a modern nation-state. Copts enthusiastically joined the march, which climaxed with the 1919 Revolution and the ensuing constitution. But the political curve started taking a downward turn as early as the late 1920s. The battle of modernity vs. 'Islam' has since been decisively won by 'Islam.'

Political scientists and media have elaborated, over the past few decades, the terminology of 'Radical Islam,' 'Political Islam,' Fundamentalist Islam,' 'Islamism,' 'Islamo-fascism,' etc. as ideologies behind a spectrum of manifestations ranging from the 'less violent' (the Brotherhood is often given in the west as an example) to the myriad of terrorist organizations such as Al-Qaida, Islamic State (I.S.I.S., I.S.I.L., Daesh), Boko-Haram, Abu-Sayyaf, etc.

But there is no clear terminology for a state that takes Islam for a reference of its political system. 'Islam' here means being adopted as a religion of state, or more generally that *Sharia*, Islam's codified legal system, being taken as a source of legislation. We propose, hence, the term '*Islamocracy*' to fill this terminology void.

Islamocracy is fundamentally a totalitarian system. Many people use the term 'totalitarianism' in the sense of dictatorship, tyranny, and oppression. It is not a matter of linguistic or intellectual sophistry, but if every totalitarian regime is authoritarian, the reverse is not true: not every authoritarian regime is totalitarian.

In *The Origins of Totalitarianism*,[261] political theorist, Hannah Arendt, examined the issue, on which she is considered to be *the* reference. The world fell prey in the 20th century to three types of totalitarianism: Communism, a totalitarian based on working-class rule and dominance; Fascism (or 'pan-movements' in general), which relished the supremacy of the nation; and Nazism, whose ideological foundation was the supremacy of race. What is more striking is that all three models were brought about, or supported, by the masses — even though these have, in each case, later paid a heavy price. Here are very brief highlights of Arendt's findings:

1. Totalitarianism is a phenomenon of masses not related to class or socially synthetic structures. It does not arise merely from manipulations. Usually, it is a result of some major social and political upheavals.
2. Masses can give up vital current interests for the sake of absolutist ideas, and can easily resort to hatred, death or suicide to achieve the ultimate victory.
3. Eventually, what attracts the masses most is the feel of power and enjoyment of violence. In the heart of the movement lies chaos and destruction.
4. Totalitarian parties use propaganda and intimidation. They proclaim the existence of laws and imperatives that no one could alter that must be implemented and spread.
5. Manipulation of the 'truth' and the 'real' spreads. Ultimately, resort to myths, tales and fantasies in a self-feeding collective mania.
6. 'Those who do not belong to us' are rejected as outsiders.
7. The common public domain becomes limited, then vanishes. Opposition suppressed. Laws modified as needed. Suspected loyalty harshly dealt with.
8. Terror spreads, fundamental freedoms eliminated. Interference in personal freedoms, even to the smallest details, and ultimately their oppression.

9. False rhetoric that no one dares to get out of. Ultimately, death unites with life.

It is not difficult to demonstrate how most if not all of these criteria of totalitarian movements fit perfectly the situation in Egypt—and beyond, across the Islamic world. In fact, Egypt is a perfect example of an *Islamocratic* system. The problem is not one of 'an extremists minority,' 'some people who do not know truly know their religion,' 'a few fanatics,' or 'impoverished groups venting their anger,' etc.

It is a matter of an entire system, including the masses.

In an Islamocracy, the strategic aim of the state and its organs (political, military, diplomatic, educational and judiciary), as well as the various 'deep state' agents, is to uphold, protect, and advance Islam's cause.

In an Islamocracy, democracy will automatically turn into a religion-based hegemonic majoritarian system. It becomes a system of 'democratization of terror and terrorization of democracy.'

In an Islamocracy, it is impossible to have equality between Muslims and non-Muslims (or even Muslims belonging to another sect other than the dominant majority).

In an Islamocratic nation-state, the 'nation' becomes merely the '*ummah*' (community of 'Believers'), and the 'state' becomes the tool to impose *Sharia*.

In an Islamocracy, the vertical dimension, which is the vertebral column of the state's authority, aims at imposing Islam on every citizen as the 'Law of the Land.'

In an Islamocracy, the horizontal dimension, which comprises the societal and communal interactions, the Islamic populace take the law in their hand to ensure the hegemony of Islam rather than social cohesion.

In an Islamocracy, Islamist movements are empowered in politics and society, leading to even more sectarian polarization in society.

In an Islamocracy, internationally accepted standards of human and minority rights, even the most basic and even if these may be beautifully enshrined in constitutional articles, remain null and void, mere ornaments; because they do not emanate from or comply with 'Islam.'

In an Islamocracy, 'Islam' represents the infrastructure that shapes the societal and legal structures and superstructures of the country.

In an Islamocracy, social Darwinism is applied, with the 'Believers' situated at the top of the 'racial' ladder, while subjugated groups are to live in submission, and face delegitimization and dehumanization.

In an Islamocracy, religion (Islam) is the basis of legislation, with a direct result that the law itself becomes an instrument of persecution rather than justice.

In an Islamocracy, religion (Islam) is 'weaponized' to justify a variety of odious and oppressive laws, policies, and acts.

There was some hope in Egypt and other Muslim-majority countries that the secularization of a country like Turkey would provide an example to follow. However, it is sadly clear that after eight decades of efforts, how easy it was to turn Turkey into an Islamocracy.

There was some who claimed that progress would come when—and only when—enlightened Muslims succeed in reforming and modernizing Islam. Even then, those engaged in that effort represent an infinitesimally small minority, and are not only (quite naturally) rejected by the religious establishment, but also by the masses. Moreover, most of their efforts seem to have focused on improving the 'image' of Islam or even the Islamization of modernity rather than modernizing Islam.

***

The story of the Copts, Egypt's indigenous population, over fourteen centuries in *Dar al-Islam* is at the same time one of tragic loss, and survival. Loss of their language, with its cultural specificities; loss of members (through relative demographic decline); loss of societal position; loss of dignity and elementary rights; loss of opportunities to develop and flourish, rather than spending their energies to merely subsist; loss of 'memory' to the point of not knowing their real history; and loss of the urge to resist and stand up for their rights. On the other hands, they—miraculously—survived, despite trials and tribulations to the point that the community came to view itself as the suffering 'church of the Martyrs.' Overall, they were supple—and stubborn—enough to withstand serious challenges and to bounce back from especially difficult times that often brought them near the brink of extinction as an independent identity.

The Copts, who submitted to Islamic domination (without resistance, since mid-ninth century), rose up with enthusiasm over one full century (from mid-19th to mid-20th centuries) to participate in building a modern nation-state. They engaged in the modernization movement of the late 19th century. They fully participated in the nationalist revival movement of the early 20th century. After some initial reluctance, they quickly joined in the 2011 uprising that ended with toppling Mubarak's regime, and also in the 2013 (army-backed) popular movement that ended with toppling the Brotherhood regime.

In all these cases, their hope was to build—or at least to set the foundation for—a more inclusive, equitable, and egalitarian system. Yet, at the end, most of the Copts have come to realize that they were chasing after the wind.

Preserving identity and survival are also matters of transmission. Transmission of culture, with its composing elements; transmission of memory; and transmission of ideals. Quoting Churchill's adage,[262] "Those who fail to learn from history are doomed to repeat it." But worse still is dropping out of history and disappearance through pure and simple assimilation and melting away.

Are they condemned to live in uncertainty? Uncertainty of whether they would, one day, become able to live in their fatherland as equal citizens, with their own specific culture and identity. Or perhaps the certainty that such a dream, however modest, is just impossible to realize in an Islamocracy?

On the other hand, there is a crucial role for the Diaspora Copts to play. For the first time in 15 centuries, since Chalcedon, when the Egyptian church chose its lonely path and when the common folks followed their leaders and withstood much oppression, the 'Copts' will need an identity that transcends Egypt. The immigrant community, now vastly larger than what it was 40 years ago, will likely play a major role in the evolution of the church, constructively or otherwise. The question will be as to what end is the value of social freedom and economic prosperity if they are not harnessed to affect a wider cultural improvement?[263] Will they be able to shape their identity and, equally important, will they positively influence the status of their kin in Egypt?

***

Copts have neither oil nor suicide bombers to attract attention, so what options do they have left for them? There is always the famous Islamic 'trilogy' of options: 'conversion; *Jizya;* or the sword,' and their 'modern' extensions: 'submission; or migration.'

Unless, of course, the long-awaited miracle happens!

The dictum that truth and justice always triumph over persecution is one of the pleasant falsehoods which men repeat after one another, but which all experience refutes.[264]

Yet, there is still hope, if people of good will stand up. For, "Silence in the face of evil is itself evil: God will not hold us guiltless.

Not to speak is to speak.

Not to act is to act."[265]

One last thought: What is perhaps most fascinating about the story of the Copts is that it has lessons for everyone. Lessons of things to do. And of things *not* to do.

Afterword

With Egypt's Copts targeted as part of a bloody and systematic campaign of genocide against the ancient churches of the Middle East, Adel Guindy has produced a timely and authoritative account of their story. It deserves to be widely read.

As the co-founder and first president of Coptic Solidarity, the leading U.S.-based advocacy group for Copts, he has given testimony before Congressional committees and is uniquely well-placed to provide this highly accessible account.

He has entitled his brief history of the Copts under Islamic Rule, *A Sword Over the Nile*.

For the Christian, it is not the *sword,* but the *cross* that provides the clue to their *faith*. In the old Latin phrase, *'Crux Potestas Dei'*— *the cross is the power of God*.

Today, in this 21st century, the great challenge for Islam and Christianity is whether the *cross* and the *sword* can live alongside one another in peace and mutual respect.

The harrowing story of the Copts illustrates what happens when religious and political leaders fail to embrace the fundamental importance of freedom of religion and belief. The West needs to be aware of the implications of ignoring this central challenge.

My interest in the Copts began while I was a member of the British House of Commons.

In the 1990s, during my work with the human rights organization, Jubilee Campaign, I was asked to write a report on the discrimination and persecution faced by the Coptic Church of Egypt.

I saw plenty of examples of discrimination and persecution — and warned that left unaddressed this would morph into something far worse.

But I also discovered the hidden treasures of the Coptic tradition and came away inspired by its extraordinary and remarkable history, its beautiful liturgies, and by its contemporary work—not least by women like Maggie Gobran—Mama Maggie—the Mother of Cairo—working indefatigably in the squalid shanty towns of Cairo.

Coptic, of course, simply means Egyptian in the pre-Arabic language of the country.

This ancient church was founded two millennia ago by St. Mark, one of the four Gospel writers—although, Egypt had been home to Jesus Himself, after his refugee family fled the slaughter of the Holy Innocents and had found a safe and secure home in Egypt: surely a story with significance for every family and every refugee fleeing persecution in these troubled times.

In 1996, at St. Mark's Cathedral in Cairo, I met His Holiness, Pope Shenouda III. Shenouda had suffered grievously at the hands of politicians, having been banished to an ancient desert monastery.

I recall remarking to him that we, in the West, had done too little to speak up for the ancient churches.

He could not understand the indifference of Christians living in the affluent West.

We recalled that this indifference had its origins in the failure to respond to the genocide of the Armenians and other Christians. Between 1915 and 1917, 1.5 million Armenians and hundreds of thousands of Assyrians and Greeks had died.

Following recent events in Northern Iraq and Syria (and across Northern Africa from Sudan to Nigeria), we need an appropriate sense of humility at our failure to act.

We should listen far more carefully to communities like the Copts, the Chaldeans, the Armenians, and the Assyrians—who have so much wisdom, have so much to teach us, and who have suffered so much.

We must listen, but we must also speak and act in solidarity.

Perhaps Adel Guindy's timely and excellent book will act as a wakeup call.

It is a moral outrage that vast swathes of humanity have been subjected to genocide and crimes against humanity, while we wring our hands.

Whole families have been murdered, terrorized, victimized, intimidated, deprived of their homes or belongings—and in places like Mosul and Nineveh —where Christians had lived in diversity and common respect for 2000 years —their homes were confiscated, marked for appropriation with the letter 'N' for Nazarene—simply because of their faith; the way in which they worship God.

After the horrific slaughter by Islamic State of 21 Coptic Christians, on February 12th, 2015, who died on a beach in Libya, professing their faith, a service of remembrance was held in the Palace of Westminster, which I attended.

The Coptic Archbishop of London, Angaelos, reminded us that *"These men paid the ultimate price, but gave us a cause to advocate for all those who are persecuted. They also showed us that there was a level of evil that we must all stand in solidarity against—and a level of courage, faithfulness, and defiance that we must all aspire to."*

Eighteen months later, at the annual Nayrouz Service held in St. Margaret's church, in Westminster, we learnt how a Coptic priest had been murdered in Cairo, *"drenched in his own blood and a cross marked onto his forehead."*

At that Service, I said that civilized countries must uphold freedom of religion and belief, and insist that those responsible for *"pestilential crimes against the region's ancient churches must be held to account and face justice."*

The Coptic New Year begins on the first day of the Month of Thoout, and is marked by the celebration of *The Feast of El-Nayrouz.*

This is the day on which Coptic Orthodox Christians honor those who have bravely stood and confessed their faith in God and whose lives have been taken.

Copts celebrate the New Year by eating red dates. The red symbolizes the martyrs' blood and the white heart of the date heart symbolizes the martyrs' purity.

Nayrouz is a word of Coptic origin and means '*the rivers.*'

Its symbolism is connected to the way the waters of the River Nile usually rise in mid-September and the faithful pray that the river's water will irrigate the land and enable abundant new crops to grow.

The title of Adel Guindy's book reminds us that there is also a sword hanging over Egypt's famous river—and that too much blood has already been allowed to flow. This offers no prospect of new life; only death and suffering.

As religious and civil authorities consider the kind of country they want Egypt to be, they should reflect that countries that crush diversity, that refuse to uphold *difference*, and that turn a blind eye to persecution and intolerance are always the most backward countries, always the poorest economically, and always the worst places to live.

Adel Guindy reminds us that historically, the Copts have been Egypt's beating heart and that Egypt's future, without them, would be bleak indeed.

David Alton
Professor Lord Alton is a Member of the British House of Lords

Appendices

1. The Impact of the 'Forgotten of History' on Civilization[i]

Péroncel Hugoz[ii] once called the Copts, 'the forgotten of history.' One of the reasons for that unfortunate fact is the conscious neglect of that history by the educational system of Egypt where history seems to jump from the Pharaonic phase all the way to the Islamic age, with hardly any mention of a thousand years deemed insignificant.

But in fact, were it not for the Copts and Alexandria, the history of Western civilization would have been totally different. The Copts' influence, though pervasive, is sometimes difficult to discern because during the better part of two millennia, they were either a subject people or a *Dhimmi* minority. Examples of the Copts' impact are:

1. Doctrinal Differentiation of Christianity

Following the war between Mithridates of Pontus and Rome (89 B.C.), Athens 'witnessed an exodus of philosophers' to Alexandria which continued to be the undisputed cultural queen of late antiquity, where the *'Greek genius was deflected'* from Athens. Alexandria was also the first and most important city of Jewish biblical scholarship of late antiquity. It utilized Greek and produced the first translation of the Hebrew Bible that became known as the Septuagint (because of the 70 Jewish scholars who worked on it).

---

[i] This Appendix is based on: *The Impact of the Copts on Civilization,* by Amin Makram-Ebeid, M.D. The reader is invited to consult this rich and well-researched article:

http://www.copticchurchreview.com/Coptic/Home_files/1999%20Winter.Vol20.%234.pdf

[ii] A prominent French writer and journalist who was the correspondent of *Le Monde* in Egypt for years, until he was expelled in October, 1981.

The stage was thus set for Alexandria to become the leading Mediterranean center of Christian theology and philosophy. For it is out of this milieu that the first major Coptic achievement occurred, namely the growth of the first theological university in antiquity (c. 180), which became known as the catechetical school of Alexandria. It is also important to remember that it is that school that was responsible for the indubitable ascendance of the Coptic Church during the first major ecumenical councils.

It was that school where the Christian beliefs, that were eventually adopted by the Universal Church throughout the globe, were explained, codified, and crystallized. It was the young Athanasius who was influential in producing the most basic document in church history, namely, the Nicene Creed.

The Chalcedon schism (451) deprived the Coptic Church of its universal leadership and restricted it to a national institution increasingly persecuted and marginalized.

2. Monasticism and the Western Civilization

When Rome succumbed first to the assault of the Barbarians and then to chaos and de-urbanization by the end of the sixth century, Western civilization seemed about to expire. Civilization was saved, by reiterating the universally accepted answer that gives most of the credit to Europe's monasteries. Yet, that institution may never have appeared in the west, were it not for St. Athanasius' biography of St. Antony, the founder of monasticism in Egypt, as well as his visit to Rome (in the fourth century). Up to the eighth century, Athanasius' *Life of St. Antony* was not only the most read, but also the most imitated book in the west after the Bible. A great part of the Hellenic heritage was thus, jealously preserved for future generations to utilize, and create the radiance of the Middle Ages that was to flower in the glorious renaissance which eventually evolved into the most advanced civilization the world has ever known.

The Egyptian origin of European and Irish monasticism is well-documented. Moreover, the books that kept civilization alive traveled from the workshops of Egypt and Syria by way of Ireland and Britain and, finally to the continent of Europe.

Coptic influence on Celtic Christianity in both Ireland and Scotland is illustrated through the Celtic wheel cross which is a Coptic invention. The

Irish litany of Saints remembers the seven Coptic monks of Desert Uilaig and the life of (the Coptic) St. Paul the Hermit is still depicted on a Pictish stone at St. Vigeans near Dundee (in Scotland). The role of the Copts was also acknowledged by the famous monk Alcuin (c. 735–804), advisor of Charlemagne, who described the Celtic Culdee (servants of God, or monks of Ireland and Scotland) as '*pueri Egyptiaci*,' the children of Egypt.

The fact that Christian civilization was saved for Europe by the Irish and the European monastic institutions, (and hence, by the Copts!) was to assume momentous importance in the eighth century at Poitier, when Islam's advance was checked by Charles Martel (732). The Saracen forces would have encountered little resistance if Europe did not benefit from the cohesiveness of its Christian heritage and its resurrected Greco-Roman culture; both kept alive by unnamed monks copying manuscripts, and preserving all the treasures of civilization they could salvage from the ruins and devastation left by the barbarians. It is thus, possible to assert that even though the Copts were defeated by the Arabs in Egypt in 642, they were present in force at Poitier, armed only with books!

3. Philosophy

In that all-embracing discipline, the uniqueness of Origen has been an intellectual light not only for the church, but also for the way the Mediterranean mind evolved. In *Science and Creation*, Stanley Jaki, a Jesuit priest and physicist, advanced the very convincing thesis that the cyclic cosmogonies of the Far East, Pharaonic Egypt and even Greece were the major reasons for stifling the intellectual development of antiquity. But in Coptic Egypt, Origen, following in the footsteps of Clement of Alexandria and preceding Augustine of Hippo, insisted that reality is the intellectual highway to knowledge, and that can only be reached by breaking through the cycle of eternal recurrences and pantheism, and transforming history into an evolving linear progression that demands a*meliorative* culture.

Most authorities agree that no one did more to ensure the spiritual and intellectual victory of Mediterranean Christianity and culture than did Origen. It could also be argued that the intellectual maturity of Christianity thus achieved elevated the followers of Jesus from a mere sect into a cohesive social religious force that was soon felt to be a threat to the Roman Empire. In other words, the Church became 'a universalistic alternative' to the empire itself and actually 'a far more dynamic and better organized alternative,' and thus, it 'had to be exterminated or accepted.' That climate was to usher the age of martyrs.

To better understand the Coptic philosophic contribution to the Mediterranean culture, it is important to realize that Egyptian Christianity managed to preserve what was best in its Pharaonic inheritance, and at the same time, shed its archaic superstition and its sterile concepts.

Christianity did not bring material prosperity or national pride to the people of Egypt, nor was Christianized Egypt ever to shine again as an independent power. Yet, the Copts were about to offer the world spiritual and cultural treasures that carry more glory than many world empires. The Copts, as represented by the towering figure of Origen, prefiguring many philosophers-theologians, were responsible in shaping the mind of future civilizations by marrying spiritual concepts to the rational mind to which all possible questions demand an answer.

That inquisitiveness was made possible by the unique intellectual climate of Alexandria that made it the undisputed cultural capital of late antiquity, because it succeeded in synthesizing into a harmonious whole the three cultures it inherited. Like the Jewish philosopher, Philo, the early Copts were able to draw on the Hellenic philosophic heritage in order to insist on the necessity of the rational mind that can be transcended but never abolished. It is that curiosity of the uninhibited mind that the west eventually inherited, (and which the east seems to have left dormant).

4. Science

Alexandria was the center for an intellectual framework that permitted the development in various scientific fields. Alexandrian mathematics reached its peak with the work of Euclid, but it also included the first work on Algebra. The astronomic Ptolemy (c. 120–180) could not have formalized the mathematics and techniques of astronomy such as astronomic trigonometry in an intellectual vacuum. Again, it must have been the Copts who transmitted their ancestors' astronomic observation and empiric mathematical knowledge that helped flower the Alexandrian Hellenic genius. The medical school also developed because the Copts kept their medical genius alive and offered the right milieu that witnessed the growth of Herophilus and Erasistratus.

The influence of the Copts on Islamic medicine was also significant. The very first scientific work written in Arabic was a medical treatise initially written in Greek by an Alexandrian Christian priest named Ahrun, which was then translated to Syriac and then to Arabic in 683.

5. Music, Art, and Architecture

Coptic music has been considered by some musicologists to be the foundation of Gregorian chants and hence, of Western music. The Coptic Church has preserved the most ancient-surviving ecclesiastic music in existence, a fete attributed to the very conservative nature of the Egyptian Church. Moreover, it seems to be the prolongation of Pharaonic music, which was transmitted orally and thus, salvaged exclusively in the Coptic liturgy, and remained purely Egyptian and thus, minimally influenced by Arabic tunes.

The Copts (along with Sassanid Persians) helped shape Byzantine art and architecture and introduced arched domes and vaults, which will be adopted with glorious effect in both the Islamic East and the Christian West. Coptic architecture has influenced both the construction and decoration of the earliest mosques both of which relied on Coptic know-how.

6. Textiles and Crafts

Another fascinating Coptic contribution resided in the perfection of textiles, which was universally considered to be superb. In fact, Durant favorably compared its earliest productions at the dawn of the Christian era to that of the Goblin factories more than a millennium-and-a-half later. Laurence Albert also affirmed that weaving was a 'Coptic invention' since the ancient Egyptians were ignorant of the technique of weaving patterns or designs and used to either paint or embroider their fabrics. The Christians of Egypt continued to innovate and developed the technique of stamping print patterns on textile with wooden blocks during the reign of the Fatimids. That concept is believed by Durant to have been carried from Egypt to Europe by the Crusaders and may have shared in the development of printing.

Coptic impact is still visible today in the so-called 'lesser arts.' For instance, Egyptian Christians were the first to have perfected manuscript illumination, which they inherited from Pharaonic Egypt, and which no doubt influenced that art in the Islamic East, as well as in the Christian West. Also, the Muslims of Egypt learned from the Copts the technique of wood Marquette and the art of decorating boxes with ivory and bone inlay. Indeed, Laurence Albert asserted that 'woodwork and sculpture remained a Coptic specialty even under the Arabs.'

7. A Fourth Century 'Red Cross'

St. Verena, a native of Garagoss (near Thebes in Upper Egypt), seems to have accompanied the Theban Legion[i] (c. 286) as a nurse. She lived the rest of her life in Zurzach (in present day Switzerland) and was a kind of fourth-century Florence Nightingale[ii]. She taught the Alemanni, the principle of hygiene, and spent the rest of her long life educating the people of what is now the Canton of Aargau, ministering to the poor and caring for the lepers. She is represented today on the coat of arms of the city of Stäfa (in the Canton of Zurich), where she is depicted holding a water jug in one hand and a comb in the other. Zurzach is a famous Swiss spa saturated with St. Verena, and one could witness the emblems of sanitation (the comb and the water jug) that she brought to the primitive Germans, proudly carved on stone or on wood above shops, in the streets, and in the Verena-Munster where her crypt is situated.

St. Verena (probably Coptic for Berenice) is credited with many miracles of healing, including that of the Roman Governor who spared her life. Died in 320, she is venerated as a saint by the Roman Catholic, Eastern Orthodox, and Coptic Orthodox Churches. She is also venerated in many European

---

[i] The Legion was the garrison of Thebes (current day Luxor) in Upper Egypt, who were ordered by Emperor Maximian to assist him against the rebels in Gaul. Refusing to offer sacrifice to the emperor's gods nor to kill innocent people, they were 'decimated' (each tenth of its men was put to death). The legion's commander has his name given to cities to cities such as St. Maurice-en-Valais and St. Moritz in the Engondine, in Switzerland, as well as some 650 places in France and Switzerland.

[ii] Nightingale (1820–1910), was an English social reformer and the founder of modern nursing. Her experience during the Crimean War (1854–1856) inspired not only her work to transform health care, but also laid the groundwork for the creation of National Red Cross Societies, and the founding of the I.C.R.C. in 1863 to ensure protection and assistance for victims of armed conflict and strife.

cities, and was one of the main patron Saints of the Hapsburg dynasty. Verena represents what is best in Christianity: a virgin Saint, living among barbarians and soldiers. She exemplified feminism at its most sublime level. By teaching hygiene and caring for the sick, and as a result of her educational zeal, she introduced the Alemannic barbarians to the elements of Mediterranean civilization. But her crowning achievement was that she contributed greatly to the spread of Christianity among the Alemannic.

2. Who Was 'Al-Muqawqis'?

The Arab sources talk about a dignitary personality, referred to as 'Al-Muqawqis,' or the 'The Great One (Chief) of the Copts,' who would have ruled Egypt at that time of the conquest, and even as early as 628.

It is claimed that this 'Al-Muqawqis' received an epistle from Mohammed (possibly apocryphal, reported by one Islamic source; Ibn Abdel-Hakam[i]) in 628, informing him of his prophethood and inviting him to espouse his new religion. It is also claimed that Al-Muqawqis responded by mid-628, to say, "I read your letter and understood what you have written. I know that the coming of a prophet is still due. But I thought he would be born in Syria. I have treated your messenger with respect and honor. I am sending two (slave) maidservants for you as presents. These maids belong to a very respectable family amongst us. In addition, I send for you clothes and a mule for riding…"

It is often claimed that 'Cyrus,' the Patriarch sent by Heraclius, is this Muqawqis. Cyrus was a bishop of Phasis, a city in the eastern side of the Black Sea, Caucasia, in current-day Georgia. In 631, he was sent to Alexandria by the Emperor as a Melkite Patriarch and possibly also as the prefect of the province around it. So, the assumption goes, the term Muqawqis would be an Arabization of 'Caucasian.'

If the person in question here is Cyrus, and apart from the fact that he was installed in 631 (after the Persians were chased out of Egypt by Heraclius in 629), which is *subsequent* to the presumed date of the message in 628, it appears highly unconceivable for a Christian bishop to voluntarily accept the claims of a prophet from the desert, and—contrary to Christian beliefs—talk about a 'still-due' prophet. Worse still, he would send to Mohammed two girls (Maria and Sirin), from a 'respectable family' as slaves. One of these two girls, Maria, is the one said to have given the prophet a son (Ibrahim)

---

[i] 800–871.

who was supposedly born in June, 630, and died eighteen months later, in January, 632 (five months before the death of the prophet, in early June).

On the other hand, it is known that at the top of the five administrative provinces of Egypt, the ruler was often referred to as *Pagarch* (prefect), who was the civil governor, to whom the local administration was confided, but not the army and the clergy who were outside his control. The complimentary title given to these *pagarchs* was *mega ukés,* [i] which signifies 'his excellency.' The Arabs at the time of the invasion took this title for part of the actual name of the *pagarch* who treated with Amr for the surrender of Babylon; and thus, might have referred to him as Muqawqis.

It is possible that this 'Muqawqis' be the one to correspond with Islam's prophet some ten years before the conquest, and not Cyrus. But then, why would a mere 'prefect' of one of five provinces, exchange such messages with a leader of a tribe living in a desert place over two-thousand kilometers away?

The whole story looks mysterious—or even invented at a later date…

---

[i] μξγαυχησ

3. The Historical Responsibility of the Copts

It would be dishonest to deny or brush over the historical responsibility of the Copts and the Coptic Church in what befell the Copts. But if it may be too easy in hindsight to give lessons about the past, there seem to be a number of situations where actions, probably justifiable at the time, led to unforeseen, and even disastrous, consequences.

We can identify four key signposts where certain popes inadvertently played a particularly detrimental role in this national saga. Luckily, the Coptic Church does not believe in the infallibility of her popes.

Pope Dioscorus (444–454)

Most disastrous events in history have simple beginnings. The 'Original Sin' of what happened to the Copts dates back to the theological debate that led to the Chalcedon Council and the schism that followed. Without going into details, the fact that fifteen centuries later, the two main sides of the schism agreed that they were initially using different formulations to express the same concept,[i] shows that conflict of personalities, as well as some circumstantial issues, might have been at the roots of the rift.

---

[i] Refer to chapter above on *Who Are the Copts*. Pope Shenouda III met with the Roman Catholic Pope (Paul VI) and, on May 10th, 1973, and they signed a common declaration that states their common confession. Background of that event: Franz König, the Cardinal of Vienna and president of Pro Oriente foundation, visited Pope Shenouda in Cairo with the aim of initiating dialog on the Christology of the Council of Chalcedon. At their meeting (according to one member of the Roman delegation, who recounted the story to this Author in June 2007), König asked Shenouda to write down, in English, the confession of the Coptic Church. The next day the document, prepared with bishop Gregorios, the Coptic top theologist, was handed to König by Shenouda. Upon reading it he murmured (in German), "but this is exactly our belief!" He cut his visit short and returned to Vienna. A few days later he was with Pope Paul VI, in the Vatican, whose reaction to the document was identical. He then invited the Coptic Pope to co-sign the document as is.

The matter started at the Second Council of Ephesus (August, 449, attended by 198 bishops), convened to discuss the argument between Flavian, the Patriarch of Constantinople, and Eutyches, a monk and the archimandrite of a monastery in the same city, over a heresy by the latter. Dioscorus, who presided the session, rushed the procedures before the arrival of other main delegates, and is said (by most historians) to have humiliated his fellow archbishops. After presenting his case, Eutyches was declared guiltless and restored to office. Disgraceful scenes ensued, and Flavian was declared deposed, as well as archbishops of Antioch and four other cities. Flavian himself was so brutally manhandled that he died soon afterward, and papal legates (representing Pope Leo) were insulted and fled the assembly.[266] Afterward, Dioscorus even excommunicated the Roman Pope, Leo.

A council was convened in 451 and held at Chalcedon to review the matter. Eutyches' teachings were declared a heresy (something that the Coptic Church has adhered to since a long time) and Dioscorus was deposed[i], mostly on canonical grounds related to his behavior and irregularities at the Ephesus II Council, rather than on theological formulations. The issue turned afterward into one of 'national pride' with the native Copts supporting their Patriarch irrespective of anything. Multiple attempts to close the gap were not successful, more due to personal factors rather than doctrinal rectitude. As put by a contemporary theologian, the non-Chalcedonian and Chalcedonian differences were not a matter of 'two dogmas,' but of 'two nuanced interpretations of the same dogma.'

It is rather telling that the *History of the Patriarchs* does not give such crucial issues as the biography of Pope Dioscorus, the tumultuous events of the Ephesus II Council and the Chalcedon Council more than few lines, simply saying that his biography was not recorded after being deposed and banished, and that the Chalcedon Council's theology was heretical

---

[i] All bishops present (whose number was 500 according to most sources) voted in favor, except for the 13 Alexandrians, who (being in a 'delicate situation') petitioned to 'excuse themselves from endorsing or rejecting the decisions of the council,' presenting a 'statement of profession of faith' During the session, they asked to postpone the signing until an archbishop was appointed for Egypt. Later on, some of them accepted the council's resolutions, but decided to stay in Constantinople, while some others (four?) accepted the resolutions and returned to Alexandria to consecrate a replacement in place of Dioscourus. Refer to *The Council of Chalcedon Re-Examined*, by Fr. V.C. Samuel, P-103, P-120.

('corrupted'). This, we believe, might indicate a degree of discomfort or even division within the Coptic Church about the whole issue.[i]

Pope Benyamin (623–662)[267]

In 629, Heraclius turned his attention to the recovery of Egypt, having chased away the Persians from Egypt and other parts of the Levant. Experience, however, had taught him that he could not retain his hold in that country without conciliating the National Church, and in so doing, the bulk of the population. Therefore, on his way back from a victorious campaign, he consulted Patriarchs Athanasius of Antioch, Sergius of Constantinople, and Cyrus, Bishop of Phasis[ii], who represented three different shades of religious opinion, as to the best means of doing so.

After much discussions and subsequent exchanges of letters, it was decided not to mention the Council of Chalcedon, since openly to accept or reject that council would inevitably offend one of two parties beyond retrieval; but it was determined to draw up an Act of Union, which should affirm 'One Will' in Christ instead of 'One Nature.' This compromise was accepted by the three bishops, of whom one was a 'Monophysite' (rather a 'Miaphysite') and the other a 'Chalcedonian' and the emperor promptly appointed the third of them (Cyrus) as Patriarch of the (Byzantine, Melkite) Church of Alexandria, and sent him off to that city with full powers to effect the hoped-for reconciliation.

Cyrus met upon arrival with several representatives of the Egyptian (Coptic) laity and many of the clergy, who found no difficulty in his task as far as they were concerned. They readily agreed to accept the Act of Union, and to communicate with the state (Melkite) church. However, Cyrus was dismayed to find that the Coptic Patriarch coldly refused to discuss the

---

[i] There exists *The Life of Patriarch Dioscorus*, in Syriac, but the Arabic version remains unpublished. In it, one can find a report on the Council of Chalcedon from a Coptic point of view, with an aim to prove the correctness of Coptic belief by demonstrating the holiness of Dioscorus. Theological discussion does not play the deciding role; the theory promoted is that a 'holy man who performs miracles and sees visions must be correct in his belief' and that such 'supernatural' evidence is considered more sufficient than any dogmatic or historical argument. See Gabra, P. 17, entry by Samul Moawad.

[ii] A Caucasian city in the eastern side of the Black Sea, in current-day Georgia.

matter, or to accept any theological compromise coming from the emperor. When the bulk of the Egyptians, as it seemed to Cyrus, gladly accepted his terms, he did not hesitate to banish the Coptic Patriarch, Benyamin, for refusing. But this only made the refusal and disapproval of Benyamin patent to all Egypt, and from that day, the Act of Union was doomed. Slowly, the inert mass of public opinion (without really grasping the intricacies of the debate) swung back from the emperor, and Cyrus began to perceive that he had failed.

History would probably have changed course if the Act of Union was accepted, and the Copts were engaged more forcefully in fighting the Arabs who came invading less than a decade later.

After the surrender of Alexandria, Benyamin is reported[i] to have returned from the monastery in Upper Egypt, where he had been, and to have held a cordial meeting with Amr (in about 644). He would have prayed for Amr, who was 'about to go to the west and to Pentapolis[ii] and take possession of them.' He is also reported to have offered thanks to the Lord for defeating the 'Godless heretics' (Byzantines). Barely a few decades later, the Copts saw that what happened to them at the hands of the invading Arabs was a sign of the End of Time.[iii]

Pope Yousab I (830–849)

This was the time of the Abbasid Caliph, Abdullah Al-Mamoun, the son of Haroun Al-Rashîd. The Peshmurians, in northern Egypt, successfully fought the *Wali* who had forced them to pay *Jizya* that they could not afford[iv]. The Patriarch wrote, warning them, so they would 'repent and stop resisting the Sultan.' He did not cease writing to them day after day, quoting to them chapters from the Books (from the Epistle of Saint Paul). These letters had been sent to the leaders of the insurgents by bishops, who added their exhortations to submission. But, for once, the authority of the Patriarch had been defied. The insurgents taunted him and his bishops with cowardice, and announced their intention to die fighting, rather than live as slaves.

---

[i] In the *History of the Patriarchs*.

[ii] The 'Five Cities' in North Africa (Libya and Tunisia), under the Church of Alexandria.

[iii] Refer to Appendix five.

[iv] See more details in the chapter on the *Abbasids*.

Al-Mamoun, fearing the total loss of one of the richest provinces of his empire, then concentrated all his resources of men and treasure on the subjugation of the insurgents. So, he came to Egypt, accompanied by the Patriarch of Antioch. Abba Yousab, along with all the bishops, went to greet him at Al-Fustat. Al-Mamoun was satisfied when he found out about the Patriarch's writings to the Peshmurians, deterring them from defying the Caliph's orders.[i]

Al-Mamoun then marched with his army (accompanied by the two Patriarchs) and ordered the gathering of everyone who knew the ways of the Peshmurians from the surrounding cities and villages. When his army succeeded to reach the Peshmurians, they annihilated them, killing them with the edge of the sword, pillaging, destroying, and burning their homes with fire, and destroying their churches. Furthermore, the conquerors revenged themselves with pitiless ferocity throughout the length and breadth of Egypt.

In accompanying Al-Mamoun during his campaign, Abba Yousab sent a direct message to the Copts in the area to help the army against the rebelling Peshmurians, and leading to the perfectly predictable massacre and what followed. The question that remains is why did Abba Yousab betray his beleaguered people, rather than stand up against their brutal oppressor?

Pope Ghobrial II (1131–1145)[ii]

He prioritized the use of Arabic translation[iii] of the Gospel and the rest of the liturgical books. He also allowed the use of Arabic during the public reading of the Gospels and preaching in all churches, after they had first been read in Coptic. Thus, the clergy began to use Arabic to teach the parishioners, and they gradually stopped studying the Coptic language. Pope Ghobrial may have had the good intention of wanting to have liturgical and catechetic books accessible to those who spoke Arabic better than Coptic. But his efforts simply helped weaken the Coptic Language. That was how, by the end of the Fatimid State, the Coptic language began its path of decay. In addition, given the scarcity of theological and spiritual books in Arabic, clergy became less and less knowledgeable in their own doctrines. This

---

[i] For more details, refer to the chapter above on the Abbasids, starting p. 73.

[ii] Before becoming Patriarch, he had been a layman, named Abul-Alaa Said Ibn Tureyk, a senior scribe in the Fatimid state.

[iii] Partial use of Arabic had started under Pope Zakharias (979–1003).

resulted in a general decline in people's understanding of their faith, thus facilitating the process of conversion to Islam.

Furthermore, in adopting Arabic, certain theological terms became confused, like translating 'God' (*Theos*) into '*Allah*' (rather than *Al-Ilah*[i]), making it sound—at least for uneducated people—that the Christian and Islamic concepts of deity were equivalent[ii]. It is certainly not a coincidence that conversion accelerated during subsequent two centuries.

The strongest pillar of Coptic identity, their very ethos, received a serious blow when Copts abandoned their national language. In fact, the pillars of all Egyptians' identity collapsed, especially that adopting Arabic as one's language is not a condition for converting to Islam (for the Persians, Turks, and others maintained their languages after Islam).

---

[i] There is no system of capital vs. small letters in Arabic. Whereas '*ilah*' means simply (a) 'god,' one needs to use a definite article 'the' to denote God, 'the (only) god.'

[ii] The term *Allah* may have been used by Christian Arabs (in the Palestine-Jordan-Levant region) to denote Godhead, but as they had conceptually associated the term with their Christian theological background, they were still capable of making a distinction with Islam's deity. In the case of Copts, such linguistic transition did not exist and Allah was introduced to them as the direct and equivalent translation of Theos.

4. Distinctive Identity and Provinciality

The renowned authors of the phenomenal book HAGARISM[i] devote some pages to the Copts. Their analysis, summarized here, is worthy of exploring and should incite more retrospection within the community.

The Egyptian identity was an extremely neat product of geography, ethnicity, language, religion and polity; all the various components defining precisely the same entity. Geography (or the Nile) was god-given and carried Egypt undivided right through the millennium.

Christianity tightened the loose relationship between Egypt, 'Alexandria at Egypt,' and the Roman Empire of which both were part. Egypt found itself caught by the rigid doctrinal and organizational structures of the Hellenized church, and whereas Greek Alexandria could retain both its identity and its intellectual supremacy within these structures, the Egyptian countryside was faced with mere absorption. The same doctrinal and organizational structures with which Egypt was caught for the Graeco-Roman world could also be used to articulate an Egyptian identity within it.

The first effect of Christianity was to defuse the political tension between Alexandria and the Roman Empire while at the same time exacerbating the cultural tension between Egypt and the Graeco-Roman world at large. On the one hand the Egyptian passion for flaunting their native martyrs in the face of the persecution (303–312) led to the formation of the Church of the Martyrs, predominantly Upper Egyptian in support. On the other hand, the native search for loopholes in the Graeco-Roman net led the Egyptians to drop out of civilization altogether, rejecting its spiritual and material culture alike: in Alexandria Ammonius might fight for his Greek wisdom and Origen

---

[i] *HAGARISM: The Making of the Islamic World,* by Patricia Crone & Michael Cook, Cambridge University Press, 1977, Pp. 50–55, 113–115

read it into his scriptures, but St Anthony refused to acquire it. Likewise, Alexandrians might enjoy the comforts of civilization, but the ascetics rejected both man-made shelters and man-made food as part of the same contaminated world they were trying to forget.

The crucial change was the development of cenobitic monasticism. We find St Anthony gathering his followers into semi-cenobitic communities; with Pachomius the caves gave way to large monastic settlements, the lonely hermits to thousands of inmates, solitary autonomy to the rules and regulations of increasingly powerful abbots. By the fifth century Egypt all but unanimously subscribed to the cenobitic ideal. Solitude, excess of zeal in prayer and in mortification of the flesh, and the quest for martyrdom were all discouraged in favor of communal life, obedience and, above all, work. Henceforth all monks worked so as to provide for themselves and the poor.

As a result Christian Egypt came to have two distinct and potentially rival components: on the one hand Alexandria, the seat of the patriarch who ruled his compact diocese with all the organizational and intellectual resources of the Hellenized church; and on the other the desert, the seat of the monks who ruled the same diocese with all the emotional resources of the Egyptian peasantry. However, this rivalry was suppressed by mutual interests. Without the support of Alexandria, the monks could not be able to articulate their own provincial identity. But equally, without the support of the monks, Alexandria could not control the diocese, let alone impose its own concepts on the Graeco-Roman world. Consequently there was an alliance: the patriarchs received monastic support in their efforts to maintain Alexandrian intellectual preeminence, the monks received patriarchal support in their efforts to find an Egyptian faith: Dioscorus defended the Monophysite creed with a small army of monks at the Council of Ephesus in 449, and the patriarch in return became the Pharaonic leader of the Copts.[i]

It was this alliance between a Greek patriarchate and an Egyptian peasantry which made the Coptic church (after the Chalcedonian schism), and from it follow its three main characteristics.

In the first place the social keynote of the Coptic church is village rusticity rather than urban elitism. The ethnically mixed and culturally Greek

---

[i] After the Chalcedonian crisis, patriarchs gradually started to be almost exclusively chosen among monks. In modern times, seated bishops cannot be candidates for the patriarchal office.

aristocracy could hardly claim to represent Holy Egypt; so it was not they but the peasants who shaped the local church.

In the second place, the emotional keynote of the Coptic church is ethnic and linguistic chauvinism: the honor of Egypt invoked in the Coptic account of Cambyses' invasion reappears as the ethnic solidarity of 'Monophysite' monks against Heraclius' persecution of the Copts, the linguistic pride of Coptic Christians in resistance to the inroads of Arabic, and the glory of Egypt in the eulogies of Egyptian saints.

In the third place, the intellectual keynote of the Coptic church was no more Alexandrian philosophy but rather peasant 'unsophistication': Cyril was the last Alexandrian theologian of note, John Philoponus the last philosopher, and the surviving Coptic literature is emotionally vibrant but also intellectually not so bright. The insulation of Egypt from Alexandria which had ensured an impressive survival of the Egyptian identity was at the same time an isolation of the Egyptian heritage from Greek thought which secured only a scant survival of Egyptian truth. Coptic Egypt (after the schism) produced practical men in the style of Pachomius or Shenute, but no thinkers.

This is not to say that without the Arab conquests Egypt would have seceded from the Byzantine Empire either politically or culturally. It is true of course that the emperor was a figure extrinsic to Holy Egypt, and that the Egyptians insisted on dating from Diocletian's persecution, not Constantine's conversion, but the 'kibbutzniks' in the desert needed an emperor in Constantinople to keep the barbarians off.

The characteristics of the Coptic church provided the components of a highly distinctive provinciality: an Egypt distinguished from the rest of the world by its peculiar sanctity yet linked to it as an example for mankind – in other words, an Egypt distinguished from the rest of the world by its peculiar ethnicity and semi-native aristocracy yet linked to it as a member of a Graeco-Roman empire.

In Muslim Egypt, the Coptic identity was intact; its initial resilience is striking. The rusticity of the Coptic church meant that the province converted slowly. The Copts being accustomed to looking to peasant leaders, whether in the village or the monastery, the departure or decline of the aristocracy did not affect them; and when exposed to the pressure of Arab taxation, they fled from their villages to other districts or to monasteries, but not to Arab cities. The result was an impressive Coptic resistance to conversion; and despite occasional waves of apostasy, it was only after fiscal pressure that the destruction of village organization and the ensuing repression finally cleared the way for the slow but inexorable conversion of Egypt to Islam.

The Copts did of course survive as Copts despite their adoption of Arabic, and they retained the title deeds to their Pharaonic past. But they eventually became in effect exiles in their own country: the willingness of the Copts to ingather their Muslim neighbors in the name of Egypt was often met with [alienation] by the Muslims.

5. Pseudo-Apocalyptic Writings as 'Political Resistance'

As the viciousness of the Arab-Islamic rule increased, and in addition to the revolts mentioned previously, Copts were intent on protesting, and finding explanations, as to what befell them. Fearing retaliation, they devised a tactic of 'political projection,' whereby some would describe their current situation in the form of prophecies attributed to famous church fathers. Apocalyptic writings that became popular attributed the events to God's wrath because of excessive sins by the people and—especially— their clergy, and linked the lot to the imminent return of the Messiah.

A particularly important text was the *Prophesy attributed to St Athanasius (d. 373) about the Arab Conquest* (or the 'Pseudo-Athanasius'). It is thought to be written by an anonymous monk in early-to-mid eighth century.[268]

It takes form within a homily, allegedly given by Patriarch Athanasius of Alexandria, on the occasion of the feast of the archangel, Michael. The chief concern of the work is to emphasize to church officials the need to fulfill their duties and heed their responsibilities with regard to both God and their flock. This message occupies the first six sections of the homily, and it is driven home forcefully in the next five sections where the speaker relates the trials of the End of Time, which happen, he insists, "On account of the sins of the priests and monks who will corrupt their way before God." In the 12th and concluding part, there is a final plea to eschew evil, "So that we shall inherit the kingdom of heaven forever by the prayers and advocacy of the great archangel whose feast we celebrate today."

The signs of the end do have a recognizably historical basis to them and begin with the Persian assault:

After these things, the good God will become angry, because they had altered His true faith. He will divide the unity of the kingdom of the Romans and of their empire in return for their having divided His great might into two natures... He will give the power to the kings of Persia for a little while and they will afflict the earth in their days... After this, God will remove the kingdom of the Persians and will stir up upon the earth a mighty people, numerous as the locusts. This is the fourth beast which the prophet Daniel saw... That nation will rule over many countries... It is a brutal nation with no mercy in its heart... (numerous iniquities detailed) *... Many Christians, Barbarians, Greeks, Syrians, and from all tribes will go and join them in their faith, wanting to become free from the sufferings that they will bring upon the earth. They will dwell in many countries and become the masters of them, and they will inherit them. Their leader shall live in the city called Damascus... They will gather all the gold, silver, precious stones, bronze, iron, lead, and the beautiful garments. The name of that nation is Saracen, one which is from the Ishmaelite's, the son of Hagar, maidservant of Abraham.*

The Persian and Arab occupations are, thus, depicted in very general terms, bar the notices on apostasy of Christians to the Arab 'faith' and on the location of Arab government at Damascus, a fact which yields a *terminus ante quem* for the work of 744, when Marwan transferred the capital to Harran. Four specific charges are then made against the Arabs:

First, that nation will destroy the gold on which there is the image of the cross of the Lord, our God, in order to make all the countries under its rule mint their own gold with the name of the beast written on it, the number of whose name is 666. Afterward, they will count the men and write their names in their documents, and set upon them high taxes... Afterward, they will measure the whole earth with the fields and the gardens, and they will count the cattle... At their end...they will take the strangers in the cities and the villages, and wherever they find them, they will call for their return and they will throw them into prison, for many at that time will leave their cities and their villages and go abroad because of the violence of the oppression of that nation.

The above four complaints are of a more concrete nature. The minting of coins with the name of the beast, that is, Muhammad,[i] refers to the monetary reforms of Abd al-Malik in A.H. 77/696, when he began to replace images on the gold and silver currency. Census may refer to that of Ubayd Allah in 724. Reference to actions of Al-Asbagh who taxed monks for the first time, and of Abd Allah ibn Abd al-Malik, who gathered all youths of 20 years and under, may be intended. A land survey was carried out at the outset of Usama ibn Zayd's stint as governor (715–17). And the problem of fugitives bedeviled the terms in office of Qurra ibn Shreek (709–14) and Usama, to the extent that Qurra had to appoint a man 'to gather the runaways from every place, take them back and bind them, punish them and return them to their place.'[ii]

Another Coptic Apocalypse written at the end of the seventh century, but attributed to the fourth/fifth century monastic leader, Shenouda, 'predicts' that the 'children of Ishmael' will 'rebuild the temple which is in Jerusalem,' after which the Antichrist will appear. This seems to refer 'Abd Al-Malik' construction of the Dome of the Rock (completed in 692) on the site of the Temple, from which height it overshadowed the Church of the Resurrection.[269]

Yet another document, the *Apocalypse of Samuel of Qalamoun*,[270] thought to have been written in the tenth or 11th century, in which the writer puts on the mouth of Samuel (d. 695), complaints about what the future holds for the Copts:

For myself, I prefer silence, my dear children, and I do not want to describe to you what the Christians will suffer from the Arab emigrants during their reign. May God make it that you do not recall their name in the middle of us today, for this is an arrogant race whom we should not name in the assemblies of the saints. Ah! This name! That of the Arabs, and their domination, contrary to our laws! These haughty kings who will reign in their day! These sorrows which will affect future generations because they will act like them! (..)

---

[i] The value of the letters in the Coptic spelling (MAMETIOC) is 666, the number of the beast according to Revelation 13: 18.

[ii] Refer to chapter on *Umayyads* above.

In truth, my children, the angel of the Lord has revealed to me hard times and sorrows without number to which this arrogant nation will subject the children of men. (..)

So know, my children, that this nation will commit a great number of iniquities and injustices on the land of Egypt: its domination will be greatly consolidated, its yoke will press like iron and its people will multiply like grasshoppers; it will seize several countries which will undergo its domination, and its injustice will increase greatly in Egypt, so much so that the land will be ruined by it; they will eat, drink, amuse themselves; they will dress like husbands; they will praise themselves much, while saying: "No nation will ever dominate us." They will subject the ground to the land register and hit it with taxes; from this will result a huge cost to live on the land; a great number will perish of hunger and will remain on the ground without anyone to give them the last burial.

(It will also happen) that those who will lie down for the night in their own houses, will each find, on awaking in the morning, three ushers at their door, each of them claiming some kind of tax. At this point in time, a great number of important cities, regions, hamlets, and ports will be destroyed, and this land of Egypt, rich in trees and in gardens, will become a salted land, wooded and sterile, because of the multiplicity of the taxes levied on the country by the Arabs; because they form an arrogant nation, little inclined to mercy. Their yoke will weigh like iron. They will molest their subjects in their greed for gold: they will make a census of the citizens, great and small, they will inscribe their names on the registers and will claim the capitation tax from them. The inhabitants will then sell their clothing and their effects to discharge the taxes, [and their masters] will lay hands on all their possessions [and] they will oppress them. The population transport themselves from one city and country to another, seeking peace without finding it.

There is also the apocalypse attributed (retroactively) to Bishop Pesynthios of Coptos (598–632), which highlights the mistreatment by the Muslim rulers of the church and the Copts in general. It enumerates the bad conditions in which the Copts lived and mentions the conversion of many to Islam to escape persecution. The most interesting thing is the prophecy of the victory of the Byzantine Empire over the Muslims in Egypt, which reflects the strong desire of the Copts at that time to become liberated from Islamic authority. [271]

6. Patriarchs of the Coptic Church

	Pope	Western pronunciation	Date	Period *	
				Y	M
1	**Mar Morcos the Apostle**	**St. Mark the Apostle**	45?–68		
2	Inianos		68–83	15	
3	Milieus		83–95	12	
4	Kerdonous		95–106	10	9
5	Epriemous	Primus	106–118	13	1
6	Iostos	Justus	118–129	10	10
7	Oumenios	Eumenes, Hymenæus	129–141	12	3
8	Markianos		141–152	10	2
9	Kalavtianos		152–166	14	6
10	Aghreppinios	Agrippinus	166–178	11	6
11	Yulianos	Julian	178–188	10	
12	Demetrios I	Demetri	188–230	42	7
13	Yaraklas	Heraclas	230?–246	16	1
14	Dionysius		246–264	17	2
15	Maximus		264–282	17	5
16	Theona	Theonas	282–301	19	1
17	Botros I (*Last of Martyrs*)	Petros, Peter I	301–311	9	10
18	Archelaos	Archillas	311–312		6
19	Alexanderos I	Alexander I	312–328	15	9

20	Athanasius I (*The Apostolic*)		326?–373	45	
21	Botros II	Petros, Peter II	373–379	5	9
22	Timothaos I	Timothy I	379–385	6	4
23	Theophilus I		385–412	27	2
24	Kyrillos I (*Pillar of Faith*)	Cyril I	412–444	31	8
25	Dioscorus I		444–454	10	1
26	Timothaos II	Timothy II	457–477	20	10
27	Botros III	Petros, Peter III	477489	13	2
28	Athanasius II		489–496	6	9
29	Yoannes I	John I	496–505	8	7
30	Yoannes II	John II	505–516	10	11
31	Dioscorus II		516–518	2	4
32	Timothaos III	Timothy III	518?–536	17	3
33	Theodosios I		536–567	31	4
34	Botros IV	Petros, Peter IV	567–569	1	11
35	Damianus	Damian	569–605	36	
36	Anastasius		605–616	11	6
37	Andronicus		616–623	6	
38	Benyamin I	Benjamin I	623?–662	39	
39	Aghathon		662?–677?	15	9
40	Yoannes III	John III	677–686	9	
41	Is'hak - Ishak	Isaac	686–689	2	
42	Simon I	Simeon I	689–701	10	
	(*Vacancy*)			4	
43	Alexanderos II		704–729	25	9
44	Kosman I	Cosmas I	729–730	1	3
45	Tawadros I	Theodoros / Theodore I	730–742	11	7
46	Khail I		743–767	23	6

47	Mina I		767–776	8	10
48	Yoannes IV	John IV	777–799	22	
49	Morcos II	Mark II	799–819	20	2
50	Yacoub	Jacob	819–830	10	9
51	Simon II	Simeon II	830–830		5
52	Yousab I	Josephus I	831–849	17	11
53	Khail II		849–851	1	4
54	Kosman/Qozmas II	Cosmas II	851–858	7	4
55	Shenouda I	Sanutius I	859–880	21	3
56	Khail III, (Mikhail I)	Michael I	880–894	27	1
	(Vacancy)			*15*	
57	Ghobrial I	Gabriel I	909–920	10	9
58	Kosman III	Cosmas III	920–932	12	
59	Makarius I		932–952	19	11
60	Theophaneos		952–956	4	4
61	Mina II		956–974	17	11
62	Abraam (Efram, *Ibn Zaraa*)	Abraham	975–978	3	11
63	Philotheos		979–1003	24	7
64	Zakaria	Zacharias	1004–1032	27	11
65	Shenouda II	Sanutius II	1032–1046	14	7
66	Khristodolos (*Christ's servant*)	Christdoolos	1046–1077	31	
67	Kyrillos II	Cyril II	1078–1092	14	6
68	Mikhail I	Michael I	1092–1102	9	7
69	Makarius II		1102–1128	26	1
70	Ghobrial II	Gabriel II	1131–1145	14	2
71	Mikhail II	Michael II	1145–1146		8
72	Yoannes V	John V	1147–1166	18	8
73	Morcos III	Mark III	1166–1189	22	6
74	Yoannes VI	John VI	1189–1216	26	11

	(Vacancy)			*20*	
75	Kyrillos III	Cyril III	1235–1243	7	8
	(Vacancy)			*7*	
76	Athanasius III		1250–1261	11	1
	(Vacancy)			*7*	
77	Ghobrial III	Gabriel III	1268–1271	2	2
78	Yoannes VII	John VII	1271–1293	29	1
79	Theodosios II		1294–1300	5	5
80	Yoannes VIII	John VIII	1300–1320	20	3
81	Yoannes IX	John IX	1320–1327	6	6
82	Benyamin II	Benjamin II	1327–1339	11	7
83	Botros V	Petros, Peter V	1340–1348	8	6
84	Morcos IV	Mark IV	1348–1363	14	4
85	Yoannes X	John X	1363–1369	6	2
86	Ghobrial IV	Gabriel IV	1370–1378	8	3
87	Mettaous I	Mathew I	1378–1408	30	5
88	Ghobrial V	Gabriel V	1409–1427	17	8
89	Yoannes XI	John XI	1427–1452	24	11
90	Mettaous II	Mathew II	1452–1465	13	
91	Ghobrial VI	Gabriel VI	1466–1474	8	10
	(Vacancy)			*3*	
92	Mikhail IV	Michael IV	1477–1478	1	
93	Yoannes XII	John XII	1480–1483	3	4
94	Yoannes XIII	John XIII	1484–1524	39	11
95	Ghobrial VII	Gabriel VII	1525–1568	43	2
96	Yoannes XIV	John XIV	1571–1586	15	4
97	Ghobrial VIII	Gabriel VIII	1587–1603	15	10
98	Morcos V	Mark V	1603–1619	16	2
99	Yoannes XV	John XV	1619–1629	9	11
100	Mettaous III	Mathew III	1631–1646	14	6
101	Morcos VI	Mark VI	1646–1656	10	
	(Vacancy)			*5*	

102	Mettaous IV	Mathew IV	1660–1675	14	8
103	Yoannes XVI	John XVI	1676–1718	42	3
104	Botros VI	Petros, Peter VI	1718–1726	7	7
105	Yoannes XVII	John XVII	1727–1745	18	3
106	Morcos VII	Mark VII	1745–1769	23	11
107	Yoannes XVIII	John XVIII	1769–1796	26	7
108	Morcos VIII	Mark VIII	1796–1809	13	2
109	Botros VII	Petros, Peter VII	1809–1852	42	3
110	Kyrillos IV (*Fr. of Reform*)	Cyril IV	1853–1862	6	7
111	Demetrios II	Demetri II	1862–1871	7	7
	(Vacancy)			*4*	
112	Kyrillos V	Cyril V	1874–1927	52	9
113	Yoannes XIX	John XIX	1929–1942	13	6
114	Makarius III		1944–1945	1	6
115	Yousab II	Josephus II	1946–1956	10	5
116	Kyrillos VI	Cyril VI	1959–1971	11	10
117	Shenouda III		1971–2012	40	4
118	Tawadros II	Theodoros / Theodore II	2012–		

(*) Table compiled with help from various sources besides the *History of the Patriarchs*, especially: https://st-takla.org/Saints/Coptic-Synaxarium-Orthodox-Saints-Biography-00-Coptic-Orthodox-Popes/Coptic-Popes-History_000-index_.html

In certain cases, there might be a dating discrepancy between different sources.

7. Glossary

Abba	Greek, from Heb, for father. It is used as a title for the Bishop.
Agha	Senior or chief officer, in Ottoman system.
Amir *or* **Emir**	Prince. A root for the term is 'amr' (order), giving 'Aamer' for giver of order, or commander. Orthographically, both words are close leading to confusing the two senses.
Anba *or* **Amba**	From old Egyptian Anbar, for 'father,' then became Apa in later Coptic.
Archon	Greek, for notable or holder of senior public office. Used here to designate community leader, who is usually more affluent and holder of a post in the administration.
Ardabb	A unit of measurement equivalent to about 39 gallons.
Ashraf	*Pl.* of sharif; 'honorable.' Usually denotes being a descendent of the Prophet.
Azan, *or* **Adhān**	The Muslim call to ritual prayer, typically made by a Muezzin from the minaret of a mosque.
Baksheesh	Turkish, for tip, gratuity, perquisite.
Bayt al-mal	*Lit.* 'house of money.' A central treasury for the Islamic State, managing its finances and expenditures, according to *Sharia* rules (theoretically), and to the extent the rulers could separate personal from 'public' finances.
Bek *or* **Bey**	A title of Turku-Mongol origin, lower than Pasha, denoting chief, lord, or dignitary.
Daftardar	*Lit.* 'book-keeper.' The most senior position in the Treasury in the Ottoman system.
Da'wa	The proselytizing or preaching of Islam.
Dhikr	A form of devotion, associated chiefly with Sufism, in which a person is absorbed in the rhythmic repetition of the name of Allah.

Dhimmi   Refers to Jews and Christians who are tolerated to live in an Islamic state as long as they live in submission and pay Jizya, making them effectively second-class citizens.

Dinar   From Greek 'dinari.' Common coin in Middle Ages. One dinar was about four grams of gold. One dinar usually equaled 37 dirhams.

Dirham   From Greek 'drachma.' Common coin. One-dirham coin is about three grams of silver.

Divân   A council chamber, royal court.

Effendi   A title of nobility meaning Master, comes lower than Bek; Effendina: Our Master.

Feddan   Acre; a unit of area equivalent to 4200 square meters. A feddan is divided into 24 kirats (karats), each equal 175 sq. m.

Fat'h   Usually translated as 'Conquest,' but it literally signifies 'opening' with an implicit sense of being peaceful and bringing in civilization and good news (Islam) to the 'opened' territories.

Fatwa   A legal opinion or decree handed down by an Islamic religious leading scholar, or jurisprudent, *faqih*.

Fitnah   Sedition, commotion, strife, tumult.

Ghazwa   *Lit.* invasion. A battle associated with the expansion of Muslim territory. The term often refers to those (27) that took place during the life of Islam's prophet. *Pl.* ghazawat.

Hajj   From Greek 'hagios' (sacred, devoted to the gods), used to refer to Muslim's pilgrimage to Mecca that takes place in the last month of the Hijra year, and that all Muslims who can afford it are expected to make at least once during their lifetime.

Hanafi   One of the four main Sunni Islamic schools of jurisprudence (*o*), along with Maliki, Shafii and Hanbali.

Hudud   The five *Sharia* bodily retributive punishments of thieves, adulterers, etc. They include flagellation, hand (and, sometimes foot) amputation, crucifying, and stoning (or hanging).

Imam   Prayers' leader. The caliph is, by definition, the supreme imam.

Janissaries   In the Turkish Ottoman language, yeñiçeri means 'new soldiers' or 'new army.' They were an infantry army division who formed their own special order. They were the strongest and most influential Ottoman army divisions. They were usually

	made up of boys and young men taken captive in war. They were reared according to the teachings of Islam.
Jihad	*Lit.* striving. A war fought by Muslims to defend or spread their beliefs.
Jizya	*Lit.* penalty. Thought to be Arabicized from the Persian Kyzyat, meaning a levy. Refers to head or poll tax demanded (as stipulated in the Quran) from non-Muslim subjects; to be paid 'in humiliation.' Rooted in verb 'to requite,' meaning to retaliate from non-Muslims for their Kufr.
Kashif	District governor or prefect.
Katkhoda	A deputy of the Wali.
Kharaj	Taxes on buildings and farmland. Sometimes refers to taxation in general.
Khedive	A title largely equivalent to the English word viceroy.
Kingdom *or* **King**	Chroniclers may use such terms to describe realities in the Islamic state, which normally refer to Caliphate or Caliph/Sultan, respectively.
Kufr	*Lit.* 'covering' or denying God or, more generally, the 'True Faith.' It usually refers to deliberate unbelief (in Islam), which often carries grave consequences.
Kuffar	*Pl.* of Kafir. Those who adopt Kufr. According to *Sharia* rules, their life and property becomes lawful to take.
Maghrebi	*Lit.* from the western lands. Inhabitants of current day Morocco and parts of Algeria and Mauritania; mostly descendants of Moors and Arabs.
Mahdi	The expected 'messiah' of (Shia) Muslim tradition.
Maks	Impost, custom duty, tax on commerce; *pl.* Mokous.
Mamluk	*Lit.* owned one, i.e. a slave. Generally, warrior slaves who, when liberated, can have their own battalion of mamluks.
Mar	Used for Saints, from Chaldean origin meaning Lord. Mari— my Lord.
Melkites	Followers of the Greek Orthodox (Chalcedonian) rites. Referred to as the 'Orthodox Byzantine' Church before the Arab Conquest.
Miḥrāb	A semicircular niche in the wall of a mosque that indicates the qibla; that is, the direction of the Kaaba in Mecca and hence the direction that Muslims should face when praying.

Misr   Egypt in Arabic and Semitic languages. It may also refer to the
                  city that is currently known as 'Old Cairo.'

Moallem   *Lit.* teacher, educator. Denotes 'erudite,' 'principal,' or
                  'knowledgeable.' Equivalent to 'doctor' (a learned or
                  authoritative teacher) in Latin and related languages. Used as a
                  title for leading Coptic scribes, especially those occupying high-
                  level state positions.

Moshrekîn   Those who practice Shirk (idolaters or polytheists).

Moslemani   Used in Egypt in early days after the Arab conquest, denoting
                  Christian who converted to Islam. Sometimes also referred to as
                  Mouwali (loyal to); often appears in Coptic papyri as *Mouléus.*

Muezzin   A Muslim crier who calls the hour of daily prayers.

Mujahed   *Lit.* one who strives against. A Muslim who is willing, perhaps
                  desires, to fight and maybe die for the sake of Islam.

Muḥtaseb   A person assigned to ensure that the rules of *Sharia* are
                  enforced, and polices public conduct. This includes tasks like
                  inspecting commercial market dealings.

Pasha   Ottoman title for someone of high rank or office, or of high
                  nobility or dignity.

Piaster   (Kuruş), silver Ottoman coin. One golden Lire (livres, pounds)
                  equals 100 piasters. One 'bag' or 'sack' (keis) contains 500
                  piasters and is the equivalent of five golden pounds.

Qibla   The direction (of Mecca) that Muslims face when they do their
                  prayers.

Ridda   *Lit.* going back on an agreement. Usually means apostasy.
                  Ridda Wars; the attacks by Caliph Abu-Bakr, after the death of
                  Mohammad, against some allied tribes that broke away.

Roum   Byzantines.

Sanjaq   Head of an administrative unit, such as district, part of a
                  province, or a governorate, in Ottoman system.

Shahada *or* The Muslim profession of faith ('there is no god but Allah, and
Shihada   Muhammad is the messenger of Allah').

Sharia   (Islamic) Law based on Quran and the tradition of the Prophet
                  (sayings and acts) prescribing religious duties and
                  personal/societal rules, including retributive penalties.

Sheikh   *Lit.* elder. Religious title of Muslim prayer leaders or scholars.

Shia	One of the two main branches of Islam, followed especially in modern day Iran that regards Ali, the fourth caliph, as Muhammad's (first) true successor.
Shiite	An adherent of the Shia branch of Islam.
Shirk	Practicing idolatry or polytheism.
Simony	The buying or selling of ecclesiastical privileges or positions.
Sufi	A Muslim mystic.
Sultan	*Lit.* authority, power. Title of rulers in the Islamic state who had almost full sovereignty in practical terms, short of the overall caliphate. Started during the Abbasids as the second person in the state, but gradually became the de facto ruler, with the caliph a mere religious figurehead.
Sunna	The body of Islamic custom and practice based on Muhammad's words and deeds.
Sunni	One of the two main branches of Islam, followed by about 90% of Muslims.
Takbīr	Proclaiming the phrase, 'Allāhu Akbar.' The expression may be used in various contexts by Muslims; in formal prayer, in the call for prayer (adhān), as an informal expression of faith, or to express resolute determination or defiance.
Talbiyah	A Muslim prayer invoked to portray conviction or readiness to perform an act for the glory of Allah.
Tawhid	The Muslim doctrine of the oneness of God.
Umma	*Lit.* nation, but in Islamic contest it refers to the nation of Muslim believers, united by faith irrespective of any other aspect.
Wali	Custodian. Administrative title of a regional governor or governor-general.
Zakat	Obligatory (tithe) payment made annually under *Sharia* on certain kinds of property and used for charitable and religious purposes.

Bibliography

Core Reference

Hekayat Al-Ihtilal wa Tas'heeh Ba'ad Al-Mafaheem ('Stories of Occupation and Correcting Some Givens'), by Adel <u>Guindy</u>, MEFF, Cairo 2009. It includes extensive excerpts from *Tarikh Misr min Khilal Makhtoutat Tarikh al-Batarekah, li Sawiris Ibn Al-Muqafa' (The History of Egypt Through the History of the Patriarchs' Manuscript of Sevirus)*, by Abdel Aziz <u>Gamal Al-Din</u>, verification and research; Publisher: Madbouly, 2006, six volumes. These excerpts have been translated afresh and included in this book (refer to the Introduction).

Primary References

—*Al-Kafi fi Tarikh Misr al-Qadim wal-Hadith*, ('The Sufficient in Egypt's Old and Recent History'), by: Mikhail <u>Sharubim</u> Bek[i], First edition (1898), Second edition in the series of *'Safahat min Tarîkh Misr* ('Pages From the History of Egypt'), 2004, Publisher: Madbouly, Cairo.

—*Al-Hurreyah fil Asr,* ('Freedom in Captivity'), By Adel <u>Guindy</u>, Merit, 2007.

—*Aqbat wa Moslemoun Mundh al-Fat'h al-Arabi ela 1922,* ('Copts and Muslims from the Arab Conquest to 1922');* by Jacques <u>Tagher</u>, Karrasat al-Tarikh al-Masri ('Egyptian History Brochures'), Cairo, 1951. Translated to English under *'Christians in Muslim Egypt. An Historical Study of the Relations between Copts and Muslims from 640 to 1922'*), by Jacques Tagher, D. Ryan, Altenberge, 1988.

---

[i] The author, Sharubim Bek, was the (maternal) grandfather of Dr. Boutros Boutros-Ghali, who personally invested in having the second edition of the book published.

—*Correspondance générale de Napoléon Bonaparte*, par la Fondation Napoléon, Tome deuxième, Fayard, 2005.

—*In God's Path — The Arab Conquests and the Creation of an Islamic Empire,* by Robert G. Hoyland, Oxford University Press, 2015.

—*Les Fondations de l'Islam Entre Écriture et Histoire*, par Alfred-Louis De Prémare, Seuil, 2002.

—*Seeing Islam as Others Saw It*, by Robert G. Hoyland, The Darwin Press, Inc. Princeton, New Jersey 1997.

—*The Chronicle of John, Bishop of Nikiu*, translated from Zotenberg's Ethiopic text by R. H. Charles, D. Litt, D.D., 1916 (http://www.tertullian.org/fathers/nikiu1_intro.htm)

—*The Coptic Encyclopedia,* Ed. Aziz S. Atiya, Macmillan, 1991, eight volumes.

—*The Coptic Papacy in Islamic Egypt,* by Mark N. Swanson, AUC Press, Cairo, 2010.

—*The Copts in Egyptian Politics (1918–1952),* by B. L. Carter, published by American University in Cairo, 1986.

—*The Story of the Church of Egypt,* by L.E. Butcher, London, Smith, Elder, & Co., two volumes, 1897.

Other References

—*Ahkam Ahl Al-Dhimma*, ('Regulations Regarding Dhimmis'), by Ibn Qayyim al-Jawziyya, Dar Algile, Beirut, 2001.

—*Ahl Al-Dhimma fil Islam* ('Dhimmis in Islam'), by Hassan Habashy, Cairo, 1949.

—*Al-Aqbat 'Abr Al-Tarikh* ('The Copts Across History'), by Dr. Selim Naguib, Dar Al-Khayyal, Cairo, 2001.

—*Al-General Yaqob wal Faris Lascaris – Mashrou' Istiqlal Misr fi 1801* ('General Yaqob and Knight Lascaris – Project for Egypt's Independence in 1801'), by Mohamed Shafik Ghorbal – First published in 1932. Ed. Dar al-Shorouk, 2009.

—*Al-Ikhwan wa Ana* ('The Brotherhood and Me'), by Brig. General Fouad Allam, Akhbar Al-Youm, 2013.

—*Al-Khutat: Al-Mawa'ez wal I'tibar bi Dhikr Al-Khutat wal -Aathar* ('The Plans'), by Taqey Aldin Al-Makrizi (1364–1442), Ed. Madbouly, Cairo, 1998.

—*Al-Muqaddimah* ('Prolegomena'), Ibn Khaldun, 1377, Ed. 2004.

—*Al-Thawrah Al-Mudadah fi Misr* ('Anti-Revolution in Egypt'), by Dr. Ghali Shoukri, Al-Ahaly, Cairo, 1987.

—*Al-Madhamma fi Iste'mal Ahl Al-Dhimma* ('The Slander of Employing the Dhimmis*)*, Imam Mohammed Ibn Al-Naqqāsh (d. 1362).

—*Aqbat Al-Mahgar* ('Copts in Immigation Lands'), by Magdi Khalil, Dar al-Khaiyal, Cairo, 1999.

—*Coptic Civilization*, edited by Gawdat Gabra, AUC Press, Cairo - New York, 2013.

—*Copts and the British Occupation,* by Samuel Tadros, (https://www.alhurra.com/a/copts-and-british-occupation/419843.html)

—*Copts and the Security State: Violence, Coercion and Sectarianism in Contemporary Egypt,* by Laure Guirguis, Stanford University Press, 2014.

—*Copts at the Crossroad*, by Mariz Tadros, AUC Press, Cairo, 2013.

—*Copts in Context,* Ed. by Nelly van Doorn-Harder, Univ. of South Carolina Press, 2017.

—*Crucified Again*, by Raymond Ibrahim (Regnery Publishing, 2013).

—*Falsafat Al-Thawrah* ('The Philosophy of Revolution'), Gamal Abdel Nasser.

—*Family Status Issues Among Egypt's Copts: An Overview,* by Adel Guindy, (http://www.rubincenter.org/2007/09/guindy-2007-09-01/)

—*Futuh al-Buldan* ('Conquests of the Lands'), by Ahmed Al-Balathury (d. 892).

—*Futuh Misr* ('Conquests of Egypt*) by* Ibn Abd Al-Hakam (d. 871).

—*Guerre au cœur de l'islam,* par Gilles Kepel, Gallimard, 2004.

—*Hadarat Misr fil 'Assr Al-Qibti,* ('Egyptian Civilization During the Coptic Era'), by Dr. Murad Kamil, Al-'Alam Al-'Arabi, Cairo, 1967.

—*Hagarism: The Making of the Islamic World,* by Patricia Crone & Michael Cook, Cambridge University Press, 1977.

—*Hawamish al-Fat'h al-Arabi li-Masr. Hekayat al-Dokhoul* ('Footnotes on the Arab Conquest of Egypt: Stories of their Entrance*')* by Sanaa El-Masry, – Dar Sina, Cairo.

—*Histoire des Coptes d'Egypte,* par Magdi S. Zaki, Éditions de Paris, 2005.

—*The Islamization of Egypt,* by Adel Guindy, Gloria Center, 2006, (https://historynewsnetwork.org/article/29855)

—*La violence et le sacré,* par René Girard, Pluriel 2011.

—*Les débuts de la piraterie anadalouse en Méditerranée occidentale,* Par Pierre. Guichard, (http://www.persee.fr/doc/remmm_0035-1474_1983_num_35_1_1981.

—*Marcus Simaika: Father of Coptic Archeology,* By Samir Simaika.

—*Misr fi 'Assr al-Wilah* ('Egypt in the Era of the Walis'), By Dr. Sayeda Kashef, 1988.

—*Muqadimmah fi Fiqh Al-Lughah Al-Arabeyah* ('Introduction to Arabic Language Philology'), by Dr. Louis Awad, Cairo, 1980.

—*Mukademmah fil Folklore al-Qibti* ('Introduction to Coptic Folklore'), By Essam Stati, Library of Popular Studies, # 127, Cairo, 2010.

—*Orality as Resistance Among the Persecuted Copts,* by Fatin M. Guirguis, 2014.

—*Seeing Islam as Others Saw It* by Robert G. Hoyland, The Darwin press, Princeton, New Jersey 1997.

—*Sword and Scimitar: Fourteen Centuries of War between Islam and the West,* by Raymond Ibrahim, Da Capo Press, New York, 2018

—*Subh al-A'sha* ('Dawn of the Dim-Sighted'), by Ahmed Al-Qalqashandi (d. 1356).

—*Symbolic Victims in a Socially Regressing Egypt: The Declining Situation of the Copts,* by Adel Guindy, (http://www.rubincenter.org/2010/03/guindy-2010-03-07/).

—*Tarikh Ahl Al-Dhimma fi Misr Al-Islameyah* (History of *Dhimmis* in Islamic Egypt'), by Dr. Fatima Moustafa Amer, Cairo, 2000.

—*The Apocalypse of Pseudo-Athanasius* (Ar.), Christine F. George, ASJ, 2013.

—*The Coptic Question in the Mubarak Era,* by Sebastian Elsässer, Oxford University Press, 2014.

—*The Copts,* by Abdel Latif El-Menawy, Gilgamesh Publishing, U.K., 2017.

—*The Council of Chalcedeon Re-Examined,* by Fr. V.C. <u>Samuel</u>, Xlibris Corp. 2001.

—*The Emergence of the Modern Coptic Papacy,* by Magdi <u>Guirguis</u>, Nelly van Doorn-Harder, AUC Press, Cairo, 2011.

—*The Impact of the Copts on Civilization,* by Amin <u>Makram-Ebeid</u>, M.D.
http://www.copticchurchreview.com/Coptic/Home_files/1999%20Winter.Vol20.%234.pdf

—*The Origins of Totalitarianism*, by Hannah <u>Arendt</u> (1906–1975); 1985 print by Harcour Books.

Sites Accessed:

– http://www.ahram.org.eg/Index.aspx

– https://www.alhurra.com/a/copts-and-british-occupation/419843.html

– http://www.almasryalyoum.com

– https://www.britannica.com/biography/Amalric-I

–   https://www.elhaq.com/kashef/41-rights-od-ahl-zumma-in-islamic-jurisprudence

– http://eipr.org/sites/default/files/reports/

– https://genographic.nationalgeographic.com/reference-populations-next-gen/

– http://www.hrw.org/news/2013/08/21/egypt-mass-attacks-churches

– http://memory.loc.gov/diglib/ihas/html/coptic/copticgallery-introduction.html

– http://www.moyak.com/papers/ancient-alexandria.html

– http://shamela.ws/browse.php/book-11404/

_   <u>https://st-takla.org/Saints/Coptic-Orthodox-Saints-Biography/Coptic-Saints-Story</u>

–   <u>http://www.vatican.va/roman_curia/pontifical_councils/chrstuni/anc-orient-ch-docs/rc_pc_christuni_doc_19730510_copti_en.html</u>

–   <u>http://www.wataninet.com</u>

Notes

[1] *Éloge de l'oublie*, par David Rieff, Première Parallèle, Paris, 2018.

[2] *Mythscapes*, article by Duncan Bell,
(https://www.researchgate.net/publication/10760719_Mythscapes_Memory_mytho
logy_and_national_identity)

[3] As Joan Ramon Resina puts it, quoted in:
https://conservancy.umn.edu/bitstream/handle/11299/184381/hiol_11_02_crameri_
history_written_by_the_losers.pdf?sequence=1&isAllowed=y

[4] George Orwell, in "1984." He pertinently adds: "Who controls the present controls
the past"

[5] Johannes den Heijer, the Coptic Encyclopedia, p 1241

[6] Referred to as 'Footnotes' when quoted in this book.

[7] http://www.moyak.com/papers/ancient-alexandria.html

[8] https://genographic.nationalgeographic.com/reference-populations-next-gen/

[9] *The Story of the Church of Egypt*, by L.E. Butcher, 1897, Vol. 2, p 280

[10] Essam Stati, '*Mokademma fil Folklore al-Qibti*' ('Introduction to Coptic
Folklore'),   Library   of   Popular   Studies,   #   127,   Cairo,   2010
(http://www.gocp.gov.eg/UserDir/Slasel/selselaM/مقدمة20%فى20%الفولكلور20%القبطى
.PDF)

[11] http://memory.loc.gov/diglib/ihas/html/coptic/copticgallery-introduction.html

[12] Butcher, V-1, Pp. 90, 388, V-2 P. 392.

[13] Butcher, V-1, P 90

[14]   http://www.vatican.va/roman_curia/pontifical_councils/chrstuni/anc-orient-ch-
docs/rc_pc_christuni_doc_19730510_copti_en.html

[15] The Coptic Encyclopedia, P 1786.

[16] Butcher, V-1, P 330

[17] Butcher, V-1, P 377

[18] Sanaa El-Masry, *Hawamish al-Fat'h al-Arabi li-Masr. Hekayat al-Dokhoul*,
('Footnotes on the Arab Conquest of Egypt: Stories of their Entrance') – Dar Sina,
Cairo — 1996, p 58.

[19] John, Bishop of Nikiu. London 1916. English Translation from Zotenberg's
Ethiopic text, R.H. Charles, Fellow of the British Academy, published by the Text
and Translation Society. (http://www.tertullian.org/fathers/nikiu1_intro.htm).

[20] *'In God's Path,'* by Robert G. Hoyland, Oxford Univ. Press, 2015, P 74.

[21] Ibn Abdul Hakam, *Futuh Misr* ('Conquests of Egypt'), P. 87.

[22] *Les Fondations de l'Islam*, par A-L. De Prémare, P. 211

[23] http://shamela.ws/browse.php/book-11404/page-200

[24] Hoyland, P. 45

[25] *The Arab Conquest of Egypt and the Last Thirty Years of the Roman Dominion*, by Alfred J. Butler, Oxford, The Clarendon Press, 1902, P. 490, and the Arabic version, Madbouly, Cairo, 1990, P. 501.

[26] Butler, P. 368

[27] Butcher, V-1, P. 374.

[28] De Prémare, P. 223–4

[29] De Prémare, P. 214

[30] *Al-Kafi*, Part 2, P. 140–141.

[31] *Al-Kafi*, Part 2, P. 144.

[32] Footnotes *'History of the Patriarchs'* Abdul Aziz Gamal Al-din, Part 1, P. 331.

[33] Footnotes, Part 2, Pp. 8, 9, and 592.

[34] Footnotes, Part 2, Pp. 160 and 636 quoted from Abu 'Ubaid Al-bakri in *'Al-Mogharreb fi Zikr Bilad Afriqya wal Maghreb'* P. 38.

[35] Reported in *Subh al-'Asha* of Al-Qalqashandi (1355–1415). The English text quoted here is edited from Tagher, P. 37

[36] *'Ahkam Ahlul Dhimma,'* ('Rulings Concerning Dhimmis'), by Ibn Qayyim al-Jawziyya, P. 212.

[37] *Tarikh Ahl Al-Dhimma fi Misr Al-Islameyah* (History of *Dhimmis* in Islamic Egypt), by Dr. Fatima Moustafa 'Amer, Cairo, 2000, P 33.

[38] Footnotes, Part 2, P. 91.

[39] *Al-Kafi*, Part 2, P. 160.

[40] Footnotes, Part 2, P. 750 quoted from: *Alkandi*, Page 73, and *Al Maqrizi Plans*, Part 1, P. 79.

[41] Footnotes, Part 2, P. 751 quoted from: *Ibn Al Hakam*, P. 156, *Al Maqrizi Plans*, Part 1, P. 74, and *Al Suyuti, Hosn Almuhaadrah*, Part 1, P. 63.

[42] *The Coptic Papacy in Islamic Egypt*, by Mark N. Swanson, P. 15.

[43] *Ibid,* P. 16. Also refer to Appendix-3.

[44] *Al-Kafi*, Part 2, P. 165.

[45] Footnotes, Part 2, P. 751 quoted from *Al Maqrizi Plans*, Part 1, P. 79.

[46] Footnotes, Part 2, P. 753 quoted from: *Alkandi*, P. 102, and *Abu al-Mahasin*, Part 1, P. 325.

[47] Footnotes, Part 2, P. 753 quoted from: *Alkandi*, P. 116, and *Al Maqrizi*, Part 1, P. 79.

[48] Footnotes, Part 2, P. 599.

[49] *Al-Kafi*, Part 2, Pp 171, 184.

[50] *Al-Kafi*, Part 2, Pp 171, 184.

[51] '*Seeing Islam as Others Saw It*' by Robert G. Hoyland, The Darwin press, Princeton, New Jersey 1997, P. 27

[52] *Al-Kafi*, Part 2, P. 186.

[53] *Al-Kafi*, Part 2, Pp. 203, 208.

[54] Swanson, Pp 32–3

[55] Swanson, Pp 32–3

[56] Swanson, Pp 32–3

[57] Swanson, Pp 32–3

[58] Footnotes, Part 2, P. 826.

[59] Tagher, p 80, quoting *Chronique de Michel le Syrien*, 3–83

[60] *Al-Kafi*, Part 2, P. 237.

[61] According to A. S. Tritton, Ar. Tr. by Hassan Habashy '*Ahl Al-Dhimma fil Islam,*' Cairo, 1949.

[62] Footnotes, Part 2, P. 769, quoted from Ibn Al-Naqqāsh, *Al-Madhamma fi Iste'mal Ahl Al Dhimma (The Slander of Employing the Dhimmis)*, P. 86.

[63] Swanson, Pp 32–3

[64] Footnotes, Part 3, P. 19.

[65] Footnotes, Part 3, P. 19.

[66] Footnotes, Part 3, P. 19.

[67] *Al-Kafi*, Part 2, P. 334.

[68] Footnotes, Part 3, P. 507, quoted from Sayed Karim, architect and renowned Egyptologist.

[69] *Al-Kafi*, Part 2, P. 365.

[70] Dr. Sayeda Kashef, '*Misr fi 'Asr al-Wilah*' ('Egypt in the Era of the *Wali*s'), 1988.

[71] *Al-Kafi*, Part 2, P. 426.

[72] *Al-Kafi*, Part 2, P. 426.

[73] Footnotes, quoting *History of Ibn Al-Raheb*, and the *Chronicles of the Holy Church* by Mawhoub Ibn Mansour.

[74] *Al-Kafi*, Part 2, P. 444.

[75] Butcher, V2- Pp. 105–6, quoting Al-Maqrizi

[76] Butcher, V2- Pp. 105–6, quoting Al-Maqrizi

[77] Butcher, V-2, P. 106

[78] Butcher, V-2, P. 106

[79] Butcher, V-2, P.108

[80] Footnotes, Part 3, P. 1216.

[81] Footnotes, Part 3, P. 1216.

[82] Footnotes, Part 3, P. 1266.

[83] Butcher, V-2, P. 133

[84] Footnotes, Part 3, P.1249, from Ibn Waṣil.

[85] Footnotes, Part 3, P.1249, from Ibn Waṣil.

[86] Butcher, V-2, P. 207

[87] Footnotes, Part 4, P. 40.

[88] Footnotes, Part 4, P. 40.

[89] Footnotes, Part 4, P. 41.

[90] Footnotes, Part 4, P. 41.

[91] *Al-Kafi*, Part 2, P. 538.

[92] Footnotes, Part 3, P. 1578.

[93] *Al-Kafi*, Part 2, P. 530.

[94] *Al-Kafi*, Part 2, P. 530.

[95] *Al-Kafi*, Part 2, P. 530.

[96] *Al-Kafi*, Part 2, P. 530.

[97] Footnotes, Part 4, P. 839.

[98] Footnotes, Part 4, P. 839.

[99] *Al-Kafi*, Part 2, Pp. 554–557.

[100] Footnotes, Part 3, P. 1587.

[101] Footnotes, Part 3, P. 1589.

[102] Footnotes, Part 4, P. 855, and *Al-Kafi*, Part 2, P. 572.

[103] Butcher, V-2, Pp. 210–211

[104] Butcher, V-2, P. 216

[105] Footnotes, Part 4, P. 1580.

[106] Butcher, V-2, Pp. 217–8.

[107] Butcher, V-2, Pp. 217–8.

[108] Footnotes, Part 4, P. 875.

[109] Butcher, V-2, Pp. 224–7

[110] Footnotes, Part 4, P. 7.

[111] Swanson, P. 124

[112] Swanson, P. 124

[113] Footnotes, Part 3, P. 1591.

[114] Footnotes, Part 3, P. 1595 quoting *Al-Sakhawi*.

[115] *Al-Kafi*, Part 2, Pp. 611–613.

[116] *Al-Kafi*, Part 2, P. 616.

[117] The Coptic Encyclopedia, ed. Aziz Atiya, McMillan, 1983, P. 618

[118] Surat 48 'Al-Fath' (The Victory), verse 1.

[119] Surat 61 'Al-Saff' (The Ranks), verse 13.

[120] Surat 17 'Al-Isra,' verse 15

[121] Footnotes, Part 4, Pp 103–115, and *Al-Kafi*, Part 2, P. 630, and Part 3, P. 31.

[122] *The Emergence of the Modern Coptic Papacy*, by Magdi Guirguis and Nelly van Doorn-Harder, AUC Press, Cairo, 2011, P. 12.

[123] Footnotes, Part 4, Pp. 1101–1112.

[124] Maniscript #153, *Bibliothèque nationale de Paris*, pp. 445-452

[125] *Al-Kafi*, Part 3, Pp. 79 and 87.

[126] *Al-Kafi*, Part 3, P. 102.

[127] Butcher, V-2, P. 251

[128] *Al-Kafi*, Part 3, P. 112.

[129] *Al-Kafi*, Part 3, P. 132.

[130] Butcher, V-2, P. 278

[131] Footnotes, Part 4, P. 1109.

[132] Appendix – *History of the Patriarchs*, Part 4, Pp. 1115 and 1122.

[133] *Al-Kafi*, Part 3, P. 137.

[134] Footnotes, Part 4, P.1109.

[135] Footnotes, Part 4, P. 1113.

[136] *Al-Kafi*, Part 3, P. 192.

[137] Footnotes, Part 4, P. 1102.

[138] Footnotes, Part 4, P. 1111.

[139] Footnotes, Part 4, P. 1114.

[140] Footnotes, Part 4, Pp. 1081–1087.

[141] *Al-Kafi*, Part 3, P. 181.

[142] Butcher, V-2, Pp. 311–4

[143] Footnotes, Part 4, Pp.1090–1095.

[144] *Al-Kafi*, Part 3, P. 182.

[145] *Al-Kafi*, Part 3, P. 215.

[146] Footnotes, Part 4, P. 1102.

[147] *Al-Kafi*, Part 3, P.191.

[148] *Al-Kafi*, Part 3, P. 241.

[149] Footnotes, P. 1104.

[150] *Al-Kafi*, Part 3, Pp. 249–252.

[151] *Al-Kafi*, Part 3, Pp. 249–252.

[152] Footnotes, Part 4, Pp. 1104–1105.

[153] Footnotes, Part 4, Pp. 1104–1105.

[154] Footnotes, Part 4, Pp.1133–1137.

[155] *Al-Kafi*, Part 3, Pp. 279–300, and Footnotes, Pp. 1148–1182.

[156] *Correspondance générale de Napoléon Bonaparte*, par la Fondation Napoléon, Tome deuxième, Fayard 2005.

[157] *Correspondances,* L. 4068 (notes).

[158] *Correspondances,* L. 4476, of 27 June 1799, addressed to the *Divân*.

[159] Footnotes, Part 4, P.1319.

[160] *Corresondances,* footnote to Letter No. 2664 by Napoleon,

[161] *Al-Kafi*, Part 3, P. 360.

[162] *Al-Kafi*, Part 3, Pp. 328–339 quoting *'Gaeb Al-Athar* (Wonders of Events).

[163] *Al-Kafi*, Part 3. Pp.359–365.

[164] Doctoral dissertation *The Jizya in Egypt and its Effects on Dhimmis from 1713 to 1865 AD*, Ayman Ahmed Mahmoud, Faculty of Arts, Cairo University (November 2008).

[165] *Al-Kafi*, Part 3, Pp. 365–405.

[166] Butcher, V-2, P. 356–9.

[167] Footnotes, Part 4, P. 1203.

[168] Butcher, V-2, P. 361

[169] Butcher, V-2, P. 367

[170] Butcher V2, P. 369

[171] The preceding sections are quoted from *Al-Kafi*, Part 3, P.407; Part 4, Pp. 12–138.

[172] Tagher, Pp. 231–235, and 261.

[173] Footnotes Part 2, P. 1231 from Johann Ludwig Burckhardt (1748–1814). This information is also confirmed by Ali *Pasha* Mubarak in his *Al-Khutat* (Plans), (Part 17, P. 25).

[174] *Al-Kafi*, Part 4, Pp. 142, 146, and 164.

[175] *Al-Kafi*, Part 4, P. 169.

[176] *Al-Kafi*, Part 4, Pp. 155–160, and 171.

[177] *Al-Kafi*, Part 3, Pp.147–155 and Footnotes, Part 4, Pp. 1354–1357.

[178] *Al-Kafi*, Part 4, Pp. 177–218.

[179] Footnotes, Part 4, P. 1416.

[180] *Al-Kafi*, Part 3, Pp. 269–438.

[181] Butcher, V-2, Pp. 416–30.

[182] Tadros, https://www.alhurra.com/a/copts-and-british-occupation/419843.html

[183] Tadros, *Ibid*

[184] Samuel Tadros, https://www.alhurra.com/a/coptic-conference/420973.html

[185] *The Copts in Egyptian Politics 1918–1952*, by B. L. Carter, published by American University in Cairo, 1986 (Routledge Library Editions: Egypt), P. 290

[186] Carter, Pp. 14–15

[187] http://www.startimes.com/f.aspx?t=13555811

[188] Carter, Pp. 62–63.

[189] Carter, Pp. 137–141

[190] *The Coptic Question in the Mubarak Era,* by Sebastian Elsässer, Oxford University Press, 2014, Pp. 211–9

[191] Carter, Pp. 16–18, and 95

[192] Carter, P. 132

[193] Guirguis and Doorn-Harder, P. 115

[194] Carter, Pp. 223–229

[195] Carter, Pp 212–222

[196] Carter, Pp 230–236

[197] Carter, Pp 239–240

[198] Carter, Pp. 153, 209, 132–133, 153

[199] Carter, Pp. 105–107

[200] Carter, Pp. 273–274

[201] Carter, P. 275

[202] Carter, Pp. 108–109

[203] Carter, Pp. 276–278

[204] *'Excluded and Unequal: Copts on the Margins of the Egyptian Security State,'* Michael W. Hanna, https://tcf.org/content/report/christian-exclusion-from-egypts-security-state/

[205] *'Falsafat Al-Thawrah'* ('The Philosophy of Revolution'), Pp. 94, 114. This was a book nominally authored by Gamal Abdel Nasser, but actually written by Mohammed H. Heikal.

[206] http://www.almasryalyoum.com/news/details/193233 (Jan. 13, 2013)

[207] *'Family Status Issues Among Egypt's Copts: An Overview'* by Adel Guindy, http://www.rubincenter.org/2007/09/guindy-2007-09-01/

[208] *Autumn of Fury*, by Mohammed Heikal, Andre Deutsch, 1983, P. 158

[209] *'The Islamization of Egypt,'* by Adel Guindy, Gloria Center, 2006, https://historynewsnetwork.org/article/29855

[210] *'Al-Ikhwan, wa Ana'*, ('The Brotherhood and Me'), by Brig. General Fouad Allam, retired director of Egypt's State Security Investigation, Cairo, 1996.

[211] Heikal, P. 162–3.

[212] *'Al-Thawrah Al-Mudadah fi Misr'* ('Anti-Revolution in Egypt'), by Dr. Ghali Shoukri, Al-Ahaly, Cairo, 1987

[213] Heikal, Pp. 217–223

[214] http://www.wataninet.com/2013/04/ال-غرست-السادات-عهد-فى-الطائفية-الفتنة/80207/

[215] Heikal, P. 239

[216] *Symbolic Victims in a Socially Regressing Egypt: The Declining Situation of the Copts*, by Adel Guindy, http://www.rubincenter.org/2010/03/guindy-2010-03-07/

[217] Elsässer, Pp. 211–9

[218] http://eipr.org/sites/default/files/reports/pdf/Naga_Hammadi_Report2010.pdf,

[219] Record compiled by researcher Soliman Shafik. See: https://www.facebook.com/soliman.shafik.3/posts/2017051398512835)

[220] Elsässer, Pp. 211–9

[221] *Coptic Civilization*, edited by Gawdat Gabra, AUCPress, Cairo-NewYork, 2013, P. xxi.

[222] *Copts at the Crossroad*, by Mariz Tadros, AUC Press, Cairo, 2013.

[223] Human Rights Report: http://www.hrw.org/news/2013/08/21/egypt-mass-attacks-churches

[224] By Professor Lord David Alton:
https://www.copticsolidarity.org/2013/10/14/egypt-s-kristallnacht/
[225] Guirguis and Doorn-Harder, P. 161.
[226] John of Nikiu, Chapter 120, section 36.
[227] De Prémare, P. 214
[228] Al-Maqrizi, *Al-Khutat (Plans)*, Part 1.
[229] De Prémare, P. 214, quoting Al-Balazry's *Fûtûh* P. 305
[230] Gabra, P. 16. Refer also to Appendix 4.
[231] Butler, P. 490
[232] Ibn Khaldun (Arab historiographer, 1332–1406), *Al-Muqaddimah*, Part 1, P. 138.
[233] '*A New Challenge for the Copts: Answering the Controversies against ttheir Culture*,' by Dr. Ashraf Sadek, paper presented at Coptic Solidarity 10th Annual Conference.
[234] Ibn Khaldun, an Arab historiographer and historian (1332–1406), who lived in Tunis; *Al-Muqaddimah* (The Introduction), Part 1, Chapter 21.
[235] Swanson, P. 103
[236] As Imam Al-Sarkhsi (d. 1096) puts it, https://www.elhaq.com/kashef/41-rights-od-ahl-zumma-in-islamic-jurisprudence/251-2009-09-03-12-30-57?showall=1&limitstart=
[237] 'Amer, P 40.
[238] Tagher, En., Pp. 227–33, Ar. Pp. 258–264.
[239] Swanson, P. 124
[240] Swanson, P. 41
[241] Swanson, P. 38
[242] Swanson P. 102
[243] *Hadarat Misr fil 'Assr Al-Qibti*, ('Egyptian Civilization During the Coptic Era'), by Dr. Murad Kamil, Al-'Aalam Al-'Arabi, Cairo, 1967, P 126. This literature was marked by apocalyptic writings: refer to Appendix 3 for more details.
[244] 'Amer, P. 235
[245] *Al-Kafi*, Part 2, P. 141.
[246] Third Preface, 116, from:
http://www.tertullian.org/fathers/severus_hermopolis_hist_alex_patr_01_part1.htm #FIRST_PREFACE
[247] Swanson, P. 60
[248] *Resistance Through Orality Among the Persecuted Copts*, Fatin M. Guirguis, Florida Atlantic University, 2010, Dissertation. Ref is also made to T. El-Leithy, *Coptic Culture and Conversion in Medieval Cairo*, A.D. 1293–1524, Diss. Princeton University, 2005, P. 9.
[249] Swanson, P. 73.

[250] *Muqadimmah fi Fiqh Al-Lughah Al-Arabeyah* ('Introduction to Arabic Language Philology'), by Dr. Louis Awad, Cairo, 1980.

[251] Muhammad M. Pickthall, ed., *The Quran* (Medford, MA: Perseus Digital Library, Surah 5:51).

[252] Ibn Qayyim al-Jawziyya, *Ahkam Ahlul Dhimma*, ('Rulings Concerning Dhimmis'), P. 212.

[253] 'Amer, Pp. 93, 108, 114, 118.

[254] https://salamamoussa.com/2018/08/21/king-of-the-copts/

[255] Elsaässer, P. 212–9

[256] http://www.abc.net.au/religion/articles/2013/09/15/3848945.htm

[257] Al-Ahram, 13.11.2018 (http://www.ahram.org.eg/News/202768/27/670706/) and https://akhbarak.net/news/2019/05/18/20071020/articles/36710140/-تفاصيل-زيادة ميزانية-الأزهر-بعد-اجتماع-الطيب-ووزير

[258] Elsässer, P. 219.

[259] https://www.brainyquote.com/quotes/arthur_schopenhauer_103608

[260] '*La violence et le sacré*', par René Girard, Pluriel 2011.

[261] *The Origins of Totalitarianism* (1951) by Hannah Arendt (1906–1975); 1985 print by Harcour Books, Pp. 527–32

[262] Rephrasing George Santayana.

[263] https://salamamoussa.com/2018/08/21/king-of-the-copts/

[264] John Stuart Mill

[265] Dietrich Bonhoeffer

[266] The Coptic Encyclopedia, entry written by W.H.C. Frend, P. 963.

[267] Butcher, V-1, Pp. 349–355

[268] *Seeing Islam as Others Saw It*, by Robert G. Hoyland, The Darwin Press, Inc. Princeton, New Jersey 1997, Pp. 282–5

[269] Swanson, P. 16.

[270] *The Apocalypse of Samuel of Kalamoun*, Revue de l'Orient Chrétien 20 (1915–17), Translation, Pp. 392, 396, 398, http://www.tertullian.org/fathers/apocalypse_of_samuel_of_kalamoun_02_trans.htm

[271] Gabra, P. 16, article by Samuel Moawad.

Adel Guindy is author of three books in Arabic and numerous articles in Arabic, English, and French about Coptic issues, current affairs in Egypt and Middle East, political transformation in Egypt, and Islamism. He provided expert input to Ph.D. theses, including in Germany and France.

He is the co-founder and first president (2010–2015) of *Coptic Solidarity*, the leading US-based advocacy group for Copts, and its affiliate in France. In his capacity, he gave Congressional testimony. He was the international senior editor (2003–2011) of *Watani*, the Cairo-based leading Coptic weekly newspaper.

Previously, he had over three decades management career with a large multinational company in the Energy technology sector, spanning the Middle East, Europe, Africa and the Far East.

CPSIA information can be obtained
at www.ICGtesting.com
Printed in the USA
LVHW082032260720
661580LV00006B/233

9 781643 787602